AF552606

SUPPLY CHAIN MANAGEMENT

Theories and Applications

SUPPLY CHAIN MANAGEMENT

Theories and Applications

DR. ANIL KUMAR CHOJAR

Senior Consultant—Supply Chain, Marketing and Operations Management
«**drakc**» Consulting, New Delhi

Formerly

Director, Disha School of Management, Raipur (C.G.)
Director, Disha Institute of Management and Technology, Raipur (C.G.)
Director, SJS International Institute of Management, Samalkha,
Panipat Distt., Haryana

Foreword by

PROF. DR. B.S. BHATIA

Director-General—RIMT Institute of Management and Computer Technology,
Mandi-Gobindgarh, Punjab
Formerly, Dean-Academics, Dean-Research, and Registrar
Punjabi University, Patiala

DEEP & DEEP PUBLICATIONS PVT. LTD.

F-159, Rajouri Garden, New Delhi - 110027

SUPPLY CHAIN MANAGEMENT
Theories and Applications

ISBN 978-81-8450-411-8

Typeset by THE LASER PRINTERS, 8/15, 3rd Floor, Subhash Nagar, New Delhi-110027.

Printed in India at MAYUR ENTERPRISES, WZ Plot No. 3, Gujjar Market, Tihar Village, New Delhi-110 018

Published by DEEP & DEEP PUBLICATIONS PVT. LTD.,
F-159, Rajouri Garden, New Delhi-110027. Phones: 25435369, 25440916.
E-mail: ddpubs@yahoo.com • ddpubs@gmail.com
Sales Showroom: 2/13, Ansari Road, Daryaganj, New Delhi-110002
Phone/Fax: 23245122

Dedicated to:
The memory of my mother Late Mrs. Kamla Chojar
My dear father Mr. Yash Pal Chojar for his blessings
My wife-Meena, son-Aditya and daughter-Bhavya for their continued support, love and affection, while I was busy with the development of this book.
My brother Arun Chojar and his family for their best wishes.
God bless us all!

CONTENTS

FOREWORD

I have known Dr. Anil Chojar for the past more than 15 years, and it has come as a pleasant surprise for me to know that he has put in his industry and academic experience together to bring out a useful title on *Supply Chain Management: Theories and Applications*. This book has a strong focus on supply chain concepts, coupled with real life applications in the form of industry analysis, case studies, and summary of several research studies. I feel it must have been a challenging experience for him to handle the vast information and literature, and present the main issues in a more direct and brief manner. The book is sure to benefit students of MBA, and PGDM programs, including Post-Graduate management students having specialization in Agri-business management where supply chain management is part of the curriculum. Since the subject matter in this book has direct relevance to commercial firms also, managers handling supply chain coordination and collaboration will benefit from it.

This book is divided into two parts. While first part is devoted to concepts that are spread over eight chapters, the second part has eleven chapters. The Part I, starts with introduction to Supply Chain Management (SCM), role of chain partners, focus of SCM, its objectives, key issues, logistics, supply chain uncertainty and bullwhip effect besides drivers of supply chain performance, inventory control systems, and followed by a full chapter devoted to importance of inventories, various inventory models, need for manufacturers to manage inventories, and their placement and distribution. A separate chapter highlights JIT and lean operations, use of visual "Kanban" systems, and followed by a chapter on distribution management that presents the role of Distribution centers and warehousing, third party logistics, transportation economics, role of warehouses in product-mix assortments, and packaging, besides warehouse layout and design, and requirement for material handling equipment. Further, the role of purchasing, its interface with other departments, particularly with logistics, supplier relationships, supplier selection and evaluation has been handled very well. In next chapter, the role of information in supply chain is described in detail with the concept of auctions, reverse auctions and catalogue hubs among various other topics. It is followed by a chapter on supply chain design for customer order fulfillment which covers concepts and discussion on virtual supply chains, development of integrated supply chains, and so on. The last chapter of Part I covers the role of logistics, its scope and contribution to manufacturing and marketing departments in the organization besides coverage on various logistics channels.

In Part II, the first chapter deals with the application of supply chain concepts in agri-business along with extensive review of literature and two case studies that are presented in brief. The next chapter relates to contract farming, followed by a chapter on a project study proposal submitted to a well known corporate sector—manufacturing and trading company that is active in agri-business, for assisting this company in developing supply chains to procure fresh horticultural produce for its network of retail operations. It is followed by two chapters that are related to managing supply chain with the help of E-commerce and analyzing the impact of information integration in multi-dimensional food chain. Further, the role of supply chain networks in the food industry is analyzed. In this analysis, the supply chain network management model for smooth functioning of the network as well as the firms in a collective manner is presented. The chapter that follows these two chapters describes the impact of globalization on supply chains and integration of small farmers in cross border supply chains. There is an interesting chapter on the management and control of international supply chains with reference to exports of horticultural products from Africa to Europe in the form of two case studies. Additionally, there is a chapter on factors that affect the food quality and safety in food supply chains, which is followed by a chapter on the salient features of the Collaborative, Planning, Forecasting and Replenishment (CPFR) model for improving the supply chain coordination. The last chapter in Part II presents the analyses of Indian agricultural sector for meeting the demand for primary food products by highlighting the production potential, prospects, price policy, food management, procurement of food-grains and role of buffer stocks, post-harvest management, and processing sectors.

The book is therefore strongly recommended for all professional managers and management students specializing in operations, and supply chain management. The book is easy, interesting and to the point.

Have a happy reading!

PROF. DR. B.S. BHATIA
Formerly, Professor and Head, Punjab School of Management Studies
Dean-Academics, Dean-Research, and Registrar
Punjabi University, Patiala, Punjab
Presently, Director General, RIMT Institute of Management and
Technology, Mandi-Gobindgarh, Punjab

PREFACE

With the liberalization of Indian economy in nineties and thereafter, the supply chain management and logistics businesses have expanded to support the growth in the major sectors of the economy. These include industrial and consumer goods sectors, mining, agricultural commodities and food processing industries besides various services sectors.

The expansion is noteworthy as India is now integrated with the global economy. As a result, many major multinational companies have set up their base in India to meet the demand for their industrial and consumer durables in the domestic market as well as use India as an export base for their products to the neighbouring countries. Additionally, with the rapid pace in urbanization resulting from real estate sector expansion, backed by infrastructure development and up-gradation of rail, road and air networks, coupled with the setting up of production hubs and industrial parks in various parts of the country, the role of supply chain and logistics management has assumed greater importance and significance. Business organizations are no longer working on individual basis, they are now part of supply chains that ultimately satisfy either the B2B end-customer or the retail customer in urban and in rural areas.

During my career with the industry, I have had been directly and indirectly involved in the field of supply chain management and logistics planning activities. My experience with the industry has given me conceptual insight and opportunity to develop my ideas in the form of this book entitled *Supply Chain Management: Theories and Applications*. The real involvement in this subject came when I became part of management education and research. I shared my knowledge and experiences with MBA and PGDM students to whom I have taught this subject along with Operations Management. Interaction with students brought me in contact with vast literature that I consulted, and interestingly I went through a re-learning process. During literature search and consultation, I have been impressed by the expertise of several Indian and global authors, including authorities on this subject, whose works I hold in high esteem.

Supply Chain Management: Theories and Applications is an introductory book on the subject in its basic edition. It is written in a very simple language, and is meant for post-graduate students of management who have taken up Operations management and Supply chain management either as core or specialization subjects. Besides, it will enrich the knowledge base of practitioners and managers across various industries—be it industrial or consumer products, including agro-industrial products, food products, commodities and services.

Broadly, the book is organized in two parts. Part I deals with the theoretical concepts, and Part II is totally application oriented comprising application of SCM concepts and practices in India as well as on the international level.

Book Organization

Part I is sub-divided into eight chapters. Chapter 1 is the introductory chapter that covers supply chain management concepts, upstream and downstream supply chain members from raw material suppliers to processors, manufacturers, traders/wholesalers and end-customers. It describes the main considerations, objectives and key issues of SCM; logistics and process view of supply chains, push and pull processes, supply chain of manufacturers and service providers, need for managing supply chains, Bullwhip effect and supply chain uncertainty, strategies for handling bullwhip effect, customer and supplier relationship processes, drivers of supply chain, requirements of inventory management and inventory control systems.

Chapter 2 deals in detail with inventory management with regard to its importance, functions, reasons for maintaining low or/and high inventories by some organizations, inventory related costs, resource utilization, types of inventory, various inventory models, forward placement of inventories, vendor managed inventory, collaborative distribution, and various inventory measures.

Chapter 3 covers topics related to JIT and lean operations, their main features and scope, major components of lean systems, JIT purchasing, manufacturing and delivery, advantages and disadvantages, pull and push systems, visual systems such as "Kanban" and their operations, inventory storage and JIT, and ABC classification system.

Chapter 4 provides details on downstream portion of the supply chain with respect to distribution and transportation management, distribution requirements planning, distribution centers and warehousing, warehouse management systems, distribution outsourcing, third-party logistics (3-PL), transportation economics, its costing, pricing and services; warehousing, break-bulk, sorting, mixing, assembly and cross-docking operations; reverse logistics, value added services, warehouse layout and design, its objectives, packaging and materials handling equipment.

Chapter 5 gives details on the role of purchasing in SCM, its importance to an organization, purchasing process, interface with other departments of the organization, particularly with the logistics; supplier certification, supplier relationships, supplier partnerships; centralized *versus* decentralized buying; supplier selection criteria and supplier evaluation: sourcing and out-sourcing.

Chapter 6 describes the role of information in the supply chain; the use of IT technologies in improving the various functional aspects of supply chain, E-business, internet role in SCM, E-procurement, Electronic data interchange, Electronic market place, auctions and reverse auctions, and catalog hubs.

Chapter 7 deals with supply chain design for customer order fulfillment by the virtual supply chains, consolidation of orders from many suppliers, larger product variety offering to consumers; integrated supply chain development-role of purchasing, production and distribution; different phases in the integrated supply chain development.

Chapter 8 is devoted to the role of logistics in supply chains with reference to value addition role to the organization, scope and contribution to manufacturing organizations, interface with the marketing department; logistics in products promotion role via push and pull systems to meet consumer demand; logistics channels, logistics links-nodes and links, diagrammatic presentation of multi-party logistics channels to complex logistics channels.

Part II has eleven chapters from Chapter 9 to Chapter 19 on various application topics.

Chapter 9 is an extension of SCM concepts along with their application to supply chains operational in India and in other countries. It gives an analysis of growing importance of SCM and identifies factors responsible for SCM coordination and its successful operation. It also highlights the role of SC partners in developing countries, and reviews several partnerships in food industry and how Supply chains link farmers to markets in India and in other parts of the world. Two brief case studies in the form of ITC's e-Choupal, and Italian Coffee company Illycaffe's supply chains are also presented.

Chapter 10 relates to contract farming; it highlights the role of buyer and supplier and identifies the critical elements of contractual agreement between the two. It gives a factual analysis in terms of problems and prospects of cultivation of medicinal and aromatic crops in Southern India. Apart from suggesting solutions, there are two appendices which are on Contractual agreement on the supply of medicinal plant species to a buyer company, and a proposal from a private cooperative for the supply of medicinal plants to a buyer pharmaceutical company.

Chapter 11 is based on building supply chain networks for supply of fresh vegetables and fruits to ITC's proposed retail operations across the country. Several options for organizing the cultivation and coordination of supply chain creation are discussed. Inventory handling and storage coupled with logistics planning is also dealt with analytically.

Chapter 12 is on managing supply chain management with the help of E-commerce. The study is drawn from a survey of Dutch companies, and the results show the relevance and application of IT technologies in E-business in enhancing efficiency, information sharing, effectiveness and responsiveness of chain partners. The competition is no longer between organizations but it is between their supply chains, and web based chains, as traditional one-to-one partnerships are being replaced by many horizontal and vertical SC partners.

Chapter 13 is also based on survey of farmers in Holland with the objective of analyzing the impact of information integration in multi-dimensional food chain. It covers vertical channel comprising partners who produce and distribute products to meet customer needs, and horizontal channel partners who complement each other to jointly develop resources and business processes. Intra-enterprise integration was at physical hardware, data and application level with standardized communication interfaces.

Chapter 14 explains the role of supply chain networks in the food industry in relation to firms in western Europe, particularly in context of German environment; network formation and collaboration by firms; role of focal firm in managing the supply chain system; coordination and cooperation among firms; network goals *versus* firm level goals; supply chain network management model is presented using Balanced Score Card methodology. The appendix at the end of this Chapter gives details about the Balanced Score Card method.

Chapter 15 briefly describes the impact of globalization on supply chains; integration of small farmers in cross-border supply chains; reasons for SC partner collaboration; building supply chains; supply chain competence; SCM benefits; role of government in public-private partnerships, international organizations' role in capacity building, and training of small farmers in developing countries.

Chapter 16 deals with the management and control of international supply chains. The first case study is on pineapple export chain from Ghana and the second one is on table grape export chain from South Africa. Both supply chains are characterized by the involvement of a large number of producers who had to comply with international market demands, mostly in the European countries. Case studies presented in this chapter highlight the stimulus of market demand on technology application and systems innovation to improve production, storage and chain systems, besides development of governance structures in developing countries such as Ghana and South Africa.

Chapter 17 presents the analyses of factors affecting the food quality and safety in agri-food supply chains. Identified factors include: production, post-harvest management and handling, packaging, transport and storage facilities. There is a brief discussion on Food standards in the Global supply chains, and revision of Food regulations in India, besides Implementation of Food Safety and Quality under Government of India's 11th Five Year Plan Schemes. The Appendix at the end of this Chapter is devoted to the Hazard Analysis and Critical Control Point (HACCP) system.

Chapter 18 deals with the salient features, and participants' role in the CPFR model for improving the supply chain coordination. It deals with supply chain complexities, problems and key issues concerning demand, forecasting, and collaboration among SC members, besides networking, distribution strategies and logistics. Collaborative Planning, Forecasting and Replenishment (CPFR) model is explained in detail with its limitations and slower adoption rate in Europe and elsewhere as it was principally evolved in the U.S. under business conditions prevailing there.

Chapter 19 presents the challenges facing the Indian agricultural sector for meeting the demand for primary food products. It analyses the production prospects for the 2008-09 crop (marketing year 2009), rainfall, price policy, food management, procurement of food-grains, and buffer stocks. It also provides brief discussion on horticulture, post-harvest management, and processing sectors.

The Appendices at the end of this Chapter provide statistical data on various foodgrains and commercial crops, and other agro-economic indicators.

DR. ANIL KUMAR CHOJAR

ACKNOWLEDGEMENTS

Dr. B.S. Bhatia, Director-General, RIMT Institute of Management and Computer Technology, Mandi Gobindgarh, Punjab, Formerly Dean-Academics and Dean-Research, Registrar, and Professor and Head, School of Management Studies, Punjabi University, Patiala, Punjab; Ex-Director School of Management, Apeejay Institute of Technology, Gr. Noida.

Dr. D.S. Sidhu, Member-PAU Governing Board, Ludhiana, formerly Dean-Post Graduate Studies, and ex-Head, Department of Economics and Sociology, and Professor of Marketing, Punjab Agricultural University, (PAU), Ludhiana, Punjab. Dr. Joginder Singh, Senior Economist-Extension and former Head, Department of Economics and Sociology, Punjab Agricultural University, Ludhiana, Punjab.

Dr. A.P.S. Gill, Consultant-Floriculture, Seeds, Greenhouse, and Floral crops management, formerly Consultant UNDP and Professor-Floriculture and Landscaping, Punjab Agricultural University, Ludhiana, Punjab.

Dr. G.S. Batra, Professor, School of Management Studies, Punjabi University, Patiala, Punjab. Dr. S.P. Narang, Professor of Eminence, Indira Gandhi National Open University, School of Management Studies, New Delhi (Formerly CEO and Secretary-Institute of Company Secretary of India, Ex-Executive Director, Apeejay Institute of Technology, Gr. Noida).

Dr. Peter J. Batt, Curtin University of Technology, Australia; Dr. Van der Vorst, J.G.A.J, Netherlands; Dr. Sjaak Wolfert, LEI, Wageningen UR, P.O. Box 29703, Den Haag, 2502 LS, The Netherlands; Dr. J.van Roekel, Director, Agri Chain Competence Center, The Netherlands; Professor Sabine Willems, Agri Chain Competence Center, The Netherlands; Dr. Dave M. Boselie, Wageningen UR, Agricultural Economics Research Institute (LEI), The Netherlands.

Dr. Jacques Trienekens, Professor, Management Studies Group, Wageningen University, Hollandseweg 1, Wageningen, 6706 KN, The Netherlands. Professor Christina Steinbauer, Johann Heinrich von Thünen-Institut (vTI), Federal Research Institute for Rural Areas, Forestry and Fisheries, Bundesallee 50, 38116 Braunschweig, Germany; Mr. Achel D. Gyingiri, formerly Project Coordinator and Business Development Manager, Bio-Resources Inc. (BRI), Accra, Ghana; Mr. Mohamed Elkoussaimi, Chief Executive, Al Kawthar Import and Export, Casablanca, Morocco; Mr. Alfred Kamokwe, General Manager and CEO, Afridis, Douala, Cameroon.

Mr. Pravin Gupta, General Manager, APEDA, New Delhi; Dr. T. Vasantha Kumar, Senior Scientist and Head-Medicinal Crops, Indian Institute of Horticulture Research Institute (IIHRI), Bangalore, Dr. S. Ganeshan, Senior Scientist and Head-Biotechnology, IIHRI, Bangalore.

I would like to thank my former organization Foreign Agricultural Service, U.S. Department of Agriculture, New Delhi and Washington D.C. offices for giving me opportunities to visit and tour several procurement, production, processing, warehousing and distribution facilities of large and medium commercial organizations and companies in India and USA.

This includes ITC, Godfrey Philips, Godrej, NDDB-Amul, and Monsanto, Specialty Grains, and Roberts Rice Mill, Arkansas Industrial Commission among several companies/organizations in various states/locations in the U.S. besides storage and handling systems, for example around New Orleans port that I visited. I also extend my thanks to my former organization Cebeco International Projects, b.v. Netherlands for facilitating my visits to client sites in India and in Holland to learn about their operations, including visits to NDDB-SAFAL retail supply chain projects, major wholesale horticultural produce markets in different metropolitan cities of India, seed potato project in Orissa, major seed potato suppliers in Punjab, and Indo-American Hybrid Seeds, Bangalore and Nath-Sluis Seeds, Aurangabad, Tasty Bites, in Pune to name a few. Besides I visited Rotterdam port in Holland, and several processing and production facilities of companies like Aviko, SVZ, Flamingo, farm equipment and tractor manufacturing firms, potato harvesting and storage operations.

I would like to thank Sami Labs Ltd., the Bangalore based Phyto-pharmaceuticals company for giving me an opportunity to work in the key position of managing the supply chain operations to align company's procurement and outsourcing processes with the production planning processes at its production facilities in Kunigal and Mysore, to assist company efforts in meeting export targets. In this context, I owe my thanks to Dr. R.K. Bammi, Chairman, Sami Group of companies for his support and guidance. I also take the opportunity to thank Dr. S. Natarajan, Executive and Senior Vice-President who was always available for consultation on matters related to quality control and new product development. I wish to express thanks to all my former colleagues at this company in all Departments, including Production, Finance and Accounts, Research and Development, Commercial, IT and Systems, Warehouse and Logistics, who cooperated with me to meet the schedules and helped me in bringing innovations in the supply chain processes to add value to company operations by enhancing production efficiency and customer satisfaction in export markets. I would also like to thank my company's suppliers in Ghana, Morocco, and in Cameroon for facilitating my visits to set-up procurement and supply chain operations in those countries. At the same time, I extend my thanks to my colleagues and contacts in Karnataka Government and University of Agricultural Sciences, GKVK, Bangalore, and Association of Medicinal and Aromatic plants, Department of Biotechnology, Indian Institute of Horticultural Research,

Bangalore for their support and best wishes. I am also thankful to my former company's cultivation organizers in Tamil Nadu, particularly in Salem and adjoining districts besides in some areas of Karnataka for helping me in organizing supply chain operations through contract farming projects. My thanks also go to R&D and developmental institutions like FRLHT, and CIMAP besides Pharmacy Institutes in Bangalore and several suppliers across the country, who supported me in supply chain operations.

I wish to convey my thanks to my former colleagues at Disha Group of Management and Engineering Institutions, Raipur, and Apeejay Institute of Technology, Gr. Noida for their best wishes.

Lastly, I would like to extend my special thanks to Mr. G.S. Bhatia, Managing Director, Deep & Deep publications Pvt. Ltd. for his valuable suggestions, and his production and editorial staff, for their support and efforts for working on drafts of this book with enthusiasm. Ideas for expanding the scope of this introductory book further in the next edition have already started coming to my mind. Suggestions from readers are also welcome.

New Delhi

DR. ANIL KUMAR CHOJAR
E-mail: anilkrchojar@yahoo.com

List of Abbreviations Used

API	Active Pharmaceutical Ingredient
BSNL	Bharat Sanchar Nigam Limited
CIMAP	Central Institute of Medicinal and Aromatic Plants
DC	Distribution Centre
FCI	Food Corporation of India
FG	Finished Goods
FRLHT	Federation for Revitalization of Local Health Traditions
IBD	International Business Division
IOC	Indian Oil Corporation
ITC	India Tobacco Company
MTNL	Mahanagar Telephone Nigam Limited
NDDB	National Dairy Development Board
OFP	Order Fulfillment Partner
PDS	Public Distribution System
POS	Point of Sales System
RM/R.M.	Raw Materials
ROP	Re-order Point
SC/S.C.	Supply Chain
S.Cs.	Supply Chains
SCM	Supply Chain Management
TQM	Total Quality Management
WIP inventory	Work in-Process Inventory
WMS	Warehouse Management System
3-PL	Third Party Logistics

PART I

Key Concepts and Theories

1

SUPPLY CHAIN MANAGEMENT

Supply chain management consists of all activities that are associated with procurement and transformation of goods and services along with associated information flows from raw materials stage to the final customer. In brief, it consists of all tangible assets, information flows and processes that extend from suppliers and producers to final customers.

A Supply Chain (S.C.) network is made-up of inter-related organizations starting with raw material suppliers, the product or service provider, the distribution channels and ending with final customer. We can also say that supply chain is a sequence of business processes and activities which run from suppliers through customers that provide products, services and information to the satisfaction of customers.

Thus a Supply Chain can be thought of an extended and integrated enterprise that is dedicated to receival, production, storage, and movement of raw materials, finished goods and service, along with information and cash flows.

S.C. is made up of four fundamental processes. These are:

— Acquiring customer orders
— Processing materials and components received from suppliers
— Producing or manufacturing products
— Fulfilling customer orders

For example, for making and supplying tomato paste to its B2B customers, Nijjar Foods Company goes to farmers for contract farming to procure its desired variety of tomatoes that have higher TDS (total dissolved solids) contents.

To achieve the desired efficiency, these procurement processes must operate in alignment with product-development processes to deliver products, services and the required information which meet with customer's needs at the lowest cost.

SUPPLY CHAIN NETWORK

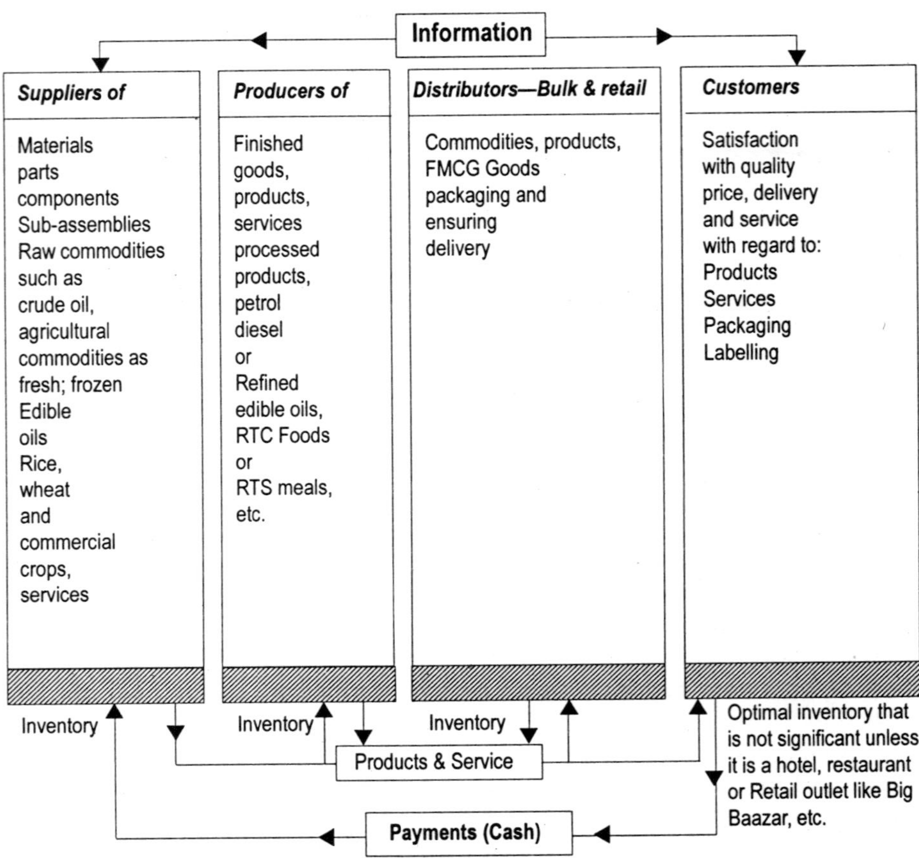

The figure given above illustrates the various stages or components of S.C. from suppliers, producers, to distributors and customers.

While suppliers are referred to as *upstream Supply Chain* members, distributors, delivery people/organizations and warehouses are called *downstream* S.C. *members*. Each member of S.C. has an inventory to insulate or shock-proof himself/herself from the unrelability of other members of Supply Chain. Information, a key factor in managing and coordinating S.C. flows in both directions, indicates that communication happens from both sides. Thus, each member (or component) of S.C. provides other members with information to help them achieve overall objective that drives the supply chain aimed at satisfying customer needs and wants. The payments made by customer in cash flows back *upsteam* in S.C.

The figure could be representative of a *single producer* directly linked to one level of suppliers and one set of end-users *i.e.* customers. A *food mart* e.g. Food World/Reliance Retail which sells grocery, fruits and vegetables besides processed food products/finished product may be buying directly from farmers cooperatives or producer-manufacturers (no brokers, etc.) and selling them directly to customers.

On the other hand S.C. of a company can consist of series of suppliers and customers in a manner that every customer is a supplier to the next in a supply chain and it continues upto the final user of products and services. For example, India-based Bridge stone-automobile tyre manufacturer buys *Rubber and related materials* from suppliers (who source their supplies from Kerala, Maharashtra and from countries like Malaysia and Indonesia) and produces tyres which it sells to Mahindra/Tata/Toyota/General Motors who in turn assemble cars and vehicles for purchase by final customers through dealers.

What we Learn from Supply Chain Network Diagram?

It demonstrates that the delivery of a product or service to a customer is a complex process, as it makes use of many different inter-related processes and activities.

It consists of following steps:

— Demand for a product or service is forecast (or to be determined)

— Plans and schedules are made to meet demand within a given time frame (By Production process)

— A given product or service can require multiple suppliers, who in term produce and ship various components, parts to manufacturing or service sites. e.g. G.M. has 2500 suppliers who supply to its 120 parts plants, and 30 automobile and truck assembly plants. Components and materials suppliers who supply directly to G.M. are *First-tier* suppliers', suppliers who supply to there suppliers are *Second-tier* suppliers and so on.

Parts and materials are transformed through complex processes into final products or services. These products can be stored at a distribution center or a warehouse. Finally, these products are transported by carriers to external or internal customers. Interestingly, this may not be the final step as customers may transform the product or service further and ship it on to their customers. All of these activities are part of their supply chain i.e. flow of goods and services from materials stage to the end-user.

For Example

Biocon →	Bulk →	Ranbaxy →	Use in →	Distributors
(A pharma-	Drugs	for	↓	↓
ceutical	such		Formulations	Retailers
products	as		which	↓
related	Atorvastation		are	Customers
company)	Calcium		moved	
produces	for sale to		to	

Supply Chain Management (SCM) Explained and Defined

Owing to fierce competition in today's global markets, and with the introduction of products with shorter life cycles coupled with increased expectations of customers have forced business organizations including retail chains to develop their own *supply chains*. Further, the continuing advances in communication and transportation technologies e.g. mobiles, high speed. Internet, and using freighters/cargo planes and shipping vessels for faster deliveries have helped in the continuous development of S.Cs. and the methodologies to manage them as well.

In a typical S.C., raw materials and components are procured and items are produced at one or more production units/factories, shipped to warehouses for immediate storage, and then transported/shipped through a distribution channel to retailers and/or customers.

In order to reduce costs and improve service levels. effective S.C. strategies must consider interactions at various stages of a S.C.

Formally, SCM can be defined as:

> SCM is a set of approaches or methodologies that are employed to efficiently integrate suppliers, manufacturers, warehouses and stores with a view to distribute products or services in the required quantities or volumes to the designated locations on right time, while minimizing system wide costs and meeting or satisfying service level requirements.

The supply chain is also referred to as the *Logistics network* which consists of suppliers, manufacturing plants, warehouses, distribution centers, and retail outlets. Further, raw-materials, work-in-process (WIP) inventory and finished products that flow between these up stream and downstream members of S.C. or these facilities are also part of *logistics network*.

Main Consideration of SCM

- It takes into account every facility of an upsteam and downstream member of S.C. that has an impact on cost and plays a vital role in making the product conform to customer requirements. In some S.C. analysis, it may become important to account for suppliers' suppliers and customers' customers because they may have an impact on S.C. performance.
- S.C. has to be efficient and cost-effective across the entire system in terms of total system-wide costs, from transportation and distribution to inventories of raw materials, WIP inventory and finished goods, that need to be minimized.

The definition of S.C.M. is similar to logistics management definition which is as follows:

> The process of planning, implementing and controlling the efficient, cost effective flow and storage of raw materials, work in process (WIP) inventory, finished goods (FG) inventory and related information from a

point of origin to point of consumption with a view to conform to customer requirements.

Objectives of Supply Chain

— To maximize overall value generated; value is the difference between what final customer pays and the effort executed by S.C. in fulfilling the customer's requirement.

— For commercial S.Cs., value is correlated with "supply chain profitability" (SCP).

SCP is difference between revenue generated from customer and overall costs incurred across the supply chain.

SCP is also the total profit to be shared across supply chain stages. Higher the S.C. profitability, more is the interest in maintaining S.C. or the more successful is the S.C. It is to be remembered SCP is to be measured across the S.C. and not at individual stages.

What is the main focus of Supply Chain Management (SCM)?

SCM focuses on managing flow of goods and services, and information through the S.C. in order to achieve synchronization level that will make it more responsible to customer needs while lowering total costs. In a highly competitive global market place, the success of a company is determined by the cumulative effect produced by the combined capabilities of each member of the supply chain. The producer/manufacturing company or department alone cannot achieve the desired results in terms of quality, lower (system wide) costs, timely delivery to fulfill the customer orders. The entire activities of supply chain have to be synchronized to achieve the maximum competitive benefit.

In order to be effective, synchronization requires close coordination, cooperation and communication. In this context, suppliers and customers have to share information by communicating to each other, and must have mutual trust and identical goals in terms of design of supply chain and meeting supply/demand parameters for quality goods/services coupled with timely deliveries/receipts of those goods and services.

Examples

Some companies attempt to manage their S.Cs. through vertical integration by owning and controlling different stages along with S.C. from materials and parts procurement to delivery of final products to end-uses/customers.

Taj Group of Hotels and Oberoi Group of Hotels own and operate their poultry farms to produce broiler chicken in their processing units, use storage and delivery systems for their own kitchens to prepare chicken based dishes for their esteemed customers.

Venky's Operations

Similarly, Venky's maintain their own network of poultry farms for procurement of broiler-chickens, processing cum poultry meat production units, frozen/cold storage units, maintaining cold chain through the distribution systems till the retail level to meet customer needs. Also, dairy brands like AMUL and MOTHER DAIRY have their own networks of milk procurement, processing units for pasteurization, UHT systems, cold chains for distribution network and finally marketing and selling through their own retail and other dealer networks. In case of fruits and vegetables, SAFAL, an offshoot of Mother Dairy follows the same strategy for vertical integration.

Inspite of total vertical integration, different operating units and departments of a company may operate in an independent and uncoordinated manner looking out for their objectives rather than total organizational goals and objectives. In whatever way S.C. is designed, SCM still should focus on coordination, communication and co-operation in order to be effective at the market place.

Key Issues in Supply Chain Management

Strategic Decisions

These decisions leave a long-lasting effect on the company, which includes decisions made on number, location, and capacity of warehouses and manufacturing plants besides flow of materials through the logistics network.

Distribution Network Configuration

This is quite a challenging issue as the management of a firm has to select warehouse locations and their capacities, which are to be based on production levels of each product at a manufacturing facility and plan transportation/ material movement flows in such a manner that it minimize inventory and transportation costs besides meeting service level requirements.

Supply Contracts and Outsourcing

Relationships between buyers and suppliers are established by both parties agreeing upon terms of supply contracts that specify quantity, price, quantity discounts, delivery lead time, quality, etc. The issue is whether price discounts or price incentives can improve supply chain performance by way of buyers placing more orders, which directly or indirectly helps in increasing supplier profits.

Also decisions have to be made on by a firm regarding what items are to be outsourced and what items are to be manufactured in-house. In this context, what risks could be faced with outsourcing, and how these risks could be minimized? How internet can be used for implementing management strategies is also to be decided by the management.

Distribution Strategies

These strategies refer to actions of companies which pay more attention and importance to special distribution strategies such as *cross-docking* where warehouses perform the role of coordinators of supplies and act as trans-shipment points for incoming order from external vendors, but these warehouse do not stock items and materials themselves. The issue is whether and special distribution strategies are better than the classical distribution strategy where warehouses hold inventory, or material should be directly shipped from suppliers to stores.

Supply Chain Integration and Strategic Partnering

Designing a supply chain at global level is not only difficult but also challenging to make it operational owing to conflicting objectives of supply chain partners. However, due to pressures of competition, supply chain members either find it convenient or are forced to enter into strategic partnering to make the entire chain successful to ultimately meet level customer needs or fulfill their service requirements. The challenge for supply chain members is to find out what information is to be shared and how to do operational planning to make strategic partnering really successful for a given situation.

Information Technology and Decision-support Systems

Since information technology is a critical component of supply chain management, opportunities can be exploited by analyzing data that is available on worldwide web. The issue here is which data is important and what data have to be transferred, or shared, and what data is to be ignored. Also a firm has to decide what IT technologies and decision support systems are to be used in order to achieve competitive advantage.

Customer Value

Customer value is the index of company's contributions to the customer. It is based on company's products, services and other intangibles that constitute company's offerings. The question is how to measure customer value, and how it affects the supply chain and how the supply chain can enhance customer value? Also, how the price and brand name relationship in conventional marketing differs from 'on-line' brand promotion and pricing? Answer to these questions are important to integrated the various supply and demand processes to enhance customer value, and satisfaction.

A typical supply chain, consists of:

— Suppliers
— Manufacturing centers
— Warehouses
— Distribution Centres
— Retail outlets and
— Raw materials, work-in-process (WIP) inventory and Finished products that flow between these facilities.

Supply Chain (SC) takes into amount every facility that has an impact on cost, and which has a role in making the product conform to customers' expectations and requirements. Facilities extend from suppliers to manufacturers through warehouses, distribution centers, retail outlets and department stores or supermarkets. It is also important to consider suppliers' suppliers and customers' customers because they have impact on SC performance.

The objective of SCM is to be efficient and cost-effective across the entire system which rangers from transportation and distribution to inventories of raw materials (RM), WIP goods and finished goods. The concept is to take a complete view of the supply chain system and manage in a manner to ensure timelines in arranging supplies and their distribution including deliveries besides being cost-effective while managing system-wide operations.

This means SCM aims to integrate suppliers with manufactures or manufacturing units, warehouses and retail stores. Therefore, SCM covers a company's activities at many levels, especially strategic level and at tactical level while performing SCM operations.

SCM can also be defined as:

> It is a set of approaches or techniques that are used efficiently and effectively to integrate suppliers, manufacturers, warehouses and retail stores in a manner that products are produced and distributed in fixed or pre-decided quantities that are received at designated locations on a fixed time to satisfy service level requirement besides minimizing system-wide costs.

Logistics Management is defined as:

It is the process of planning, and controlling the cost effective and efficient flow and storage of raw materials, WIP inventory of finished goods, and related information from point-of-origin to point-of-consumption for the purpose of conforming to customer requirements.

Process View of Supply Chains

Traditional Flow method (Cyclic Flow or cycle process)

- — Customer places an order with Retailer
- — Retailer replenishes stocks
- — Distributor arranges supplies
- — Manufacturer/Assembler produces the Product-mix
- — Procurement process starts when supplier supplies the manufacturer with Raw-material/components

Push and Pull Processes

Supply Chain Processes can be either executed in response to customer order or in anticipation of customer order

Pull processes are initiated in response to customer order, and

Push processes are executed in anticipation of customer orders

Pull processes are reactive processes as they are in response to customer demand

Push processes are purely speculative as they are in response to potential/forecast demand rather than actual demand.

Strategic Fit of the Supply Chain

When competitive priorities of an organization align themselves with its supply chain capabilities and strategies, the concerned S.C. is said to be having a "strategic fit" in terms of S.C. design that is aimed at meeting customer's priorities and requirements.

To achieve this kind of equilibrium, the functional strategies of different departments must match with the competitive strategies of a firm.

For achieving strategic fit, the steps to be followed are:

Step 1: Understanding the customer and supply chain uncertainty with respect to:

— Quantity
— Response time
— Variety of products
— Service level e.g. construction industry/Real estate
— Price of the product
— Innovative design of the product

Demand Uncertainty

(a) From the customer, who places only an emergency order; it results in mismatch between supply and demand in terms of quantity and specifications which customer is looking for; supplier margins could suffer.
(b) For regular customer, demand forecasting could be either accurate or inaccurate in short-term, but resulting margins could be high, as the purchase quantities during the specified period might be profitable.

Step 2: Understanding the supply chain

When we are dealing with a supply chain, we have to deal with *Responsiveness* and *Efficiency* issues. As a result, the SCM has to trade-off between *Responsiveness* and *Efficiency*.

S.C. Responsiveness should have the following attributes:

— Ability to respond to wide ranges of quantities demanded
— Handle short lead times
— Supply a variety of products
— Develop a high quality service level
— Ability to handle uncertainty in supplies

In actual practice, the *responsiveness* is associated with costs. To handle and respond to large quantities, capacity has to be the increased, which means incurring higher costs. This increase in costs leads to a lower *supply chain efficiency when it* comes to manufacturing/assembling and delivering the ordered product mix to the customer.

For example, booking the orders for a product and then supplying the same—Zenith computers, and other example is: Booking discount tickets for airlines in the service industry prior to departure for an overseas holiday tour.

Step 3: Achieving the strategic fit

The SCM manager must ensure that S.C. operation is consistant with customer needs and is able to strike balance between customer's needs on one side, and supply chain uncertainty on the other side. Also, he should be able to trade-off between S.C. *responsiveness* and *efficiency* which may vary from situation to situation.

Supply Chain for Manufacturers

The major purpose of design of supply chain for manufacturers is to control the *inventory size* by managing and regulating the flow of materials. According to an estimate (Krijewski and Ritzman), 50-60% of revenue realized from sale of products is spent on purchase of raw materials and services, compared with 30-40% spent by a service provider. Therefore, a reduction in cost of materials brings in more than proportionate increase in profits for a manufacturer. This explains why supply-chain management is a competitive weapon.

Inventory is a stock of materials used to satisfy customer demand or to support production of goods and services. With each S.C. member, there is always an inward and outward flow of either raw-materials, components, assemblies or finished products and services. With increased inward flows, just like water in a storage tank, inventories rise. With increased outward flow, inventories level declines or dips. During summer, water levels in lakes, rivers or dams decline fast as there is a slower or no re-charge till rains come. Therefore, *inward and outward flow of inventory determines the level of inventory.*

From the figure given below, it we can understand as to why companies follow *six-sigma* and *TQM* programme to reduce defective materials in the inventory. This is because if outward flow of "scrap" materials is high, we would require higher volume/amount of inward flow of materials required for obtaining given level of output.

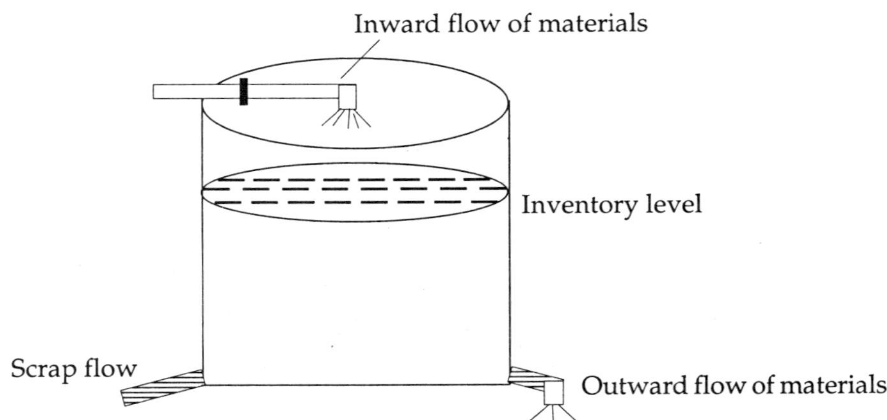

Inventory exists at three aggregate levels, which are useful for recording purposes.

Raw Materials (RM) are the inventories required for the production of goods or services. They are regarded as inputs to the transformation processes of a firm, whether they produce a product or service.

Work-in-Process (WIP) inventory consists of materials, items such as components, or assemblies required for a final product in manufacturing. WIP is also found in some service operations, such as restaurants, repair workshops, check processing centers, and package delivery services.

Finished Goods (FG) inventory found in manufacturing plants, warehouses and retail outlets are items sold to the company's or firm's customers. Interestingly, finished goods of one manufacturer may be raw materials, or components of another manufacturer.

e.g. Radiator → RM for car manufacturer
(FG)
Zips → RM for Jeans manufacturer
(FG)
Bulk drugs → RM for formulation units and/or other pharma company
or
APIs
of a Pharma Producer — RM for pharma companies for their formulations or products sold to consumers as tablets or capsules

API: Active Pharmacautical ingredient extracted from a natural product/herb.

The figure (below) illustrates as to *how inventory* can be held in different forms at various stocking points. In the example exhibited in the figure, *raw*

INVENTORY AT SUCCESSIVE STOCKING POINTS

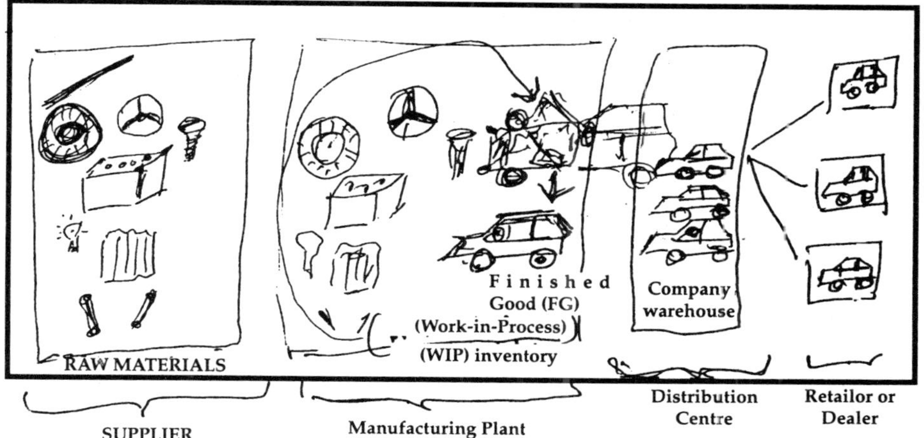

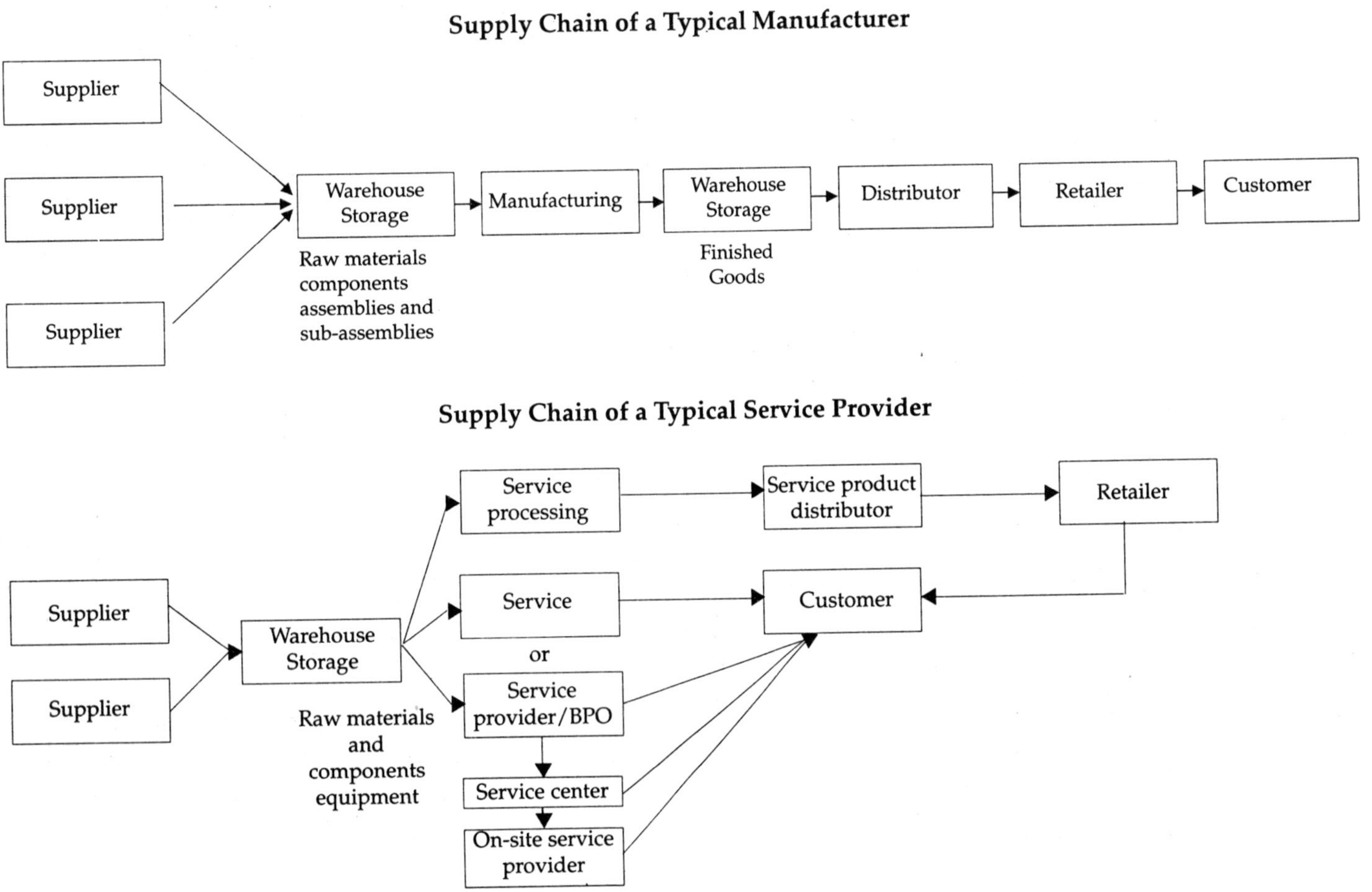
Supply Chain of a Typical Manufacturer
Supplier
Supplier
Supplier
Warehouse Storage
Raw materials components assemblies and sub-assemblies
Manufacturing
Warehouse Storage
Finished Goods
Distributor
Retailer
Customer
Supply Chain of a Typical Service Provider
Supplier
Supplier
Warehouse Storage
Raw materials and components equipment
Service processing
Service
or
Service provider/BPO
Service center
On-site service provider
Service product distributor
Retailer
Customer

materials (which are) the finished goods of the supplier—are held both by the supplier and manufacturer. Raw materials at the plant pass through one or more processes, which transforms them into various levels of WIP inventory. Final processing of this (WIP) inventory yields finished goods inventory. Finished goods (FG) can be held at plant, the distribution center or warehouse owned by the manufacturer and finally retail points or with dealer.

Every business organization is a part of at least one supply chain, and many are part of multiple supply chains. Generally, the *member-partner and type of organizations* in a supply chain are determined by whether the supply chain is manufacturing or service oriented. Supply chain are sometimes referred to as *value chains*. The term *value chains* reflects the concept that value is added to goods and services as they progress through the chain.

Highlights

- Supply/value chains consists of separate business organizations rather than just an single organization. Moreover, the *value chain* has two components for each organization.
  - Supply Component
  - Demand Component
- The *supply component* starts at the *beginning* of the chain and ends with internal operations of the organization.
- The *demand component* of the chain starts at the point where the organization's output is delivered to its immediate customer, and ends with final customer in the chain. In fact the *demand component* is the sales and distribution portion of the supply chain.
- The length of each component depends upon the position of the organization in the chain. The closer the organization is to the final customer, the shorter is demand component and longer is its supply component.
- Except for beginning stage supplier(s) and final customer(s), the organizations in a supply chain are both customers and suppliers.

The goal of the supply chain management is to link all components of the supply chain so that the market demand is met efficiently across the entire chain. This requires *matching supply and demand* at each stage of the chain.

Why there is a Need to Manage a Supply Chain?

In past, many firms or business organization did little to manage their supply chains; instead they concentrated on their own operations and their immediate suppliers. Listed below are factors that make it desirable for business organization to actively manage their own supply chains.

Need to Improve Operations

In the last 10-15 years, many business organizations adopted practices such as lean production and TQM and they were able to improve quality and brought in reduction of the excess costs at the same time. Although there is still a room for improvement, opportunities lie with procurement, distribution and *logistics in the supply chain.*

Increasing Levels of Outsourcing

In order to lower costs and concentrate on their core competencies coupled with trading opportunities on the horizon or just increasing the organizational efficiency in terms of final products marketed, companies or business firms have resorted to out-sourcing i.e. buying goods or services instead of producing themselves. With-outsourcing, firms are spending time/money on supply related activities such as grading, sorting, packaging and wrapping besides processing the raw materials or semi-finished products.

Increasing Transportation Costs

Transportation costs are increasing and they need to be carefully managed.

Competitive Pressures

Competition at market place has led to development of new products, shorter product development cycles and increased demand for customization. In some industries like pharmaceuticals, electronics, computers-hardware and software, product life cycles are relatively short. Further, quick-response strategies and shorter lead times are required.

Increasing Globalization

This development has increased the physical length of Supply Chains. A global S.C. increases the challenges of managing a S.C. of far-flung customers and suppliers. It also means longer lead times and greater opportunities. Monetary fluctuations and different currencies, besides cultural differences need to be taken into account for balancing the smooth flow of a S.C.

Increasing Importance of e-Commerce

It has added new dimension to business buying and selling and it has also brought up challenges.

Bullwhip Effect on S.C. Inventories

Tier 2 supplier | Tier 1 supplier | Producer | Distributor | Retailer | Final customer

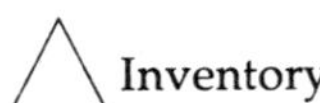

Complexity of Supply Chains

S.C.'s are complex and dynamic, yet there are many inherent uncertainties which can adversely affect the S.C. performance such as inaccurate forecast, late deliveries, sub-standard quality, equipment breakdown, and cancelled or revised orders.

Need to Manage Inventories

Inventories play a major role in success or failure of a S.C. Therefore, it is important to coordinate inventory levels throughout a S.C. as shortages can disrupt work flows and cause underproduction of goods and services (customers may cancel orders and shift to other suppliers). On the other hand, excess inventories add to unwanted costs. It is not unusual to find inventory shortages in some portions of S.C. or with some members of S.C., and excess inventories with other members of S.C.

The inventory phenomenon which can occur without good S.C.M. is called *Bullwhip effect*. Inventory stockpiles become progressively larger when looked backwards through the S.C. from the final customer at the demand-component side. The bullwhip effect increases inventory costs and hence final costs.

Supply Chain Objective

One of the major objectives of S.C. is to align and synchronize:

* The flow of materials, components, assemblies or sub-assemblies from (upstream) suppliers having production or manufacturing units, with downstream distribution (channels) in order to respond to an uncertainty in customer demand without creating an expensive inventory, or putting excessive money in huge inventory, and locking the scarce capital which would be used elsewhere.

Factors which result in uncertainty and variability in S.C. are:

Variations or inaccuracies in demand forecasting, lead times, batch ordering, price fluctuations and inflated orders could occur. The negative consequences of uncertainty and variability often introduces "LATENESS". For example, if flow of goods and services from suppliers are either late or incomplete or received in uneven batches, they slow-down the flow of goods and services through the S.C. which ultimate result in poor-quality customer service.

In order to prevent or reduce uncertainty levels, companies build up inventory of supplies. Supply chain members usually carry inventory at various stages of S.C. to minimize the negative effects resulting from uncertainty. This helps in smooth flow of goods and services from suppliers to customers. For example, if Maruti Udyog Ltd. or TATA Motors receives radiators, clutch and gear box assemblies which it ordered, late for the current production schedule, then it can rely on the inventory for such a situation. Since inventory keeping is costly business, companies try to maintain minimum inventory. Depending upon the customer-orders, status and efficiency of suppliers, inventory could be held for a month, 2-weeks, one-week or no-inventory to facilitate JIT production operations e.g. Toyota Motors.

Incomplete information, or even absence of any solid information from one side of S.C. to the other is one of the principal causes of uncertainty and it can lead to (i) excessive inventory, (ii) poor customer services, (iii) lost revenues, (iv) missed production schedules, (v) wrong capacity planning (vi) ineffective transportation and (vii) high costs. Distorted information throughout the supply chain is result of a common phenomenon called *bullwhip effect*. *Bullwhip effect* phenomenon take place when slight to moderate demand uncertainties and variability become magnified when viewed through the eye of managers at each link in supply chain. If each member of S.C. keeps "ordering" and takes "inventory decisions" of his department's or organizations as supreme objectives and then inflates the actual need required by the level of uncertainty, stockpiling may occur. This can occur at 3 or 4 or more places in the S.C. resulting in *excess inventory* throughout the chain.

Example: Foodgrains (mainly wheat and rice)

Drought scenario or bad weather forecast by metrological department can lead to excessive procurement of food grains by food processing units or millers, and paying high prices for early arrivals. The information from upstream that customer demand is likely to outstrip supply, forces wholesalers, sub-wholesalers and processing units to "stock-up" inventory in anticipation of worst scenario. Later on, monsoon arrives resulting in a normal crop, and causes prices to fall to normal levels.

* Each of these S.C. members can be a part of same or different supply chains but catering to needs of the same customer. Either customer buys 'atta' (wheat flour) or wheat from retail units for processing into 'Atta' for making Indian brcad (chapati) at home, or customer buys baked bread for consumption directly from the distribution chain. This bread processing unit is an additional member of S.C. besides miller who converts wheat into 'Atta'.

Supply Chain Dynamics

What causes fluctuation in supply chains and what are the consequences? Bullwhip effect is explained in detail below.

Facts

- Each firm in supply chain depends on other firms for materials, services or information required to execute supply to its external customer in the value chain.
- Since firms are independently owned and managed, actions of downstream members of S.C. can affect operations of upstream members. It is observed that upstream members react to the demands placed on then by downstream members of S.C. Normally, these demands are a function of corporate policies, these firms have set for replenishing their inventories, which in turn are also

dependent on the actual level of those inventories coupled with, demands of their customers, and accuracy of the information received. If we analyse the order patterns of firms/organization in S.C., it is observed that variabilities in order quantities increase as we proceed upstream. The increase in variability is called *Bullship effect*. The tip of whip gets widest action. It gets its name from the action of a *Bullwhip*.

- The slightest change in customer demand can run through the entire S.C., with each member receiving more variability in demand from member immediately downstream.

External Forms Responsible for Disruptions

A firm has least control over external customers and suppliers. Therefore, a firm must design processes with the understanding that they may have to respond to disruptions caused by external supplier or customers. External disruption include the following:

- Volume changes (by suppliers or customers)

Orders quantities may change by specific date or schedule, or there may be more demand for a product, or composition of product-mix may change.

Short lead times to supply customer needs may also cause suppliers to respond quickly in the form of inventory build-ups.

- Service and product mix changes can happen from Brand A/ Product A (40%) Brand B/Product B (60%) to Brand A/Product A (60%) and Brand B/Product B (40%)
- Late deliveries receipts of raw materials/component at production plant
- Partial shipments (from suppliers)

Internal Causes

Internally generated shortages (of components, spare parts, etc.) could be due to:

(a) machine breakdowns
(b) inexperienced workers
(c) QC problems
(d) labour shortages
(e) Transportation problems
(f) Others

Engineering Changes

Changes to the design of products (or services) can impact supplies (and suppliers) of various components and machinery.

New Product Introductions

New products (or series) may require a new supply chain or add new products to the existing supply chain, or addition of new member in S.C. e.g.

for transporting milk, the refrigerated or insulated container trucks for holding liquid milk will have impact on owner companies of such trucks for maintenance of new service.

Product Promotions

These measures often make use of price discounts, which result in sudden (increase) in demand which is felt in entire S.C. e.g. MTNL/BSNL's discounts on broadband service resulting in increased connections making customers to wait for the connection to be installed on account of shortage of equipment and manpower to handle sales. Price structuring according to usage also encourage efficiencies in a S.C. if they promote the cost cuts in S.C. to reduce wasteful expenditure that could be eliminated. The introduction of new technologies or supporting equipment also brings about efficiency and speed in the supply chain due to coustomer interest in newer and improved products required for their convenience and better performance.

Information Errors

Errors in demand forecast can cause a firm to order higher or lower materials components or products. There forecast errors induce suppliers to react more quickly to avoid shortages in supply chain.

Strategies for Handling Bullwhip Effect

1. Reducing Uncertainty

One of the methods to decrease the impact of bullwhip effect is to reduce uncertainty throughout the supply chain. This can be achieved by providing true picture with regard to each stage of supply chain with exact/actual customer demand.

It is to be noted that bullwhip effect can still exist because each stage while using the same demand data may use different forecasting methods and different material buying practices.

2. Reducing Variability

The bullwhip effect can be reduced if we could reduce variability in consumer demand process, which could be handled at the retail level itself. This will help in reducing variability in demand at the wholesale level.

3. Lead Time Reduction

It has been observed that increase in lead time often results in the variability of demand at each stage of supply chain. On the other hand, lead time reduction reduces the variability and bullwhip effect throughout the chain.

There can be two parts of lead time. The first one is *order lead time*, which means the time it takes to produce and ship the item, andthe second is *information lead time* which is the time it takes to process an order. We can reduce the order lead-time by using cross-docking technique, and information lead time can be reduced with the help of Electronic Date Interchange (EDI) system.

4. Strategic Partnerships

The strategic partnerships help in sharing information and managing inventory within the supply chain, with the objective of reducing the bullwhip effect. In a vendor managed inventory (VMI) system, a given manufacturer manages the inventory of his product at the retail outlet, and thus he is able to determine how much inventory he has to keep on hand and how much to ship in a given period to the retailer. Therefore, manufacturer does not rely on the retailer's orders and this way he minimizes or eliminates the bullwhip effect.

Designing the Customer Relationship Process

The customer relationship process (CRP) is the interface between the firm and its customers downstream in the supply chain. The purpose of CRP is to identify, attract and build relationships with customers and to facilitate transmission and tracking of orders.

The key nested processes are:

Marketing Process

The key features of Marketing Process are:

- It focuses on customers to target.
- It develops the methodology to target customers.
- It decides what products and services to offer to customers.
- It determines how to price the products.
- It works out how to manage promotional campaigns.

Order Placement Process

It determines the activities required to execute a sale e.g. use of sales force by visiting existing or potential customers

- Record specifics of customer order requirements
- Confirm the acceptance of order
- Track the progress of order until it is completed or executed

Designing the Order Fulfillment Process

It consists of activities required to deliver a product or service to a customer. This process can be used to address the issues of competitive priorities such as cost, time, quality and flexibility.

- The order placement and the order fulfillment process are closely linked and in many cases they occur at the same time. e.g. buying a book at a store or buying a mobile phone handset from a retail counter of Mobile store vis-à-vis buying it through dealer website, where order placement process and order fulfillment process are separated. Therefore, receipt of products through a web-site order placement may face a delay in receipt of products, or services. Thus order fulfillment process can have competitive implication. Other example is that of Domino's Pizza. Pizza deliveries are so time competitive that it is generally convenient to order it for home delivery rather than having it at their retail outlet.

Designing the Supplier Relationship Process (SRP)

SRP focuses on the interaction between a business firm and upsteam suppliers. The major nested processes are:

Design Collaboration Process

It focusses on jointly designing new products or services with suppliers. The process aims to eliminate costly delays and errors/mistakes done by suppliers when they design service packages or manufacture components independently based on their own judgment. Therefore, the use of information and interaction between supplier and its customer is very important, otherwise end-results could be disastrous.

Servicing Process

This process selects and evaluates suppliers and manages the supply (or purchase) contracts and orders.

Negotiation Process

It focuses on obtaining an effective contract (purchase contract or supply contract) that meets with the price, quality and delivery requirements of the buyer's *internal customers* e.g. production or marketing department.

Buying Process

This consists of actual procurement of the service or material from a supplier—e.g. pesticide spray services provider. This process includes creation, management, and approval of purchase orders.

Information Exchange Process

This process facilities the exchange of pertinent operating information such as forecasting, schedules and inventory levels between the firm and its suppliers.

Drivers of Supply Chain Performance

There are facilities, inventory, transportation and information.

1. Facilities

These are places in S.C. network where product is stored, assembled or fabricated. Major facilities include production sites and storage sites. Regardless of function of facilities, decision regarding location, capacity, and flexibility of facilities leave a significant impact on supply chain performance. For example, if LG electronics has more warehouses, near to its customer-base, it will increase its responsiveness but lower its efficiency. On the other hand, maintaining fewer warehouses will increase the efficiency but affect LG's responsiveness.

2. Inventory

This refers to all raw materials, work-in-process (WIP) items and finished

Supply Chain of a Typical Shirt Manufacturer

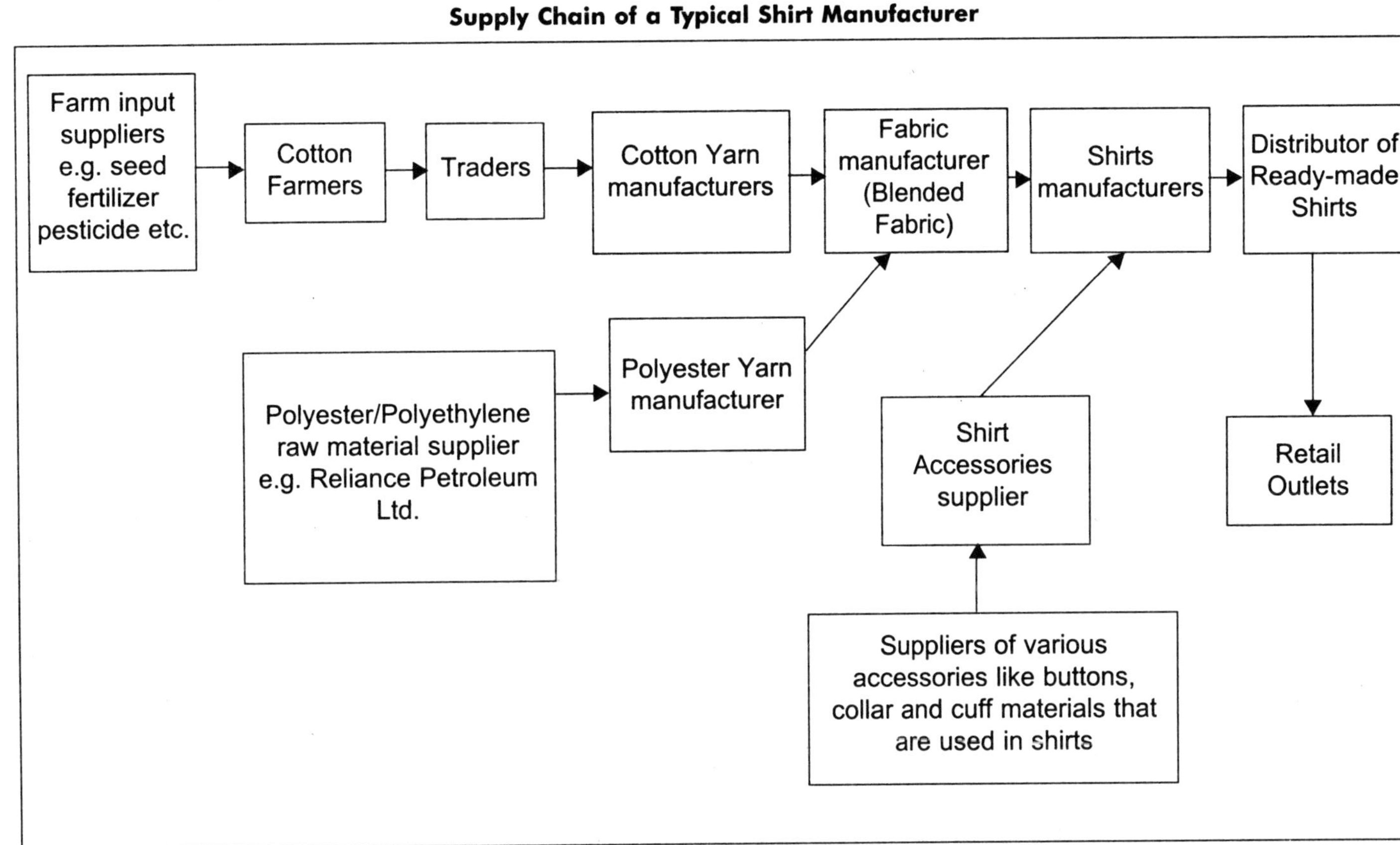

goods within a supply chain. Inventory is an important S.C. driver because changing inventory policies can significantly change S.C.'s efficiency and responsiveness. For example, Vishal Megamart makes itself more responsive by stocking large inventory of a range of consumer products to satisfy consumer demand for different products from its shop floor. However, it increases its cost, thus making it less efficient. Reduction in inventory makes Vishal Megamart more efficient but it will slow down its business and (negatively) affect its responsiveness by turning away its customers who would like to choose and buy more when store is fully stocked.

Transportation

The use of transportation results in physically moving the inventory from point to point in a supply chain. It can make use of various modes and routes of transportation, with each mode or route having its own characteristics. The choice of transportation can have a large impact on S.C. responsiveness and efficiency. e.g. ground transport/water transport versus Air transportation and so on.

Information

It consists of data and analysis related to facilities, inventory, transportation and customers throughout the S.C. It is the biggest driver of S.C. performance as it significantly affects the other drivers. Information is like opportunity management to make S.C.'s more responsive and efficient.

For example, with information on demand pattern of Electronic goods, company like LG or Samsung can produce and stock various consumer electronic items in anticipation of consumer demand which will make their S.C. responsive to meeting customer needs when latter requires these electronic goods. Information on demand is available from demand forecast which can make company like LG or Samsung efficient as it will produce only required quantities of differentiated products.

Requirements for an Effective Inventory Management

The basic requirement of the management of any commercial firm is to keep track of its inventory levels and to decide how much and when to order. In order to successfully manage, inventory operations, the following points need to be considered:

1. Develop and implement a system to keep track of inventory levels.
2. Develop a reliable forecast of demand with a forecast error that must be built into the system.
3. Estimate of lead times and variations in lead time.
4. Estimates of inventory holding costs, ordering costs and shortage costs must be done.
5. A classification system of inventory items should be implemented.

Inventory Control Systems

Broadly, inventory control systems seek to address the following:

- How much to order and its level of replenishment.
- When to order.

There are two basic types of inventory systems:

A **continuous (or fixed-order quantity) system** and a **periodic (or fixed-time-period) system**:

(A) In continuous system, an order is placed for the same constant amount whenever the inventory with the organization decreases to a certain level.

(B) In a periodic system, an order is placed for a variable amount after specific regular intervals. It is also called **Periodic Inventory System**, and **Fixed-time-Period System**.

Fixed-time-period System

It is a physical count of inventory done at periodic intervals i.e. weekly fortnightly or monthly or yearly depending upon the item as well. It is commonly used at retail or big stores and estimate is made on quantity required/ demanded which is then converted into an order that will bring inventory back to a desired level.

Advantages

(1) As requirements of items occur at the same time, it helps in achieving economies in processing and shipping orders.

Disadvantages

(1) The interval between periodic reviews to have the information on existing and required inventory of items ignores the shortages that might happen. As a result, extra stock may be required to exercise control over shortages of key items.

(2) It results in a larger inventory levels for a retail store following periodic inventory system than in continuous system. Higher inventory levels are required to prevent stock outs

Fixed Order Quantity System

These systems are also called:

- **Continuous inventory system**, and
- **Perpetual inventory System (i.e. continual system)**

It keeps track of removal of items from an inventory on a continuous basis, so that the system provides current an up to date information an existing levels of inventory of each item.

When the inventory level reaches the pre-determined minimum level, a fixed-quantity Q is ordered. It is also called a **Re-order point**.

Advantages

(1) Control is provided by continuous monitoring of inventory withdrawals. Such system is useful for critical items which need to be replaced often. Hospital consumables, automobile spare parts in a workshop come under this category.

(2) Another advantage is the requirement of fixed order quantity, which helps the management in determining **optimal order quantity**.

Disadvantages

These mainly relate to:

(1) Costs incurred on record keeping. e.g. Banking records.

(2) Moreover, physical counting is still needed to confirm the data and eliminate any errors in data reporting/changes, occurring owing to pilferage, spoilage and other factors like expiry dates of many items that can reduce inventory.

Perpetual systems range from a simple to very sophisticated inventory control or counting systems. In a two-bin system (a very elementary system), two containers for inventory are used.

Items are withdrawn from first bin until they are exhausted. It is then time to re-order. Sometimes, the re-order card is placed at the bottom of the bin. The second bin contains enough stock to satisfy expected demand until the order is fulfilled. Also, it gives an extra cushion of stock to prevent stock-outs if either order is late or demand is more.

Advanatage

There is need to record withdrawals from inventory.

Disadvantage

Re-order card may not be replaced due to variety of a reasons e.g. forgetfulness on the part of person responsible, or it might be misplaced.

Perpetual systems (fixed-order-quantity system) also called continuous inventory system) can be either batch-or online systems.

In batch systems, inventory records are collected periodically and entered into the system. On the other hand, in on-line systems inventory records are recorded immediately, and they are always up-to-date. In batch system, a sudden increase in demand could reduce inventory below the re-order point between the periodic intervals.

A more sophisticated example of a perpetual system is the computerized system installed at the payment point with cashier, or it could be only checkout system at exit point where a laser scanner is used by super markets and big retail outlets. The laser scanner 'reads' the Universal Product Code (UPC), or bar code from the product package. Thus the transaction or sale is instantly recorded, and the inventory level updated. This system is not only accurate and fast, it provides the supermarket/retail store manager with continuously updated information on the inventory level status of various items.

Many manufacturing organizations, suppliers and distributors use bar code system and hand held/portable laser scanners to 'measure' inventory level of materials, components, equipment, in-process parts and finished goods (FGs).

Role of demand forecasts and lead-time information in inventory management

1. Since inventories are used to satisfy demand, therefore it is important to have reliable estimates of quantity required and timing of demand.
2. At the same time, it is essential to know how long it will take, or how much time it will require, for orders to be delivered.
3. Besides, it is essential for a manager to know the variation between demand and lead-time. Lead time is the "time interval" between submitting an order and receiving it. The greater is the potential variability, between demand and the lead-time, higher is the need for keeping additional stock to reduce the risk of shortage.

In this context, point of sales system (POS) require special mention, as it electronically record sales. Information about actual sales can greatly enhance forecasting and inventory management. This system helps a manager and the management to make adjustments with regard to re-stocking decisions, and it serves as an important input to creating an effective Supply Chain Management by sharing the information with suppliers as well.

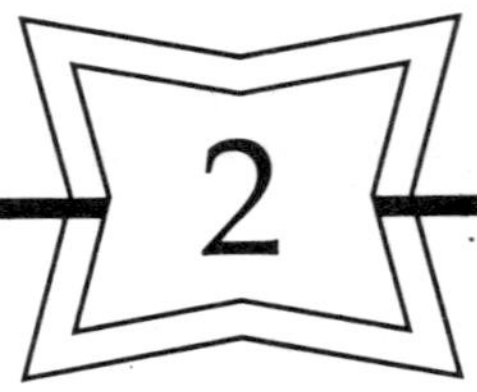

INVENTORY MANAGEMENT

What is Inventory?

Inventory is a stock of materials, goods, components, parts, or finished products. Depending upon requirements, business firms stock a range of items starting from basic products like paper, chips, pins, pencils, screws, nuts and bolts to spare parts, electronic items, machines, trucks, textiles, pharma products, food items, construction equipment, hospital equipment and related consumables. The list is endless. Armed forces stock tanks, warplanes and missiles. Many of these items could be part of the business requirement the firm is engaged in. For armed forces, war equipment and associated hardware is an essential requirement for country's security while big firms like Reliance require executive jets and helicopters for its top executives and management.

A typical car manufacturer carries supplies of purchased parts, assemblies, tyres, fuel pumps, radiators, batteries, various lubricants/oils, bearings, Rims, steerings, bulbs, wire (electric) harnesses, seats, etc. besides spare parts of machines, tools and other supplies that go into its manufacturing and assembly plants. These all items constitute inventory of car components, and parts, including minor spares and consumables required for operating assembly line equipment.

Alternatively

Inventory is created when receipt levels of materials components or parts or finished goods exceed their distribution levels. Inventory is depleted or finished when distribution levels (or issues) exceed their receipt levels.

Importance of Inventories

Inventories are a vital part of any business operations as they ultimately contribute to customer satisfaction. The inventories in volume terms differ considerably from a company to company, but a typical firm may have locked in about 25-30 per cent of its assets and 80-90 per cent of its working capital invested into inventory.

Since return on investment (ROI), which is profit after taxes divided by total assets, is used to measure managerial performance, a reduction in inventories can result in a significant increase in ROI.

The main source of revenue for retail and wholesale business is the sale of marchandize (i.e. inventory) because in value terms, the inventory of goods held for sale is one of the largest assets of a merchandizing business.

A typical manufacturer usually carries the following types of inventories:

— Raw materials, and purchased parts
— Partially completed goods, called work-in-process (WIP) goods
— Finished goods inventories held by manufacturing firms or merchandise firms (retail stores and wholesale business)
— Replacement parts, tools and supplies
— Goods-in-transit to warehouses or customers

Note: Service firms usually carry small amount of inventories (pipeline inventory); For example, Nursing homes carry inventories of consumables and equipment required for patient care.

Functions of Inventory

1. *To meet anticipated or expected industrial and/or consumer demand.* For example, demand for industrial products and FMCG products.

2. *To balance the seasonal fluctuations in demand.*

Products whose demand is seasonal, their inventories are built up during off-season or pre-season when raw-materials are stored as inventory. The production run is executed during off-season and the products are stored for sales to meet demand later on in the season. For example, processing of fruits and vegetables is undertaken when supplies of raw materials exceed the demand. Other examples include moving surplus potatoes to cold storage for sales in summer months and converting excess supplies of fruits to juices or ready to use products during off season. Other example is that of electronic goods inventory which is built up for Diwali and Christmas/New year sales.

3. *To decouple operations or to meet the production losses during machinery break down, strikes and non-availability of vital inputs/raw-materials.*

Inventories are used as buffers between successive operations to maintain continuity of production, which could be disrupted due to machinery breakdown, technical problems, strikes, compulsory shutdowns due to internal/external causes.

Thus, raw material buffers are used to maintain production owing to disruption of supplies from suppliers. Similarly, finished goods inventories are used to buffer sales/marketing operations from production breakdowns/shutdowns.

4. To protect against stockouts. Delayed deliveries and unexpected increases in demand increase the risk of shortages.

Reasons for delay include:

- Weather conditions
- Supplier stock-outs
- Delivery of wrong materials
- Quality problems
- Other factors

The risk of shortages can be reduced by holding safety stocks which are stocks held in excess of average demand to compensate for variabilities in demand and lead-time.

5. To take advantage of order cycles. In order to minimize purchasing activity, and ordering costs, a company buys materials in quantities that exceeds its immediate requirements. This makes it necessary to share some or all of the purchased amount for use later on, e.g. kitchen items, department store specializing in children's or men's wear.

Similarly, if it is economical to produce in large rather than small quantities, the excess output has to be stored for later use. What we infer is that inventory storage enables a company/firm to buy or produce in "economic lot sizes" without having to try and match purchases or production with demand requirements in the short run. This results, in periodic orders, or order cycles. The resulting stock is also called 'cycle stock'. Therefore, periodic orders/order cycles are not always based on economic lot sizes.

In some situations, it is practical or economical to group orders and/or to order at fixed intervals.

6. To hedge against price increases. Occasionally a firm will "anticipate" a substantial price increase is going to occur, and resorts to higher than normal purchases to hedge against price increases. This also enables the firm to take advantage of price-discounts for larger orders.

7. To facilitate production operations. As production operations involve certain amount of time, it means that there will be some work-in-process (WIP) inventory besides raw materials, semi-finished items and finished goods at production sites. Additionally, there are goods stored in warehouses. All this leads to pipeline inventories throughout the production distribution system.

8. To take advantage of quantity discounts. Suppliers 'often give discounts on large orders in quantity or volume terms.

Inventory Concepts

Inventory is created when the receipt levels of materials, parts, components or finished goods exceed their distribution levels. Inventory is depleted or finished when the distribution levels (or issues) exceeds their receipt levels. In this discussion, we shall focus on factors responsible for maintaining low and high inventories.

Reasons for Maintaining Low Inventory Levels

The manager is involved in conflicting objectives which call for keeping costs low on one hand while determining the appropriate inventory levels in situations that requires a mix of both low and high inventory levels.

The main reason for keeping low inventories is due to the fact that an inventory represents a temporary monetary investment in materials and goods on which a firm must pay interest. Inventory holding cost (or carrying cost) is the variable cost incurred on keeping items stocked, which includes storage and handling costs, interest, taxes, insurance and shrinkage/losses, etc. When components of this variable cost change with changes in inventory levels, the holding cost also changes. Business firms express an item's holding cost at per period of time as a per cent of its value.

The annual cost to maintain one unit in inventory usually ranges from 20 to 40% of its value. (Stevenson, 2006).

Interest or Opportunity Cost

To maintain an inventory, a company may obtain a loan and/or surrender or forgo an opportunity of an investment that promises an attractive return. Interest or opportunity cost is the largest component of the holding cost, and it could be as high as 10-15% + 2-3%.

For example, a car dealer may obtain loan at 10% to finance an inventory of cars and forego a return the MF investment at an expected return of 12-15% per annum.

Storage and Handling Costs

Inventory takes space and it has to be moved in and out of storage. Therefore, storage and handling costs are incurred when a firm rents space either on a long-term or short-term basis. There is also an opportunity cost for storage when a firm could use investment in a more productive manner.

Taxes, Insurance and Shrinkage

A firm may be required to pay more taxes if year-end inventories are high and insurance costs increase with increase in inventory assets. Further, some commodities (biologicals, fruits, vegetables natural products) may undergo shrinkage, natural losses or some items are vulnerable to thefts, pilferage either by customers or employees. This could be significant percentage to total sales.

The other form of shrinkage is obsolescence which means an inventory can not be sold or used on full-value basis owing to model changes, engineering modifications, on unexpected low demand.

Obsolescence is a big expenditure in retail clothing, consumer electronics, computer industry, shoes etc. where drastic discounts are offered at the end of season or when new models and designs hit the market. Some items undergo deterioration due to physical spoilage. Food and beverage products come under this category. Other example could be woollen garments inventory which could be spoiled on account of termite attack, flash foods or due to humidity, etc.

Inventory Costs

Holding or Carrying Costs

These costs relate to having materials or items physically in storage. These costs include: interest, insurance, taxes (e.g. state government taxes) depreciation, obsolescence, deterioration, spoilage pilferage, breakage and warehousing costs comprising heat, light, cooling, refrigerator rent and security besides record keeping and transportation. They also include opportunity costs associated with funds which would be used somewhere else instead of being "locked-up" in the inventory.

The significance of various components depends upon the type of material, component or item involved. Some items like floppies, CD-Rom drive, pen-drives, calculators, etc. can easily be stolen. On the other, fresh foods like dairy products, seafood, meats and poultry products are subject to rapid spoilage. Similarly, products like batteries and films have limited life.

Note: Total carrying costs are determined by adding all the individual costs as mentioned above on a per unit basis per time period such as month, quarter, or on half-year basis.

Holding costs can be expressed as: Percentage of unit price, or per unit rupee amount on annual basis i.e. in rupees/unit on annual basis. Typical annual holding costs could range from 10-40% of the value of a manufactured item or percentage of average inventory value. It means to hold an item worth Rs. 1,000 in inventory, one may be required to spend Rs. 100-400 on an annual basis.

Ordering costs are the costs associated with ordering and receiving inventory or replenishing the stock of inventory held. These costs vary with the actual placement of an order, and the number of orders placed. In addition to shipping (or transportation) costs, they also include costs for estimating requirements with respect to determining how much material (including grades and specifications) is needed; preparing purchase orders, inspecting goods upon arrival for checking quality and noting variations in quantities ordered compared with quantities received. These costs also include costs of temporary storage before they are moved to the regular warehouse. For example, storing raw materials in leased premises close to production as it enables the material to undergo grading, inspection and packing etc. Ordering costs are expressed as a fixed expenditure in Rupees per order, regardless of order size.

Note: Ordering costs are inversely proportional to carrying costs. When a firm produces its own inventory instead of ordering it from a supplier, the costs of machine setup (e.g. preparing the equipment for the job by adjusting the machine or changing cutting tools etc.) are similar to ordering costs i.e. they are expressed as a fixed charge per production run, regardless of size of the run.

Shortage costs also called stockout costs, when customer demand cannot be met because of insufficient inventory. These costs occur when demand exceeds the supply of inventory available.

These costs include:

- Loss of customer goodwill.
- Opportunity cost of not making a sale or selling the product resulting in permanent loss of sales and loss of profits.
- Late charges and other such charges.
- Loss of production or downtime if there is a shortage of an input/ breakdown of an equipment considered crucial for production e.g. raw material or an assembly line. These costs can run into lakhs of rupees on per day or per week basis.

These costs one difficult to measure and they can be measured or estimated subjectively.

Note: Shortages occur because carrying inventory can be expensive. Thus, shortage costs are inversely related to carrying costs. With increase in inventory. shortage costs decrease, while carrying costs increase.

Important Objective

The objective of inventory management is to employ an inventory control system that will indicate how much quantity/volume should be ordered. Timing of the order in very important as we tend to minimize (sum of) these inventory related costs as discussed.

Reasons for Holding high Inventories

The fact that Food Corporation of India (FCI) has to hold high levels of foodgrains inventories shows that there are adequate reasons for holding such inventories despite the expense involved and subsidy bill paid by the Government.

Seasonality and Consumer Demand

Owing to seasonal nature of consumer items such as foodgrains and in some situations dairy products, the organizations such as NDDB created daughter organizations Mother Dairy and State Dairy Cooperatives like Prag, Verka, Amul, etc. who are able to meet consumer demand when procurement of liquid milk is low due to environmental factors resulting from extreme summer, drought, flood, etc. Holding of large inventory by FCI helps in on-time deliveries of wheat and rice to traders and millers. Similarly NDDB held stocks of milk powder and butter oil are supplied to state milk cooperatives or dairy federations to sell the re-constituted milk to consumers.

For other industrial items, inventory reduces potential for stock outs for critical items and back orders which are the concern of wholesalers and retailers. A stock out occurs when a popular item that is normally stocked is not available to satisfy the demand when it occurs, resulting in loss of sale. A back order is a customer order that cannot be executed when promised, but is executed or fulfilled later on. Customers may wait for back order once or twice but they may do their business elsewhere next time, when back order is not executed on-time.

Ordering Cost

Each time a business organization/firm places an order it incurs an ordering cost that includes the cost of preparing a purchase order or a production order for the supplier. For a given item, the ordering cost is same, regardless of the order size. The purchase department must decide in conjunction with production department as to how much to order and select a supplier and negotiate terms. Time spent on paper work, follows-up and receivals is also counted towards this cost. In case of a production order for a manufactured item, a blue-print/design and routing instructions generally accompany the (shop) order.

Set-up Cost

The cost involved in changing over a machine to produce a different item is the set-up cost. It includes labour and time spent to make the changeover, clearing and installing new tools or fixtures, remove scrap, or rework cost which can be substantially higher at the start of the production run. Set-up cost is independent of order size, so there is usually pressure on a manager to order a large supply of items and hold them as an inventory.

Resource Utilization

Labour and Equipment Utilization

By building inventory, management can increase the workforce productivity and facilities' utilization in three ways:

- By placing a large production order, it reduces (or eliminates), the number of unproductive setups, which add no value to a service or the product.
- By holding inventory the chances of costly rescheduling of production orders within the organization or for an external customer is reduced because the components needed to make the product are available in the inventory.
- By building inventories, the firm improves the resource utilization by stabilizing the output rate when demand is cyclical or seasonal.

The firm thus uses the inventory built-up during slack periods to handle extra demand in peak periods and minimizes the needs for extra shifts, hiring, overtime, and requirement for additional equipment.

Transportation Cost

In some situations, outbound transportation costs can be reduced by keeping higher inventory levels. This is because by having comfortable (higher) inventory, a manager can undertake more truckloads/shipments at one time, which would be economical rather than piece-meal shipments, or choosing to send consignments by more expensive modes such as air-transportation or half truck loads.

Inbound Transportation

Costs may also be reduced by creating more inventory, or by procuring higher amounts of material, as fewer truck trips results in discounts on transportation costs. e.g. whether one should book half or full truck load, charges would be same because there are industrial items which can not be sent along with other goods. Trucks normally carry an assortment of various goods, over long-routes and take more time for deliveries. Therefore, one should combine small orders into a single large order to decrease transportation and landed raw material costs.

Payments to Suppliers

A business firm can take advantage of prices by placing a large order during the time when prices are low or just before they are about to be increased by the supplier, or on account of some external factors such as shortages, excise duty changes or tariff increases, etc.

Types of Inventory

There are four types of inventory for an item:

(1) Cycle inventory
(2) Safety stock inventory
(3) Anticipation inventory and
(4) Pipeline inventory

A manager cannot identity the type of inventory by physical inspection alone. However, the distinction can be made on conceptual basis.

Cycle Inventory

The portion of total inventory that varies directly with lot size is called cycle inventory. The determination of frequency of placing an order and in what quantity is called lot sizing. Two conditions are applicable. These are:

1. The lot size, Q, varies directly with the elapsed time (or cycle) between the orders. If a lot is ordered every three weeks, the average lot size must be equal to three weeks' demand.
2. The longer is the time between orders for a given material or an item, the greater will be the cycle inventory.

Note: At the beginning of the (time) interval, the cycle inventory is at its maximum, or say at Q level. At the end of the interval i.e. just before a new lot arrives, cycle inventory drops to its minimum or 0. Therefore, the average cycle inventory is: $Q+0/2 = Q/2$.

This is the average of these two extreme values.

The formula of Average cycle inventory ($Q+0/2 = Q/2$) is good only when demand rate is constant. Nevertheless, this provides good estimates even while there are fluctuations in demand rates. There can be estimation errors, for example, on account of scrap losses when this simple formula is used.

Safety Stock Inventory

Safety stock inventory refers to surplus inventory that protects against uncertainties in demand, lead time and supply. Safety stockes are desirable when suppliers fail to deliver the desired quantity by the specified date or the supplier is unable to meet quality specifications, or when manufactured/un-manufactured items have either scrap or impurities/ungraded items present in them. Safety stocks ensure that operations are not disrupted when such problems occur. Therefore, replenishment order can be placed for delivery much ahead of time when the material or component is typically needed.

Suppose the average lead time of given item from a supplier is 3 weeks but a firm places an order 6 weeks in advance to be safe in terms of stock availability required for processing/assembly operations. This will create safety stock equivalent to three weeks supply.

Anticipation Inventory

Inventory that is used to adjust to uneven rates of demand or supply, which business firms often experience is referred to as an anticipation inventory. The demand patterns which could be predictable owing to seasonality factors often result in build up of anticipation inventories by S.C. members.

Also uneven demand may force a manufacturer to build-up anticipation inventory during low demand period in order to keep production levels steady (or normal) when demand increases or peaks. Anticipation inventory is useful when suppliers or manufacturers experience capacity limitations.

Pipeline Inventory (P.I.)

Inventory flowing from point to point in the materials flow system is called pipeline inventory. Materials shipments move from suppliers to a manufacturing plant. At plant, materials move from one operation to another, and from plant to a distribution center/distributor and then to a final customer.

Pipeline inventory also consists of orders that have been placed but not yet received. P.I. has two points for either production or transportation, which can be measured as the average demand during lead-time, denoted by $\bar{D}_L$

$\bar{D}_L$ is the average demand for the item per period (d) multiplied by the number of periods in an item's lead time (L) to move between two points.

$$\text{Pipeline inventory} = \bar{D}_L = d \times L = dL$$

where d is demand on daily, or weekly basis (per period) and L is lead time in days, or weeks.

Note: The lot size does not directly affect the average level of pipeline inventory. Increasing Q increases the size of each order, and if order has been placed but not yet received, there is more pipeline inventory for that lead time. On the other hand, lead time can also increase but we are assuming it will be constant for a given size of Q.

However, the increase in Q is negated by a proportionate decrease in number of Orders placed per year.

The lot size can 'indirectly' affect pipeline inventory if increased Q causes the lead time to increase. In this situation, $\bar{D}_L$ will also increase.

Determining how much to order

Economic Order Quantity (EOQ) Models (Stevenson, 2006)

EOQ models are aimed at determining the optimal order quantity by minimizing the sum of Annual Costs that vary with order size. The most popular order size models are explained below:

1. The basic EOQ model (Also referred to as Economic-Lot Size model)
2. The Economic Production Quantity (EPQ) model (Also referred to as Production Lot Size model)

1. EOQ Model

It is used to identify the fixed order size, (optimal order size) that will minimize the sum of Annual Costs of holding inventory and ordering inventory. It is to be noted that unit purchase price of items is generally not included in total cost because unit cost remains unaffected by the order size unless quantity discounts are a factor.

Assumptions of EOQ Model

1. Only one product is considered in this model.
2. Annual demand requirements are known.
3. Demand is evenly spread throughout the year, therefore demand constant.
4. Lead time does not vary and is thus known.
5. Each order is received in a single delivery.
6. There are no quantity discounts.

The figure on next page illustrates a few inventory cycles.

A cycle begins with the receipt of an order for Q units. They (units) are drawn at a constant rate over time; when the quantity on hand is sufficient to meet demand during lead time, an order for Q units is placed again with the supplier. Since usage rate and lead time do not vary (see assumptions), the order will be received at the exact time when inventory on hand falls to zero. Thus orders are timed to avoid excess stocks and stockouts. The optimal order quantity reflects a balance between carrying costs and ordering costs. When order size varies, one type of cost will increase while other type of cost decreases.

A small order size will require frequent orders which will increase annual ordering costs. On the other hand, ordering large quantities infrequently will bring down annual ordering costs, but will increase inventory levels and thus it will result in increased carrying costs.

Therefore, the ideal situation will be to determine the order size that will either prevent the necessity of placing a few large orders, or relying on placing many small orders, but will be "in-between" these two extremes. See the figures on the next page. The exact amount/volume of order will depend upon the relative magnitude of carrying and ordering costs.

Now to compute Annual carrying cost we do the following calculations:

Average amount of inventory x. Carrying cost of one unit for one year

Average Inventory Q/2 is simply half the order quantity as the amount on hand steadily decreases from Q to 0 (zero) units therefore average of (Q+0)/2 = Q/2.

Denoting Average Annual carrying cost per unit by Symbol 'H' the total annual carrying cost is given as:

Annual carrying cost = Q/2 × H

The Inventory Cycle/Profile of Inventory Level over a Period of Time

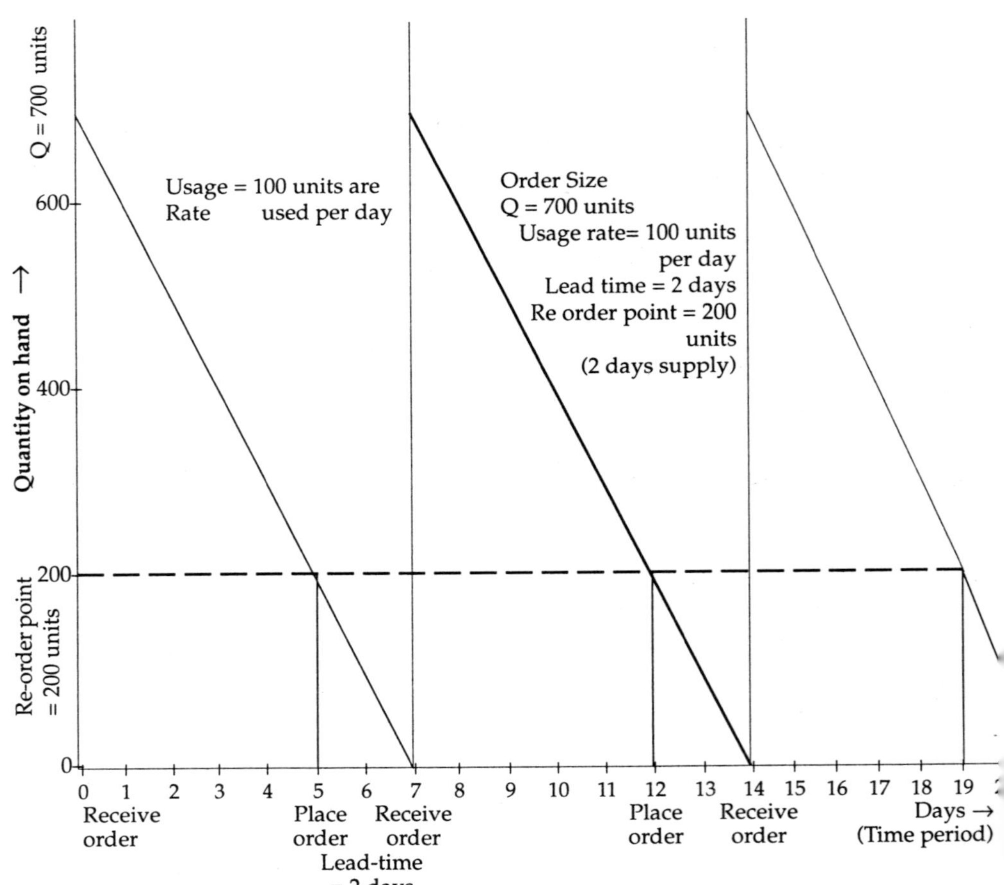

where

Q = Order quantity units

H = Holding (carrying) cost per unit

Thus, we can see, carrying cost is a linear function of Q. Carrying costs will increase or decrease in direct proportion to changes in order quantity Q. See figure on page 41. On the other hand, Annual ordering cost will decrease as order size increases because for a given level of annual demand, denoted by D, larger the order size (Q), fewer will be the number of orders required.

Unlike carrying costs, ordering costs are relatively unaffected by order size. However, certain tasks/activities such as determining how much quantity is required periodically, evaluating sources of supply or vendors and preparing purchase order, and invoice etc. besides inspection of goods, and sampling tests, are required to be undertaken by the firm. Therefore, annual ordering cost is a function of the number of orders placed per year and the ordering cost incurred per order.

Annual ordering cost = $D/Q \times S$

Many Small Orders Result in a Low Average Inventory

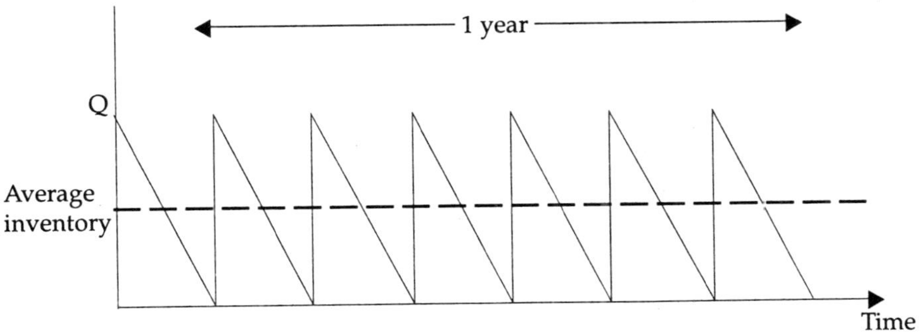

Few Orders Produce a High Average Inventory

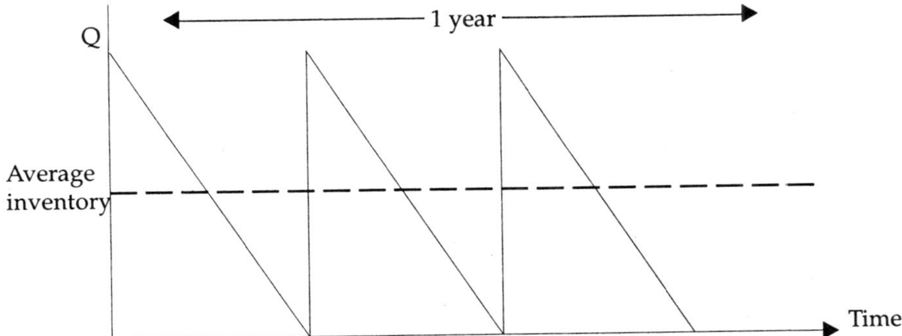

where

D = Demand, in units per year,
S = Ordering costs, and
Q = Order quantity (or order size) in units.

Since the number of orders per year i.e. D/Q tend to decrease as Q increases, Annual ordering cost is inversely related to order size. See figure B on the page 41.

The total Annual cost incurred (or associated) with carrying and ordering costs when Q units are ordered each time is given by the formula:

$$TC = \text{Annual Carrying Cost} + \text{Annual Ordering Cost} = \frac{Q}{2} \times H + \frac{D}{Q} \times S$$

Note: D and H must be in same units e.g. months, year, etc.

Figure C shows that total cost curve is U-shaped i.e. convex with one minimum point, which coincides with the optimal order quantity (Qo) point where carrying and ordering costs are equal (see figure C for observing point of intersection between two costs). At this point, and total cost curve is at its minimum.

Using calculus, an expression for optimal order quantity (Qo) can be determined. The resulting formula is:

$$Qo = \sqrt{\frac{2DS}{H}}$$

Qo (also written as EOQ) = Optimal Value of Q, i.e. order size or quantity.

Thus, given annual demand, ordering cost per order, and annual carrying cost per unit, one can calculate the optimal (economic) order quantity. The minimum total cost is computed/determined by substituting Qo for Q in formula

$$TC = \frac{Q}{2} \times H + \frac{D}{Q} \times S$$

The length of an order between cycles i.e. (time between orders) is as follows:

(Some authors also label it as TBO i.e. Time between orders)

Length of order cycle = Qo/D, i.e. Q/D

Annual demand = EOQ/D = EOQ/D × 12 months (or working days in a year)

Numerical

A car tyre dealer expects to sell about 9,600 radial tyres for Maruti Swift model during 2011. Annual carrying cost is estimated at Rs. 16/Tyre, and ordering cost is Rs. 75/- order. The dealer will operate for 288 days in 2011.

Figure A: Carrying Costs are Linearly related to Order Size

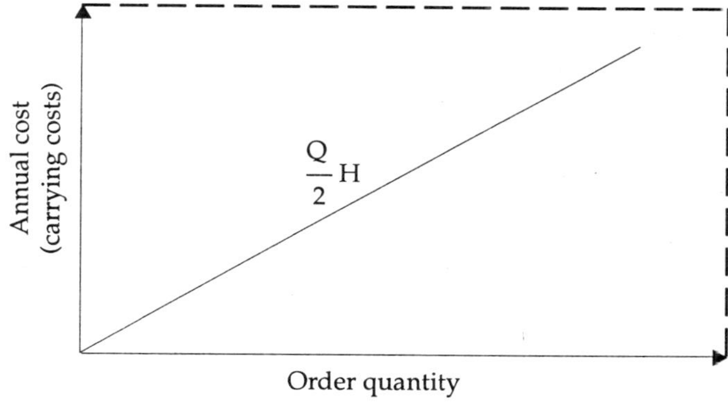

Figure B: Ordering Costs are Inversely (and non-linearly) related to Order Size

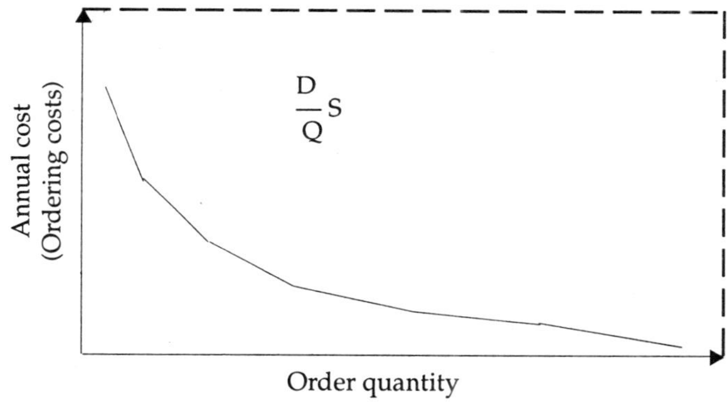

Figure C: Total Cost Curve is U-shapted

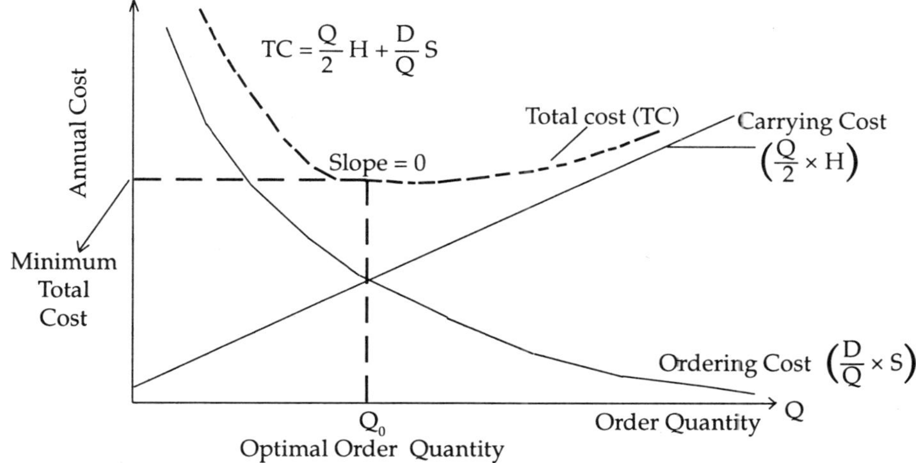

Calculate his:

(a) EOQ
(b) How many times, the dealer will reorder on per year basis
(c) What is length of order cycle
(d) What is total cost of EOQ quantity ordered

Solution

D = 9600 Tyres; H = Rs. 16/Tyre/year; S = Rs. 75/-

(a) $Qo = \sqrt{\dfrac{2DS}{H}} = \sqrt{\dfrac{2 \times 9600 \times 75}{16}} = 300$ tyres

(b) No. of orders per year: $\dfrac{D}{Qo} = \dfrac{9600 \text{ tyres}}{300 \text{ tyres}} = 32$ tyres

(c) Length of order cycle $= \dfrac{Qo}{D} = \dfrac{300 \text{ tyres}}{9600 \text{ tyres}} = \dfrac{1}{32}$ of 2011 (year)

$= \dfrac{1}{32} \times 288$

$= 9$ working days

(d) Total cost (TC) = Carrying cost + ordering cost
= (Qo/2) H + (D/Qo) S
= (300/2) 16 + (9600/300) 75
= Rs. 4800/-

Numerical

Lotus Corporation assembles protective Goggles for Indian army for use on Siachen Glacier. It purchases 3,600 Goggle frames for Rs. 650 each. Ordering costs are Rs. 310, and annual carrying costs are 20 per cent of purchase price. Compute optimal quantity and the total annual cost of ordering and carrying the inventory?

Solution

D = 3,600 Goggle frames
S = Rs. 310/-
H = Rs. 650 × 20 per cent = Rs. 130/-

$Qo = \sqrt{2DS / H} = \sqrt{2(3600(310) / 130}$ = About 131 Goggle frames

TC = Carrying costs + Ordering costs
= (Qo/2) H + (D/Qo) S
= (131/2) 130 + (3600/131) 310
= 8515 + 8519
= Rs. 17,034/-

Note: 1. Carrying cost (as seen above) can be stated as percentage of purchase price of an item rather than Rupee amount per unit. As long as percentage is converted into Rupee amount, the EOQ formula will be appropriate.

2. Holding and ordering costs, and annual demand are estimated values from accounting department/records. Holding costs are sometimes 'designated' by the firm rather than computed. Therefore in such cases EOQ should be regarded as approximate quantity rather than exact quantity.

When to re-order with EOQ ordering: EOQ models can tell us how much to order but not tell us as to WHEN to order. Therefore, one has to make use of models which identify the *Reorder point* (ROP) in terms of quantity. The *Reorder point* occurs when the quantity on hand drops to a *pre-determined amount*. This amount covers *expected demand* during lead time and some extra cushion of stocks may be used to prevent the probability of stockouts during the lead time.

Note: In order to know the re-order point, *continuous inventory system* (Also known as *perpetual* and a *fixed-order-quantity* system) is required. In this system, a continuous record of inventory level of each item is maintained. When the inventory level decreases to a pre-determined level, which is referred to as a *re-order* point, a new order is placed to replenish the inventory. The order that is placed for a fixed amount is known as economic order quantity. It is the one that minimizes the total inventory costs. The decision for placing an order is when amount of inventory on hand is sufficient to cover demand or requirement during the *lead time* (i.e. time difference between placing an order and receiving of an order).

There are *four determinants of reorder point* quantity:

1. Rate of *demand* (usually based on a forecast).
2. *Lead time.*
3. External to known demand and/or *lead time variability.*
4. Degree of stockout risk acceptable to management.

If demand and lead *time* are both constant, then re-order point is an given by:

ROP = d × LT

where

d = Demand rate (in units per day or week),
LT = Lead time in days or weeks.

Note: LT is also written as L by some authors.

Example 1

Mr. Uday takes two multivitamin tables daily which he receives at his residence by the Chemist sales person 3 days after an order is placed. At what point Uday should Re-order?

Usage rate = 2 tablets a day
Lead time = 3 days
ROP = Usage × Lead time
= 2 Tablets/day × 3 days
= 6 Tables of multivitamin

Mr. Uday should Re order when he is left with 6 tablets.

Example 2

Jagdeep store which keeps several styles of carpets in its inventory, operates for 305 days a year from its South Delhi retail outlet. If the annual demand for carpets is 6,500 units, determine its re-order point from its supplier craftsmen, given that it takes a lead time of 15 days to receive an order.

RoP = d × LT
= (6500/305) × 15
= (21.31) × 15
= 319.67 or approx. 320 carpets.

where RoP = Re-order point and

$$d = \frac{\text{Annual demand}}{\text{No. of days store operates in a year}}$$

Therefore when inventory level falls to 320 carpets, a new order is to be placed. Please note that re-order point is not related to *optimal order quantity* or any of the inventory costs.

Safety Stocks

When variability is present in demand or lead-time, there is a possibility that actual demand will exceed the expected demand. Therefore, it becomes important to have or carry an additional inventory called *safety stock* to reduce the risk of running out of inventory (a stock out) during the lead-time. The re-order point increases by the amount safety stock is to be held.

For example

RoP = Expected demand + safety stock during lead-time
= 100 units + 10 units

Therefore, RoP in this example = 110 units

Let us consider Example 2 given earlier when the re-order point for *carpet stock* reaches 320 units, the inventory in stock will be depleted at a constant demand rate in a manner that new order quantity will arrive at exactly the moment the inventory level reaches zero.

In reality, both demand rate and lead time show variations. The figure on next page shows uncertain demand and a constant lead time with re-order point.

As can be observed in the second order cycle that a stock out takes place when demand exceeds the available inventory in stock. As a hedge (or insurance) against stockouts when demand is uncertain, a safety (or buffer) *stock* of inventory is frequently added to the expected demand during the lead-time.

Service Level (Russell and Taylor, 2004)

There are several ways to find out the amount of safety stock. One commonly used method is to establish a safety stock that will meet the requirements of a specified *service level.*

The service level is the *probability* that amount of inventory on hand is sufficient, during lead-time, to meet the expected demand. In other words, there is a good probability that a stock out will not occur. We use the term *service level* because there is a higher probability with inventory on hand that the customer's demand is likely to be met. In other words, customer can be *served*. A service level of 90 per cent means that there is a 0.90 probability that demand will be met during lead time, and the probability of stockout is 0.10 or 10 per cent.

The service level is a policy decision of the organization that is based on number of factors like dependability of a business firm to its customers, carrying costs for extra safety stock and lost sales if a customer demand can not be met.

Illustration of 90% Service Level

Service level = 100 per cent – stockout risk

90% = 100% – 10%

Note: 100% indicates the availability of stock/inventory during lead-time.

Re-order Point with Variable Demand

To estimate the re-order point with a safety stock that will meet a specific service level, let us assume that demand during each day of lead time is uncertain, independent and can be described as a normal distribution. The *average demand for lead time* is the *sum of average daily* demand for the number of *days in the lead time period.*

Similarly, the variance of distribution is sum of daily variances for number of days in the lead time. Using these parameters or variables, the re-order point to meet a specific service level can be computed by the following formula:

$$R = \bar{d}LT + Z\,\sigma d\,\sqrt{LT}$$

Variable Demand with Re-order Point

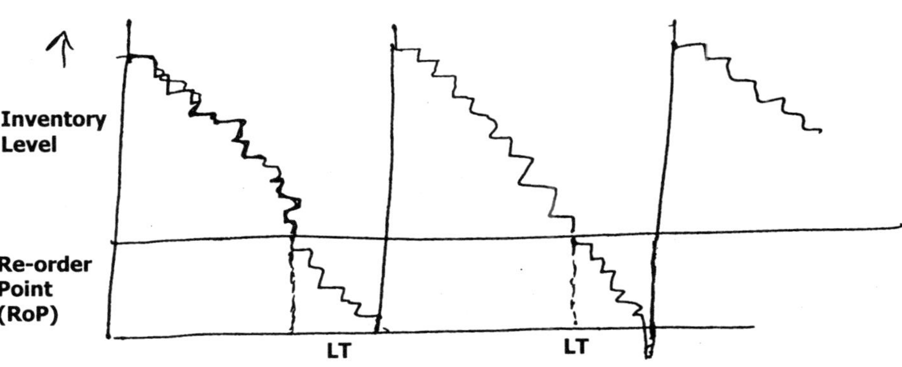

Re-order Point with Safety Stocks

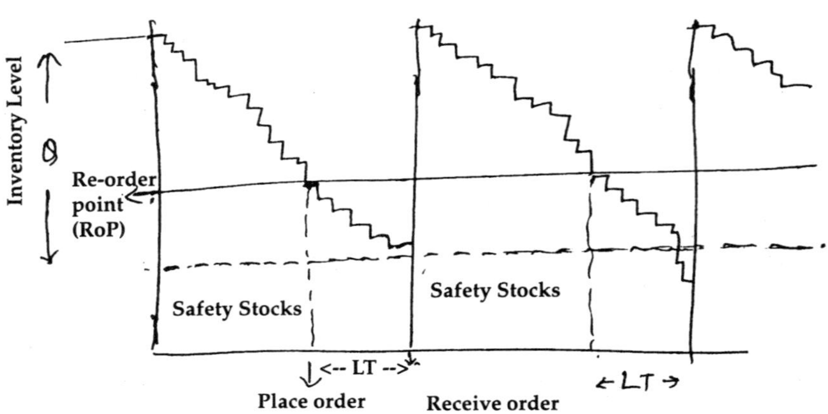

where:

$\underline{R}$ = RoP = Re-order point,

$\bar{d}$ = average daily demand,

L = Lead time,

σd = Standard deviation of daily demand,

Z = No. of standard deviations corresponding to the service level probability,

$Z\,\sigma d\,\sqrt{LT}$ = Safety stock.

Note: LT is also referred as L by some authors.

The term $\sigma d\,\sqrt{LT}$ used in this formula for the re-order point is the square root of the sum of daily variances during lead time.

Variance = (daily variance) × No. of days of lead time

$$= \sigma^2_d\sqrt{LT}$$

$$\text{Standard Deviation} = \sqrt{\sigma^2_d\,LT}$$

$$= \sigma_d\sqrt{LT}$$

The re-order point relative to service level is shown in the figure on next page. The service level is indicated by the shaded area, or probability to the left of RoP.

Example 3

In a example of Jagdeep Stores dealing in designer carpets of various styles stocked by the store, we will assume that daily demand of 20 carpets with standard deviation of 5 carpets per day. We will also assume that daily demand is normally distributed.

The lead time for receiving new order of carpets is 15 days. Determine the Re-order point and safety stock if store wants a service level of 95% with a probability of a stockout equal to 5%.

$\bar{d}$ = 20 carpets per day
LT = 15 days
σd = 5 carpets per day

For a 95% service level, the Z value is 1.96. The Re-order point is computed as follows:

$$\begin{aligned} RoP/R &= \bar{d}LT + Z\sigma_d\sqrt{LT} \\ &= 20(15) + (1\text{-}96)\ (5)\ \sqrt{15} \\ &= 300 + 9.8\ (\sqrt{15}) \\ &= 300 + 9.8 \times 3.87 \\ &= 300 + 37.92 = 337.92 \\ &= \text{or } 338 \text{ carpets} \end{aligned}$$

The safety stock is the second term of the re-order formula

$$\begin{aligned} &= Z\sigma_d\sqrt{LT} \\ &= (1.96)\ (5)\ (\sqrt{15}) \\ &= 9.8)\ (3.87) \\ &= 37.92 \text{ carpets or } 38 \text{ carpets} \end{aligned}$$

Figure: Re-order Point for a Service Level

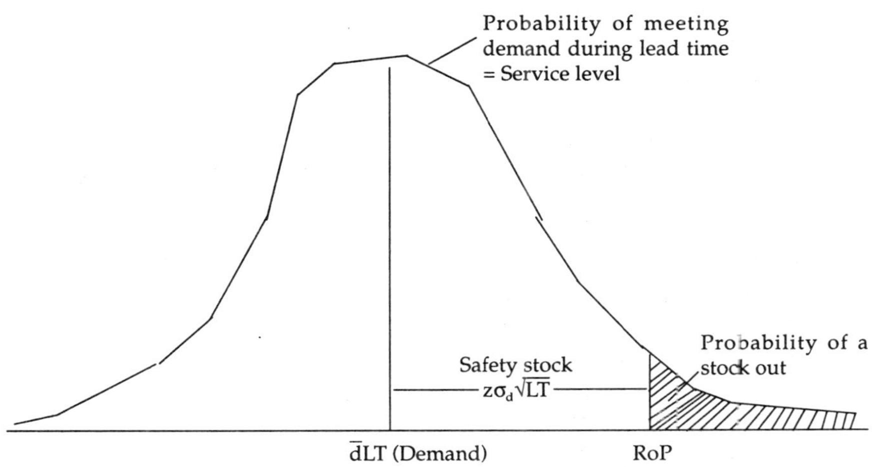

Economic Production Quantity (EPQ) Model (Stevenson, 2006)

It is a variation of EOQ model with non-instantaneous receipt. As we know, the batch mode of production is generally used in production operations. This includes manufacturing as well as assembly line operations, where production work is done in batches.

This is on account of the fact that capacity to produce a particular part/component exceeds the part's/component's usage or demand rate. Thus as long as production continues, inventory will continue to build up. Therefore, it makes sense to *periodically produce* such items in *batches*, or *lots* instead of producing it continuously.

Assumptions of EPQ would be similar to EOQ model except that instead of orders being received in a single delivery, orders in the form of units are received incrementally during production phase.

Assumptions of EPQ Model

1. Only one item is involved
2. Annual demand is known
3. Usage rate is constant
4. Usage or consumption occurs continuously, but production takes place periodically.
5. Production rate is constant
6. Lead time does not show variation
7. There are no quantity discounts

Key Features of EPQ Model

The order quantity is received gradually over time, and the inventory is depleted at the same time it is being replenished. This situation is common where *inventory user* may be inventory producer. For example, part produced is used in assembly operations. This situation can also occur when orders are delivered gradually over time, or when a retailer is also producer.

During production phase of the cycle, *inventory builds up* at a rate equal to the difference between production and usage rates. We can assume 'p' to be production, and 'u' to be usage rates.

For example, in a firm

$p > u$ and $p - u > 0$

$p - u$ = inventory

Production rate = 30 units/day

Inventory usage rate = 5 units/day

therefore,

Inventory build-up rate = 30 – 5 = 25 units/day.

As long as production continues, inventory level will continue to build-up. Inventory begins to decrease when production stops. At the same time, inventory level will be maximum at the point where production stops. When the amount of inventory on hand is depleted, production is resumed and the cycle repeats itself.

Point to Note

Since the company produces the product itself, there are no ordering costs as such. However, with every production run (batch), there are set up costs. Such costs are incurred to prepare the equipment for the next job, and include costs on cleaning, adjusting and changing tools and fixtures. Set-up costs are similar to ordering costs because they are independent of lot (run) size. Therefore set-up costs are treated in the same way as ordering costs. With larger (production) run size one would or company would require lesser number/frequency of production runs, therefore the *annual set up costs will be lower.*

The number of production runs or batches per year will be D/Q and the Annual set up costs will be as follows:

= No. of production runs (batches) per year × set up costs, per production run

$= D/Q_o \times S$

Note: Q is Q_o → optimal quantity
D → demand in units per year
Q → Quantity of order/batch size

EPQ Model (EOQ Model with Incremental Inventory Replenishment)

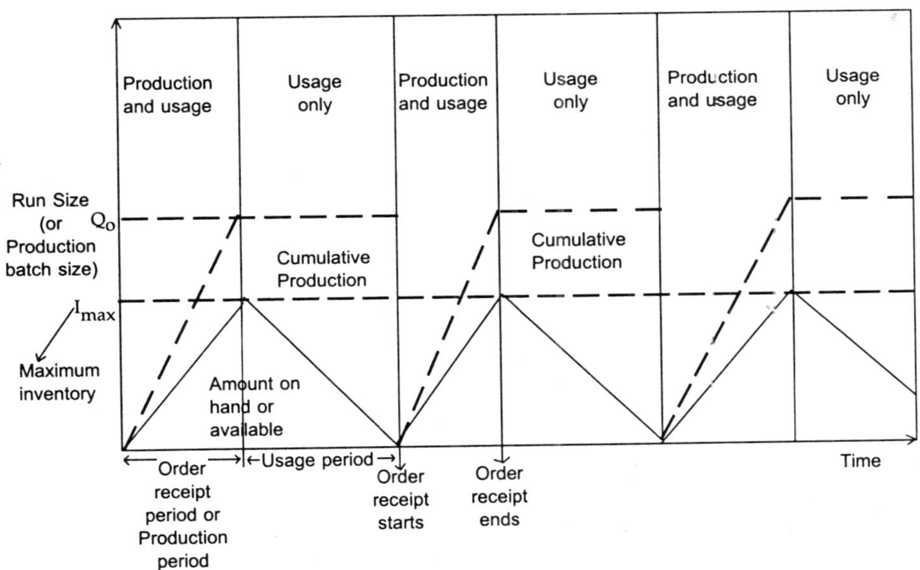

Notes:

1. Cumulative production: It is assumed that there is no usage and production adds entire units to inventory i.e. lot size Q_o.
2. Imax : $p - u > 0$.
(production rate – usage) is equal to inventory for that period or day.
3. At I_{max} production stops; usage occurs, and inventory declines.
4. I_{max} refers to maximum inventory level.

Total Costs are to be minimized:

TC_{min} = Carrying cost + Set-up cost

$= (I_{max}/2)\ H + (D/Q_o) \times S$

where:

I_{max} = Maximum inventory

The Economic run quantity is:

$Q_o = \sqrt{2DS/H} \times \sqrt{p/p-u}$

where

p = Production or delivery rate

u = usage rate

The cycle time (i.e. time between orders or beginning of production runs) for the economic run size model is a function of run size and usage (demand) rate:

Cycle time (Ct) = Q_o/u

Similarly, the run time (production run time) i.e. production phase of the cycle is a function of the run (lot) size and production rate:

Production phase of cycle (Length of production run)

Run time (Rt) = Q_o/p

The maximum and average inventory levels are:

$I_{max} = Q_o/p \times (p - u)$ and

I average = $[I_{max}/2]$ or $[Q_o/p\ (p - u)\ /\ 2]$

Numerical

A home invertor/power-back up system manufacturer uses 48,000 batteries per year for its popular Eagle brand of invertors. The company makes its own batteries, which it produces @ 800 units per day. The inverters are assembled uniformly over the entire year. Carrying cost is Re 1 per battery a year. Set up cost for a production run of batteries is Rs. 45. Assuming that this company operates 240 days per year, find out

(a) Optimal run size

(b) Minimum total annual cost for carrying and set-up cost

(c) Cycle time for the optimal run size

(d) Run-time

Solution to the Numerical based on EPQ Model

D = 48,000 batteries per year

S = Rs. 45/-

H = Rs. 1 per battery a year

p = 800 batteries per day

u = 48,000 batteries per 240 days, or 200 batteries per day

(a) $Q_0 = \sqrt{\frac{2DS}{H}} \sqrt{\frac{p}{p-u}} = \sqrt{\frac{2\,(48000)\,45}{1}} \times \sqrt{\frac{800}{800-200}}$

$= 2400$ batteries

(b) Tc_{min} = Carrying cost + set-up cost

$= (Imax/2)\,H + (D/Q_0)\,S$

Let us compute I_{max} first

$Imax = Q_0/p\,(p-u) = \frac{2400}{800}(800-200) = 1800$ batteries.

$$TC = \left(\frac{1800}{2}\right) \times \text{Rs. } 1 + \left(\frac{48000}{2400}\right) \times \text{Rs. } 45 = \text{Rs. } 1800/-$$

(c) $\text{Cycle Time} = \frac{Q_0}{u} = \frac{2400 \text{ batteries}}{200 \text{ batteries per day}} = 12 \text{ days}$

(d) $\text{Run Time} = \frac{Q_0}{p} = \frac{2400 \text{ batteries}}{800 \text{ batteries per day}} = 3 \text{ days}$

Inventory Placement/Inventory Pooling

The basic issue facing a manager in S.C.M. is to decide the location of inventory of Finished Goods (FGs) strategically. For example, the international manufacturing (MNCs) or trading companies locate the *distribution centers* (DCs) of their products in such a manner that they handle the local competition by reducing delivery time to their customers. Examples are from computer industry and electronic goods manufacturers such as HP, Compaq, LG and Sony for their products. The local computer brands include HCL and Zenith, who have even dealers for their products. In Electronics, it is Sony and Samsung brands who are in competition with other MNCs and local TV and white goods manufacturers like Panasonic and Philips besides Godrej and Onida, which are Indian brands in white soods and in electronic items category.

However, the real issue for any company producing standardized products is where to position the inventory in Supply Chain. On one hand, the company could keep the inventory of FGs at its manufacturing plant and ship the FGs directly to its customers. This results in a "phenomenon" called inventory pooling, which is a method employed to reduce inventory and safety stocks on account of merging of variable demands from the various customers.

A higher than expected demand from one customer will neutralize lower than expected demand from other customer. One disadvantage with this method is that smaller orders or uneconomical orders shipped directly to customers will add to costs to service customers located over long distances.

Forward Placement

Another approach employed by manufacturers is to use a practice called *forward placement*, which means locating *inventory* (or stock) closer to customers at a *warehouse*, Distribution Center (DC), and with wholesaler or retailer. It has two advantages: (1) Faster delivery for order fulfillment process time and (2) Reduced transportation costs. These two together can boost sales of the products. As a result, a company can transport its large inventories at economical transportation rates to the Distribution Centers and the service to customer becomes efficient.

Vendor Managed Inventory

Distributors (i.e. buyers) traditionally place orders with manufacturers (i.e. vendors) when they need products. The timing, size of order, and the inventory plan are decided by the distributors. In Vendor managed inventory (VMI), the manufacturers instead of distributors generate orders. Under VMI concept, manufacturers receive data on stocks and sales electronically through internet. Thus the data analysis, both for past and present periods are analysed and forecasting about growth (or changes) is undertaken with respect to various items and thus an inventory plan is made. VMI concept presents the "role reversal" as the responsibility for planning inventory shifts to a manufacturer.

VMI usually signals a first step towards supply chain collaboration. The manufacturer i.e. vendor has more control over supply chain and the buyer i.e. distributor/customer is relieved of management or administrative functions, which enhances supply chain efficiency because the distributor focuses on promotions and sales. Both manufacturers and distributors benefit from such cooperation and data errors are also reduced due to computerized communication and data exchange environment. Therefore, distributors have lessor stock-outs; planning and ordering costs are reduced and distributors have the right product at the right time. At the same time manufacturers get data on sales on daily basis (or point-of-sales data) which makes forecasting tasks earier.

Collaborative Distribution

Collaborative planning, forecasting, and replacement (CPFR) is the next phase of VMI. Compared to VMI, CPFR concept ensures that responsibility is shared and is collaborative in nature. CPFR enhances VMI's role and combines it with "continuous replenishment" through the incorporation of joint forecasting. Under CPFR concept collaborative partners exchange information and supporting data on past sales, trends, point of sales (PoS) data, on-hand inventory, scheduled promotions and forecasts. The joint forecasting helps in reducing differences in forecast numbers between the two parties that are involved in the collaborative process.

The data is reviewed together and causes of discrepancies are removed. The purchase order can be sent to the vendors without any problem as both parties (i.e. vendors and distributor-customers) work together and jointly fix the problems. This way both parties are able to reduce inventories as the joint working tends to reduce the "bull whip effect" as well.

The collaboration can extend to logistics and transportation management as well. The objective here would be to reduce transportation costs to both manufacturers and distributors. Internet can be used as a coordination tool between manufacturers-carriers and distributors-customers (retailers). Software which is compatible with internet usage has a role to play in order to smoothen coordination among S.C. partners.

Distribution Outsourcing

In order to focus on their core competencies, manufacturers and producers/assemblers are "outsourcing" distribution activities, which they used to perform earlier themselves. This way they take advantage of expertise of distribution companies. While distribution outsourcing helps in reducing inventory levels of manufacturers, it also reduces distribution costs and time, as well as enhances production efficiency of manufacturers. Additionally, flexible and more responsive product delivery helps in meeting cusotmer needs.

Example

Nabisco with US$ 9 billion annual turnover and 800,000 buyers (retailers inclusive) with a range of processed foods/confectionery items with in-coming raw material shipments, outsources distribution and transportation activities with more than US$ 200 million to third party warehousing and logistics 3-PL companies. Nabisco has links with more than 100 third-party firms.

Distribution outsourcing helps this company to focus on marketing. It is thus able to manage variations in demand levels efficiently, and adapt to market place changes efficiently.

Source: www.cbyrnedc.com/outsourcedSpl.html

Measuring Inventory (Krajewski and Ritzman, 2007)

Methods that begin with measuring inventory include physical count of units in numbers, or by volume or by weight. In inventory analysis, we report data on inventories by expressing them in (1) Average aggregate inventory value (2) Weeks of supply, and (3) Inventory turnover.

Average aggregate inventory value is the total value of all items held in inventory by a company in Rupee (or dollar) terms at a cost by adding the individual values of all raw materials, work-in-process (WIP) inventories and finished products. It is to be noted that final sales value in Rupees can not be used for all items, as it is meaningful for final products that can be sold.

It is an average value because it generally represents the inventory investment over a certain period of time. For example, there are products A and B, and we want to measure average value of inventory. In order to simplify, we can put the expression in an algebraic form to arrive at the final value.

Average Aggregate inventory value = [No. of units of item A held in inventory] × [Value of one unit of item A] + [No. of units of item B held in inventory] × [Value of one unit of item B]

If we add value of all items held in inventory, the total value arrived at indicates to managers as to how much of company's assets are "locked-up" in inventory. Generally, manufacturing companies have about 25 per cent of their total assets held up in inventory vis-à-vis wholesalers and retailers who have about 75% of their assets or capital "locked-up" in inventory.

Further, the average aggregate value indicates to managers whether it is too low or high in comparison with industry standards or by comparing historical values while evaluating company's performance in terms of sales versus inventories held or ratio of inventories to production achieved.

Another measure called *weeks of supply* takes demand into account, is obtained by dividing *average aggregate inventory value* by sales per week at cost. It is to be noted that in some low inventory situations, days or even hours are a better unit of time for measuring inventory.

$$\text{Weeks of supply} = \frac{\text{Average Aggregate inventory value}}{\text{Weekly sales (at cost)}}$$

While numerator includes the value of all items ranging from raw materials, work-in-process (WIP) inventory, and finished goods, the denominator indicates the finished goods *sold at cost* rather than sale price after mark ups or discounts. This cost is called "cost of goods sold."

Inventory turnover is an inventory measure obtained by dividing annual sales cost by average aggregate inventory value (all inventory held) during the year.

$$\text{Inventory turnover} = \frac{\text{Annual sales (at cost)}}{\text{Average Aggregate inventory value}}$$

For practical purposes, the most appropriate inventory level can not be determined or chosen easily. For this, benchmarking with leading companies in the industry is to be done.

Links to Financial Measures

Inventory is an investment because it is required for current and future use in a commercial organization. Since it ties-up funds that might be used profitably in other operations.

Return on Assets (RoA)

Return on Assets is an important financial measure which is net income divided by total assets.

Reducing the aggregate inventory investment will reduce total assets in the balance sheet of a company. Consequently, ROA will increase. However, the objective of a company should be to have an appropriate amount of inventory for optimizing business operations and not the least amount of inventory. ROA can also increase by reducing costs in the value chain which would increase the net income.

Working Capital

It is the money used to finance on going operations. Decreasing weeks of supply or increasing inventory turns reduces the working capital required to finance inventories. Reductions in working capital can be achieved by improving customer relationship, order fulfillment and supplier relationship processes.

Reduction in lead times from suppliers can reduce weeks of supplies required and could help in increasing inventory turns.

Total Revenue

Increasing the percentage of on-time deliveries to customers tends to increase *total revenue* because satisfied customers are expected to buy more products from the company. Higher percentage of on-time deliveries from suppliers tend to reduce costs of inventories, which lead to improvements in sales value and consequently surge in company margins.

Cash Flow

Cash to cash is the time lag between paying for raw-materials, components or sub-assemblies/assemblies needed to produce a product and receiving payment for it. Shorter the time-lag better is the position of a company in terms of cash flow because the requirement for working capital is decreased. Some companies re-engineer order placement process so that either full or partial payment is received at the time of order placement which reduces the time lag. In a situation, where customer pays for product before the company has to pay for raw materials required to produce the product is called Negative cash-to-cash situation. Dell computers is one example in this regard which pays for materials as it uses them.

Inventory Productivity

Inventory productivity measures the amount of sales revenue generated from the inventory. It is measured in *inventory turns* computed as sales divided by the average value of inventory in Rupee (or dollar) terms. A higher number of turns indicate that a given amount of inventory on an average has generated greater sales value.

Improving inventory turns results in reduced costs related with inventory, better profit margins, reduced assets and improved RoA (Return on Assets). Increasing inventory turns generally leads to reduction in inventory. It is to be noted that all inventory items do not contribute to the same value to the business.

Some items could be very important while others are taking valuable space in the warehouse. Inventory turnover increase should be done in a manner that it does not affect the service quality or delivery reliability.

JIT AND LEAN OPERATIONS

The term *just-in-time (JIT)* refers to an operations system, where materials and services are moved and delivered with the precise timing that coincides with each step of the process just when those materials and services are needed. Initially, the term JIT was used to refer to movement of materials, parts and semi-finished goods within a production system. Over a period of time, the scope of JIT broadened and the term became associated with *lean production*.

Now the two terms are used inter-changeably to refer to a highly co-ordinated and repetitive manufacturing or service system designed to produce a high volume of output with fewer resources than more traditional repetitive systems, but with ability to accumulate more variety than traditional systems.

History

The JIT approach was developed at the Toyota Motor Company, Japan. The development of JIT was influenced by the fact that Japan was a crowded country with few natural resources. Despite that, Japanese are very sensitive to waste and inefficiency. They regard scrap and re-work as waste, and excess inventory as an evil because it takes up space and scarce resources, including capital (funds).

A widely held view of JIT is that it is simply a system for production scheduling that results in low levels of work-in process (WIP) inventory and it aims to reduce overall inventory. But actually, it is a philosophy that encompasses every aspect of process, from design to production, and after sales service of a product. The philosophy is aimed to pursue a system that functions well with minimal levels of inventories, minimal waste, minimal space requirements and minimal transactions. As such, it is a system that is not prone to disruptions and should be flexible in terms of product variety and volume it should be able to handle.

Briefly, it can be said that a system that was originally meant to reduce inventory levels eventually became a system for continuously improving all aspects of manufacturing operations.

As the JIT production system has developed with the objective of eliminating waste, it is composed of the following in elements:

1. Flexible resources
2. Cellular layouts
3. Pull production system
4. Kanban production control
5. Small-lot production
6. Quick set-ups
7. Uniform production levels
8. Quantity at source
9. Total productive maintenance
10. Supplier networks

In the lean systems, quality is given utmost importance in manufacturing the final product and to the process that is used to transform various inputs, parts or components into the final product. Companies that use lean operations have achieved a level of quality that enables them to function with small batch size and tight schedules. Lean systems have reliability as major sources of inefficiency and disruptions are eliminated and workers are trained not only in their functional areas but also to continuously improve the system.

Just in Time (JIT) Manufacturing

JIT has many definitions but it can be explained and defined as:

> "JIT manufacturing is a system where we produce and deliver finished goods just in time to be sold, sub-assemblies are assembled JIT into finished goods, fabricated parts are used JIT to put together sub-assemblies, and purchased materials are ordered/received JIT to be transformed into fabricated parts."

JIT is a disciplined approach to improve manufacturing quality, flexibility, and productivity through elimination of waste and the total involvement of people. JIT is meant not only to reduce inventory but the overall objective is to improve quality. To realize the benefits of JIT, certain conditions must prevail in the organizing. There are:

— Respect for people, creating a stable environment, motivation and trust, all round management, use of Robotics (wherever required), quality circles, and sub-contractor networks.

— The employees (not management) operate JIT. Employees work on problems and solve them, and improve product quality.

Elimination of waste is achieved through a better focus in the production

Major Components of the Lean System vis-a-vis its Objectives

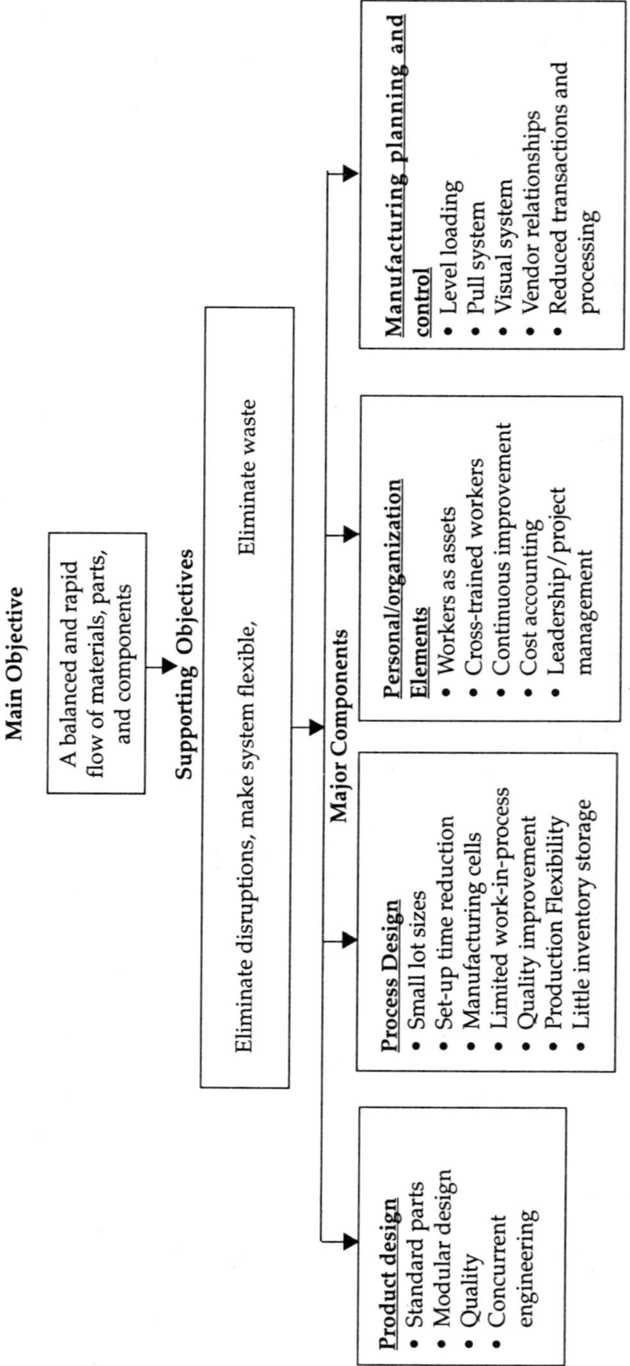

units/factories, use of group technology, quality control on site, KANBAN (implementation), minimization of set-up times and uniform plant loads. The implementation of such programs results in reduction of inventories in the organisation.

Three Components of JIT

— **JIT purchasing:** It ensures usage of materials, immediately after their arrival.

— **JIT Manufacturing:** It ensures that goods which are manufactured are sent for immediate shipment/or It ensurers that manufactured sub-assemblies are sent for immediate assembly, and fabricated parts are sent for immediate use in sub-assemblies.

— **JIT delivery:** It ensures to transport goods in a manner to meet tighter transit time schedule and reliability standards of JIT operations.

All three components must work together so that the organisation benefits from them.

JIT reduces cost on account of application of *Experience curve* and *economics of scales*, as the higher volume of the given product is manufactured by using same resources. This reduces the per unit cost by spreading fixed costs over higher number of units produced or assembled.

As JIT uses the *learning concept also*, which explains that with each doubling of cumulative production it brings in reduction of unit cost. This is on account of the fact that employees, including technical manpower, gain experience in the process, as they make less mistakes and make use of better equipment and improved technology to increase production.

Fewer mistakes mean lower reworking costs and lower staffing needs. Fewer mistakes smoothen the production rate, reduce buffer inventories and associated costs. Each positive effect of JIT gets embedded into other areas of production leading to further cost reduction. Higher productivity is realized by requiring less input for the same output levels.

Disadvantages

JIT has certain shortcomings as well. Some companies assume that if their competitors have JIT, then they should also have it. JIT is most effective in repetitive manufacturing environment, but not well adapted to other manufacturing techniques. JIT also requires supplier involvement, as the supplier must provide quality material just when needed. As JIT advocates flexibility and broadly defined jobs, employees who know more are paid more under JIT philosophy.

Transportation can be a problem unless the carriers serving the plant and warehouse provide JIT delivery. Transportation costs may increase until all parties feel comfortable in that role. JIT does not work well in a global trade, which requires buffer stock because of long lead times.

Note: JIT system will work anywhere but it should be adapted to specific environment. In some situations, where some experts advocate *zero safety* stocks and nearly no raw material inventory, the system will not be JIT but will be a failure owing to production department going out of stock when sudden customer orders are received. Therefore, we can say that JIT is required for continuously aiming for increased product quality, and its overall benefits that make JIT to operate successfully.

Pull System

The term *push* and *pull* systems are used to describe two different systems for moving work through the production process. In traditional system, a *push* system is used when work is finished at a particular workstation; the *output* is pushed to next work station, or in case of final operation, the final output is pushed on to the *inventory*.

On the other hand, in a *pull system*, each workstation *pulls* the output from *preceding* workstation as needed, and the output of final operation is pulled by customer demand. Thus work moves on in response to demand from the next stage in process whereas in *push system*, work (output) moves on as it is completed without next station's readiness for work. Consequently, the work may pile up at workstations that fall behind schedule on account of, say, equipment failure or detection of a problem related to quality.

In JIT system, communication moves backward from work station to workstation. Each workstation (i.e. customer) communicates its need for more work to do the preceding work station (i.e. supplier) and thus assures that supply equals demand.

Work moves "just-in-time (JIT)" for next operation; as a result work is coordinated and the accumulation of *excessive inventories* between operations is avoided. Therefore, by design, each workstation produces just enough output to meet the anticipated demand of the next workstation.

Visual Systems

In a pull system, work flow is dictated by "next step demand". A system can communicate such demand in a variety of ways. The most commonly used device is "*kanban*" card. *Kanban* in Japanese Language means "*signal*" or "*visible record*" when a worker needs material or work from the preceding station, he uses or needs a *kanban* card, which in fact authorizes him to move or work on parts. In *kanban* system, no part or lot can be moved without use of one of these cards, which are referred to as "Kanban" cards.

How this System Works?

A *kanban* card is fixed to each container; when a workstation needs to replenish its supply of parts, a worker goes to the area where these parts are stored and draws one container of parts. Each container holds a predetermined quantity. The worked removes the *kanban* card from the container and "posts" it in a designated spot where it will be visible, and the container is moved to workstation. The "posted" *kanban* card is picked up by a *stock person*, who replenishes stock with another container. Demand for parts triggers a replenishment, and parts are supplied as per usage/requirements. Similar "removals" and "replenishments" are all controlled by *kanbans* up and down the line from vendors to finished goods inventories.

In case some inventories are building up, supervisors can withdraw some kanbans from the system. In case system appears to be tight, some additional 'kanbans' can be introduced.

What is observed is that:

Vendors can influence number of containers.

Trip times can influence the number i.e. longer trip times may lead to fewer but larger containers while shorter trip times may involve a greater number of small containers.

Since 'kanban' cards number is an important variable, one can use the following formula to compute the ideal number of 'kanban' cards

$$N = \frac{DT(1+X)}{C}$$

where

N = Total No. of containers (1 card per container)

D = Planned usage rate of using work centre

T = Average waiting time for replenishment of parts plus average production time for a container of parts.

X = Policy variable set by management that reflects possible inefficiency in the system (the closer it is to '0', more efficient is the system)

C = Capacity of a standard container (should not be more than 10 per cent of daily usage pattern)

Note: D and T must be in same units. (*Source*: Adapted from "Operations Management" by William Stevenson, Tata McGraw-Hill, 2004).

Numerical

At a truck manufacturing factory usage of "clutch assembly" at a work center is 300 parts per day, and a standard container holds 25 parts. It takes 0.12 day for a container to complete a circuit from time a 'kanban' card is received until the container is returned empty. Compute the number of *kanban* cards (containers) needed if X = 0.20

Solution

We have to find N

D = 300 parts/day

T = 0.12 day

C = 25 parts/container

X = 0.20

N = = 1.728

(Round it off to 2 containers)

Limitation: Rounding up will cause system to be relaxed, and rounding down will cause system to be tighter. Usually rounding up is used.

Kanban system usually have small lot sizes, short lead times, high-quality output, and is an example of team-work. *Kanban* is essentially *a two-bin* type of inventory. Supplies are replenished when they reach a pre-determined level. Materials Requirement Planning (MRP) is more concerned with projecting requirements and with planning and scheduling operations.

A major benefit of kanban is its simplicity, while the main benefit of MRP is its ability to handle complex planning and scheduling. It addition, MRP II enables management to answer "what if" questions for capacity planning.

Kanbans can also be used *outside the factory* to order materials from suppliers. The supplier brings the order e.g. filled container directly to its point of use in the factory and then picks up an empty container with *kanban* to fill and return it later. It is not unusual to observe 5,000 to 10,000 of these supplier *kanbans* in a typical JIT style unit to rotate between factory and suppliers. To handle this volume of high transactions a special kind of kanban "post-office" can be set up, with 'kanbans' sorted by each supplier. The supplier thus checks up his "mail box" to pick up new orders before returning filled containers to the factory. Bar-coded *kanbans* and Electronic kanbans, can also be used to facilitate communication between customer and supplier. The kanban system is actually similar to Re-order point system. The difference lies in its application. While the *re-order* point system attempts to create a permanent ordering policy, the *kanban* system aims for continuous reduction of inventory.

The number of kanbans required can be calculated on the basis of demand and lead time information, which is as follows:

$$\text{No. of kanbans} = \frac{\text{Average demand during lead time + Safety stock}}{\text{Container Size}}$$

$$N = \frac{dL + S}{C}$$

N = No. of kanbans (or containers).

D = Av. Number of units demanded over the given time period

L = Lead time, the time taken to replenish an order (expressed in same units as demand) i.e. time etc.

S = Safety stock, usually given as a percentage of demand during lead time.
But it can be based on service level and variance of demand during lead time (refer to "re-order point" inventory model in continuous inventory system).

C = Container size.

Source: Adapted from "Operation Management" by Russell and Taylor, PHI, 2004).

To enforce improvement process, the container size should be smaller than demand during the lead time. At many Japanese companies, containers can hold roughly 10% of a day's demand. Benefits involve the reduction in number of kanbans; if required smaller number of kanbans help in identification of problems that are then solved by managers.

Example

At Sun pharmaceuticals company in Ahmedabad, a technical worker processes 200 bottles of dental preparation per hour through his workstation. If one kanban is fixed to every *container* that holds 20 bottles, it takes 20 minutes to receive new bottles from previous workstation. Since the factory uses a safety stock factor of 10 per cent, how many kanbans are required for the bottling process?

Solution

D = 200 bottles per hour
L = 20 minutes = 20/60 = 0.3 hour
S = 10% i.e. 0.10 (200 × 0.3)
= 6 bottles
C = 20 bottles

$$N = \frac{dL+S}{C} = \frac{(200\times0.3)+6}{20} = \frac{60+6}{20} = \frac{66}{20}$$

= 3.3 kanbans or containers

We can "round up" to 4 which will relax up operations slightly, or "round down" to 3 to improve operations.

Inventory Storage and JIT

JIT systems are designed to minimize inventory storage, as in JIT philosophy inventory storage is waste. Inventories are buffers that tend to cover up recurring problems that are never resolved because first, they are never obvious and secondly presence of inventory makes them, i.e. problems look less serious. When machine breaks down it will not disrupt the system if there is sufficient inventory in store from machine's previous output to feed the next workstation.

The use of inventory as the "solution" can lead to increasing amounts of inventory if breakdowns increase. The better solution is to find the 'cause' of machine break downs and focus on removing them. Similarly problems related to quality, unreliable vendors and scheduling can also be solved by having sufficient inventories to fall back upon. But carrying all that extra inventory increases cost burden and requirement for more space; and allows problems to go unresolved.

The JIT approach is to reduce down inventories gradually in order to 'uncover' the problems with a view to solve them, which leads to removal of more inventory. As a result JIT system solves more problems and so on. Low inventories are due to a *process* of problem solving that occurs over time. Since problems continue to occur, there is a need to identity and solve problems within a short time to prevent new problems from disrupting the smooth flow of work through the system.

One way to minimize inventory storage in JIT system is to have deliveries (from suppliers) go directly to production floor, which eliminates the need to store incoming parts and materials. At the other end of process, completed product units are shipped out after they are ready, which minimizes the storage of finished goods. Along with low WIP inventory, these JIT features result in systems that operate with little inventory.

Advantages of lower inventory are: lower carrying costs, lesser space requirement, little tendency to rely on buffers, lesser re-work requirements and reduced need to "work-off" current inventory before implementing design improvements.

Risks of less inventory: If problems arise, there is no "safety net". There is a possibility of missed opportunities if the system is unable to respond quickly to those opportunities.

The ABC Classification System

The ABC classification system is a method employed by business firms for classifying inventory according to importance of materials and items. This system is usually based on annual value (in rupees terms) i.e. Re value/unit of materials/items multiplied by annual consumption or usage or off take rate of these materials/items. Typically, three categories of items are used:

A → Very important
B → Moderately important
C → Least important

The actual member of categories may vary depending on the needs of a company as to how many categories it wants to differentiate towards its inventory control efforts.

In general, 5-20 per cent of total inventory items account for 70 to 80 per cent of the total value (in Re terms) of inventory. These are classified as *class A items*.

Class B items account for about 25-30 per cent of total inventory units but contribute about 15 percent of total inventory value in rupee terms.

Class C items account for 50-60 per cent of total inventory items but account for 5-15 per cent of total value of inventory.

In ABC classification systems, each class of inventory, requires different levels of inventory control i.e. higher the value of inventory, tighter will be the control. Therefore, class A items require much higher control than class B and perhaps for class C items control is somewhat relaxed i.e. it requires much less attention.

The first step in ABC analysis is to make list of all items and classify them into class A, B, or C category items. Assign a value (in Re terms) to each item by multiplying cost (or price) of the item/unit by annual demand for that item. Thereafter, all items are ranked as per their annual Re value. Roughly top 10 per cent items (based on their value contribution to total items) are classified as class A items; the next 30 per cent as class B items and the last 60 per cent as class C items.

These percentages very from company to company, but in most cases a relatively small number of items will account for a large share of the value or cost associated with the inventory, and these items should receive more attention or control by reviewing the stocks (inventories) on hand and control over withdrawals should be exercised to make sure customer service levels (both for internal and external customers) are attained.

Since the value of class A items is higher, accurate demand forecasts should be made for their consumption in order to minimize high inventory, and close attention should be paid to the purchasing policy.

Class B and C items, require less stringent control. Since carrying costs are usually lower for class C items, higher inventory levels can be sometimes maintained with larger safety stocks.

Please note that class C items are not un-important as stock-out for class C items such as nuts and bolts used for manufacturing can result in a shut down of an assembly line.

Although cost is an pre-dominant reason for A-B-C classification of inventory, other factors such as scarcity of parts, difficult in arranging a supply, longer lead times may also be the reasons for giving items a higher priority.

DISTRIBUTION MANAGEMENT

Distribution

It is the "downstream" portion of a supply chain, comprising distribution channels, and processes, including warehousing, which a product must pass through on its way to the final customer (end-user). Distribution is the actual movement of products and raw materials/components between locations. Distribution management involves handling of raw materials and products at receiving stations and/or at docks, storing and packing them and to carry out orders shipment to customers. The objective of distribution is to under take *order fulfillment,* which means delivery of customer's order on-time at the specified location.

"Distribution and transportation" are often called *logistics.* Logistics management interpretation in a broader sense is similar to that of supply chain management. However, it can be explained in brief as an area or sub-set of SCM, which is concerned with transportation and distribution of materials and products. The driving force behind *"distribution and transportation"* is *speed of service.* Owing to customer demand who wants to get or buy things "now", the requirement for vendor is to find out stock-position with respect to different raw materials/components or finished goods at the warehouse located in the vicinity of the service area. This also puts pressure on transportation company to answer whether it has trucks and schedules available to pickup goods and execute deliveries at the desired customer locations.

We can also say that *information* is key to distribution speed. Commercial firms are making use of IT technology to speed up the distribution processes, which includes the use of Electronic Data Interchange (EDI), bar code technology and the Internet to increase the responsiveness to meet customers' requirements.

Distribution is an important supply chain component of internet dot-coms i.e. virtual companies like e-bay.com, amazon.com, rediff.com and yahoo.com, etc., whose supply chains consist entirely of supply and distribution processes. These companies have almost no production processes, they *market and distribute* products they acquire (or buy) from suppliers. They are driven not from the front-end i.e. website but from the back-end i.e. distribution. Their success depends on their capacity to *ship orders* when customer wants them.

Distribution Requirements Planning (DRP)

It is a system employed for inventory management and distribution planning, which is found to be useful in multilevel warehousing systems existing at factory levels and regional levels. The concepts of MRP (Material Requirements Planning) are extended to multi-level warehouse inventories. The demand is worked out from downstream channel members and then it moves upwards through the warehouse system to obtain time-bound replenishment schedules in order to move inventories through the warehouse network. DRP is often used to plan and coordinate transportation, warehousing, manpower/ workers, equipment and financial flows.

Distribution Centers and Warehousing

Distribution Centres (DCs) incorporate the warehousing or storage functions. These are buildings or premises that are used to receive, handle, store, process and package products for shipping them to customers.

For example, IOC facilities for petroleum products: FCI warehouses for grains distribution i.e. wheat and rice for deficit states or PDS shops for retail level distribution to needy segments of population. NDDB's storage of dairy products i.e. milk powder for use during lean period. Mother dairy's central storages in different Metros for procurement and distribution of vegetables and fruits through its horticultural products division called "Safal". Intel Computers Distribution Channels in different parts of the world to distribute/ market processors and motherboards for manufacturers.

With the latest developments in IT technology and e-commerce, warehousing and distribution management is undergoing a change. As a result, there are more frequent orders, even smaller orders, and with rising consumer expectations, responsiveness factor to customers has come under pressure for the vendors. To speed up processing and delivery of orders on time, material handling equipment (usually automated) requirements have increased.

Instead of buying goods in bulk and storing them, Retailers have pushed inventories and storage to upstream members in the supply chain. They expect vendors or suppliers (including distributors) to make frequent delivery of merchandize with wide range of product-mix that is labelled, picked and shipped in store-ready conditions and configurations.

Another interesting development is the handling of entire range of components of high-tech goods, say for example, electronic and computer industry products and white good industry related products at the DC level who take up or are given the responsibility of assembling final goods on receipt of confirmed orders from customers. That is DCs do not stock finished goods but components of goods, and in such instances manufacturing moves away from manufacturing plants to match the orders from customers and discourage piling up of FGs inventories.

Also, to successfully manage retail level requirements, DCs are expected to manage cross-docking, automated sorting, customized labeling, packing and processing of goods inventory.

Warehouse Management Systems

To handle and manage pressures of distribution management, commercial firms employ *warehousing management systems* (WMS) to run routine and daily operations of DC and keep track of inventory levels of different items. The *WMS* system places an item at a specific location in storage; locates and takes an item out of storage; packs and ships it via a *carrier*. WMS confirms that an item is available to ship; otherwise it will inform when an item would become available to ship.

Components of WMS

- **Transportation Management**—It facilities the DC to track in-bound and out-bound shipments, it builds up the economical loads, selects the best carrier based on cost and service.
- **Order Management**—It helps DC to accept, add, change or cancel orders in available time. If item is not available, it will took into supplier's production schedule and finds out when it would become available.
- **Yard Management**—Controls activities at the facilities dock point, and schedules dock deliveries or their times to reduce bottlenecks.
- **Labour Management**—Controls, plans and manages the performance and working of warehouse personnel
- **Warehouse Optimization**—Optimizes the "placement" of items in a warehouse; it is called "Slotting" which is based on demand, product groupings and physical (including chemical) characteristics of the item.
- **WMS Handles Cross-docking**—Saves on costs by undertaking location specific storage, picking and packing operations to fulfill outgoing orders. WMS undertakes customized labeling and packaging as well.

Distribution Outsourcing

It is similar to production outsourcing, where companies turn to suppliers or manufacturers-cum-suppliers to supply them with products, which were once manufactured/assembled in-house. Just the way these suppliers are cost efficient suppliers of products owing to better utilization of time and resources, the manufacturing companies are turning to external suppliers to take over distribution and warehousing operations of their products. Outsourcing allows companies to focus on their core-competencies, and allows them to take advantage of expertise that these distribution companies have developed. Distribution outsourcing helps in reduction of inventory levels (raw materials, components or FG's whatever the case may be) and helps in reducing costs for the firm that is outsourcing distribution operations.

Third-Party Logistics (3-PL)

3-PL term refers to the outsourcing of logistics management responsibilities to an external company to perform either all or part of company's materials management and product distribution functions. Product distribution is carried out along with transportation activities. Also, there can be *inbound logistics* and *outbound logistics.*

Modern 3-PL arrangements involve long-term commitment and often multiple functions. For example *Ryder Dedicated Logistics* a U.S. based company had 5 years agreement with *Whirlpool* to design, manage and operate inbound logistics. Such agreements are operation in India also. In some situation, a few companies like TVS have their logistics company dedicated to distribution logistics. On the other hand, exporting companies routinely use or have contracts with them for out-bound logistics. "DB Schenker"is one such award winning 3-PL Company

3-PL providers come in all sizes and shapes from small companies with

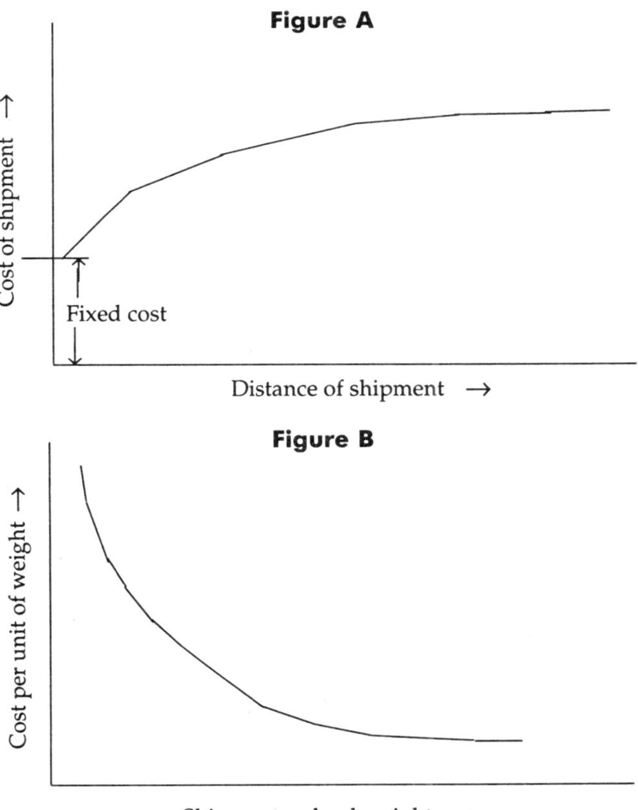

Figures A and B: Charts depicting Transportation Economics Related Curves

turnover in millions to huge companies with revenues in billions. Many of such companies are bound to manage many stages of supply chain and are SCM solution provides to manufacturing and trading firms.

Transportation Economics

Transportation economics is a function of the following factors:

Distance

It is a major factor contributing to the cost in the form of fuel, vehicle maintenance and labour involved. However, there are fixed costs involved with shipment pick up and delivery irrespective of distance to be covered for delivery. Cost curve on the other hand increases at a decreasing rate as distance increases.

Weight

Transport cost per unit of weight decreases as shipment load increases because of fixed costs of consignment booking and pickup, administration charges and delivery get spread over the increased shipment load or weight.

Density

Product density is a combination of weight and volume. A consignment or shipment may have more weight than volume vis-à-vis a consignment with larger volume than weight. A shipment with higher volume may result in higher costs per unit volume/weight than a shipment with higher density occupying less volume/space in a container or truck as the cubic capacity of truck/container can be utilized further. In actual situations, a manager may have to trade off between these two situations as per unit price of the product with higher volume may be lower which can justify the economics as far as landing cost per unit of weight may still work out to be cheaper assuming, for example, the whole truckload has been utilized for purchasing the in-bound material. This means freight costs per unit of higher volume material get lower on purchase of full truckload equivalent material. On the other hand, the material could be made more dense by processing or assembling at the site, if factors and facilities could be made available, to reduce freight costs.

Shipment/Product Dimensions

Uneven package sizes and shapes including excessive length, breadth and or height dimensions may not fit properly resulting in wasted volume or cubic capacity of the container or truck. Therefore, effort should be made at raw material or manufacturing stage to manipulate dimensions to fit the consignment in the designated space or arrange special vehicles such as in the case of transporting military, and industrial equipment, including odd size steel rods and railings. In case of components of various sizes the same could be packed in a manner that the whole consignment accommodates more units of such material.

Costing

Fixed Costs

These costs remain unchanged the short-run and must be paid by the transporter even while he is not operating. These involve staff salaries, vehicle maintenance and insurance, administration charges of office and office equipment, information systems and other associated charges which a transportation company has to pay in terms of license and state permits for service operations.

Variable Costs

These costs are related to the movement of cargo or shipment with each pick-up and delivery trip. These costs typically include labour, fuel, and maintenance charges, which are higher when vehicles are put to use due to wear and tear. It is the minimum amount a transport/carrier company must charge to recover daily operational expenses. Otherwise it may not remain in business.

Up and Down Trip Costs

These costs are supposed to be incurred on the basis of carrier vehicle making a return trip "without" finding the shipper from the "delivery point" to "point of origin" of shipment. In such situations, costs of two way trip-back and forth trip must be borne by the original shipper or back return shipper. Customers must be found to stay in business and yet compete in the logistics services provider market.

Pricing Decisions

Cost of Service

This approach is used when a transport company fixes a rate based on the cost of service provided plus a profit margin. This approach is used for hauling low-value shipments or while facing a competitive environment.

Value of Service

This approach is more appropriate for high worth or high value consignments which are more valuable to a shipper consigner than low value truck loads of routine items. Though competition in this segment is limited to a few freight companies such as DHL, Fed Express, etc., value of service charges are still higher than normal consignments charged by other service providers like DTDC, On-Dot courier service, First Flight Courier, etc.

Commodity Rates

When a large quantity of an either un-graded or graded commodity/ shipment moves between any two of the several destinations on regular basis, it is common practice to publish a *commodity rate*. Commodity rates are published on a point to point basis and apply to particular products or destinations. See *The Hindustan Times* commodity page that appears on a fixed day of the week in this newspaper.

Rates-based on Classification

All products that are transported are generally grouped into uniform classifications. The classification takes into account the characteristics of a product or a bulk commodity that can be a factor in the cost of handling and transportation. Products with odd sizes, dimensions, density, liability such as petroleum products can be grouped into a particular class. This helps in fixing the freight rate.

Special Rates and Services

When a consignment of different products, or assortment of different products is transported, an average price rating is used for total shipment.

When a shipment moves under the tariff (rate) of a single carrier, it is called *local rate*. When multiple carriers are involved *joint rate* (up and down trip rate) may be applicable.

Transit services allow a shipment to be stopped at an "in-between" point between "point-of-origin" of shipment and the "destination" to facilitate loading storage, and/or processing.

For various business and other unforeseen reasons, a shipper may change routing, destination or even consignee after a shipment is made/or when it is in transit. *Diversion* means changing the destination of shipment before it could arrive at its "originally specified" destination.

"*Re-consignment*" refers to a change in consignee prior to the delivery. Both services can be provided by road and rail carriers.

A *split delivery* means when a "portions or parts" of a shipment are required to be delivered at different destinations.

Demurrage charges refer to holding the consignment at the warehouse of Logistics Services provider (by rail and road carriers) beyond 48-72 hours. After this, the charges are to be borne by the Consignee.

Environment Services

This refers to taking special care of consignment with respect to ventilation, referigeration and heating in some cases. In such cases, special equipment charges may be applied to the shipper for the safety and well-being of a consignment which can be spoiled otherwise.

Warehousing

A warehouse is traditionally a place to hold or store an inventory of items, raw-materials, or even final products. With the development of transportation facilities and overall transportation system, product storage has moved from households to retailers, and wholesalers/sub-wholesalers. Warehouses generally hold inventory as a point of logistics pipeline in order to balance demand and supply.

With globalization, Indian departmental stores and retail chains like Big bazaar and even Electronic Products stores like Vivek's and Pais in South India find it difficult to manage purchases and transportation in terms of economics when buying directly from suppliers or manufacturers. The cost of moving and transporting small shipments becomes prohibitive. In order to overcome this constraint, wholesalers and integrated retailers use modern warehouse systems to support the stock replenishment logistically. The traditional warehouse has thus evolved into a *distribution centre to meet* the needs of retailers.

For manufacturers, the *distribution centres* (also called strategic warehouses) have given opportunity to reduce holding time of materials inventory. Thus warehouses have because integral part of JIT (Just-in-time) production systems that rely on little stocks. Products or raw-materials/components can be purchased and shipped to such *distribution centers* (strategic warehouses).

Since JIT aims to reduce work-in-process (WIP) inventory, the *strategic warehouses* or *distribution centres* are dependent largely on efficient logistics. Such warehouses also do sorting and sequencing for each assembly plant or production unit in order to reduce inventory during assembly/manufacturing operations.

These warehouses are also useful for creating product-mix assortments for retail customers, say for example Godrej soaps and appliances assortment of bathing soaps, detergents and personal care products besides refrigerators; LG Electronics—TV, DVD, HDTVs, Washing machines, audio systems, microwave ovens, refrigerators and so on. Another input that is important for these warehouses is the flexibility in operations. This is possible only if information is received and utilized in timely manner. Flexibility in operations also helps in creating local presence of a brand from other regions, or from other countries.

Consolidation and Break-Bulk operations at Strategic Warehouse or Distribution Center

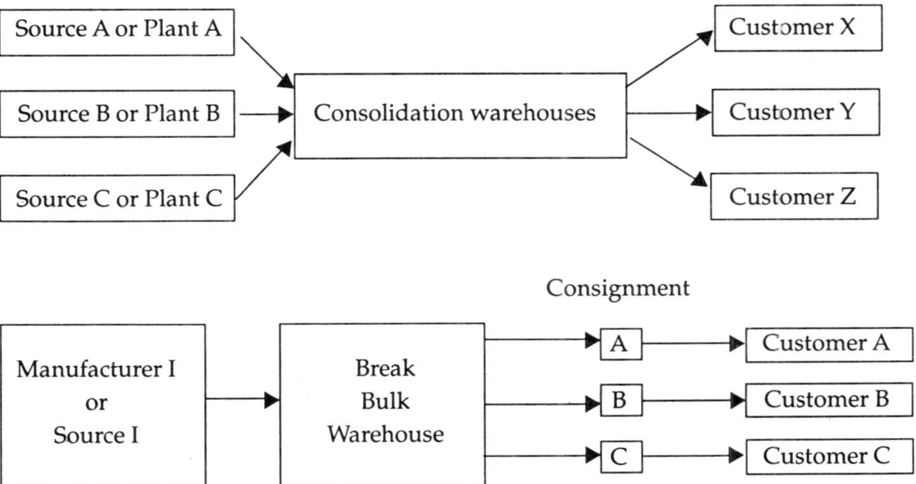

Economic Benefits

Consolidation and Break-Balk Operations

Materials which are received from multiple sources are combined into a large single shipment to match with customer requirements. This is called *consolidation* operations as it helps in reducing freight charges, and executing timely and controlled delivery at customer's premises or receiving dock. The entire operation from receiving consignments from different sources to consolidation generally helps in reducing transportation charges.

On the other hand, a *break-bulk* operation receives a single large shipment at the warehouse and is split into the individual orders to arrange local deliveries. See the diagram on the previous page. Both *consolidation* and *break-bulk* use warehouse capacity to impart efficiency to transportation efforts.

Sorting

The main aim of sorting at strategic warehouses is to reconfigure freight consignments as they flow from their origin to destinations. There are three major types of assortment—*Cross docking, mixing,* and *assembly* which are generally done in warehouses/distribution centres.

The major aim of *cross-docking* is to combine consignments/inventory from various sources into pre-specified assortment as per requirements of a specific

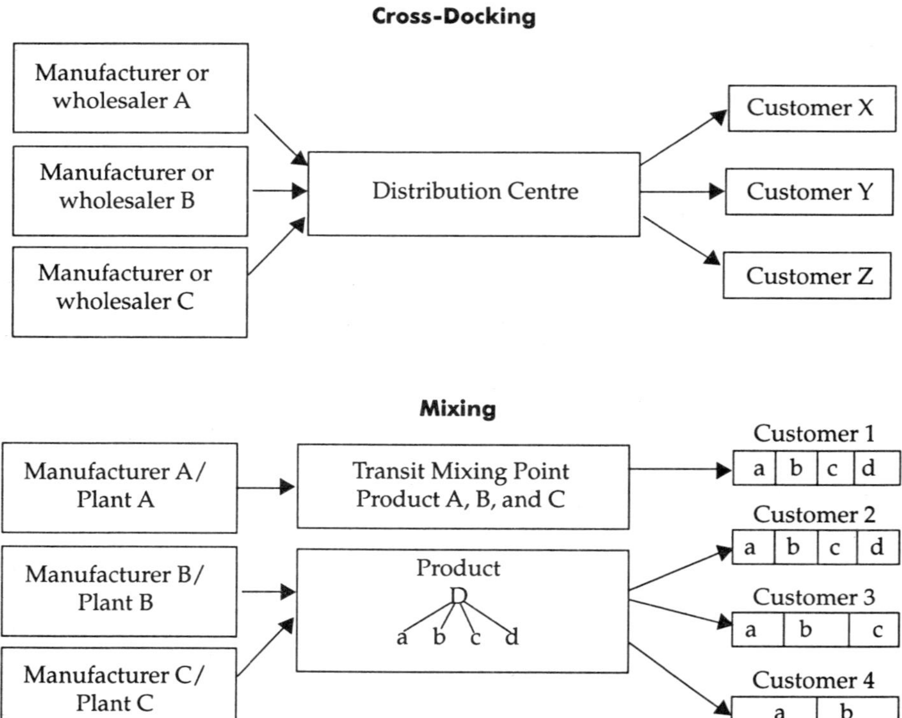

Order Assembly
Scenario 1

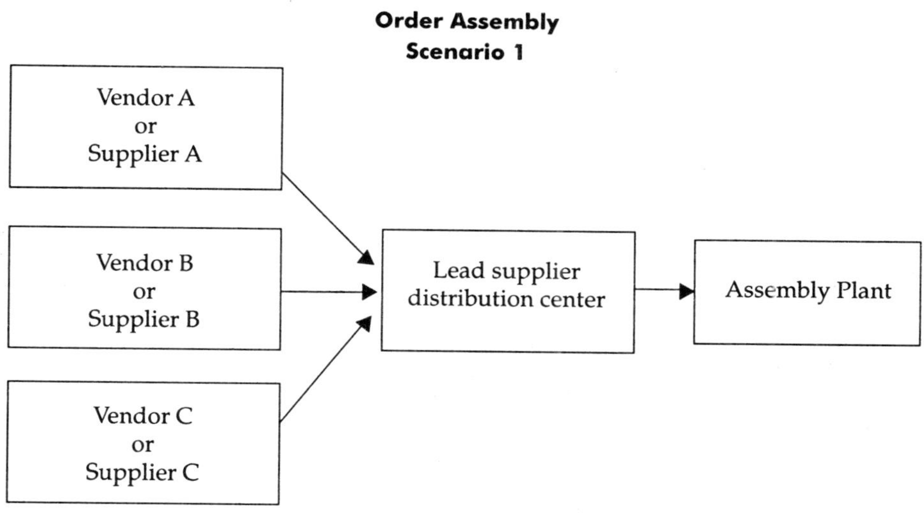

Order Assembly
Scenario 2

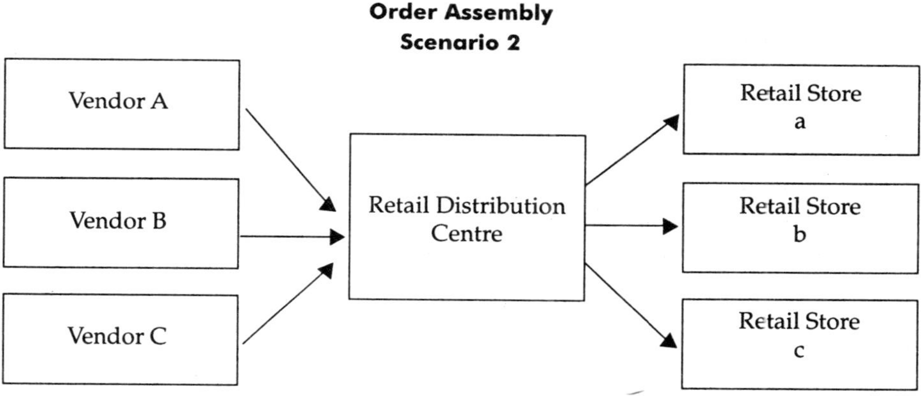

customer. For cross-clocking to succeed, on-time delivery from each source such as wholesaler, or manufacturer is required. As soon as material consignment is unloaded at warehouse, it is sorted by destination. If for example, the material has already been sorted, loaded and labeled with quantity and grade specification by each destination (or customer at a given destination), the material is transferred from receiving vehicle/truck into another vehicle dedicated to delivery destination.

Mixing operation at the warehouse is performed at a location in between shipment of origin and destination. Upon arrival at mixing warehouses, consignments of materials are unloaded and sorted into combination desired by each customer. Also, during mixing, in bound consignments can be mixed with other materials that are regularly stocked at the warehouse. Mixing operation helps in minimizing transportation costs and achieving customer specific assortments.

The aim of *assembly* operations is to assist in manufacturing operations. Materials and components are assembled from a variety of *lead suppliers*, or tier one suppliers, who are located close to the manufacturing plant. It is becoming common for manufacturers to use value-added services performed by a *lead supplier* or *integrated service provider* (ISP) to sort, grade, sequence and deliver components as per manufacturing requirements. This concept also supports JIT philosophy and helps in saving transportation time and cost as the manufacturer is able to concentrate on the main activities.

Reverse Logistics

Reverse logistics is often carried out at the warehouses in order to manage the reverse flow of:

(a) Consignments that have not met with customer specifications or have quality problems. The *returns management* or *reverse flow* would be to the manufacturing plant from where the consignment originated, or to the external manufacturer. Examples are: Pharmaceutical industry's bulk drugs, and biologicals/vitamins or supplements/nutritional products, manufactured clothes/fabrics/ leather products etc.

(b) Consignments for remanufacturing, or re-assembly after their useful life is over. The product is updated with new components and is offered at a discounted price as a re-conditioned product.
Examples—Computer and electronic products; electrical appliances, vehicle parts and components

(c) Products for re-marketing, which the original customer no longer needs them.
Examples:—Winter Garments due to late shipment to export markets are instead offered in domestic markets as they are not accepted in foreign markets after the due date is over. Marketing of second hand vehicles after some repair and refurbishing work is done.

(d) Products for *recycling* following the completion of their life-span with a view to decompose it to basic or components/materials so that they can be re-processed.
Examples: Iron, Ferro Alloys are decomposed/melted for recasting into fresh products.

Value-added Services

Owing to rising demand for highly customized services, modern distribution warehouses have been transformed into facilities that provide value added services to their customers. Value-added services generally change the physical feature or configuration of products in order to present them to customers in an unique or customized manner.

Listing of Value Added Services

- Cross-docking
- Customer service to handle 'returned' and/or high value packets ('returned' refer to some processing, stamping, QC sampling etc.)
- Labelling
- Lot control
- Mass Customization
- Manufacturing support
- Distribution
- Order assembly operations
- Transit mixing
- Mixing
- Pick and pack
- Repair and Refurbishing
- Reverse Logistics
- Sequencing
- Specialty packing
- Container management
- Store support/direct store delivery
- Home delivery

Warehouses can also indulge in light manufacturing such as ice-cream and desert manufacturing, fruit-jam manufacturing and assembly of some electrical appliances, computer parts and PC printing/copying products.

Warehouse Layout and Design

Determining Space Requirements

In order to develop basic layout and design, the management has to determine space requirements by developing a demand forecast for raw-material and/or finished products that a business firm needs to store. The forecast has to cover the period such as quarter, months or weeks or even two quarters to handle seasonal products or commodities. Products must be

Space Requirements in a Typical Warehouse

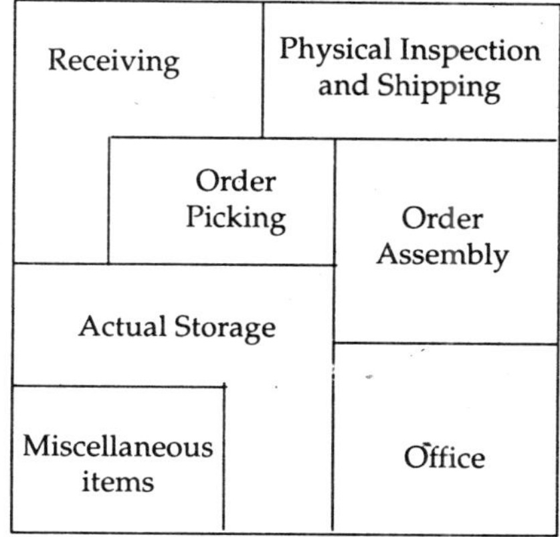

expressed in units, or by weight or by volume with a margin of 15-25 per cent to allow for growth over a period of time.

The receiving and shipping areas are quite important, and two separate areas are required to facilitate operations of material movement. Other considerations include whether to unload goods on the dock area outside the warehouse, or directly into the warehouse. Therefore design has to allow for "turn around" space for vehicles or for equipment used in material handling as space is also needed for aisles besides office space to record the in-ward and out-ward material movement data.

Space is also needed for staging goods on a specially built platform before loading them for transportation, and for consolidating shipments, by customer. Customer could be firm's internal, or external customer. Besides, there could be a separate area requirement for physical inspection and counting of the goods.

In warehouses where physical distribution operations are frequent, space for *'order-picking'* and *'order assembly'* are also required. However, space for such activities depends upon the nature of products and accommodation for material handling equipment.

Finally, the actual storage space for raw materials or components is very important, as the warehouse manager must use the entire cubic meter space that is available. Usually, the height is a factor in deriving the maximum advantage for utilizing the space in terms of volume available for storage.

Layout and Design Objectives

To Completely use the Cubic Capacity

This can be made possible by having larger and deeper storage bays with limited access. The aisles can be narrow because of low turnover products or commodities which can be put there for storage.

On the other hand, items with increased turnover makes it necessary to design smaller bays with wider aisles for efficient access to handle material movement. This aspect is useful where customer service requirements for physical distribution are high.

Separation of Hazardous Items

Items like chemicals of hazardous nature, inflammable and other items that could contaminate other products such as food products, and commodities for direct human consumption should be stored separately. Further, items that require security and protection such as special equipment for public use/ hospital use, etc. should be stored separately.

Minimization of Labour Requirements

Utilization of storage space should be done in a manner that warehouse design permits mechanization, which is also facilitated by the fact that items and storage pallets are in proper geometric shape and are easily handled leading to minimum labour requirements and costs.

Packaging

In addition to providing information about the product the package contains, the size and protection provided by packaging determine the type of material handling equipment to be used. The packaging also determines, the stacking height of the product in warehouse operations, which is an important element in utilization of warehouse capacity and for lowering costs of storage. Since packaging involves different organizational departments, coordinating packaging with warehouse is of concern to these departments such as production, marketing, quality control, shipping and exports besides legal department. For example, marketing is interested in providing product information, legal may issue warning about its consumption, and provide other information such as weight by volume, expiry date, fitness of use by age, e.g. whether product is suitable for infants and children below five years, and so on. On the other hand, production is interested in finding out the most economical cost of placing goods in a package while logistics department may like to determine how its can bring, move or transfer goods in a cost effective manner by utilizing the cubic capacity of the packaging and of the transport i.e. when one of the mode of transportation like truck, rail, ship or air transfer is to be used.

Types of Packaging and Packaging Materials

There are broadly two types of packaging "consumer packaging" and "industrial packaging".

Over the years harder packaging materials like wood and metal have been replaced by corrugated and plastic materials. Plastic materials, available in different range and types, have in fact revolutionized packaging as plastics provide cushion to the product material inside the package besides facilitating automation in packaging. Moreover, plastic provides very economical weight-to-product material ratio while shipping, thus lowering costs of transportation.

Bar Coding

Bar code symbols which an optical scanner can read have had a major impact on distribution logistics since 1970s and 1980s. A bar code is a series of parallel black and white bars—of different widths arranged in a sequence that represents letters or numbers. Barcode scanners help in finding out shipments' origin, place of manufacture product type, date, month and year of manufacture and product price.

Different industries use different barcode standards.

Bar coding can be either automatic or hand held. Automatic scanners remain in fixed position and scan packages as they move on the conveyor belt. On the other hand, a worker can manually scan packages in a warehouse by handheld scanner.

At several retail outlets and super markets, scanners are now commonly used at cash counters or "Point-of-Sales"to settle customer bills against the items purchased. The information helps in updating inventory records on continuous basis. Such information is helpful in re-ordering, stocking and for material movement besides forecasting.

Materials Handling Equipment

Forklifts

Forklifts are very common dock equipment that a company can make use of with ease. A typical forklift is individually powered and comes with different lift arrangements. Warehouses use forklifts along with pallets. Pallets are essential to materials handling operations. Pallet's main function is to provide base to hold individual items together. Once the items are stacked on pallet, forklifts can move the pallet to proper storage location within the warehouse.

Rider Trucks

Rider trucks provide a low-cost and effective method of general materials handling utility. They are used for shuttling loads between warehouses, or within a large warehouse facility. Rider trucks are widely used in consumer packaged goods warehouses.

Tractor Trailers

A typical tractor trailer is a driver driven unit that tows a four-wheel trailer attached to it. The main advantage of such equipment is that it is very flexible, and can handle a variety of load within facilities, warehouses and from other destinations which are located within reasonable distance.

Conveyor System

A conveyor system can be quite expensive. Since it is fixed at a location it lacks flexibility. However, they are common in large manufacturing firms because the conveyor systems reduce labour costs as they assist in distribution of raw materials, and final products within the facility or a warehouse.

PURCHASING IN SUPPLY CHAIN MANAGEMENT

Importance of Purchasing

Purchasing activity is important to an organization on account of two factors. These are:

- Cost efficiency, with respect to materials and components purchased, and
- Operational effectiveness of production plant.

Purchase managers with good negotiation skills and strong relationships with suppliers are able to save large sums of money for their organization while purchasing goods and materials that go into production of final products.

On the other hand, buying the right production equipment at a good (favorable) price creates a competitive advantage relative to competition, that lasts for several years. Finally, effective and sound purchasing practices avoid operational problems. In the event, inputs fail to arrive, the production stops and plant has to shut down. If the quality of inputs falls short of standards, the final product may fail to meet customer pecifications. Therefore, operational effectiveness of a firm gets affected significantly due to low quality or wrong specifications of materials, and due to late delivery of consumable and materials required for production.

We can explain purchasing as an acquisition of "right" or specified products and materials (including services) in specified quantities in the acceptable condition at the "right" time from the right source, that is able to meet with the desired service levels at the "right" price.

As a result, purchasing is getting an increased importance as organizations are placing more emphasis on supply chain management, quality improvement, lean production and outsourcing.

In a business organization, the purchasing is expected to accomplish the following objectives:

1. It should provide an uninterrupted flow of materials, supplies, and services required to operate the commercial production of goods and services.
2. Minimize inventory investment and loss
3. Maintain adequate quality standards
4. Develop competent and effective suppliers
5. Standardize the purchased materials in terms of material specifications
6. Purchase materials and components at competitive (lowest possible) prices without comprising quality or delivery schedules
7. Improve a commercial firm's competitive position in the market
8. Maintain harmony while involving with other departments in the organization
9. Accomplish the objectives of purchasing at lowest levels of administrative costs

Purchasing Process

- Recognizing a need or requirement for material or components
- Identifying a supplier or a group of suppliers
- Setting supply terms, and placing an order with the vendor(s)
- Monitoring and managing the delivery (process)/orders
- Evaluating the purchase and the supplier who is receiving and executing orders

Interface with other Departments of the Organization

Purchase department must work closely with other departments of the organization who may place many demands on purchasing. They make require

Purchase Department: Interface with Internal Customers and Information Flow

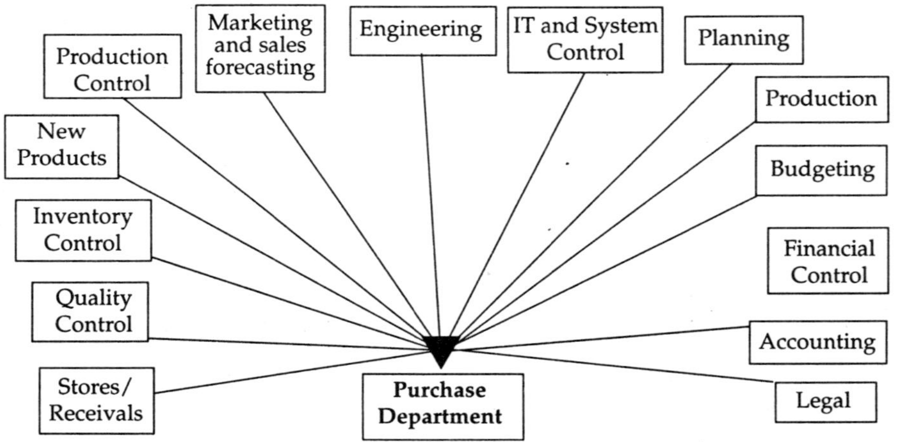

Purchase Department:
Interface with External Customers and Information Flow

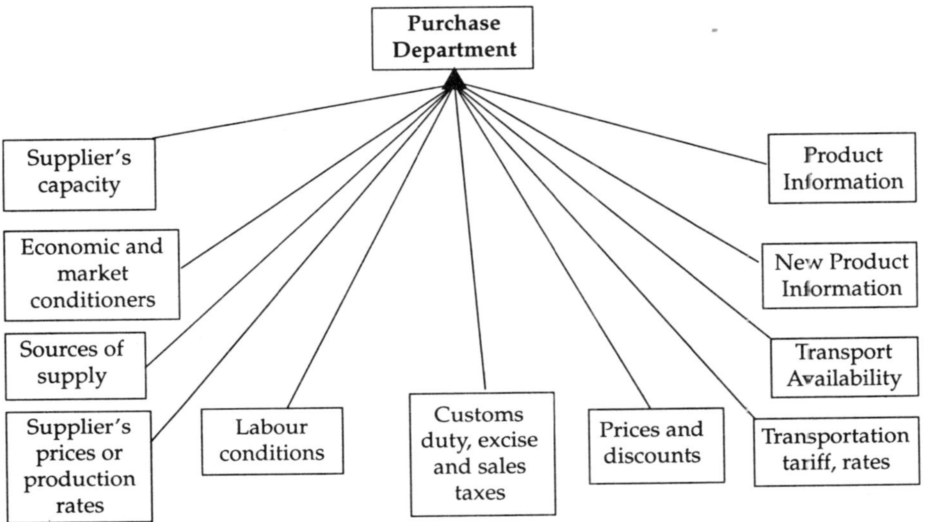

Purchase Department:
Outflow of Information to Various Departments of the Organizations

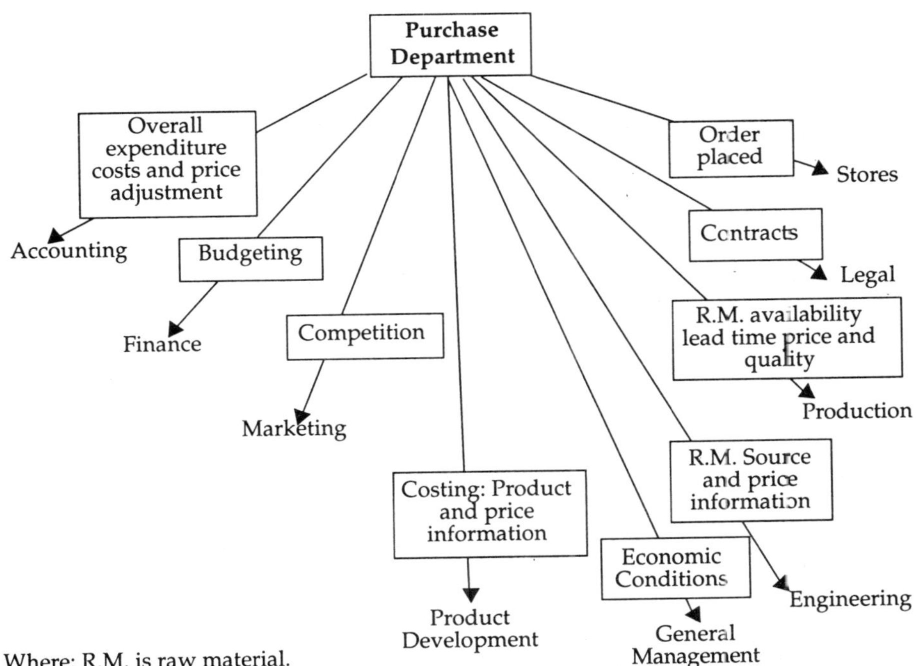

Where: R.M. is raw material.

purchasing expertise from buying a new computer with LCD/LED monitor to identifying the best sources of small and highly technical components, other raw materials, solvents, chemicals, etc. Thus the purchase department is a gateway or a common link between other departments of the organization and external suppliers who wish to sell their products to the organization.

Since the purchasing process is information driven, the two diagrams given on previous page show the role of internal and external information in purchasing.

Purchasing Interface with Logistics

Both purchasing and (integrated) logistics have common areas of activity, mainly with regard to inbound (or inward) flow of products and/or raw materials. These two activities (i.e. purchasing and logistics) must be coordinated with each other to ensure continuous flow of products through the channel of distribution. While in some companies, purchasing is part of integrated logistics, in others, purchasing (or purchase department) controls and manages the entire integrated logistics process. The coordination between purchasing and logistics may involve number of activities. In-bound transportation, raw-material and components, warehousing and inventory control are common to both purchasing and integrated logistics in many organizations. Of these, transportation receives most attention, as transportation may represent a large percentage of costs of in-bound materials. Also, transportation is crucial to on-time delivery in JIT manufacturing operations. When purchasing and integrated logistics are seen as a part of supply chain, the interdependence becomes clear, as one company's out-bound logistics is another company's inbound logistics. That is, it operates on a principle that one person's ceiling is another person's floor. For example, tyres sold by MRF or Bridgestone to a car manufacturer are *outbound logistics* for a tyre manufacture and *inbound logistics* for car manufacturer. And it goes on like this throughout the supply chain.

The coordination between purchasing and logistics is dependent upon factors as highlighted below. The coordination is aimed to ensure the continuous flow of products through the distribution-channel (or supply chain channel). Responses to the these factors are meant to address the issues related to transportation, warehousing and inventory control. The factors are:

1. Quantity or volumes of material under purchase

While warehouse location and storage space/volume in it determine the purchase quantity of materials, the processing/assembly line operations capacity determine the finished goods inventory. Further location of warehouse and processing facilities affect the mode of transportation (i.e. by Rail or Road) that will be used for carrying materials and finished goods. Higher quantity of purchase leads to quantity discounts and transportation discounts for transporting large volume, but results in increased carrying costs, including storage costs.

2. *Timing of delivery of ordered material*

- Integrated logistics must be informed as to when goods will arrive into plants and/or warehouses as storage space has to be made available.
- If *inbound vehicle* is 'empty', logistics may arrange to send outbound load in it (Depends on whether it is company's or hired vehicle on such terms that outbound load will be allowed).

Further, the date and timing of delivery must be linked to production planning and scheduling.

3. *Choice of transport carrier in delivering the purchased material*

It helps the logistics (i.e. integrated logistics) manager to choose the transport carrier that offers lower rates under the delivery contract. This may also be due to the fact that either this transport company is specialized in area specific deliveries, or it is already carrying in *outbound* logistics and thus has business reasons to oblige the purchase/logistics manager of the company.

4. *Routing for the Inbound Flow of Materials*

If the purchased materials delivery, time and location fits into transporter's route and schedule, than there is no need for choosing a new carrier. These dedicated carriers usually understand customer operations, know routes and lanes and are able to find customers facilities with ease. This means better on-time service and lower costs.

5. *Freight Movement Control*

It is usually suppliers who select the transport company to move goods/ raw material to buyer's premises i.e. plants or warehouses. But buyer firms can also exercise their choices, as they may have special rate contracts with the preferred list of carriers and may want to control transport costs, loss or damage during transit or to have more reliability in terms of time taken for delivery.

6. *Performance Measurement of Purchasing*

The common performance measures include price effectiveness, cost savings, work load, administrative control, efficiency, vendor quality, delivery, material flow control, compliance with regulations, societal measures, environmental measures, procurement planning, research, competition, inventory and transportation.

Price Effectiveness

It relates to determining actual price performance compared to the purchase plan, market price, and actual price paid besides performance among buying groups both inside and outside the organization.

Cost Savings

It refers to reducing per unit cost of item purchased. It also evaluates the new unit price quotation from a different supplier, which may be lower than the average price quoted by a existing supplier.

Work Load

It relates to measuring new work, backlog of work and work accomplished.

Administration and Control

It refers to comparing actual cost to the purchasing budget.

Efficiency measures actual purchases made, relative to purchasing inputs. Common measures include purchase orders (P.O.) issued to each supplier, Rupee (value) committed for purchase in each P.O. and contracts specified by P.O. and supplier *vis-a-vis* actual goods purchased, or supplied by the vendor/supplier.

Vendor Quality and Delivery

It indicates percent of supplied items accepted or rejected, the frequency and seriousnes of defects, and *total cost* of purchasing a single unit of product from a supplier, or group of suppliers.

Material Flow Control Measures

It measures the flow of materials from suppliers to the buying firms:

Regulatory, societal and environmental measures

It indicates whether purchases are meeting legal and societal standards. These could also include pollution control standards.

Procurement planning and research

It deals with price forecast accuracy, lead-time forecasting, and number of purchase plans proposed annually.

Competition

It refers to firm's evaluation of number of purchases made from a single source and amount of money spent in rupees in value terms as compared to purchases from multiple sources.

Inventory

Analysis pertaining to inventory turnover ratio, inventory levels, and consignments received or shipped helps in improving efficiency and revenue besides bringing cost savings to a firm.

Transportation

It makes estimation of how much material moves by *premium transportation* i.e. using more costly/expensive mode of transportation as compared with less expensive and regular mode of transportation.

Supplier Certification

Supplier certification is a detailed examination of policies and capabilities of a supplier. The certification process verifies that a supplier meets or exceeds the requirements of a buyer. This is particularly important when buyers are attempting to establish a long-term relationship with suppliers. One advantage of using certified suppliers is that the buyer can eliminate most of the inspection and testing of delivered goods and materials. Although problems with supplier goods/raw materials or services may not be eliminated, there is significantly lesser risk compared to making purchases from non-certified suppliers.

Instead of developing their own certification procedures, some buyer companies rely on the industry specifications such as ISO 9000. ISO series of certification programs were first developed in 1987. ISO 9000 requires that firms establish processes and document activities. However, it does not ensure, or even check for customer satisfaction. Neither do registration and certification guarantee quality but they are widely accepted as a sign of quality. Briefly, ISO 9000 Series programmes and their purpose is presented below:

1. ISO 9000: Quality management and quality assurance standards.
2. ISO 9001: Quality systems model for quality assurance in design and development, production and installation.
3. ISO 9002: Quality systems model for quality assurance in production and installation.
4. ISO 9003: Quality system model for quality assurance in final inspection and quality.
5. ISO 9004: Quality management and quality system elements.

Purchasing falls under ISO 9001. While being certified does not ensure quality, it ensures consistency in what is being produced. For example, a defect in an auto component is likely to be present in the entire production. Identification of the defect will eventually lead to process improvement and then in to producing components with better quality.

Supplier Relationships

Purchasing department has the ultimate responsibility for developing and maintaining good supplier relationships. The relationship is often determined by the duration (or length) of the purchase contract with suppliers. Short-term contracts involve competitive bidding by suppliers in respone to specifications and terms stated by the buyer company. Normally, suppliers are kept away from close inter-action, and business may be conducted through formal communication via letters and/or by E-mail. Medium-term contracts often happen due to on-going relationships with suppliers. Long-term contracts often develop into partnerships, with buyers and sellers cooperating on various issues that tend to benefit both parties. Also, business firms are entering into long-term relationships that are based on *strategic* considerations.

Maintaining good supplier relationship helps the buyer company a flexibility in purchases, delivery schedules, changes in specifications, packaging etc. Additionally, supplier companies help in identifying problems and often provide suggestions in solving them. Therefore, price alone can't be a factor in switching the supplier. Good relationship with a supplier also helps the buyer in maintaining competitive edge in the market as his raw material or component might have special features or specifications. The view point is that by maintaining a stable relationship with a few reliable suppliers ensures high quality supplies, precise delivering schedules and allowing flexibility with regard to changes in product specifications.

Supplier Partnerships

It has been observed that more and more business organizations are establishing partnerships with other organizations in their supply chains. This leads to lesser number of suppliers, long-term relationships involving sharing of information (e.g. forecasts, sales data, problem alerts, etc.) and cooperation in planning. Benefits include getting materials with higher quality parameters, increased delivery speed and reliability, lower inventories, lower costs, higher profits and improved operations.

Shortcomings to such partnerships include: hesitancy on part of suppliers to enter into such partnerships with buyers, suppliers may have to incur additional investment in equipment and infrastructures which might put strain on their cash-flow. Another possibility is that organization cultures of buyer and supplier might be quite different which may pose difficulty in entering into such agreements. Additionally, supplier might be open to diversifying his customer-base to improve profitability by either selling same grade (or set of components), or diversifying product-mix which other customers may be willing to buy.

Centralized *versus* Decentralized Buying

Centralized purchasing means that purchasing is handled by one special department. Decentralized purchasing means that individual departments or branches/divisions at separate locations handle their own purchasing requirements.

Centralized purchasing may be able to bargain and get lower prices than decentralized units owing to higher volume of orders by combining individual requirements of different units to take advantage of quantity discounts offered by suppliers on large orders. At the same time, *centralized purchasing* (C.P.) may be able to get better service and closer attention from suppliers. Additionally, C.P. enables companies to assign purchase tasks to *specialist managers* in certain areas due to complex *product specializations* as these managers tend to be more efficient because they are able to concentrate their efforts and attention on a relatively fewer items instead of spreading their attention on a large amounts of materials or items.

Decentralized purchasing (D.P.) has the advantage of dealing with the issues of 'local' needs and being able to respond these needs efficiently. Thus, D.P. can often quicken response time than centralized purchasing (C.P.). D.P. is particularly useful where locations are widely scattered and is able to save time and transportation costs by buying locally which also creates a "goodwill" in the local community.

Some companies employ both C.P. and D.P. in order to take advantage of situations. Decentralized purchase is allowed to units, particularly where material is available locally at competitive prices. For example, small orders and rush orders can be handled locally by units or departments while high volume orders are handled by centralized purchasing.

Supplier Selection

Three criteria are generally considered by companies for selecting suppliers. These relate to price, quality, and delivery.

- Since companies spend a large percentage of their total income on purchase of items, selecting suppliers who supply materials at lower prices (than their competitors) is a key objective of buying firms.
- However, quality of goods purchased is also an important factor, as the hidden costs of poor quality can be high owing to rejection of the final goods at market place or by the final customers during the post-purchase phase. It is then too late to reverse the damage at that stage when full value has been added to the product. For a retailer, poor merchandize quality mean loss of goodwill and loss of future sales.
- The delivery of order with shorter lead-time and on-time delivery helps the buyer company to maintain acceptable customer service to its clients by holding less inventory.

The benefits of on-time deliveries are also applicable to the manufacturing sector. Many manufacturers demand quick, and dependable deliveries from their suppliers to minimize their inventory levels. This requirement "constraint" forces suppliers to have their raw material, component, or part plants or warehouses located in the vicinity of buyer's manufacturing operations (e.g. Tata Motors "Nano", and its component and ancillory products' suppliers).

Another criterion that is becoming important while making purchases is handling impact of raw materials and components on environment. This is called *green purchasing* which involves identifying evaluating, managing and reducing the flow of environmental waste and finding ways to minimize its impact on the environment. Suppliers are asked to be environment conscious while designing and manufacturing their products, and they should be able to substantiate their claim of supplies of materials as *Green, bio degradable materials* and *recycled* when bidding for supplier contracts.

Other Criteria for Selection of Suppliers

Purchasing managers often find it more convenient to deal with fewer suppliers rather than traditional approach to deal with more suppliers, which meant generating competition to get good service and high quality of materials to the buyer company. However, managers involved in integrated logistics think it differently because they wish to give a larger share of business to a few selected suppliers. This is due to fact that finding and developing suppliers is expensive and time-consuming process. Secondly, maintaining close relationships with those few selected suppliers makes it possible to give quality time to them vis-a-vis large number of suppliers under traditional approach. Thirdly, having a few suppliers means that each one gets more business from one buyer, which makes this buyer company more important to the supplier. Finally, managing the search for quality materials is easier with fewer suppliers. Generally buyers and suppliers usually work closely to develop new products for the major buyers (e.g. Fiat 1.3 L diesel engine for Tata Indica Vista and Maruti Swift/ Dezire car Models respectively).

Working with a few suppliers means that purchasing managers must choose them carefully. Different sources may be used to select domestic and international suppliers. Buying companies usually follow all the selection steps only for the first time a supplier is selected, or when a major re-evaluation takes place.

Supplier Selection Sources

Internal company staff	Catalogues
Trade Journals and Directories	Samples
Sales Representatives	Visits to Suppliers
Supplier and Commodity Files	Purchasing Files
Colleagues	Mail Advertisements
Yellow Pages	Trade Exhibitions
Trade Intermediaries/Government agencies	News Papers
Banks	Websites of suppliers, manufacturers
Chamber of Commerce Offices	Trade Associations

Supplier Evaluation

After reviewing the sources, the purchasing manager must reduce the initial supplier list to a more manageable number. From this short list, one or two best suppliers are chosen. The selected suppliers are subjected to detailed analysis of their operations. The investigations of their banking and credit references, financial stability, supply capabilities, technical expertise, quality assurance programs, plant facilities, management style, customer service levels

Supplier Evaluation Variables

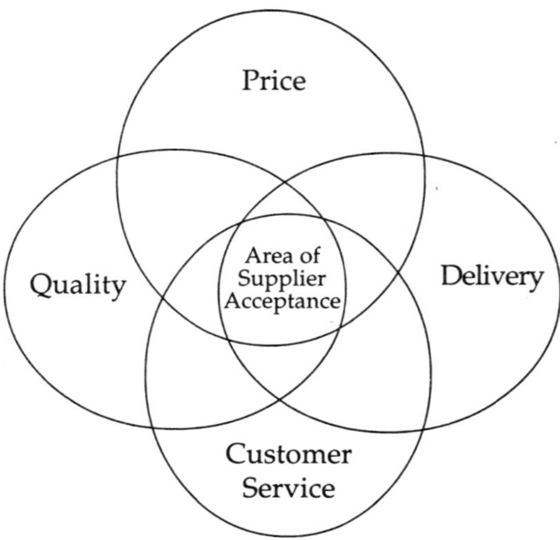

and JIT capabilities are usually undertaken. Sometimes, supplier's performance with the current and former clients (a sensitive issue) may also be checked.

A company must consider whether they wish to use single source/or multiple sources for arranging raw materials or components. Many times, a single source is preferred due to: (1) Priority in supply, (2) Price and/or volume discounts, (3) Lower costs, (4) Better quality control, (5) Lower freight costs, and (6) Lower inventory costs as the supplier is supposed to manage the inventory.

Risks in single-source purchasing are: (1) Inability on the part of supplier to execute supplies in times of shortage, natural calamities or strikes, (2) Supplier price increases, and (3) Supplier complacency about quality and customer service.

Based on several studies, suppliers are usually evaluated on *price, quality, customer service and delivery*. These are shown in the diagram which illustrates circle for each attribute or selection criteria for evaluation. The area where the four circles intersect indicates that a specific supplier meets the expectations of the purchasing manager.

The following table indicates the findings of a typical purchase manager. After having chosen which variables to evaluate, the purchasing manager must choose rating and importance scales. For example, on a rating scale '1 to 5', '1' indicates "worst" and '5' indicates, the "best", and on importance scale '0 to 5' where '0' indicates "No importance" and '5' indicates "highest importance". These two scales can be used for each variable. This method not only "Ranks" but also gives "Weights" to each variable. This way the analyst multiplies the rating rank by the importance rank to get an overall scope for that variable. For example, the purchase manager may rate price offer of a supplier as 5 (best price) and *reliability* of delivery as 5. However, the importance rankings of these variables are '3' and '5' respectively.

Therefore, reliability score of delivery $5 \times 5 = 25$ vis-à-vis price score of an order $5 \times 3 = 15$ is given higher overall rank owing to the score ratings obtained as above.

Supplier Evaluation Form (Vendor Analysis)

Suppliers and their Supply Attributes	(A) Rating of Supplier 1 = worst 5 = Best (Scale 1 2 3 4 5)	(B) Importance of Supply Attributes to the buyer co. 0 = No importance 5 = Highest importance (Scale 0 1 2 3 4 5)	(A) × (B) Weighted Composite Rating 0 = Minimum 25 = Maximum
Supplier A			
Product Reliability/Quality			
Price			
Reliability of delivery			
Flexibility			
.			
.			

(Contd.)

.

After sale service

Total for supplier A

Supplier B
Product Reliability/Quality
Price
Reliability of delivery
Flexibility
.
.
.
After sales service

Total for supplier B

.
.
.

Sourcing

Purchasing, which is also called procurement, is the process of acquiring raw materials, components, product services and other resources by companies from their suppliers to fulfill their business operations.

Sourcing is the entire set of business processes required to purchase goods and services. Sourcing processes comprise selection of suppliers, preparation of supply contracts, development of product and/or collaboration in joint designing of products required by buyer company, procurement of raw materials or components, finished products or partially finished/or assembled products, and working with the most appropriate supplier for a given product and evaluating/or supplier performance in case there are more than one or two suppliers.

Traditionally firm's purchased goods and services are based on considerations related to price and promised delivery dates. However, the relationships between suppliers and buyer companies have evolved into collaborative relationships in the last 10-15 years. In this context, identification and selection of suppliers itself amounts to *sourcing* process, as suppliers are sources of supply. This type of relationship focusses on collaboration and coordination, shared goals of quality and service, lower supplier costs and performance measurement of suppliers. Sourcing concept has evolved as a result of supplier companies focus on quality improvement and buyer companies satisfaction from acquiring material from external sources.

Single-Sourcing

With single-sourcing, a company either purchases goods and services from very few suppliers or only from a single supplier. In order to spread out the risk resulting from non-supply of goods/raw materials on time, quality or pricing related problems/issues, or production related problem with suppliers owing to any reason, buyer companies have traditionally purchased from multiple sources or suppliers.

On the other hand, benefits of purchases from a single source include: buyer company has a direct control over quality, cost, and delivery performance of a supplier in a situation where bulk of supplier's business is accounted by the buyer company's purchases. Thus both supplier and buyer enter into an agreement where supplier agrees to meet with customer's quality standards or specifications for raw materials/or products and services. The buyer company can also specify delivery schedules to the supplier with a view to reduce inventory levels. In return supplier gets a continued business with stability and peace of mind. The customer 'dictates' the cost, quality and performance to the supplier; and the supplier does the same to his supplier. Thus, the entire supply chain becomes smooth, efficient and cost effective.

Outsourcing

It refers to purchasing of goods and services that can be produced in-house but are purchased from an external/outside supplier. Outsourcing is resorted to situations when:

(1) Demand outstrips supply in the short term
(2) Break down in plants and machinery
(3) Temporary lack of capacity
(4) Increased cost of production in house due to geographical location of a plant where raw material is not available or due to higher transportation costs, or better economies of scale with external supplier
(5) Strategic decisions of a business firm either to concentrate on development of new range or generation of products, or to use plant capacity for higher value products.

It is common to see many large companies moving their production requirements, including inventory of raw materials, to suppliers.

One of the major reasons for out-sourcing is that these companies are focusing on their core competencies. By *outsourcing*, they allow suppliers to do things what the buyer company is not good at, and the suppliers are most competent in doing so. Doing all the functions related to sourcing purchasing of raw materials, parts or components, holding of inventories, and distribution of products stretches the resources of the company in a manner that it becomes unviable at times to exercise managerial control over all the activities themselves.

Thus outsourcing provides greater flexibility and deployment of resources in areas or businesses where companies have greater competencies. Also, supplier partnerships and outsourcing of products and services by the buyer companies helps them to have greater control over their businesses.

ROLE OF INFORMATION IN THE SUPPLY CHAIN

Information is the critical link between all supply chain processes and activities, which runs from suppliers, producer-manufacturers/assemblers, distributors, wholesalers and retailers to customers.

Computer and the associated IT technology has become a powerful tool to enable on line communication and exchange of data and information across the entire supply chain. IT technologies which assist in the flow of product and services throughout the supply chain are called "Enablers". IT technology not only links and coordinates with different members of supply chain but also enhances the speed of transactions and brings about cost reduction through the elimination of extra manpower, and paper based transactions that would involve the traditional postal technologies for transmission of information.

Therefore, IT technologies can be employed to improve supply chain functions in the following manner:

- Control inflow and outflow of information through the centralized coordination.
- Integrate production, transportation, distribution and ordering activities.
- Provide access to domestic and international transportation and distribution channels.
- Keep track of movement of various items in supply chain.
- Provide consolidation of purchases from different suppliers.
- Product/or services data collection at the point of origin and point of sale or distribution.
- Updation of inventory levels on continuous basis.

Application of IT Technologies in SCM

Electronic business or e-business refers to replacement of physical processes involved in traditional business with electronic ones. In e-business, interactions between business organization and/or individuals take place through different types of electronic media such as:

- Electronic Data Intercharge (EDI)
- E-mail
- Electronic Funds Transfer (EFT)
- Electronic Publishing
- Electronic bulletins
- Shared databases such as GEDES (Global Electronic Data Exchange Systems) that have been used by some MNCs
- Bar coding
- Electronic Fax transmissions
- C.D.-Rom Catalogues
- Internet and Websites

Examples of Electronic Systems in Retail

- Banking and Electronic maintenance of consumer records at banks and financial institutions
- Credit card usage for internet purchases
- Demat accounts for stocks trading
- Booking of Airlines Rail Tickets through respective websites
- E auctions
- Airlines check-in through on-line sharing of passenger and airline flight information
- Others

Benefits

The use of above mentioned electronic business methods have drastically reduced paper work, filing systems and the requirement of extensive manpower. The bonus is in form of cost and time saving. Besides the role of its intermediaries is also significantly reduced. Benefits include:

- Consumer has more choices and supply chain transactions for ordering and delivery are reduced.
- Improved services management is possible due to instant access to customers and channel partners like wholesalers and retailers.
- Creation of virtual companies like E-bay.com, Amazon.com, etc.
- Greater benefit to smaller companies which otherwise lack expensive physical infrastructure.

Internet in SCM

As a result of development of internet and its wide-spread usage, it has not only made significant impact on SCM management practices among buyers and sellers in a supply chain but it has also enabled visibility among trading partners. This aspect makes mutual collaboration and cooperation among supply chain partners relatively easier to implement. In this context, web-based tools and technologies have been specifically developed for SCM practices.

With internet creating new forms of supply chain linkages, it has transformed the traditional role of producers, suppliers and distributors by eliminating the intermediaries. It has assisted companies to access markets and suppliers on global basis which was not possible earlier. Thus the advantage has shifted from seller to buyer, as the buyer community tries to contact scores of suppliers in order to get lower prices and better services.

Also internet brings speed and accessibility to supply chain. Companies are able to reduce traditional time-wasting routines related to purchasing and ordering transactions as internet sites directly link to suppliers, distributors and customers. Internet allows firms to bring speed to ordering and delivery process and instantly update information on inventories besides getting feed back from customers. Besides, orders can also be tracked.

Advantages of internet

- Cost reduction (for processing orders)
- Revenue flow increases (e.g. credit and payments)
- Global, and 24 hour access
- Pricing flexibility (price changes can be notified quickly)

Intranets and Extranets

Intranets use the same basic technology of internet but these are internal networks of organizations. They are like *internal internets*. By using *web browsers* and *server software* with their internal systems, *intranets* make it possible for companies to link groups of *computers* and develop more effective *internal information system*. These *intranets* can be connected to global internet to form "extranets" that include company's suppliers and customers. *Extranets* allow limited access to firm's partners and customers.

Examples

- HP & P&G use *extranets* with their advertising agencies to exchange marketing plans.
- Intranet may enable a firm that is operating from multiple locations to give HR information to employees, including filling up forms for medical benefits, expenses, and travel related forms besides, leave application, etc. It can also help various departments to know about production plans and inventory levels.

Also, *intranets* allow companies to implement internal applications, which are not connected with outside customers or suppliers, and thus avoid the unwanted confusion.

Bar Codes

In bar coding, 'computer readable' codes are fixed or pasted on items passing through the supply chain including products, containers and packages.

The bar code contains information about the item like product description, item number, its source and destination, cost, order number, etc. When the bar code information is scanned by the scanner attached to the company's computer, it provides information about item's location in the supply chain. This technology is used by hundreds/thousands of companies to manage their supply chains in different situations. Supermarkets use *scanners* at cash registers to read prices, products and manufacturers from uniform product codes (UPCs). Airline use bar codes to route luggage between terminals at various landing locations. When bar codes are scanned at payment counters, it results in *point-of-sales data*, which is the instant record of sale of a product. Such information is transmitted through supply chain to update *inventory records*. This helps downstream and upstream S.C. members to understand trends in consumption which can help in arranging supplies of raw materials, components or finished/ assembled products accordingly. (Russell and Taylor, 2004)

E-procurement (or Electronic purchasing)

It is a part of the business-to-business (B2B) commerce that is conducted on the internet, where buyers make purchases directly from suppliers through their websites or through e-market places, e-hubs and other such trading exchanges.

Purchases are classified into two broad categories i.e. *Manufacturing inputs (direct products)* and *operating inputs (Indirect products)*

Direct Products are raw materials and components that are used in the production (or assembly) process of a product, and they are industry specific which involves specialized suppliers and distributors, who are aware of the requirements for such specific industries.

Indirect products do not go directly into the production of finished goods, and there are maintenance, repair and operation (MRO) goods and services. These can include PCs, furniture, electrical items, airline/rail travel tickets, etc. and such MROs cover the needs of several industries.

Buyer companies can purchase both *direct and indirect products and services* from the suppliers websites over the internet. Companies can also make purchases through the internet or e-marketplaces.

In the following section, we will discuss four approaches to e-purchasing. These are:

(1) Electronic data inter-change
(2) Catalogue hubs
(3) Exchanges, and
(4) Auctions

Electronic Data Inter-change (EDI)

EDI is a computer to computer exchange of business documents in a standard format over telephone or direct leased-lines. The use of special communication software helps in transforming (or translating, converting) documents "into and out of" generic form, which permits organizations to exchange information even while their hardware and software configurations are different. EDI can handle routine documents like invoices, purchase orders, and payments and thus replaces the requirement for surface/air mail, fax or courier. The following procedure is usually followed for e-purchasing using EDI system.

A buyer browses an electronic catalog of a supplier and clicks on items he wishes to purchase. The computer (through internet) sends the order directly to supplier, supplier now checks the payment particular which is mainly through buyer's credit card number and makes sure that items are available with him to execute in order. Supplier's warehouse, order shipping department are informed electronically to make the order ready for shipment. At the same time, supplier sends the bill/invoice to buyer electronically. (Krajewski and Ritzman, 2005).

Thus EDI system helps in time and cost saving. It not only sends the buyer's request to right Department but checks the accuracy of the documents. Besides, the EDI systems shortens the response time and can even help in managing inventories in a way that surplus inventory is avoided.

Exchanges (or Electronic Market Place)

An exchange is an electronic market place where buying and selling companies come together to do business. Exchanges are often used for "spot" purchases to meet the immediate need of a buyer at the lowest possible price. Such exchanges maintain close relationships with buyers and sellers, and they make it easier for buyers and sellers to do business. Long-term contracts are usually avoided. Commodities like grains, oil, steel, and crude fit into this category. However, they can be used for other items as well.

Auctions

The concept of exchange can be extended to include *auctions*, where companies place competitive bids to buy items which are required by them for manufacturing or trading. For example, soyabean processors in Madhya Pradesh state (Central India) may form a website, where soya processing firm with excess capacity or material, for example soya oil can be offered for sale to the *highest 'bidder'* for buying this product. Bids can either be closed or open to competition.

There is another aspect to auctions, which is referred to as *Reverse Auctions*. Under this concept, suppliers provide supply bids to their prospective buyers. This is usually done on a web-site, say for example "Free markets", where top companies do "open-bidding" for supply contracts. After the 'bid' is posted, supplier can determine as to how much lower their bid can be to remain in competition or race to ultimately win supply contracts. Each contract has details with regard to term and conditions, specifications and other standard (and non-negotiable) requirements.

How the Reverse Auction Works?

A Hypothetical example

A company posted a supply contract for supplying telecommunication equipment to a Telecom service provider BSNL for Rs. 650 million as a bench-mark starting price. Let us say there are 10 manufacturers/suppliers who participated in bidding. Within few hours of open bidding session the supply contract came down to Rs. 640 million, then 635 million and finally to Rs. 595 millions, which resulted in savings to BSNL. This is an example, we do not know whether BSNL does believe in this type of bidding.

However cost is not the only consideration. Exchanges and auctions are more useful for commodities or infrequently needed items that require short-term relationships with suppliers. It has been observed and experienced across various industries that suppliers are partners when supply requirements are significant and stable, and as a result supply contracts are extended over a period of time.

Catalogue Hubs

These are used to reduce costs of placing orders to suppliers as well as the costs of services or goods themselves. Suppliers post (or display) their catalogue of items as the hub and buyers select what they want and purchase them electronically. For certain types of items, such as technical items, specialized items, services or furniture, buyers can negotiate the prices with some specific suppliers. Interestingly, the employee of a buying firm can only see the negotiated prices on the catalog (or electronic price lists) for approved items. The system then generates the Purchase Orders (POs) which are electronically dispatched to suppliers. In some firms POs are regularized by taking signatures of authorized signatories i.e. Purchase Manager and Director on the hard copy of each P.O. A copy is given to accounts and a copy is sent to receiving warehouse or the production unit indicating that purchase order has been approved for so much quantity at so much price with given specifications and/or other related terms and conditions of supply.

In brief, the Hub connects the firm to potentially hundreds of suppliers through internet, thus saving costs of EDI, which require one-to-one connection with each individual supplier.

SUPPLY CHAIN DESIGN FOR CUSTOMER ORDER FULFILLMENT

Virtual Supply Chains

With the availability of internet facilities, many commercial firms/organizations have re-designed their supply chains to outsource a portion of their order fulfillment process by using web based electronic links. Such companies, e.g. Nike manage their order fulfillment process in a manner as if they were getting their supplies from in-house facilities. Thus, the organization structure facilitates efficient flow of both physical goods and information from over 700 suppliers across the world.

This strategy helps the company to focus on its core competencies of customer relationship management and new product development.

Additionally, internet based retail companies (like ebay.com, rediff.com and yahoo.com) are implementing the virtual supply chain concept by using a technique called *drop shipping*, where a retail company passes the order directly to wholesaler or manufacturer, who then ships the order directly to the customer with the retailer's label on it. Thus retailers save themselves the costs of holding inventories by outsourcing their warehouse operations.

Benefits of Virtual Supply Chains

- **Reduced investment on inventories and order fulfillment infrastructure.** Otherwise high sale volumes are to be achieved by the firm to pay for investment made in inventory, equipment, warehouses and personnel/manpower.
- **Increased product variety to choose from**
  It is possible due to freedom to get access and supplies from a wide variety of wholesalers, manufacturers and service providers.

- **Lower costs due to economies of scale**
  Since the supplier is responding to outsourcing needs of different retailers (or such companies) for requiring the same product/ product-mix the increased volume turnover of supplier ensures that the costs to the outsourcing firm will be much lower than if the order fulfillment process was to be done in-house.
- **Lower transportation costs**
  As the supplies are made by wholesaler/manufacturer to the customers under "drop-shipping" concept in a virtual supply chain, the outsourcing firm/retailer or such firm saves on these transportation costs.

Virtual supply chains are not solutions for all problems which manufacturers or service providers (i.e. retailers here) might face in design of their supply chains. In this context, a lack of information, or information gap between a retailer and his order fulfillment partner (manufacturer or wholesaler) with regard to whether the latter has any inventory or enough inventory to undertake sales of items booked or has enough capacity to provide a critical service to customers may become an issue. Also, the outsourcing retailer could face rationing or quota allocations from his outsourcing/order fulfillment partner (O.F.P.) owing to inventory problems with O.F.P. as he might also have to deal with number of other retailers. The other danger is that O.F.P. may by pass the retailer and reach the customer directly owing to availability of customer information from the retailer.

Therefore, supply chain designers must weigh the costs and benefits between traditional approach, which keeps the order-fulfillment process in house and the virtual supply chain. The traditional approach is followed in situations when.

- **Sales volumes are high**
  Higher sales volumes are necessary to offset infrastructure and personnel related costs. It also helps a company strategically to dominate the industry in its area of specialization.

Consolidation of Orders from Many Suppliers

In a situation, when multiple suppliers are required to satisfy a single customer's order, the coordination in virtual supply chain becomes difficult and transportation costs would increase as well. With the traditional approach, the firm can coordinate its suppliers owing to the availability of its own warehouses.

However, the need for order consolidation clears the way for third-party logistics providers. For example in construction or interior decoration business, transportation companies like Patel Roadways, Jaipur Golden, and Fed Express, Blue Dart/Gati could be used for bringing 'rough' supplies and relatively 'delicate' supplies from various suppliers respectively to the construction or customer's site in a manner that major inputs and components arrive within small range of time to help in production or assembly process. Thus members of distribution chain such as third party logistics providers as mentioned above become part of *channel assembly*, where they assume the role of assembly station in the factory.

Similarly, in pharmaceuticals industry, critical ingredients could come from different suppliers to make a formulation and *channel assembly* role could be done by an agent company, or bulk *drug wholesale distributor*, who is equipped with required facilities.

Capability for small order fulfillment

Suppliers and/or manufacturers must have capability to deal with small order fulfillment process even if it involves the use of their warehouse operations in executing the orders such as in consumer durables or FMCG products.

The virtual supply chain is useful when

Demand pattern is volatile or uneven

Volatile demand patterns could be risky for holding inventories. A least cost approach could be to locate a supplier who would be supplying the same item with uncertain demand pattern to other firms. Thus the manufacturers/ suppliers can overcome fluctuations in demand patterns when they are handling multiple orders of same item/set of items from different customers and are able to offer the product/ item at a competitive and cost-effective price.

High product variety to choose firm

Retailer through his website can offer a larger variety when he enters into partnership with a single supplier or multiple suppliers. For example, a large range of movie titles are provided by rediff.com services, which are fulfilled through virtual inventories.

The trade-offs between traditional approach and virtual supply chain in order fulfillment process are important to a business firm. There can be implications while making the choice between two. These relate to:

(i) Virtual supply chains operated by a firm passes on direct control of order fulfillment to other supplier firms. Therefore, it is important to have a contract or agreement between the members of a supply chain. Strategic partnerships and long-term contracts offer more control than the short-term contracts. As the competitive priorities of a firm (like yahoo.com) increase, it will require a higher degree of control over its supplier partners.

(ii) Virtual supply chains provide greater flexibility in changing the design of firm's service packages, or its products because it does not have the higher overhead investment in order fulfillment process. The firm needs to balance control against the need for flexibility in choosing supply chain design.

Developing Integrated Supply Chains

- Managing supply chain successfully requires a high degree of functional and organizational integration. Examples include Maruti, Tata Motors, and Mahindra & Mahindra who source components and services from various suppliers for their automobile assembly line operations.
- Such integration takes time which can take months or even years to evolve.
- Business organization usually divide the responsibility for managing the flow of materials, components and services among three departments. These are: purchasing, production and distribution.

Purchasing

Purchasing is the management of acquiring process (flow of materials, components and services) which involves the selection of suppliers for each kind and range of products, be it raw, semi-finished, processed, assembled, or fabricated. It also involves negotiations, award of contracts, and deciding where to buy i.e. locally or from outside the geographical area of plant/factory operations. Purchasing is also responsible for inventory levels, leasing maintenance, and repairs of warehousing facilities etc.

Production—It is concerned with the management of transformation process i.e. from receival of raw materials, components, services to conversion or assembly into a final product or a service. It is responsible for determining *output quantities* and *scheduling the utilization of machines* and manpower both technical and support for production of final goods and services.

Distribution is the management of the flow of services or materials from firms to external customers. It's also responsible for inventories of finished goods and selection of transportation service providers.

For developing the integrated supply chains, business organizations pass through a series of phases.

Phase 1—It is the starting point for Business firms:

- External suppliers and customers are independent of the firm in question in terms of their operations and managing business with other firms. Relations with suppliers and customers are formal, and there is hardly any sharing of information, including on costs.
- Internally, the purchase, production and distribution departments act independently and show no concern for each other.
- Each external and internal entity in supply chain controls its own inventories and often utilizes the control systems and procedures that are *incompatible* with other entities (customers i.e. both internal and external). Because of organizational and functional boundries large amounts of inventory exist in supply chain and the overall flow of goods and services is ineffective.

Modern Bakery or Brittania Biscuits Flow Chart (Hypothetical)

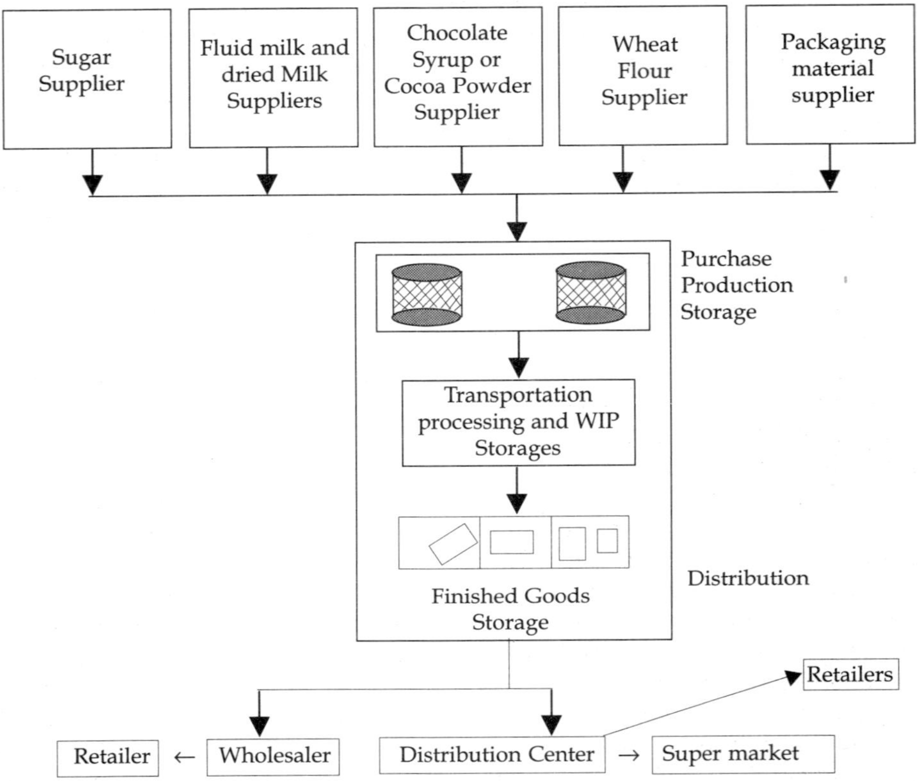

Sugar Supplier
Fluid milk and dried Milk Suppliers
Chocolate Syrup or Cocoa Powder Supplier
Wheat Flour Supplier
Packaging material supplier

Purchase Production Storage

Transportation processing and WIP Storages

Finished Goods Storage

Distribution

Retailers

Retailer ← Wholesaler

Distribution Center → Super market

Phase 2

- The business firm starts internal integration by developing a Materials Management Department. Materials Management is concerned with decisions about purchasing materials, maintaining or removing inventories, production levels, staffing patterns, schedules and distribution.

For example, the focus of Modern Bakery or Britania biscuits is on *internal supply chain* through integration of those aspects or departments or activities which come under firms control directly. Firms in this phase utilize a 'seamless' accounting information and control system ranging from purchasing, finance, accounting, and operations to marketing and distribution. Efficiency and Electronic linkages to suppliers and customers are stressed. However, the firm still considers its customers and suppliers to be independent entitles and focuses on tactical, rather than strategic issues.

- Under ***phase 3***, the internal supply chain is extended to include linkages between firm and its suppliers and customers. The supplier relationship includes purchasing and order fulfillment that extends to and involves production, distribution and customer relationship processes, as well as their internal and external linkages which are integrated into normal business routine. The firm, thus, becomes customer oriented.

Role of Logistics in Supply Chains

Logistics is the process of anticipating consumer needs and wants; acquiring the capital, materials, people, technologies, and information necessary to meet these needs and wants; optimizing the goods or service-producing network to fulfill customer requests, and utilizing the network to fulfill customer requests in a timely manner (Coyle et al, 2009). Logistics management is exercised in both public and private enterprises besides NGOs and service providing organizations like hotels, nursing homes, hospitals, banks, and restaurants.

The origin of logistics term and its management is related to military activities. During 1960s the logistics term started appearing under the domain of *physical distribution*. While the focus of military logistics as observed in Vietnam war, Operation desert storm in Iraq in 1990s and a decade later, and more recently in Afghanistan, was mainly on reliability of supplies at that time, the commercial businesses have focused on consumer goods' marketing and physical distribution of finished goods.

Thus there can be four sub-division of logistics:

- Business logistics
- Military logistics
- Event logistics
- Service logistics

The common characteristics of four sub-division are forecasting, scheduling and transportation. When viewed in a supply chain context, all these four components are dependent on *upstream and downstream* supply chain members.

Value Added Role of Logistics

Form utility: It means value addition to material goods by undertaking manufacturing or assembly process. The process of combining assembly or blending various products and materials in a final product form adds value to that product. In certain segments of business, mixing of products, and breaking bulk takes place at distribution centres thereby changing product's forms, size and packaging.

Place utility: Logistics moves goods and materials from production plants/areas to the points of consumption in other geographical areas where demand is strong for these products resulting in economic benefits to producers and dealers.

Time utility: The availability of goods to meet demand at a particular time adds value to the product and related service provided to the customer. In this context, logistics plays an important role in inventory management and timely transportation of goods to the desired location. Time utility function of logistics is particularly important for just-in-time (JIT) operations.

Quantity utility: In addition to delivering the products on time, the order must be compliant with exact quantity, number and or weight. Thus, the *time, place and quantity* become important parameters in logistics.

Scope of Logistics

It covers the following areas:

- Transportation
- Warehousing and storage
- Industrial packaging
- Materials handling
- Inventory management and control
- Order fulfillment
- Demand forecasting
- Production planning and scheduling
- Procurement
- Customer service
- Facility location
- Reverse logistics
- Scrap disposal

Contribution of Logistics to an Organization

Support to Manufacturing Operations

In order to operate with reduced inventories, production runs are generally shorter in manufacturing organizations, which do not wish to lock their capital in either raw materials or finished products. This is generally observed in manufacturing firm employing 'lean' production and scheduling operations. Thus the trend is towards "pull system" for manufacturing and logistics where products are "pulled" in response to customer demand vis-à-vis to being "pushed" out of manufacturing system ahead of demand. This kind of system not only lowers inventory costs but also costs related to logistics.

At the same time, the organization has to deal with seasonality factor wherever applicable. Therefore, 2-3 months inventory may have to be kept to meet consumer demand for finished products and simultaneously raw material inventories have to be maintained to keep production operational. Thus logistics function has to keep pace with inventory build up in advance. The manager has to take a balanced decision by working out a trade-off between inventory costs and stock-outs to prevent losing customers on one hand, and between inventory costs and production costs on the other side, in case raw material has to be arranged at exorbitant prices in the off-season to keep production going in the lean period. As a result, the responsibility of production scheduling is shared between production and logistics.

In some manufacturing organizations, the responsibility of industrial packaging is given to logistics department. Besides, logistics department's role is becoming more important in import dependent firms/products, as material has to be arranged off shore (foreign countries) to keep manufacturing schedules intact. Examples include metal ores, fertilizer base materials, crude or semi-processed oil, etc. Some automobiles manufacturers like Honda & Toyota may prefer to import certain components from Toyota facility in Japan and elsewhere to their assembly plants in Asia such as India to support "JIT" manufacturing. But recent earthquakes and Tsunami make force Japanese firms to work on alternatives.

Interface with Marketing

Logistics function interfaces with marketing with respect to price, product, place and promotion (Coyle *et al*, 2009) just as it is in case of 4 P's of marketing mix.

A brief discussion is provided below:

> **Price:** A buyer who gets a quantity discount on purchase of larger shipment from a supplier, tries to get a discount on larger shipment from the transporter in terms of weight that is to be carried from point A to point B. Thus the per kg. consignment weight rates applicable to a truckload will be lower than on the smaller and/or partial consignments which go on irregular basis between the two destinations. Therefore, the per kg. rate charged to a customer for a product will include transportation charges as well when we do the costing exercise for the product to be sold. Transportation rates are applicable to both raw materials and finished products.

To sum up, the logistics manager must provide different price schedules to the purchase department to enable the latter to make a decision on inventory to be kept and how to take advantage of lower transportation rates.

Product: The size, shape, weight, dimensions and packaging of the product jointly determine as to how the merchandize will be moved by the logistics provider. As a result of dimensions or design of the product, innovative packaging solutions are implemented for the individual unit for a "consumer good" as well as the bulk consignments of products such as Mixie-

Grinder, Television, PC system with monitor, washing machine, furniture, items etc. The dimensions ultimately help in choosing the mode of transportation—air, water, rail, or road.

Place: The decisions generally relate to physical distribution along with distribution channel decisions. Marketing division of the organizations have to take the decision whether to market the product directly to consumer through retailer or through wholesale dealers. Such decisions affect the logistics requirements of the product to be transported. For example, marketing of several brands of electronics through retail dealers vis-à-vis marketing of Dell computer system directly to a retail customer and bulk user organizations require different types of logistics arrangements.

Purchases by wholesalers are predictable and they place orders for larger quantities for maintaining their inventories which facilitate logistics movements. Retailers or retail customers individually on the other hand are less predictable and order small quantities and thus put pressure on logistics for maintaining customer service to such clients.

Promotion

The product promotion through advertisements at national level helps to create a consumer demand when the customer asks for a product to a retailer who then works through his supply chain to get the FMCG product what the consumer requires. This is the 'pull' system vis-à-vis' push system which the manufacturer adopts and shares advertisement expenses with wholesalers to move the FMCG product through the upstream of supply chain to get it downstream to the customer. Both these approaches—'pull' and 'push' systems have advantages and disadvantages.

A 'pull' system may result in erratic demand, or all of a sudden heavy demand thus and even stock outs putting pressure on logistics system or logistics department of the organization resulting in higher transportation

A Simple Logistics Channel

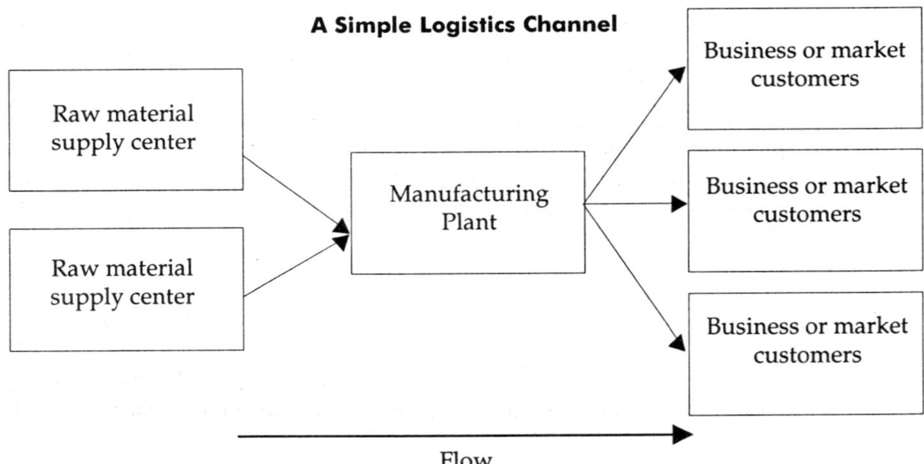

Source: Adapted from "A logistics approach to supply chain management" by Coyle *et al* (2009) Cergage Learning.

costs. The 'push' system works somewhat better as it maintains inventory with wholesalers and to some extent with retailers besides maintaining 'pipeline' inventory by involving logistics on periodic basis. In 'push' system, the manufacturer collaborates with wholesalers to keep some inventory, and put some FMCG products, including new ones on the shelf to stimulate demand.

Logistics Channels

It is the network of intermediaries engaged in transfer, storage, handling, communication and other activities that result in efficient flow of materials and goods. The logistics thus can be seen as a component of total distribution channel, which is inclusive of logistics flow and transaction flow.

The logistics channel can be either simple or complex. In simple channel, control is simple as it is exercised by the manufacturer because he deals directly with his customer.

In a complex multi-party channel comprising a market or public warehouse and retailers the control could be difficult as extra storage and transportation is provided by third-party organizations.

Logistics Systems

Nodes and Links

Nodes are fixed spatial points where materials or goods are held for storage and/or processing. We can say that nodes represent manufacturing/assembly point/facilities and warehouses. Materials at such points are converted into required finished products and delivered to customers.

Links represent the transportation network and connect the nodes in the logistics system. The network may consist of different modes of transportation i.e. rail, road, air or water (and even 'pipeline') either individually or combination of 'one or more' modes of transportation.

Nodes and Links in a Logistic a Systems are represented by:

P = (Production Plant transports finished product to warehouses)

W = (Warehouse transports finished products to market)

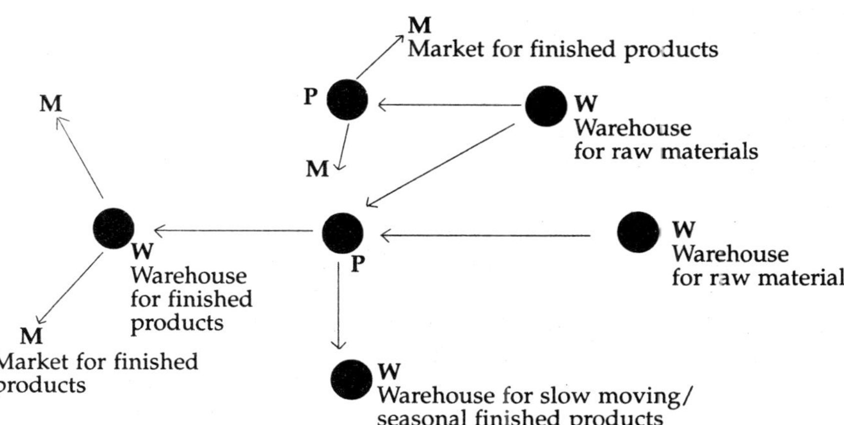

M = (Market for finished products)

Links (Warehouse transports raw-material to production plant for product manufacture/assembly)

Links (Warehouse for storage of finished products which are slow moving or seasonal)

Where: W = Warehouse; P = Production Plant; M = Market.

LOGISTICS CHANNELS

Figure A. A Multi-party Logistics Channel

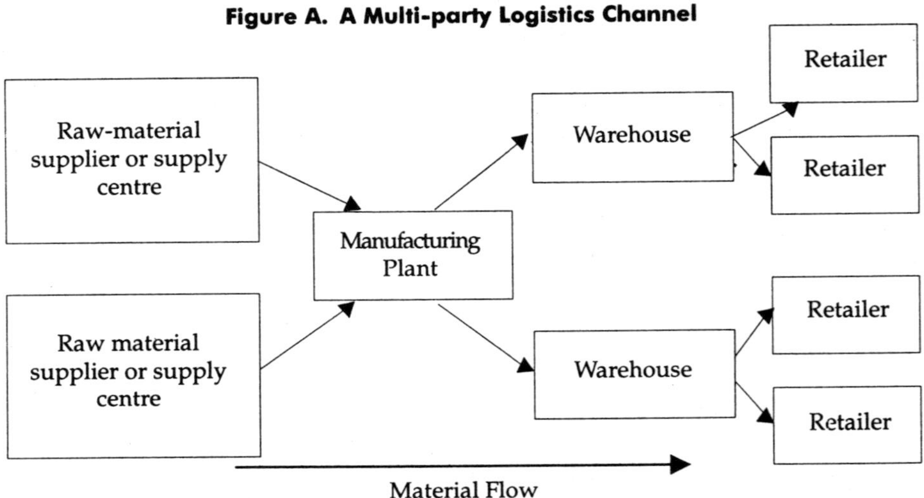

Figure B. A Complex Logistics Channel

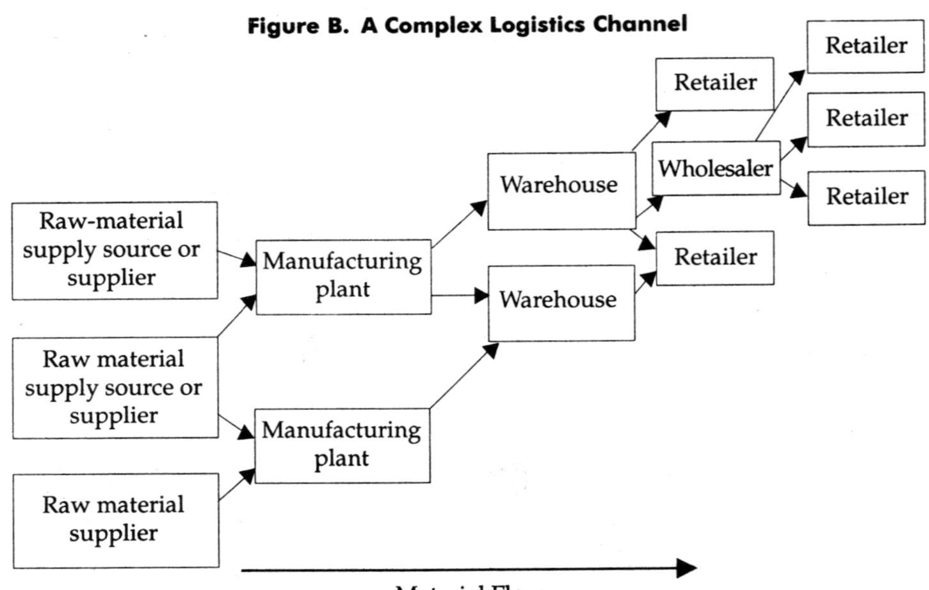

Source: Adapted from "A Logistics Approach to Supply Chain Management," by Coyle *et al* (2009) Cergage Learning.

PART II

Supply Chain Applications with Research and Case Studies

Factors Affecting the Supply Chain Management Practices in Agri-business, Integration of Concepts with Cases

Introduction

Commercial interest in supply-chain management (SCM) in agri-business is on increase in India owing to the growth in urbanization, life-style changes of consumers, and increased competition among producer cooperatives besides traders and newly formed food and agricultural commodities' business companies that are now increasingly involved in the procurement and distribution channel management. Further, the forces of globalization-as evident through the opening of several networks of Retail stores with specialized horticultural produce departments, in different regions of India have resulted in the requirement for efficient and smooth functioning of their backward linkages with upstream members of supply chain. Additionally, there is also a necessity for timeliness factor with regard to the delivery of farm products to meet the requirements of downstream supply chain members that culminate at transformed "new look" retail, or at supermarket levels. Factors responsible for development of supply chains from *"farm-gate to retail level"* in the last 5-10 years have been due to: (i) availability of greater variety of food grains, oilseeds, and horticultural products, (ii) improvements in product quality-both in raw and processed form, (iii) availability of improved rail, road and air-networks, (iv) ability to transport products in cost-effective manner, (v) overcoming seasonality factor by linking any two geographical regions having different agro-climatic conditions and crop marketing seasons,

(vi) development of cold-chains, (vii) giving option to consumers to choose a range of products-in fresh, frozen or processed form, and (viii) providing innovations in packaging to consumers for convenience in handling, storage and use of farm products in consumable form. In addition to these factors, consumer awareness about quality, safety, health and nutritional aspects of food products have also resulted in the formation of supply chains which were unthinkable 2-3 decades ago. These supply chains extend across regions within the country, and in some cases they go across borders, and are connected to chains across continents as well. As a result of these linkages, consumers have been able to exert influence on food chains that originate from different agricultural regions and end-up at retail stores or retail counters of supermarkets located in different parts of the country.

Owing to the interplay of several new variables as outlined above, there has been a significant reorientation of supply chain strategies from earlier supplier driven distribution chains to consumer driven supply chains, which are indicative of consumer power. Traditional agricultural and food businesses, which had previously focused only on prices were unable to address changes in consumer demands and preferences. Individually, the earlier chain member of the production chain represented only part of the cumulative processes involved in production of an agricultural product and its subsequent transport, processing and retailing to the consumer were left to other independently operating chain or channel members. SCM management concepts have provided means to manage changes by incorporating processes operating either in-house via a group company or outsourcing such services from a service provider or simply through the addition of another member in the value-chain as required in the system to efficiently respond to consumer needs. These changes, which require integration and efforts of all the supply chain member-partners have brought-in a trend towards consolidation of cooperatives and organizations operating at farm, processor and supermarket levels. Their activities range from organizing production to managing channel costs through economies of scale, besides gaining market share and competitive strength to survive in the global competition that has arrived on the home turf as well.

It is to be noted that in the last two decades, the general trend is for de-regulation and opening of agri-business markets by governments in many countries around the world. The drivers of change include a rapidly expanding middle class population in South East Asia with an increasing level of personal and household incomes. The educated middle class in the age bracket of 25-40 are young career minded working couples who value convenience, exhibit a greater awareness of health and hygiene, and wish to shop in a cleaner environment of the supermarkets. This has created avenues for suppliers to re-engineer the business strategies, and create new supply-chain relationships. Interest has also risen in managing quality issues through the supply chains owing to public health concerns because of the fact that India is also associated with the global trade in agribusiness products. As a field of study, SCM draws contributions from several disciplines, which includes operations management, such as logistics, materials management and inventory control, planning, scheduling and controlling manufacturing operations, besides marketing-covering both industrial/business and retail markets, economics, human resources and financial management. These are backed by engineering processes in handling and processing the merchandize at successive stages of the supply chain for the ultimate customer.

A few well known examples of successful SCM in agri-businesses operating from farm to retail level in the Indian domestic markets are National Dairy Development Board (NDDB)subsidiary Mother Dairy's *Safal*, Gujarat State Cooperative Milk Marketing Federation Ltd.-GCMMF's *Amul* and retail outlets of *Subhiksha*, besides existing retail centers of HPMC (for apple and other juices from Himachal Pradesh state Horticultural produce Cooperative Marketing Federation Ltd.), Food and retail grocery stores of *Food World*, *Nilgris* and fast developing network of the retail stores of *Reliance Retail*, and many other such retail chains, including *Spencer's* that are doing business at local and regional levels. New agri-produce retail companies floated by big business groups in India such as *Bharti* teleservices, *Tata's*, *ITC* and *DCM Shriram* are also expected to launch their regional and/or nation-wide retail networks by developing their supply chains properly.

SCM-basic Background

SCM in agri-business implies managing the relationships between the businesses responsible for the efficient production and supply of agricultural products from farm level to consumers with the broad objective of meeting consumers' requirements in terms of quantity, quality and price. Meeting customers' requirements involves integrated management of the transactions and relationships between firms as well as processes within firms. Managing these relationships provides an opportunity for negotiating the shares between chain members of the value produced within the chain. Moreover, joint planning of collaborative strategies is aimed to improve the shared value. Traditional supply chains in developing countries typically involve many players, and are tightly linked with long-standing social structures. As developing countries enter into World Trade Organization (WTO) arrangements, their agricultural industries will be subjected to increased competition in their home markets, and at the same time they will have better opportunities to meet global standards in export markets. SCM provides an integrated approach to plan the improvements required in the management of their agricultural production and marketing systems to meet future challenges.

Key Concepts in Supply Chain Management

A supply chain comprises all activities resulting in flow and transformation of goods and services from raw material stage to the finished or processed stage for the ultimate consumption of final consumer requiring those processed/manufactured goods, products, and or services. Along with flows of goods and services, the flow of information is an important attribute and requirement in the supply chain (SC). A SC is made up of raw material suppliers, including equipment and other associated raw materials required for processing various inputs, and the distribution channels that finally end up with the retail consumer. Also, a SC is a sequence of business processes of inter-related organizations, inclusive of their facilities, and activities, which are involved in producing and delivering a product or service to the final customer. Facilities are made up of warehouses, factories, processing centers, distribution centers, retail outlets, and offices. The activities of various members of SC may include forecasting, purchasing, inventory management, information management, quality control, scheduling procurement and production, distribution, delivery and customer service.

Typically, SC consist of four basic processes: Acquiring customer orders, purchasing raw materials and components from suppliers, producing products, and fulfilling or executing the customer orders. In a SC, suppliers are called upstream supply chain members, and distributors, including warehouses, up to retail or supermarket level are called downstream supply chain members. At each stage, the SC members keep an inventory to insulate them from uncertainties. Information is the key factor in managing and coordinating the supply chain at both ends in order to meet the prime objective of the chain, which is meeting the customers' requirements. A local retail store or a super market that gets its supply of eggs, milk products, vegetables directly from the farmers represents a basic level of supply chain. On the other hand, supply chains of food companies like *Brooke Bond*, and *Nestle* who produce and market food and dairy products may operate with a series of linked suppliers and customers as every customer in their SC is a supplier to the next in the chain till the final consumer buys the product from retail outlet. Interestingly, upstream chain members also have their pool of suppliers to produce or assemble their supplies.

Supply chains are also sometimes referred to as value-chains which highlight the fact that value is added as goods and services pass through the chain. Supply or value chains consist of different business organizations. Each chain member has two components of the value chain in the form of a supply component and a demand component. A supply component begins at the beginning of the chain and ends up with internal operations in the organization. The demand component of the chain starts at the point where the organization's output is delivered to the next customer. The demand component is the distribution and sales portion of the value chain. The length of each component depends upon where a particular organization is in the value chain. The closer the organization is to the final customer, the shorter is its demand component and longer its supply component. Value chain, highlights the contribution of functional parts of the chain (either within an organization or across a supply chain) to the development of customer value. While consumers constitute the market size and preference, they play little role in the management of the chain.

In addition to managing the flow of goods and services besides the information flow across the supply chain, a professional manager will try to achieve the level of *synchronization* in a supply chain that will make the chain more responsive to the needs of customers while lowering the system-wide costs. *Synchronization* means more coordination, cooperation and information sharing among SC members, which translates into speedy flow of information between suppliers, distributors and customers. Apart from sharing the same goals with suppliers, customers must be able to count on the quality and timeliness of deliveries of products and services at attractive and competitive prices. For example, a few top class luxury hotel chains comprising *Taj* and *Oberoi Group* of Hotels besides *Venky's*, an offshoot of the Venkateshwara hatcheries having a dominant share in egg layer birds, poultry meat birds and dressed chicken at retail market level, have in past managed their supply chains of food items comprising broiler chicken and selected vegetables by vertically integrating all stages along the Supply Chain (SC) from producing and rearing basic raw materials, such as a day old chicks and procuring vegetable seeds to cultivation and harvesting of various types of horticultural produce and poultry meat for further processing, deep freezing, storage, and distribution to their various hotel locations and retail outlets. Even in such types of organization structures, the individual departments may work in an independent manner, which still requires a lot of coordination among all departments in order to meet consumer needs on time.

Information Technology (IT) Revolution and Supply Chain Management

The IT technology has completely revolutionized SCM practices. As a result, the traditional marketing, purchasing and manufacturing systems are being improved to align with SCM practices. Since logistics systems have the ability to deliver products or consignments at precise times, the service failure instances of past systems are being replaced by zero defect concepts, or the six-sigma performance levels. Perfect order deliveries, which means undertaking deliveries in perfect quantities and assortments to the right location and on time, in damage free condition with accurate invoice data entries, and related papers are becoming routine as per customer expectations. The current SCM practices create conditions for firms to collaborate for strategic market positioning and achieving operational efficiencies. Logistics lies within the domain of supply chain as it involves moving and positioning the inventory within the supply chain. Logistics contributes to order management, inventory, warehousing, materials handling and packaging.

Specifically, the need and importance of SCM has increased owing to the following factors:

(i) Implementation of lean production and TQM practices in organizations aimed at improving quality and reducing operational costs, (ii) Increased levels of outsourcing from arranging supplies of products/services to sorting/grading, packaging, loading, unloading and transportation of raw materials, semi-finished materials to final products to save time and costs, (iii) Role of competition that have led to production and marketing of new products with shorter life cycles and increased customization coupled with short lead times, (iv) Increased globalization which has brought opportunities for many suppliers to widen their global market share or support the global brands by maintaining latter's supplies of key raw materials, short lead times, making use of currency differences in valuation of products and meeting the needs of products that are desired by the prevailing cultures or societies in different countries, (v) increased importance of e-commerce, (vi) need to manage and bring down shipment or transportation costs, either through bulk order movements that get the reduced transportation rates or by getting the raw material processed by forming a SC chain link with the processor when higher volume could be reduced to obtain concentrates or concentrated product, which happens in agricultural and horticultural produce, (vii) outsourcing of 3-PL (third party logistics) management activities, which means giving responsibilities of warehousing and distribution to other companies that specialize in these areas, and (viii) need to manage inventories as they play a key role in success or failure of the supply chain. Shortages can affect the work and could have far reaching consequences. On the other hand, excess inventories add to costs. Further distorted information from one end of SC can lead to excessive pile up of inventory at each stage of the SC resulting in losses to SC members by undesired investment in raw materials, semi-finished to finished products, transportation costs, wrong production capacity plans and high operational costs when real demand at the downstream side of SC is missing. Distorted information flow through the supply chain is due to the phenomenon called bullwhip effect. It occurs when slight to moderate uncertainty and variability at downstream becomes magnified when viewed by the Operational managers of each SC member from downstream to upstream at each chain link. In order to guard its own self interest, SC member at each link resorts to stock piling of the excessive inventory to meet the needs in case "demand flares up". Thus inventory stockpiles become progressively larger when viewed backward through the chain from final customer to the beginning of the supply chain.

The requirements of successful supply chain requires: (i) mutual trust among SC members, (ii) Effective communication, (iii) Supply chain visibility to access data on *inventory and shipping status, delivery time, etc.* (iv) ability to detect and manage unplanned events related to delayed shipments, low inventories, and taking corrective actions, and (v) measuring performance metrics related to quality, delivery times, response time, and inventory turnovers.

In order for the SC to be more competitive and more responsive, it requires active management initiated by one or more members of the supply chain for moving actively towards delivery of improved chain performance. In other words, all products reach consumers through a supply chain but not all chains have sufficient commitment and interaction to consistently improve efficiency, customer value and competitiveness through integrated management.

Given the diversity of consumer interests and options they have to choose products which meet their needs, factors like improved logistics, better information flows, reduced transaction costs, product quality maintenance, and integrity of chain members are known to enhance the operational effectiveness of a chain. Adopting these approaches is important in matching competitors and gaining access to export markets, and supplying to top supermarkets. However strategy should aim at bringing out innovations in product and service design that is hard for competitors to match. Other SCM strategies should aim at (i) reduction of market competition where one should work towards mutual dependence to an extent that the costs of switching over to a new supplier or customer are sufficiently high to inhibit the development of new relationships, (ii) learning how to create value together and then collaborating to consistently utilize the new value as a source of competitive advantage, (iii) developing Collaborative planning, forecasting, and replenishment (CPFR) that focuses on information sharing, planning, forecasting and inventory management. CPFR begins with agreement between major partners to develop a joint market plan, outlining what products are to be sold, promoted, and how within the given time-frame shipments/orders are to be processed and inventory is to be managed, (iv) using the established relationship to develop new range of products, and venture into new segments/markets. Chain relationships are built on the relationships developed between senior managers of the two organizations. Developing relationships requires significant effort, and the maintenance of the relationships is an ongoing commitment. As the investment in a relationship grows, so does the cost to duplicate a similar relationship. Hence, the cost of leaving a relationship increases over time, and thus it leads to interdependency.

Perspectives for Chain Partners in Developing Countries

Globalization offers opportunities to producers and exporters in developing economies. One such opportunity is the year-round provision of fresh agricultural and horticultural produce. To meet new consumer demands, transnational companies, as well as retailers and importers are expanding their international operations. This means that the demand horizon has expanded and is no longer confined to local or regional level. Fresh produce can now be shipped to many parts of the world at competitive prices.

The availability of information from various global markets, coupled with information technologies (IT) and improved logistics help traders to respond quickly to requirements related to consumer demand and facilitate in the flow of merchandize in highly complex global marketplace today. Concerns regarding food quality and safety, government-implemented trade regulations and tough retail standards have increased the requirements for quality producers and reliable supply chains throughout the world. In developing countries and emerging economies, however, companies face particular challenges in adapting to these changing requirements. Producers in developing countries/fast developing economies are capitalizing on opportunities by entering into partnerships with other businesses active in the global food/horticultural produce chain. In various cases, local farmers have linked their production activities to the interests of transnational companies, thus achieving vertically controlled operations in a cross-border supply chain.

Cross-border supply chains are the unique channels by which new forms of production technologies, labor processes and organizational relations and networks are introduced into the host country. When *Pepsico* re-entered India in eighties, it brought with it the concept and model of tomato processing by forming backward linkages in its supply chain with tomato farmers in Punjab. Since its processing requirements were higher, and wanted to keep costs of procurement and operations low, it had to introduce new farm technologies to increase the per acre yields by three to four times the average yields prevalent at that time. Similarly, fresh grapes' exports from Indian states of Maharashtra and Andhra Pradesh by producers' cooperatives that started in nineties with the NABARD's (National Agricultural Bank for Rural Development) financial assistance and APEDA's (Agricultural Processed Products Export Development Authority's) export initiative is another combined example where importers from western Europe, particularly England helped in new production technologies based on consumer preferences in those countries. Thus with the increasing consolidation of markets for agricultural, horticultural and agro-industrial products world-wide, investments and business processes in local markets are projected to increase throughout the world. Supply chains not only benefit the companies directly involved, they also stimulate social, and economic development within a region of a host country. Cross-border supply chain can stimulate the development of local agro-industry, generate employment, increase local food production, undertake value addition to products, introduce new technologies, contain waste losses, increase export earnings, and bring in improved food safety and nutrition standards by connecting chain partners.

To realize new opportunities for trade and income, chain partners in developing countries—producers, processors and exporters—must adapt to the quality and safety standards of importers and retailers in those importing countries. In order to adapt, they need to understand markets, plan their activities accordingly, have technology and management access to improve production systems, and consequently these efforts should be reflected in final products. Also, the supply chain partners are being told: (i) to minimize costs in order to meet increased worldwide competition, (ii) to optimize the supply chain performance through the intelligent handling of inventories, product variety, transportation, and (iii) by reducing warehousing costs, and intermediaries.

Developing Supply Chain Partnerships and Linking Small Farmers to Markets

The findings of several case studies, papers, and reports indicate that supply chain partnerships and alliances between upstream and downstream supply chain members in production, marketing and distribution of food products represent success through cooperation, rather than through an adversarial approach. The relationships between retailer, manufacturer, distributor and farmers have changed the way business is being done by the entire agri-business industry in the last 10-15 years.

In South Asia, the vertical partnerships are taking place between two independent producers. Horizontal alliances have been observed between two independent processors, thereby suggesting that the business control of their units remains with the individual cooperating companies involved in such mutually beneficial relationships. In fast developing economies of Asia, Infrastructure development, new channels of distribution and the emergence of professional retailing are the key drivers to allowing more products to be within the reach of consumers. Logistics and physical transportation are improving rapidly with infrastructure development. In South-Asia, the rapid growth in agri-business supply chains will come from rapidly increasing population in the 20-39 year age bracket, who are the middle class working affluent population, having preference for buying their weekly needs of food products from organized retail or supermarkets. Trade liberalization as observed through imports of foreign fresh horticultural produce e.g. apples and Kiwi fruit in Indian market, and Communications via internet, and e-commerce have shrunk the physical distances and pioneered the business communications in the food and agribusiness sector. As result, many new local players having the national level presence, and local market level players in the agri-business markets of Asia have appeared and are challenging the existing MNCs. They are even giving tough competition to the new MNC entrants (Thompson, 2001).

The food system is undergoing significant changes at local, national and international levels. New products, new business practices, and new relationships between supply chain partners are indicators of this change. Biotechnology, information technology and globalization are the major drivers of this change. Regionally and nationally, there is growing demand for natural and organic food along with some "functional" foods having special health benefits. With the evolution of food system, some segments of supply chain are either disappearing or being transformed. Thus with the formation of some specific supply chains for branded products- developed by companies representing their popular brands, genetics- based products- these refer to a product evolved from specially developed variety, and production based products-mostly produced by cooperatives, changes in food system are making managers to adopt new ways of collaborating with the trading partners. The strength of supply chain is derived from chain leadership, which affects the overall chain structure, product and information flows, and the distribution of returns and costs. For the supply chain to be successful, there has to be a system-wide efficiency, quality assurance and transparency. This may give opportunity to farmers to have larger share of consumer food-spends, but increasing concentration and market power in other segments may make it difficult to exploit this opportunity (King, 2002).

Supply chains are complex entities that not only move products from producers to consumers but they also pass ownership rights from producers to processors and finally to marketers. In return, they bring payments, and credit/working capital from consumers to producers. The supply chains and the members/participants are linked on account of shared information, mutual scheduling of orders, maintaining product quality and transaction volume commitments. Individual suppliers, producers and marketers who are associated with each other through a supply chain, create a greater value for their activities than would do otherwise if they were to operate independently. At the consumer end, chains compete primarily on the basis of price, differentiated products, and services offered with sale. At the producer end, supply chains compete with one another on account of long-term relationship between producers and other members of the chain. Conclusions derived from successful agriculture based supply chain projects include: (1) Long term relationships between partners in the chain lead to improved margins, (2) improved market knowledge for the primary producers (growers and farmers), (3) Reduction of product losses during storage and transportation, owing to improved coordination, (4) Maintenance of quality and freshness of products, and (5) Coordinated supply chains tend to generate "high value added" products which generate significant revenue as they meet with the demands of high-end markets of high income group consumers (Roekel, *et. al.* 2002).

E-commerce in agri-business is becoming popular in many countries across the globe. It involves business transactions between two business firms or companies (B2B), business firms and consumers (B2C), and between public sector firms and consumers. It is related to buying and selling of products, besides providing services, information and data through computer networks. The Internet reduces transaction costs for business firms, and provides consumers with more choices over purchasing decisions, and lower prices, in some instances. A study was conducted to understand the factors affecting the adoption of information technology and e-commerce use by Alabama agribusiness firms in the U.S. Majority of these firms were dealing in farming/ranching, grain merchandising/processing, fertilizer, feed and seed, and were categorized as manufacturers, distributors or dealers. Study findings revealed that while many agribusiness firms in Alabama had adopted e-commerce strategies, farmers were generally unwilling to buy products over the Internet owing to the issue of privacy while purchasing products over the Internet. Results showed that 41 per cent of the firms that had adopted the Internet considered the issue of privacy as a barrier to adoption of e-commerce by farmers. Further, distribution (logistics) being a major function in the supply chain, thirty per cent of those firms who had adopted e-commerce agreed that distribution issues limited the sale of their industry's products over the Internet. It was also found out that firms were more likely to adopt Internet/e-commerce strategies if product comparisons and recommendations could be done over the Internet, and achieve increase in sales through improved distribution, logistics and inventory management practices. The conclusion drawn from this study is that vertical integration or vertical partnerships are necessary for the supply chain to be "complete" in order to execute the distribution and logistics part of the supply chain, which could also handle pre-shipment samples/demonstrations/product or input displays by dealers based on the farmer enquiries before purchasing the concerned product (McFarlane, *et. al.*, 2003).

In the 21st century, the food supply chains have become a complex, interconnected system with strategies that are aimed at creating improved products to satisfy consumers' demand for safer foods. To stay competitive and ensure consumer confidence, agribusiness firms develop and implement strategies that take into account not only traditional economic factors driving the food demand, but also issues such as food safety and quality. Traceability and assurance protocols help agribusiness companies improve and refine their production processes, thus providing better control over, and transparency of food quality and safety throughout the food supply chain. A survey was designed to address questions on traceability and assurance protocols with the representatives of 17 industry members who participated in the focus interviews conducted during the 2004 IAMA World Forum and Symposium conference in Montreux, Switzerland. The industry members represented international agribusiness corporations from Argentina, Australia, Germany, the Netherlands, South Africa, Switzerland, Zambia, the U.K., and the U.S. They were involved in sectors such as farm production, handling, processing, manufacturing (including farm input supply), wholesale, retail, food service, as well as R&D and consulting. The results of this survey indicated that most of the companies that participated had at least some traceability and assurance protocols implemented within their operations to both meet the new food safety regulations, and to give better market access internationally. Results also indicated that the lack of synchronization of traceability and assurance protocols was a significant constraint in deterring companies from implementing the protocols. The majority of participants considered the private sector to hold the primary responsibility over food quality, and the public sector to provide oversight responsibility with regard to a legal framework, standards, specifications and measures for food safety (Jones *et. al.*, 2004).

The socio-economic conditions of mountain farmers in East Africa are affected by their poor access to markets and limited entrepreneurial skills for adding value to produce. To address these problems, a new kind of approach known as Participatory Market Research (PMR)—a component of the Enabling Rural Innovation (ERI) initiative—is being implemented by the International Center for Tropical Agriculture (CIAT) in collaboration with research and development partners in Uganda, Malawi, and Tanzania. PMR is a community-based approach in which rural communities become active partners in identifying market opportunities and developing profitable agro-enterprises. Although individual case studies show promising signs of success and robust results at the community level, the greater challenge lies in linking micro-level community processes to higher macro-level processes where market opportunities and institutional conditions may offer better opportunities for small-scale farmers.(Sanginga *et. al.*, 2004).

Small farmers continue to face challenges in farming even with the development of supply chains in many countries across the world. Competition and unpredictable or lower product prices in the global markets bring economic hardships to these small farmers. With the projected increase in human population by the year 2020 in the U.S., who will be demanding higher quantities of fresh and organic produce, it is being argued by some researchers that alternative outlets should come to the rescue of small farmers. Horticultural auction markets are projected to take over the role of alternative market outlets to provide small farmers with consumer linkages, and relief from lower prices (Tourte and Gaskell, 2004).

Highly cohesive supply chain partnerships between the farmer-producers, retailers and restaurants in Australia are essential for continued sustainable growth in Australian agribusiness. Trust and technology adoption have been identified as critical success factors in supply chain management. A research was carried out to determine the level and importance of the factors of trust and technology adoption focusing on the Australian meat and horticulture industry supply chains. The term level referred to the perceived performance level and the term importance related to the expected performance level for the factors of trust and technology adoption. The research findings showed that the meat and horticulture industry supply chain rated the factors of trust and technology adoption of high importance. On the other hand, research revealed that the level of trust and technology adoption was lower than the importance, presenting gaps in most of the factors of trust and technology adoption. Across both these industries, eight critical gaps were found with respect to factors of trust, which were 'Information sharing', 'Reliability', 'Timeliness', 'Customization', 'Work standards', 'Shared values', 'POS information' and 'Honesty and Integrity'. There were three critical gaps identified in technology adoption, which were 'Relative advantage', 'Traceability' and 'Trialability'. The conclusions from this research were: (a) there was a need to assess the differences between the level and importance of trust and technology adoption to identify the critical gaps in the supply chain, and (b) critical gaps in trust and technology adoption need to be eliminated or diminished to improve Australian agribusiness supply chains. (Paterson, 2006).

In Indonesia, banana farming is quite popular among small farmers in west Java. Unfortunately, the supply chain is fragmented as traders have, traditionally, paid low prices to farmers for their produce, and in turn have made good profit margins after selling the produce to urban markets such as those in Jakarta where demand for such fruits is quite high. Farmers on their part initially, did not exercise good crop management and harvesting practices. With the assistance of *Centre for Tropical Fruit Studies, Bogor Agricultural University, Indonesia and Winrock International,* crop systems improved for Nanggung farmers in west Java. Owing to an increase in productivity and quality of bananas produced, traders turned into partners of farmers in the supply chain by increasing their procurement quantities, and using plastic trays for handling produce besides improving logistics management practices to cut down losses of quality produce being purchased. Farmers on their part started organizing themselves for collective marketing with traders and thus creating a strong market linkage for mutual benefit of both the partners. Further, bananas started getting sold as per market specifications and grades, with top grades getting higher prices than other grades. Extra efforts by supply chain partners resulted in the improved quality of harvest, better prices and improved incomes for farmers, and larger procurement for traders (Tukan et al., 2006).

Himalayan Action Research Centre (HARC), an NGO-based in the mountain state of Uttaranchal in India has been building the capacity of small farmers and hill communities to bring about socio-economic change by linking them to markets in India and even abroad. The NGOs capacity building approach includes collective organizing, agricultural extension, backward linkages, production planning, market linkages and micro-finance. The formations of viable supply chains have helped farmers and rural communities to realize higher incomes than before (Baptista, 2007).

The food retail industry in industrialized countries has undergone major changes in the last three decades. During the 1970s and early eighties, food retailing companies were thought to be agents or extensions of the food processors. Nowadays, they are regarded as the most powerful segment of the whole food chain. In current situations, retailers are able to exercise monopoly powers also, which includes demand for price stability on upstream supply chain partners. The main feature of this changing business behavior is due to competition and increase in the retailers' consumer orientation. This tendency towards vertical supply chain management is on account of the fact that many retail firms have established retail brands. In the course of retail globalization, North American and European retailers such as Wal-Mart, Carrefour, Metro, or Aldi are exporting their business models to China, Vietnam, and/or India. Since raw materials have to be sourced locally mostly, these retail big names establish tighter relationships with local suppliers and they develop the infrastructure before they implement management concepts. The majority of the medium-sized and large firms in the food industry are using supply chain management in order to gain efficiency by reducing stocks, optimising logistics, and reducing waste. In addition to logistics orientation concepts, they have added the concepts such as 'efficient consumer response' and 'collaborative planning, forecasting and replenishment' by addressing the demand side to cover all supply chain management concepts. Food products are usually produced in vertical collaborations which are called either supply chain networks (SCN) or net chains. Such supply chain networks possess a focal firm that manages the system in order to realize the strategic objectives. An important point of chain management is partnering, which addresses issues that are associated with the design of relationships within a supply chain. Partnerships exhibit a certain degree of continuity and the focus of the relationships goes beyond price. Thus, both retail-brand management and processor-brand management face the same challenges. In this context the management of the focal company (i.e. retailers) has to guarantee the authenticity of the quality of the whole food chain. In order to meet the desired 'new quality definition' food processors and retailers have to re-design their food chains in such a way that all stages of the food chain are involved. Operative chain quality approaches takes care of food safety and risk issues as well as efficiency issues vis-a-vis a strategic chain quality system that can be used to achieve a qualitative competitive advantage (Hanf, 2008).

Supply Chain is one of the critical factors for the smooth functioning of McDonalds fast food business in India. Its Supply Chain model ensures on time delivery of raw materials and other supplies besides cutting-costs and maintaining quality standards of its ready to serve meals. McDonald's supply chain initiative in India, along with the deployment of the state-of-art processing technology has changed the spectrum of the Indian fast food industry. McDonalds began developing its supply chain even before it opened its first outlet in the country. The success of McDonalds India operations was due to its sourcing the required raw materials and related supplies from within the country. McDonalds did it by developing local suppliers. McDonalds India works with 38 different suppliers on a long term basis. McDonald's entered its first distribution partnership agreement with *Radha Krishna Foodland* in July 1993. At distribution centers (DCs), the company was responsible for procurement of large volumes of products, maintaining quality control, storage, inventory management, deliveries to the restaurants and data collection, recording and reporting. The DCs provide 'Cold, Clean, and On-Time Delivery' of material to McDonalds restaurants, and maintain the product freshness and quality through out the supply chain. Cold Chain was one of the unique concepts that McDonalds put in its supply chain in India. This system has benefited the farmers upstream and retail customers downstream in the supply chain. With the assured market provided by McDonalds, *Dynamix Dairy Industries*—supplier of Cheese has benefited farmers in Baramati, Pune district of Maharashtra by setting up a network of milk collection centers, thus enabling farmers improve their incomes by finding a new market for surplus milk. *Trikaya Agriculture,* is a major supplier of iceberg lettuce to McDonalds India. Application of improved agricultural management practices and provision of specialized production technology by McDonalds has enabled *Trikaya Agriculture* farms in Talegaon, Maharashtra, to cultivate this crop year round. *Vista processed foods,* a three way joint venture between *OSI Industries Inc.*, USA, *McDonalds India Pvt. Ltd.* and *Vista Processed Foods Pvt. Ltd.*, produces a range of frozen chicken and vegetable foods for McDonalds India operations. Technical and financial support provided by OSI Industries Inc., USA and McDonalds India Private Limited have enabled Vista to set up world-class infrastructure and support services. Another important supply chain partner is *Amrit Foods,* which is a Supplier of UHT Milk with longer shelf life and Milk Products for Frozen Desserts. McDonalds suppliers adhere to Indian government regulations on food, health and hygiene besides complying with McDonald specified standards. The relationship between McDonalds and its Indian suppliers is mutually beneficial and rewarding (Bisht, 2009).

After training vegetable farmers in Indian states of Punjab, Maharashtra, and Andhra Pradesh in adopting newer and innovative methods of production and post-harvest practices, USAID linked farmers in these states to markets and promoted the efficient flow of goods and services through supply chains. USAID initiative has thus helped Indian farmers to realize better prices for their produce (USAID, 2009).

There is sometimes a misplaced feeling among the social activists that the modern retailing is threatening the livelihoods of millions of farmers in many developing countries, including India. On of the reasons is that multi-branch Retail chains require massive volumes of fresh produce at the precise time as per high grading standards and specifications laid down by these chains. Earlier, it was assumed that small farmers would find it difficult to get integrated into these type of comprehensive supply chains. However, recent studies of value chains of fresh vegetables, cotton, rice, shrimps, honey, coffee, and broiler chicken have shown that small farmers have been benefited by way of increased incomes and assets as a result of being included in such value chains. The interesting thing to note is that these value chains are independent in their operations and do not depend on the "subsidies" or "corporate social responsibility" budgets of big companies. The conclusion drawn is that small producers who were grouped into cooperatives achieved "economies of scale " and improved quality of produce' besides having easier access to technical training, inputs, finance, administration and marketing (Harper, 2009).

Review of Two Case Studies

- India Tobacco Company's (ITC's) e-Choupal

ITC, which is one of largest exporters of agricultural commodities from India, through its International Business Division, developed an initiative known as e-Choupal to put in place an efficient supply chain application aimed at delivering value to its customers in domestic and international markets. The e-Choupal model has been specially designed to handle problems faced by Indian agriculture, which in general has been characterized by fragmented farms, weak infrastructure, involvement of numerous intermediaries in inputs supply, and in distribution/market channels, dependence of agriculture on monsoons, variations in production and produce quality owing to cultivation in different agro-climatic zones, and associated difficulties in selling their produce. To overcome the various problems, ITC used the information technology based intervention called e-Choupal, to tie loose-ends in inputs supply and distribution channels. It also shared information related to crop production techniques, inputs use, and on weather conditions, besides providing farmers with information on market demand for their commodities, price trends and identifying suppliers of critical inputs.

e-Choupal was launched in June 2000 with the participation of soybean growers in Madhya Pradesh. Since then, it has already become the largest internet-based initiative in rural India. *e-Choupal* services more than 3.5 million farmers cultivating variety of crops from soybean, coffee, wheat, rice, pulses, to shrimp in over 36,000 villages through 6,400 kiosks spread across nine states of India—Madhya Pradesh, Karnataka, Andhra Pradesh, Kerala, Uttar Pradesh, Uttaranchal, Haryana, Maharashtra and Rajasthan. The problems faced during the setting-up operations of *e-Choupals*, included problems on power supply, telecom connectivity and bandwidth, besides imparting on-line computer training and internet usage to farmers in far flung areas of rural India. Several hardware related backups have been provided to overcome these shortcomings. This includes Power back-up through batteries charged by Solar panels, up-gradation of telecom operator Bharat Sanchar Nigam Limited (BSNL) exchanges with pan India presence, installation of VSAT equipment, Mobile *e-Choupals* etc.

In the first season of its operations in Madhya Pradesh, farmers marketed about 50,000 tons soybeans through the *e-Choupal*, whose marketed volumes have increased two times since 2000. With regard to wheat farmers, e-Choupal has helped them to realize better prices owing to segregation of wheat into different qualities. For aquaculture farmers in coastal areas of Andhra Pradesh, *e-Choupal* has made them aware of food safety norms in importing countries, and provided information with regard to hygienic and disease free production techniques required in shrimp farming. A laboratory for disease detection has also been set up that provides customized service with regard to inputs usage, including that of antibiotics. Plans are being made to integrate bulk storage, handling and transportation facilities in order to improve operational efficiencies of logistics. As India's farmer oriented Company, ITC has taken care to involve farmers in the designing and management of the entire *e-Choupal* initiative. The active participation of farmers in this rural initiative has created a sense of ownership among the farmers.

Owing to positive response from farmers, ITC has decided to extend e-Choupal initiative to 15 Indian states in the next decade to cover 100,000 villages by installing 20,000 *e-Choupals*, and bringing 10 million farmers under the e-Choupal network. There are plans to launch micro-credit, insurance, health and education services through the e-Choupal infrastructure.

How e-Choupal Model Works

Realizing the overwhelming role played by intermediaries in Indian agriculture, e-Choupal makes use of information technology (IT) to virtually cluster all farmer-participants, and makes a value chain through the vertical integration concept. In doing this, it makes use of third party 3-PL logistics concept, by using the current intermediaries as service providers for aggregation, logistics, insurance and even financing but disassociating them from information flows with regard to market information. Village internet kiosks are managed by farmers—called *sanchalaks*, enable the agricultural community access instant information related to weather conditions, market prices, package of practices of crop cultivation methods, risk management, sale of farm inputs and purchase of farm produce from the farmers' doorsteps.

Latest information and customized knowledge provided by *e-Choupal* improves the ability of farmers to take decisions and adjust their farm output according to market demand. The aggregation of the demand for farm inputs from individual farmers gives them access to high quality inputs from reputed manufacturers at favorable or discounted prices. As a direct marketing channel, virtually linked to the wholesale markets system for higher price realization, *e-Choupal* has eliminated intermediaries, thus reducing transaction costs significantly. While the farmers benefit through improved farm productivity and higher farm gate prices, ITC benefits from the lower net cost of procurement by eliminating intermediaries and related costs in the supply chain.

- ***Cross–border Supply Chain***

Illycaffè, an Italian coffee company and its supply chain partners from Brazil

Illycaffè is an Italian coffee roaster that markets an elite arabica coffee brand on world wide basis. The company is a major buyer of superior-quality Brazilian green coffee, which constitutes around two-thirds of its coffee blend. Illy coffee is marketed in 70 countries through 40,000 outlets, which serve an estimated five million cups of coffee daily. During the early 1990s, coffee beans exported by Brazil were usually of low quality, resulting in rejections of nearly 70 per cent of its supplies. It was essential for Italian company to identify Brazilian producers who could comply with the company's quality standards and supply fine coffee beans.

In 1991, the company instituted an annual competition (Prêmio Brasil De Qualidade Do Café Para Espresso) for Brazilian growers of the best green coffee, awarding the winner with a cash prize of USD 30,000, and a 30 per cent premium price over the market price, and the second winner prize amounting to USD 20,000 and so on till the tenth place winner getting USD 1,000 as the prize money. As over 600 small and large Brazilian producers took part in this competition, incentive approach of the company stimulated the development of relatively unknown regions to start producing fine coffees. Illycaffè encouraged producers to invest in quality by paying them prices above the market average. The company buys certified Brazilian coffee beans in sealed lots directly from the producer. To expand its supplier base, the company reduced its minimum lot quantity from 150 to 100 sacks, allowing small-scale producers to aggregate their production.

For training and support services, Illy has instituted, in cooperation with the School of Economics and Business of the University of São Paulo, the Illy Coffee University (Unilly), dedicated to sharing information on coffee production as a chain of economic activities, ranging from production processes to management techniques. With the above incentives, the company has developed its supply chain by getting the supply of coffee that meets its demanding quality standards, while the Brazilian coffee industry has built up its reputation as a quality producer-exporter, and Illy growers enjoy higher profits.

Results-Conclusions and Recommendations

Success Factors

From the supply chain concepts and cases presented, the following *success* factors for cross-border supply chain projects have been identified:

(a) Development of mutual trust, commitment and transparency among SC chain partners improves information exchange,
(b) Chain partners jointly plan and control the flow of goods, information, technology and capital,
(c) Close collaboration among the chain partners,
(d) Development of models, and meeting training material to overcome problems in the supply chain,
(e) Responsibilities of quality and food safety falls into the purview of both private and public sector organizations which are associated with the Supply chain,
(f) Leadership of one or two players, that includes leadership in different functional areas, in the supply chain is very important for the continued success and operation of the projects, and
(g) The number of chain partners participating in the project should be limited.

Risk Factors

The *risks factors* that may affect the success of cross-border supply chain projects in developing countries are:

(i) Social and cultural factors between companies and countries can lead to miss-communication between chain partners,
(ii) Hidden agendas of individual companies within a supply chain may affect the success of the supply chain project,
(iii) Supply chain strategies should be translated into incentives at operational level,
(iv) Trade regulations imposed by governments and retailers may affect the chain partners who have long-established relationships,
(v) Selecting preferred suppliers means disqualifying others as many smallholders may not be able to supply high-end retailers or supermarkets.

References

Anonymous, 2007. *ITC e-Choupal: Transforming Lives and Landscapes, a Revolution Inspired by Public-private Partnership*, document accessed from URL: http://www.itcportal.com/agri_exports/Dec 15, 2005 and Feb. 10, 2007.

Baptista, Piya, 2007. *Linking Small Farmers to Markets: Case Study on the Himalayan Action Research Center, Uttaranchal, India.* South Asia Agriculture and Rural Development Department, World Bank, Washington, D.C.

Bisht, Amit, 2009. *McDonald's Supply Chain* In: Articlesbase, Marketing section, Free online articles Directory, http://www.articlesbase.com, posted January 20, 2009, accessed Sep 26, 2009.

Bowersox, D., Closs, D., and Cooper, M.B. 2008. Supply Chain Logistics Management, 2nd ed., Special India edition, Tata McGraw-Hill, New Delhi.

Food and Agriculture Organization, 2006. *Linking Farmers to Markets, Private Company Linkages,* Case studies involving nine countries from Africa, south America and south-east Asia, Agriculture Marketing Division, Agriculture Department, FAO, Rome.

Hanf, Jon, 2008. *Food Retailers as Drivers of Supply Chain Integration: A Review,* Australasian Agribusiness Review, Vol. 16, 2008.

Harper, Malcolm, 2009 Beyond retail revolution, special report In: *The Broker,* Oct 7, 2009, Leiden, The Netherlands, http://www.thebrokeronline.eu, accessed Nov 17, 2009.

Jones, *et al* 2004. *Traceability and assurance protocols in the Global Food system,* International Food and Agri-business Management Review, IAMA, Vol. 7(3).

King Robert P. 2002. *Supply Chain Design for High Quality Products: Economic Concepts and Examples from the United Sates,* Department of Applied Economics, University of Minnesota, St. Paul, MN,USA. http://www.ifmaonline.org/pdf/congress/king accessed Dec 21, 2008.

McFarlane, D., Chembezi, D. and Befecadu, J. 2003. *Internet Adoption and Use of E-commerce Strategies by Agri-business Firms in Albama,* Department of Agri-business, Albama A&M University, USA.

Paterson, Ian, 2006. *Trust and technology adoption in Australian agri-business supply chains: a gap analysis approach.* A research Thesis. Univesrity of Southern Queensland, http://eprints.usq.edu.au/2499 accesssed Nov 19, 2009.

Roekel, Jan van, Willems S. and Dave Boselie. 2002. *Agri-Supply Chain Management: To Stimulate Cross-border Trade in Developing Countries,* World bank paper on Cross Border Supply Chain Management, Washington D.C., http://www.regoverning markets.org accessed Sep 2, 2007.

Roekel, J.V., Kopicki, R., Broekmans, C.J.E. and Dave Boseli, 2002. *Building Agri-supply chains: Issues and Guidelines.*World bank paper on Agri-supply chains, Washington D.C. http://siteresources.worldbank.org/INTARD/agri-supplychains accessed Oct. 12, 2008.

Russell, Roberta S., and Bernard Taylor, 2004. *Supply Chain Management* In Operations Management, 4th edition, New Delhi: Prentice Hall of India.

Sanginga, P.C., Best, R., Chitsike C., Delve R., Kaaria, S., and Kirkby, R. 2004. *Linking Smallholder Farmers to Markets in East Africa,* Empowering Mountain communities to identify market opportunities and develop agro-enterprises, International Centre for Tropical Agriculture (CIAT), Kampala, Uganda, Vol. 24(4), pp. 288-91.

Sawhney, Mohanbir, 2007. *ITC's e-Choupal Movement Initiates Rural Development in India,* http://www.itcportal.com/rural devp_philosophy/ document accessed Feb 4, 2007.

Thomson, Glen, 2001. *Supply Chain Management—Building Partnerships and Alliances in International Food and Agri-business-* A Report for the Rural Industries Research and Development Corporation (RIRDC), KINGSTON ACT 2604; RIRDC publication no. 01/31, and project no. GLL-2A, Australia ; http://www.rirdc.gov.au accessed Nov 8, 2009.

Tourte, Laura and Gaskell, Mark, 2004. *Horticultural Markets: Linking Small Farms with Consumer Demand,* Renewable Agriculture and Food systems, Vol. 19(3), pp. 129-34.

Tukan, C.J.M, Roshetko, J.M., Buildarsono and G.S. Manurung, 2006. *Banana Market Chain Improvement—Enhance Farmers' Market Linkages in West Java, Indonesia,* http://www.globalfoodchainpartnerships.org accessed Sept. 16, 2009.

United Conference on Trade and Development, 2004. *Financing Commodity based Trade and Development: Innovative Agriculture Financing Mechanisms,* Report prepared by Trade and Development Board, Commission on Trade in Goods and Services, and Commodities, UNCTAD Secretariat, Geneva, Nov 2004.

USAID, India, 2009. *Success Story—Bringing Small Farmers Closer to Markets,* U.S. Agency for International Development, http://www.usaid.gov accessed August 7, 2009.

Woods, Elizabeth, J. 2004. *Supply Chain Management: Understanding the concept and its implications in Developing countries,* School of Natural and Rural Systems Management, University of Queensland, Gatton, Australia.

CHALLENGES IN CONTRACT CULTIVATION*

Basic Concept

The basic concept of contract farming for a given agricultural product, including livestock/dairy, poultry and horticultural products, is to reduce the risk for the buyers and producers alike. Both producers and buyers-who may be processors as well, enter into a contract to supply and buy a specified/agreed quantity of crop/agricultural product at a pre-fixed/agreed price over a period of time. The *Contract Agreement* or *Memorandum of Understanding* for an agreed crop/product covers: the quantity to be produced and purchased, season or period of production, specifications, variety to be raised, supply of inputs, if any, by the buyer such as seedlings, fertilizers, pesticides/fungicides, including credit/advance payment, the economic portion of the crop to be supplied, e.g. whether it is going to be fruits, seeds, or roots, and in what form fresh, dried or on processed basis. Further, the agreement also mentions the timing of the supply i.e. in which month and week the supply is to begin, to a specific location or warehouse or processing unit of the buyer. It also sets clearly the mode of payment to grower or organizer-supplier. For example, the first installment can be a certain percentage of the total estimated value of the crop to be purchased by the buyer. It may be paid either in advance or within 2-4 weeks after planting, if it is a field crop, followed by one or two

Source: Developed mainly on the basis of experience of contract farming projects, while author worked as General Manager (Supply chain operations and procurement, including contract cultivation of medicinal crops) at Sami Labs Ltd., Bangalore (1998-2004).

installments during the middle of the crop production season, and the balance either at the time of completing the supply of the agreed harvest, or within two weeks to four weeks after the delivery of the complete crop. By entering into a contract agreement, the buyer reduces the risk of non-availability of a new crop or not-so-commonly available product, and both producer-supplier and buyer reduce the risk of market demand and fluctuation in prices of produce.

Relevance of Contract Farming

A farmer is usually faced with difficult decisions in choosing what to produce, or how much to produce and where to market the produce. He is also faced with questions such as what combination of food grain crops, cash crops, and livestock enterprises to follow on his farm. He must have knowledge of all these based on the resources existing in terms of land, labour, machinery, farm equipment, buildings, agro-climatic conditions and working capital available with him. He is supposed to either have or acquire good knowledge of farming practices, and crop rotations that will help him in utilization of farm resources efficiently in maximizing his returns from farming business over a period of time and on continuous basis.

To reduce his market risk in terms of finding a buyer before hand who would buy at a fixed price declared in advance under the buy back agreement and much ahead of even planting, the contract crop offers a viable solution. Since a farmer in any Indian state is following the traditional crop mix, it would be worthwhile for him to integrate a contract crop in his cropping system for which production technology can be acquired from the agronomists from University or from the contract buyer himself.

The contract farming system should be seen as a partnership between agribusiness units-the buyers, and farmers. In order to be successful, it requires a long-term commitment from both parties. Exploitative arrangements by a contract buyer/organization turn out to be of limited value, and can jeopardize agribusiness investments. Similarly, farmers need to understand that honouring contractual arrangements, under normal circumstances, would result in their long-term benefit. Contract farming has become an important component of agricultural related businesses. It deals with the supply and purchase of entire crops or their products, mainly the economic portions-e,g. roots, leaves, seeds, or flowers are purchased by multinationals, large commercial organizations, smaller companies, government agencies, farmer-cooperatives or individual entrepreneurs. Contract farming has potential in areas where small-scale farming operations prevail in situations where small farmers are not competitive individually without having access to the services provided by contract farming companies. However, contract farming model is to be seen in commercial context within the framework of technical and economic realities.

Requisites for Success of Contract Farming

A Profitable Market

A market must have the capacity to remain profitable in the long-term as prices tend to be cyclical for many crops or their products. An analysis of economic viability is advisable when prices are high as the analysis would indicate different results than those obtained when prices are at season's low. Thus a "sensitivity analysis" may be required to ensure that production is viable even when prices are low. A contract farmer or contract farming sponsor/supplier can lose markets if quality standards and deliveries are not reliable in terms of timeliness, and scheduling. Exporters dealing with high-value horticultural exports also need to be sure that they can comply with the prevalent quality standards and would be able to meet projected requirements.

Profit for the Farmer

If either the sponsor or its contract farmers do not achieve consistent and attractive financial benefits, the contract farming venture would not succeed. While it is assumed that regular and attractive incomes should encourage farmers to make a long-term commitment, sponsors should note that per acre yield results from experimental plots may be higher than those from actual field conditions. Therefore, yields should be based on the mean production results in the last 3-5 years. With new technologies and improved farm management practices, the mean yield increases over time. Farmers must realize profits if average yields and agreed prices by buyers result in increased revenues covering the production costs adequately for the contract farmers.

Physical Environment

The success of the agri-business enterprise requires that there should be:

(1) A general suitability of the topography, climate, soil fertility and water availability, and
(2) suitability of the physical environment for the specific plant genotype or livestock product for which there is a market demand. The interplay of all these factors determines production yields, quality and profitability.

Communications and Utilities

A major requirement for agricultural investment in rural areas is the existence of an adequate communication system with respect to roads, transport, telephones and other telecommunication services. Reliable power and water supplies are vital for ensuring irrigation to crops, agro-processing and exports of fresh produce. While major road infrastructure may be adequate, approach (or feeder) roads to farms located in interior areas may be poorly developed or non-existent.

On the other hand, exports of horticultural crops under contract-farming require the availability of regular airfreight facilities. Fresh vegetables and cut flowers exports depend upon adequate cargo space, and availability of cooling chambers to maintain ambient temperature and humidity till they reach international markets.

Land Availability

Contract farming can experience wide fluctuations in land ownership and involve use of leased lands. Farmers under contract must have unrestricted access to land on which to plant their crops. There must be an understanding on the part of sponsor to know how farmers would gain access to land for cultivation and it should be acceptable within the framework of the contract.

Inputs Availability

In most contract farming, ventures, the sponsors recommend, procure and distribute many or all of the material inputs. Sponsors need to organize the supply of all necessary inputs for the farmers. All inputs should be identified and ordered well in advance.

Cultural Considerations

Many rural communities refrain from using modern agribusiness practices and are influenced by traditional practices as they are normally more conservative in their social and economic approach. Therefore, cultural factors need to be considered while finalizing the contract agreements with the farmers. Also, the economic success of a contract farming venture with one group of farmers may bring social problems with other groups which do not have contracts owing to limits on number of farmers or acreage of land to be considered for contract agreements.

Government Support

Progressive Governments play an important role to make contract farming successful. A relevant legal framework and an efficient legal system are preconditions. Moreover, governments agencies can help in developing linkages between investors/sponsors, and farmers. They can protect farmers by ensuring the financial and commercial reliability of firms, or sponsors.

Contracts and Agreements

Agreements, in the form of a written contract cover the responsibilities and obligations of each party. It also specifies the corrective mechanism arising due to natural calamity, and way out if the contract itself breaks down due to unforeseen circumstances. In most cases, agreements are made between the sponsor and the farmer. In case of arrangements through intermediaries or cultivation contractor, the sponsoring firm contracts directly with the cultivation contractor who makes his own contract arrangements with farmers. Four aspects need to be considered when drafting contracts:

1. *The legal framework:* The formal law of contract applicable in a particular local environment/country, as well as the manner in which that law is applied in actual practice.

2. *The main ingredients :* The clarification with regard to responsibilities, the pricing structures, contract period, and the set of technical specifications, production season, periods and destination of supply.
3. *The format:* This is with regard to the contract presentation-on legal paper or on the Company letter head of the sponsor/buyer organization, including in the local language, signing authorities from both sides, if required.
4. *The implementation:* The details with regard to putting the contract into practice with regard to commencement of the contract, inputs supply, credit, land preparation, visits of technical people, training of farmers, post-harvest practices, quality control, disease management, production schedule and management practices, including logistics services if applicable.

The type of contract used depends on a number of factors such as the nature of the product, the primary processing required, if any, and the demands of the market in terms of supply reliability. The nature of the agreement is also influenced by quality incentives, payment arrangements, the level of control the sponsor wants to have over the production process, and the extent to which the parties have capital tied up in the contract.

Market Specifications

Under a market specification contract, only quality standards are specified. The sponsors normally provide only minimal material and technological inputs. This is the most elementary type of contract, and is commonly used by individual developers under the informal model.

Resource Specifications

In this type of contract, key components such as varieties, fertilizer and pesticide rates, and agronomic practices are mentioned. Some financial and input advances are provided to farmers by sponsors.

Product Specifications

Contracts that focus on product specifications usually establish predetermined pricing structures and make heavy commitments in the form of farm input advances, technical inputs and managerial control. This formula is the most commonly used by the commercial agreements involving direct contracts or through intermediaries.

Contract Specifications

In brief, contracts will have to specify the following elements in the buyer/sponsor-farmer agreement or contract:

- Contract duration;
- Quality standards;
- Production quotas;

- Cultivation practices;
- Crop delivery arrangements;
- Pricing arrangements;
- Payment procedures; and
- Insurance arrangements.

Contract Duration

The duration of agreements depends on the nature of the crop. Contracts for short-term crops such as vegetables are normally issued and renegotiated on a seasonal basis, where as commercial crops such as tea, coffee, sugar cane, and cocoa require long-term contracts that can be amended periodically.

Quality Standards

Product quality can have far-reaching consequences in terms of market acceptance and future expansion. Most contracts contain detailed quality specifications. The produce that does not conform to the agreed criteria can be rejected.

The grading of crops/crop products are well established for several commercial commodities, and approved by Commodity Boards, and organizations like Agmark in India. However, for certain products/crops such as medicinal crops, standards are specified by the Buyer companies or intermediaries on behalf of such sponsors.

Production Quotas

Quotas are employed in the majority of contracts in order to:

- Utilize processing, storage and marketing capacities efficiently;
- Guarantee markets for all farmers;
- Ensure quality control; and
- Control excess production.

However, in times of shortages, overproduction by some farmers is welcome otherwise overproduction attracts lower prices. Sometimes, sponsor will go for overproduction by registering higher number of farmers under contracts than required in order to indirectly discourage farmers from selling the produce in open markets. In the event market prices are higher than contract prices owing to tighter overall supplies, contract sponsor or buyer benefits. On the other hand, if market prices are lower, farmers who are under contract benefit due to favorable contract prices.

The allocation of production quotas will vary according to crop and situations. If there is no alternative market for the crop and farmers have made long-term investments, the sponsor or the government agency should purchase the entire crop covered under the quota if the crop meets with the agreed quality specifications.

Cultivation Practices

When sponsors provide seeds, fertilizers and agrochemicals, they have the right to expect that those inputs will be used in the correct quantities, and there would not be any diversion. Farmers are also advised to follow the recommended cultivation practices. Of particular concern is that farmers should not apply any banned or non-recommended agrochemicals. Therefore, farm extension assumes a critical role.

Crop Delivery Arrangements

Arrangements for collection of fresh produce or dried products, or delivery by farmers differ from agreement to agreement and the situation. Some contract mention that farmers should deliver their harvest to processing plants on stipulated dates; others may include the use of the sponsor's transport to collect harvested crops at centrally located buying points. When the sponsor's transport is used there is normally no cost incurred by the farmer.

Pricing Arrangements

Pricing and payment terms are the most important components of contracts. The choice of pricing structure depends upon whether it is for local or export market or both, seasonal nature of production, competition in the marketing system, and specialized nature of crop due to its limited demand from the end-user industry. There are several ways of calculating prices offered to farmers. These are:

- **Fixed prices** as per grades, which are pre-determined before the start of the season;
- **Flexible prices** according to shape, size of the product, or active ingredients linked to basic average content/recovery rates, and in some cases international prices;
- Prices calculated on fluctuating **spot-market prices**, which may be unsatisfactory to farmers;
- Prices on a consignment basis after the product has been sold in the market; this again is controversial and makes farmers unhappy; and
- Prices based on Split pricing, which is basic price plus additional price paid based on the final market price after the product has been sold. In case of processed commodity/crop, the final price may take 4-6 weeks to calculate after the product derived from it is sold.

Payment Procedures

For all farmers the most convenient method of payment is usually cash-in- hand immediately following delivery of any part of their crops. However, this is not always possible, as in the majority of cases, payments are made periodically throughout a season, perhaps two to four times, with the final payment after the delivery of the last harvest. Depending upon the nature of contract, any material and cash advances given to farmers during the season are normally deducted from the final payment.

Insurance Arrangements

Agricultural investments always involve risk. The most likely reasons for crop failure are poor crop management, climatic conditions and natural calamities, and pest epidemics.

Identifying Suitable Production Areas

Following the choice of a suitable physical and cultural environment, sponsor must then select specific areas that can provide easy access for extension and logistics services. It is usually important for the contracted areas, or farmers to be situated relatively close to the company's processing or packing facility so that transport costs can be minimized. There are situations when it is advisable to spread production over a larger area. This may be when farmers are situated in many districts over different soil types, and irrigation facilities. The cultivation of crops in different areas can also reduce the risk of total crop failure due to irregular weather patterns or diseases. Such a strategy helps to guarantee a regular supply for processing and marketing.

Selecting Farmers

After the choice of production areas the next requirement is to select farmers. Management must decide how many farmers should be offered contracts and the criteria for their selection. Community leaders and local district/government officials are usually knowledgeable on the capabilities and attitudes of farmers in the targetted districts.

Providing Material Inputs

The provision of material inputs to farmers is an important feature of contract farming. Before the start of each season, the pesticide and fertilizer requirements for each farmer based on his production quotas or area registered are calculated. Sponsors sometimes guarantee installment payments to commercial banks and rural cooperatives agencies for purchase of heavy equipment such as tractors, harvestors, and establishment of post-harvest facilities by farmers in the event contract agreement is on long-term basis. Such payments are deducted from the farmer's crop proceeds. In other cases, advance payments made to farmers to cover production costs are deducted from the final proceeds when the entire crop is sold to the sponsor or buyer firm.

Providing Logistic Support

Another key management function is to organize input distribution, container deliveries and the strict scheduling of final produce transportation, especially around harvesting time. This is a vital area for management because logistics problems can adversely affect both the sponsor's profitability and the relationship between sponsor and farmer.

Purchasing the Product

Management must ensure that staff are available to purchase the product from farmers as scheduled. Sincere efforts should be made to avoid corruption in the buying process. Farmers must be able to verify the weights of the products they sell to the sponsor. Also, where produce is rejected, farmer should be given opportunity to inspect it.

Training

Management may consider organizing training programs for extension staff and farmers in the form of regular lectures and field days and through the use of demonstration plots. Staff training can be provided by visiting experts from agricultural universities and other such scientific institutions.

Challenges for Cultivation Organizers—Commercial Medicinal and Aromatic Crops

Facts with Farmers

Farmers are not emotional about the choice of crops. They want to grow proven crops, not only for one season but year after year. In case of any new crop, they wish to take up only if it is profitable to them. Once they are convinced, they would like to integrate any new crop into regular cropping system. Farmers once commit themselves to a crop, they would like contract buyers to purchase that crop on a long term basis.

Farmers want to be sure of the demand of the crop in the medium to long term; they do not want quick changes from year to year and they wish to stick to the recommended crop provided it comes out well on their farms. This also means that in the event, the contract buyer backs out, they would like to find its market elsewhere in the coming season.

Farmers are concerned more with the physical yields. Except for few crops like medicinal crops, sugarcane or milk sales to cooperatives, the concept of active yields in terms of active ingredients, sugar content, dissolved solids, protein or fat content, is not well understood by them.

Problems at the Cultivator Level

In case of vegetable or regular commercial crops, there can be an either non-availability or **shortage of basic planting materials**.

For any new crop, farmers are not well-versed with the production techniques or package of practices, Further, there are problems associated with anticipating average yields, production costs and eventually the per acre profits; farmers are not sure of crop performance under the existing agro-climatic conditions.

Soil types vary from area to area ; in some situations farmers may be good but the soil types like black cotton or clayey soils they have on their farms may not be good for medicinal plant based root crops.

Irrigation may be a problem; contract cultivation can not be taken up without the availability of sufficient water.

Cost of production factor bothers the farmers, and they want to be sure that contract procurement price or their sale price would be able to cover costs of production.

Opportunity cost principle operates in farmers' considerations while taking up the new crop cultivation. They like to compare its merits in loosing the existing or the best alternative crop or crop combination.

For a new contract crop, comparison with the other commercial crops in terms of per acre profits are often made.

Average size of the holding is 1 hectare or between 2-3 acres. This may constrain the farmer to take up the cultivation of a new crop for which he is not prepared. In many instances, holdings are fragmented i.e. they are spread over in small pieces and are not localized in once place.

Marketing infrastructure in terms of receivals and drying yards is not existing in many rural areas. In other words, some kind of investment is needed to create the basic infrastructure.

Problems with the Potential Cultivation Coordinators

Most of the people who approach the buying organizations for agricultural products/raw materials with the promise of arranging 100 or 200 acres land are businessmen turned farmers. These are "Fly by Night" operators. They are unable to organize farming as their sole aim is profitability through agriculture and they usually ask the buying organizations (of contract crop) for developmental funds. These people may have businesses of their own such as being fertilizer dealer, compost supplier to farmers or contract dealer for buying the produce of farmers such as mangoes, sapota or other crops for which quick profits could be made by buying large volumes at low prices from farmers.

The "available land" for cultivation is generally rocky and fragmented. Moreover, land is not available at one geographical location, the soil type differs sharply, agro-climatic conditions vary greatly. There is little availability of the existing fertile land, and the land is yet to be developed. In many cases, they want to inter-crop with the orchard crops or plantation crops, which is not the correct decision.

In many instances, traders/businessmen turned contract farming organizers look for an agreement with the buyer/buying organization as an instrument to raise money through banks or some financial institutions. Apart from getting the publicity for their other businesses, e.g. input supplies for agriculture or industry, they are unable to organize the farming business due to lack of manpower and infrastructure.

Determining Areas where Solutions are Possible

To overcome the mental blocks which farmers have with respect to new crops (e.g. medicinal crops) or varieties of existing crops such as corn (maize), wheat, rice or vegetables, buyer should encourage or develop the farms wherever farmers show interest, after ensuring that selected area has a potential of getting developed into specialized crop growing area in terms of contract crops.

The buyer can develop the practice of satellite farming system. Once an area of cultivation or a pocket is developed, it would serve as a demonstration unit to other farms, and the diffusion of agricultural technology to cultivate contract crop would take place. The expansion of area under the contract crop can take place in that district and in the neighboring districts, after farmers realize that there are genuine buyers of the cultivated material/contract crop.

To ensure increased area under the contract crop in order to match with the targeted purchase levels or requirements, and to reduce costs for supplying the plantation material to farmers, one has to develop nurseries at the farm level for the commercial propagation purposes. In this context, the tissue culture laboratory could be helpful for few crops. This could be true for banana crop in certain parts of Maharashtra and Karnataka and elsewhere. It could also be true for certain aromatic crops like *Basil, Lemongrass, Davana* in Tamil Nadu and Karnataka. In case, the propagation material or seed material is not available with the buyer organization, then buyer should hire external nursery operators who would multiply and supply the seed material for commercial plantation with farmers.

In the event, the pocket of cultivation is developed, the existing infrastructure available in the area for receiving, drying, bagging and storing the material should be made use of. The selected area for cultivation should have easy access to road and rail communications in order to move inputs and the produce, and for undertaking inspection of the cultivated area whenever required.

In order to procure the quality material, we should link the procurement price with the minimum recovery rates with respect to parameters desired. It could be fat or "solids not fat" in cow's milk, sucrose content in sugarcane, protein content in a pulses crop or soya crop, forskohlin content in the root of the medicinal crop like Coleus forskohlii. Any farmer bringing farm produce exceeding the minimum requirement for a particular parameter should be rewarded on pro-rata basis and the one whose material is below the minimum level should be paid as per content basis to reduce risks of incurring the extra costs.

How to get Started

The buying agency or organization should get started with the cultivation of a contracted crop even if the project has to start from a small acreage.

Farmers Honesty and Suitability of Agricultural Area

The important criterion is the seriousness and honesty of the farmers or agriculturally oriented persons interested in the cultivation and the suitability of the agricultural area, including the agro-climatic conditions for producing the required crop, or combination of two-three crops.

Risk Factors

Farmers in general are very careful in accepting the new crop and businessmen turned farmers avoid risk taking on their resources alone, and they do not wish to put higher area under the new crops as there are many variables involved in the cultivation equation. These variables include potential yields, production costs, profits vs. actual yields, actual costs and net profits from medicinal or horticultural crops farming.

Support to the Interested People

In this context, buyer agency or company requiring the material should support people or organizations who wish to venture into contract cultivation by taking calculated risks.

Clarity of Requirements

As there are many new products coming into domestic and export markets, the buying company should be very clear about what it requires in terms of final products, or raw materials to be obtained from contract crops. From what is feasible to cultivate in the domestic environment, not more than one crop should be selected to begin with.

Projected Requirements

And lastly, the buying agency should bear in mind that contract crops should remain in demand for next 5-10 years. The upward sloping curve will bring higher area under the contract farming, especially with regard to new varieties of wheat, corn, vegetables and new crops in the medicinal and aromatic crops sector.

REFERENCES

Eaton, C. and Shepherd, A.W. (2001). "Contract Farming-Partnerships for Growth", Food and Agriculture Organization of the United Nations, FAO Agricultural Services Bulletin 145.

GOI (2002). "Report of Inter-Ministerial Task Force on Agricultural Marketing Reforms", Ministry of Agriculture Department of Agriculture & Cooperation Krishi Bhawan, New Delhi.

FAO (2010). "Linking Farmers to Markets", In: Agricultural marketing, FAO, Rome, http://www.fao.org/ag/ags/subjects/en/agmarkets/linkages accessed April 2, 2010.

APPENDIX 1

Example of Contractual Agreement

MEMORANDUM OF UNDERSTANDING

This Memorandum of Understanding, hereinafter referred to as the MOU, is an Agreement made on this .... day of June 2003 at Bangalore.

Between

XYZ District Cooperative,
Having its registered Office at
No. 50, TPH, Greenfields,
Secunderabad-560 024
Represented by its Managing Director,

Mr. G. Shankar Reddy, hereinafter referred to as the First Party, which term shall mean and include its representatives and assignee

And

ABC Herbal Extracts,
Having its registered office at
XX, I Main, II Phase,
Industrial Area,
Bangalore-560058
Represented by its Director,

Mr. John De Silva, hereinafter referred to as the Second Party, which expression shall include its successors and assignee,

WHEREAS the First Party is a Limited Company engaged in the cultivation of medicinal plants for sale.

WHEREAS the Second Party is a recognized Export House engaged in the manufacturing and exporting of various category of natural products, fine chemicals, herbal extracts, etc. from medicinal plants and agricultural products, having 100% EOUs in the State of Karnataka.

WHEREAS the First Party has approached the Second Party and agreed to cultivate, procure and supply *Phyllanthus amarus* whole plant to the Second Party which the Second Party has agreed to buy on the terms and conditions provided below:

TERMS OF THE AGREEMENT

1. **Term**

   During 2003-04, the First Party hereby agrees to organise the cultivation of 10 metric tons, with +/- 10% permitted variation, of *Phyllanthus amarus* crop exclusively for the Second Party in 15 acres of land around Madurai or any other suitable area which the First Party chooses to cultivate this crop.

2. **Role of the First Party**

   The First Party will act as the cultivation organizer *cum* supplier and will organize the entire activity from production, harvest and supply of dried *Phyllanthus amarus* whole herb, inclusive of leaves to the Second Party. Further, it will be the responsibility of the First Party to determine the suitability of land as well as choice and number of farmers to be selected for cultivation of *Phyllanthus amarus*.

3. **Period of Supply**

   The First Party shall supply the said *Phyllanthus amarus* whole plant, dried herb during the scheduled period from August/ September 2003 and February-March 2004.

4. **Quality Specification**

   The First Party shall supply the said *Phyllanthus amarus* whole plant dried which shall be in accordance with the pre-purchase sample supplied to the Second Party. Further, the First Party shall adhere to the following specifications:

(a) Foreign matter	- Not more than 1.0%
(b) Sand & Silica	- Absent
(c) Insect infestation	- Nil
(d) Rodent contamination	- Nil
(e) Ash content	- Not more than 10% w/w
(f) Moisture content	- Not more than 10% w/w

   It is important that the dried *Phyllanthus amarus* herb should be supplied to the buyer with leaves. Material supplied without leaves or insufficient leaves will not be accepted.

5. **Price Payable**

   The agreed price payable by the Second Party for the whole plant of *Phyllanthus amarus* dried is Rs.22/- (Rupees Twenty-two only) per kg. Packing/ bagging and freight charges and tax, if any, would be charged at actuals. The material should be sent to our Mysore Unit address. Any change of dispatch address would be notified by the Second Party in writing to the First Party.

6. **Payment**
   (i) The Second Party agrees to give an amount of Rs. 22,000/- (Rupees Twenty two thousand only) to the First Party as an advance payment to be distributed to farmers to undertake basic agricultural operations for the cultivation of *Phyllanthus amarus* crop. This will constitute 10% of the total value of the cultivated material, excluding packing/bagging and freight charges. It is agreed that the amount shall be sent to XYZ cooperative in the form of a demand draft within a week from the date of signing this Agreement.
   (ii) It is further agreed that the initial advance amount of Rs. 22,000/- (Rupees twenty two thousand only) would be adjusted against the supplies of *Phyllanthus amarus* to be made by the First Party. Upon receipt of the first 5 MT material, the amount due towards it will be released between 30-40 days from the date of receipt of the material. Further the payment towards remainder 5 MT material, will be released between 30-40 days after the receipt of this material.

7. **Default**
   In the event of default by either of the parties, the affected party shall be entitled to claim all costs, damages and other expenditures incurred due to, or occurring on account of such default. However, it is agreed that if the First Party is unable to supply the said *Phyllanthus amarus* due to reasons of force majeure,

   (i) the Second Party shall reserve its right to receive the same or the balance of the supply during the next cultivable season, or
   (ii) the Second Party shall be entitled to claim the refund of the advance amount with interest @ 12% p.a.

8. **Termination of Agreement**
   It is agreed and understood that this is an agreement for specific performance and either of the parties is not at liberty to terminate this Agreement unilaterally. Termination of this agreement is possible only by way of mutual written undertaking from both the parties on such terms and conditions as may be agreed to at the time of termination.

9. **Dispute**
   In case of any dispute or difference arising out of this contract between the parties, during the progress of or after termination of the Agreement, as to the meaning of this Agreement or touching or relating to the said product or to any other matter or thing arising directly or indirectly under this Agreement, then, and in such an event, the same shall be referred to arbitration as governed by the Arbitration & Conciliation Act, 1996. The venue of the arbitration shall be at Bangalore.

IN WITNESS THEREOF the parties hereto have signed this Agreement on the day, month and year first above written in the presence of the following witnesses.

WITNESSES:

for ABC Herbal Extracts,

1.

Director

2.

for XYZ District Cooperative,

Managing Director

APPENDIX 2

Proposal for Contract Cultivation of Coleus forskohlii (medicinal crop) with ABC Labs Pvt. Ltd.

Objective

To undertake cultivation of Coleus forskohlii in 250 acres for supply of 200 tonnes of dried tubers in 2004-05.

Background

Gram Mooligai Company Limited (GMCL) promoted by FRLHT (Foundation for Revitalization of Local Health Traditions) has its head office in Bangalore. It is a public limited company with groups of farmers and herbs' gatherers as shareholders. GMCL is a medicinal plant enterprise committed to supply quality medicinal plant raw drugs to buyers in India. GMCL operates through NGOs which work with farmers and gatherers group (sanghas). In this tripartite arrangement (between GMCL, NGOs and sanghas), GMCL has the role of providing market support, technical guidance, setting standards in operating systems and quality. NGOs have the role of organizing herbal growers into sanghas, training, bringing a sense of ownership and the sanghas have the responsibility of cultivating/gathering herbs and supply as per standards and schedule. Since its inception in 2000, GMCL has undertaken cultivation of the following plants; Aloe barbedensis, Cassia angustifolia, Vinca rosea, Mucuna pruriens, Bacopa monnieri, Phyllanthus amarus, Andrographis paniculata, Coleus forskohlii and Ocimum tenuiflorum, based on market demand. Through collection source more than 15 species are being supplied in bulk from organized supply through traditional gatherer sanghas.

GMCL has standardized the package of cultivation practice for 12 species through its own in-house agro-trial program. GMCL started its cultivation program by sourcing seeds and planting material, but now it is in a position to supply seeds and planting material to others also. For the above species, a minimum of two cycle of cultivation has been completed, cultivation package standardized and suitable geographical locations selected (based on productivity, species adaptability and cropping pattern fit).

Rationale

1. GMCL has four years of experience in organized cultivation and supply of medicinal plants. Two cycle of cultivation has been completed with respect to Coleus forskohlii with a total acreage of 102 acres.
2. Package of practice, disease management, productivity enhancement techniques have been evolved for Coleus forskohlii from experience.
3. Locations where Coleus performs well have been identified.

Modus operandi

1. For supply of 200 tonnes of dried Coleus tubers, 250 acres will be taken up for cultivation.

2. Planting will be in August-September 2004 and supply will be in January-March 2005.
3. Farmers will be organized into groups of 20, cultivating 40-50 acres in one village. Two suitable locations viz., Thiruvanamali district, Tamilnadu and Natham taluk, Dindigul district, Tamilnadu have been already identified and cultivation is in progress. More location identification and farmer' selection is in the process.
4. Identification of NGOs and Organizers and training them on technical aspects, monitoring and reporting, processing (drying and dispatch) will be taken up ahead of planting.
5. Renting of drying yards, machinery for chopping and other logistics will be taken up.
6. Establishment of monitoring systems for disease surveillance, growth, advances for farmers (cash and inputs) will be completed.
7. Training will be organized for farmers, organizers on cultivation package, calendar of operations and delivery schedule and put into standard operating procedures for adoption by all involved.

Calendar of Events

For the objective to be achieved the following calendar of events has to be adopted:

S.No.	*Activity*	*Period*
1.	Contractual agreement between ABC Labs and GMCL	January 2004
2.	Finalizing package of practice for Coleus in consultation with Dr. Anil Chojar	January 30th 2004
3.	Selection of geographical locations for cultivation	15th February 2004
4.	Nursery raising in selected locations	March 2004
5.	Preparation and sourcing of inputs like Neem cake, Vermicompost, Bio-fertilizers, Fertilizers etc.	March-June 2004
6.	Identification of NGOs and Organizers	February 2004
7.	Identification and selection of farmers	February 2004
8.	Training for NGOs, Organizers	February-March 2004
9.	Training for farmers	April 2004
10.	Planting	August-September 2004
11.	Drying	January-February 2005
12.	Dispatch	January-February 2005

Human Resource at GMCL

There are two staffs at GMCL with agriculture sciences and organic farming background with experience in organized cultivation of medicinal plants. At the NGO level there is one Coordinator with forestry sciences background and two field organizers located at the site. After a review, if required staff strength will be increased.

REFERENCES

1. The agreements of contract cultivation cited in Appendices 1 and 2 are typical agreements between the buyers and sellers (cultivators) of medicinal crops.
2. Such agreement formats were developed when the author of this book worked as General Manager with Sami Labs Ltd., Bangalore (1995-2004). Sami Labs Ltd. is a phyto-pharma Company that produces and exports medicinal plants extracts, nutraceuticals, dietary supplements and fine chemicals that are useful for human health.

BUILDING SUPPLY CHAIN NETWORKS FOR ITC—A PROJECT MODEL APPROACH*

In response to a request from ITC-IBD division, Gurgaon, the following project proposal was developed to source horticultural products for this company.

Corporate Vision: To develop Supply Chains for ITC-IBD to support fresh vegetable and fruit marketing operations at retail level.

ITC-IBD Mission: To get into Retail marketing of fresh horticultural produce on commercial basis.

Objectives: (a) To form a successful supply chain of a range of horticultural products to meet customer demand at the *ITC Choupal fresh* retail centers, (b) To increase the production, procurement and marketing network of ITC in the country, (c) To ensure year around supplies of fresh horticultural produce at the ITC retail centers

Background: The pilot project for marketing the produce from retail centers had been launched in Chandigarh, Pune and Hyderabad, with procurement of produce coming from selected areas of Punjab, Maharashtra, and Andhra Pradesh.

Introduction

The above mentioned project is a typical supply chain management (SCM) exercise that will be developed from a pilot project level in three retail centers to the full blown commercial level. SCM in horticulture business will imply managing the relationships between the various networks of farmers

*Source: Developed from Project outline submitted by Dr. Anil Kr. Chojar to ITC horticulture project office, Gurgaon in April 2007 for assisting the company in developing supply chain network capabilities to support ITC's retail initiatives for its pilot project's operations in different parts of the country at that time.

who will be responsible for the production at farm level and ITC-IBD agro team who will organize the procurement and supply of horticultural produce —mostly vegetables and fruits from farm level to retail level customers. The produce must meet with consumers' requirements in terms of quantity, quality and price. Meeting customers' requirements involves integrated management of the transactions and relationships between supplier-farmers, and the buyer-ITC-IBD agro as well as the various processes within their agriculture and horticulture produce businesses. The objective will be either to remove or minimize the channels between farmers, and the ITC-IBD agro in order to lower procurement costs for the ITC agro on one hand, and help farmers realize higher share of consumer rupee. With the growing interest in Indian agricultural sector by the foreign and domestic companies, the agricultural industry is likely to be subjected to increased competition for procurement of the agricultural and horticultural produce in its home market, but at the same we may have better opportunities to meet global standards in domestic and export markets as well. SCM provides an integrated approach to plan the management of horticultural production and marketing systems.

How to Develop and Handle Production and Supplies

There are Four Options Available

(i) Contract farming is one of the major options before ITC-IBD agro to plan direct purchases of its supplies from farmers. Supplies can be arranged directly from farmers in specified quantities, qualities, grades, and at pre-determined prices.

Farmers can be given specialized varieties, and various types of horticultural produce, including exotic varieties of bell pepper, cucurbits, strawberries, special 'long and soft types' of banana variety that is typically available in certain areas such as Jalgaon in Maharashtra. However, new orchards for some fruit crops like mangoes, grapes, pomegranates, and sapota need to be developed for which long term contracts have to be made with farmers directly.

(ii) A certain percentage of supplies can also be outsourced through a network of knowledgeable traders in wholesale markets by entering into contracts with them before the start of season by providing them with a list of horticultural items required. This will help in reducing the pressure on average prices that rise during the season, and managing supplies in the event shortages occur. Also, the horticulture produce, particularly some vegetables and a few fruits, which are easily available and are not of special type can be outsourced through these traders, while special varieties can be contracted out for production to farmers.

(iii) Supplies can be built up to overcome seasonal or unexpected shortages due to high demand for certain types of vegetables or fruits, by doing direct purchases from wholesale markets adjoining metros like the one in Delhi and Rai, and around Pune and

Hyderabad to begin with. Also, at time of shortages, direct farm gate purchases of certain fruits, or vegetables from farmers who are located in interior areas of states like Andhra Pradesh or Karnataka can also be organized to overcome shortages of mangoes, papaya, grapes, and melons. Later, these farmers can also be developed for contract farming if found suitable.

(iv) Direct plantations of fruits and vegetable crops can be done on leased land on long term basis, if available at affordable rates.

ITC-IBD may require to exercise fifth option also, which is as follows:

Geographical areas: In order that supplies are available throughout the year, ITC agro may have to go in for contract production or contract purchases in additional areas from Uttaranchal, Himachal and North-east to arrange for winter and spring season vegetables in warmer seasons of North and South India, and summer season fruits from other states in Southern India when winter season is on in northern India. For example, we can think of supplying cabbage, cauliflower and leafy vegetables like spinach and bell pepper in north Indian markets in summer, besides melons, watermelons, and even mangoes in winter season. For that matter, cooler areas of north-east, and higher altitude areas of Maharashtra and even southern India need also to be explored for developing the network.

ITC-IBD also needs to look at Central Indian states of Madhya Pradesh, Chhattisgarh and Haryana, particularly the areas where irrigation and river/ canal irrigation water is likely to be available.

Similarly, surplus horticultural produce can be fed to the common grid from southern or western India to north India, and winter crops of north can be supplied to western and southern markets to add variety and availability of different vegetables across India to an ITC-IBD consumer.

Inventories

ITC-IBD need to manage inventories of horticultural produce as they play a key role in success or failure of a supply chain. Shortages can affect the chain and the image of the retail center, and result in loss of customers. On the other hand, excess inventories add to costs and problems in case of perishables commodities like fruits and vegetables. It might be a good idea to plan slightly surplus production to meet the consumer demand and keep the retail centers fully stocked, and process the unsold "Old" stock before they are spoiled by forces of nature. For this ITC-IBD should enter into agreements with some the food processing companies who will act as service providers. For example, we may talk to Nijjar Agro in Amritsar.

Logistics, Warehousing and Distribution

Apart from the advantages of having ITC owned fleet of refrigerated vans/trucks with insulated/perforated or window type containers that are especially beneficial in summer, outsourcing of 3-PL (third party logistics) management activities can be done, where responsibilities of warehousing and distribution can be given to other companies that specialize in these areas. Along with this, a distribution center in the form of cross-docking point can be set up to undertake supplies immediately after the receipt of horticultural produce from the farm, or wholesale markets. However, this is possible only when grading has taken place at farm level.

Getting Started

Define what is to be produced: ITC –IBD *Choupal fresh* must lay down its product mix in terms of fruits and vegetables with regard to what is to be marketed and what is being produced in the currently selected states of Punjab, Maharashtra and Andhra Pradesh.

Identify the customer base: ITC-IBD must identify the consumer segment for whose benefit the horticulture produce will be marketed through the retail centers, and prices the consumers will be willing to pay for the high quality, and graded products. For this costs-benefit analyses, and price-spread analyses need to be done.

Layout of Retail center. In addition to keeping quality horticultural products, layout planning has to be extremely good to make consumer attracted and feel comfortable, while purchasing the produce. It will be useful to keep some other processed items under the ITC label to develop the customer loyalty for ITC brand of products.

Creating an Effective Supply Chain

In order to create an effective supply chain from " farm to retail ", we need to link supplier- farmers, with bulk buyer like ITC directly or in some situations through a cultivation organizer or a trader cum distributor. Since vegetables are perishable products, they need to be stored in ambient temperatures to extend their shelf lives, or some quantities sent for processing in the event they are close to finishing their shelf lives.

One of the main requirements of a supply chain is to enable all participant farmers to achieve significant gains, and thus giving them incentive to cooperate. In other words, it should be a win-win situation for both sides to develop a long-term association. Incentives can be provided through a combination of factors like profitable prices, production technology, financial assistance, provision of inputs, storage technology in the form of common shared equipment at the centre of collection, logistics, and eventually profits. Further, it may be useful to exchange information with farmers on forecasts related to production, consumption/off-take, inventory and on quantities to be sold in the coming season so that they could do their production planning work in advance.

Requirements for a Successful Supply Chain

Goals setting: ITC-IBD agro must involve farmers in long-term partnerships ranging from 7-10 years, and even beyond to develop a mutually rewarding relationship, as farmers are not sure of benefits of short term association. It also helps them to do investment on their farms related to farm equipment, mechanization, irrigation, including installing micro-irrigation systems.

Trust: Both farmers and ITC-IBD should trust each other, feel confident of each other, and share common goals with regard to increased production and sales turnover.

Effective Communication: There should be effective communication between farmers, and ITC through its field officers, extension workers and by installing an integrated network of IT technology to share information related to crop management, weather conditions and warning farmers of any pest attack etc.

Supply Chain (SC) Visibility: This means that SC partners can connect with any part of the chain comprising farmers, collection centre, processing/ grading centers, cold stores/chain, and retail centers on data sharing to plan the supply/marketing of product-mix accordingly.

Event Management Capability: It is the ability to detect and respond to any unplanned event such as a delayed shipment, surplus procurement, lower grade availability, or warehouse running on a short supply of an item in demand etc.

Strategic Partnering: It takes place when two or more business organizations have complementary products or services that will strategically benefit the customers, who agree to join with a purpose of realizing a strategic benefit. This should happen with farmers and the input suppliers such as top quality seed producers.

Performance Drivers. Apart from handling issues related to cost, quality and customer service, the ITC-IBD agro should have flexibility to adjust to changes in quantity, quality, variety selection, delivery time, and product or service requirements to satisfy customers. The same thing applies to individual farmers in the sense that they should be flexible under certain situations.

SWOT Analysis for Introducing Organized Retailing in Horticultural Produce

Strengths

Increased urbanization, life-style changes of consumers, globalization of local markets, consumer spending power, consumer eye for quality and convenience in shopping for farm fresh produce

Weaknesses

Seasonality of production, competition from other crops, economics of existing crop patterns and rotations may still be in favor of wheat, rice, coarse cereals-maize and millets-jowar, and bajra mainly, pulses, and cash crops like oilseeds, sugarcane, tobacco, cotton, and some selected vegetables.

Opportunities

(i) Introduce a range of graded horticultural products of the latest varieties for quality conscious consumers, (ii) organize production from different geographical areas to "overcome" the seasonality factor for many vegetable and fruit crops, (iii) ability to transport products in a cost-effective manner and in a timely manner to retain freshness of the produce, (iv) to make use of cold chains in preserving the produce, and giving option to consumers to choose a range of products that are aimed at meeting quality, safety, health and nutritional aspects of food products, (v) Position and develop the brand image of ITC Choupal fresh in the mind of customer.

Threats

Presence of a number of large Indian companies, and MNCs or subsidiaries of foreign companies who wish to diversify into retail business, including for horticultural produce, in a big way; increased competition from the traditional horticultural produce retail markets, and vendors.

Implementation Points

Form ITC-IBD agro producers' cooperatives in the various districts of the concerned states. Do a business tie-up with the experienced seed producing companies like Indo- American Hybrid seeds, Beauscape farms, Rallis India, Mahyco, Nath Sluis, Astra Zeneca and others, whose seeds are known, or proven to produce high yielding crops of different vegetables and fruits, which possess healthy uniform physical shape, features and attractive natural colours, as desired from consumer point of view. For example, well shaped cucurbits, bitter gourds, gourds, onions, tomatoes, watermelons, melons, grapes, papaya and so on, fetch not only good customers but also command premium prices.

• With the help of these seeds companies choose the district level cultivation organizers under the ITC umbrella who will enter into agreements with the farmers lower down the order from the targeted areas to match with the per acre productivity per crop and meet with the cumulative targets from these districts on continuous basis as per given season of each crop. To benefit the cultivation organizer, monetary incentives could be considered as the company will get into agreements with these cultivation organizers to control the farmers as they will be familiar with local conditions.

• Develop the crop calendar to organize production and procurement, and storage wherever possible on continuous basis. Farmers will deliver their produce to the ITC-IBD sponsored cooperatives' collection points, who will procure the produce, issue a provisional receipt on quantity procured of each variety, its procurement price-farmers get paid within seven days from the date of delivery, consigns it to ITC processing centers for grading the produce. The harvested vegetables and fruits crops are transported to the retail center markets, where they are sold to consumers.

Testing: Sample of the final produce is sent to the ITC-IBD funded laboratory in the University center for analyses and advice, and feedback is given to the farmers for improving the quality by adhering to better crop management practices.

Farm Inputs: The cumulative purchase order should be sent to various input providers/dealers/companies for receiving discounts on bulk purchases.

These should be stored in ITC-IBD leased stores, and distribution should be done under the guidance of ITC-IBD employee. Further, a schedule of production/agronomic practices should be shared for each crop among farmers.

Training and support services: ITC-IBD agro cooperatives should participate in training programs organized by the Technical committee comprising technical experts from the Agricultural University on horticulture, plant protection, soils, selected extension workers, seed companies' representatives, and fertilizer companies besides experts on organic farming.

NGO and organic farming: We can also involve some NGO in addition to some expert on organic farming for imparting training to farmers' in agro-ecological practices to promote organic farming and to foster the spirit of cooperation among the members of rural communities.

Irrigation and phyto-sanitary management: Irrigation has to be used judiciously and automated-sprinkler and drip irrigation systems are to used to avoid wastages especially on large orchards, and there has to be proper use of pesticides to control various pests and insects.

Incentives: Farmers will be paid according to quality parameters laid down in contract agreements with respect to per acre yields (so that there is no diversion outside), physical shape, external colours and features, taste and internal colour of the produce wherever it matters in terms of consumer rating, and timely deliveries. A proper weighing system will be developed to allot bonus payment to farmers.

Funding the projects: As ITC-IBD agro will enter into long-term agreements with the farmers on marketing the produce, or procurement in terms of hundred per cent buyback, involve NABARD in the funding of infrastructure projects for setting up cold chains, processing centers or distribution centers. In addition, commercial banks and rural cooperative societies can also be involved for extending the farm credit.

ROLE OF E-COMMERCE IN THE FOOD SUPPLY CHAINS*

Supply chain management (SCM) deals with the integrated planning, co-ordination and control of all logistical business processes and activities in the supply chain to deliver superior consumer value while lowering the system-wide costs. In the last 10-15 years, new information and communication technologies (ICT) have emerged to support SCM management concepts. E-business, e-commerce, e-sourcing and e-fulfillment are some of the new terms used in the literature. In general, they refer to doing business electronically (Huff *et al.*, 2000). E-business is about substantially restructuring and reconfiguring the traditional supply chains. Traditional SCM activities focus on improving the efficiency and effectiveness of existing supply chains. However, E-business can be used as an enabler for these activities, by implementing electronic data interchange (EDI) systems (Van der Vorst, Jack G.A.J. *et. al.*, 2002). While making it easy and speeding-up exchange of information, internet enables improvements throughout the entire value chain. (Porter, 2001). E-business can be used to establish new partnerships and new ways of working. Through the Internet, new markets and new clients and suppliers can be identified to facilitate the logistics and/or information management process. In fact, supply chains may be referred to value webs (Tapscott *et al.* 2000) or even as business webs (b-webs), as they come together on the Internet to create value for customers and wealth for their shareholders.

**Source*: *Based on paper by* Vorst, van der, J.G.A.J., Dongen, van S., Nouguier S. (2002). "E-Business initiatives in Food Supply Chains; Definition and Typology of Electronic Business Models", *The Journal of Logistics: Research and Applications*, Vol. 5, No. 2, pp. 119-38.

Business webs refer to a distinct system of suppliers, distributors, commercial services providers, infrastructure providers and customers that use the Internet for their primary business communications and transactions.

From Value Chain to Value Web (Holland *et. al.*, 2000)

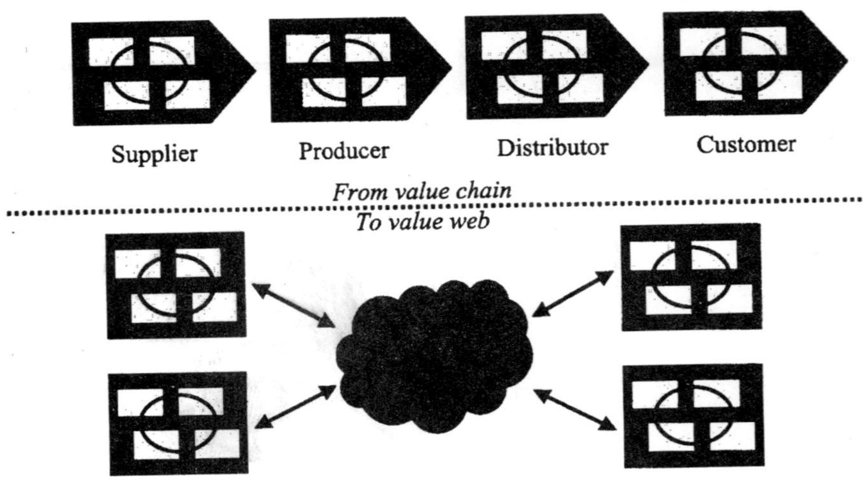

The term e-business can be used in different contexts, such as business-to-business (e.g. electronic market-places), business-to-consumer (e.g. home shopping services), business-to-employee (e.g. tele-working systems) and business-to-authority (e.g. tax collection systems, education) approaches. One can also observe buyers' market-places, sellers' market-places, electronic auctions and chain information systems (Van der Vorst, Jack G.A.J. *et. al.* 2002).

In order to understand "What type of B2B e-business" is good for a business organization, Van der Vorst, Jack G.A.J. *et. al.* 2002 studied the concept of an electronic business model that covers all relevant elements of b-webs by reviewing 16 major e-business initiatives in Dutch food supply chains, and analyzed the impact that e-business had on the design and management of those supply chains. The study followed the case study approach to illustrate the e-business model elements, and general typology of business web.

Objectives of the study were:

1. To study e-business and its differences with SCM management.
2. To study the specific characteristics of the food industry and agribusiness.
3. To study the impact of e-business on design and management of food supply chains.

Results and Discussion

E-business and Supply Chain Management

A survey of 903 companies in the Netherlands showed that almost 75% found e-business to be strategically important. About the definition of e-business, 44.8% referred to having a website, and 44.6% to having an e-mail connection with supply chain partners (Mostafi, 2000). The following Table presents a brief overview of different definitions for e-business.

Some Definitions of E-business

Source	*Definition*
Archer & Yuan, 2000	Technologies that provide effective and efficient ways in which corporate buyers can gather information rapidly about available products and services, evaluate and negotiate with suppliers, implement order fulfilment over communication links and access post-sales services
Chopra & Meindl, 2001	The execution of business transactions over the Internet
Gartner Group, 2001 (gartnergroup.com)	A combination of: electronic commerce, technology-enabled relationship management and SCM
Roelofs, 1998	The streamlining of all business processes in the value chain using Internet technology to improve the efficiency and effectivity of the complete supply chain

Internet-based e-business is interactive, allows for spontaneous relationships or transactions to occur, has many potential users and can create both a delivery mechanism and a market-place (Thompson *et al.*, 2000).

The Table below presents an overview of general revenue and cost opportunities of Internet-based e-business.

Impact of E-business on Supply Chain Performance (Chopra & Meindl, 2001)

Revenue-enhancing Opportunities	*Cost Reduction Opportunities*
Offering direct sales to customers	Reducing product handling with a shorter supply chain
Providing 24-hour access from any location	Postponing product differentiation until after an order is placed
Aggregating information from various sources	Decreasing delivery cost and time
Speeding up time to market; implementing flexible pricing	Reducing facility and processing costs
Allowing process and service discrimination	Decreasing inventory costs through centralization
Facilitating efficient fund transfer	Improving supply chain co-ordination through information sharing

The major perspective of e-business from a SCM view point is the intensive and efficient information transfer between companies in a value chain, which increases the responsiveness owing to changes in customer demand. However, SCM activities are still required for information exchange through the co-ordination of decision policies among channel partners.

Mainly Two Forms of e-business can be Distinguished

1. *Improving the efficiency and/or effectiveness of existing supply chains.* This refers to the electronic exchange of demand, inventory and/or production data between companies in the value chain to improve responsiveness. However, roles can shift between supply chain partners by introducing vendor managed inventories (VMI).
2. *Establishing new business models; towards dynamic supply chains.* This form of e-business results in new supply chain structures. Typical business roles in the supply chain can be eliminated or trusted third parties in new business roles can be introduced. Depending on customer requirements, the market dynamism is converted into dynamic chain configurations where partners are selected with accompanying roles. In E-business, 1:1 partnerships are abandoned by selecting more suppliers. Depending on the new business model, suppliers are selected via global electronic market-places. Often price differentiation becomes the main order winner (Van der Vorst *et. al.*, 2002).

Food Industry and Agribusiness

In general, there are two main types of food supply chains:

1. *Supply chains for fresh agricultural products* (such as fresh vegetables, flowers, fruits). In general, these chains consist of growers, auctions, wholesalers, importers and exporters, and retailers. The main processes are handling, storage, packing, transportation and trading.
2. *Supply chains for processed food products* (such as snacks, juices, desserts, canned food products). In these chains agricultural products are used as raw materials for producing consumer products with higher added value. In most cases, conservation and conditioning processes extend the shelf life of agricultural products.

Participants in both types of chains realize that original good quality products can easily deteriorate unless another chain participant takes action. Thus, agricultural food supply chains are characterized by shelf life constraints, quality and quantity variations due to biological variations, seasonality, weather and pests (Van der Vorst *et. al.*, 2002). Since in agribusiness about 70% of the production value is accounted for by the costs of raw materials (van Weele, 1988), it is vital for industrial producers to contract suppliers to guarantee quality and coordinate the supply of the right raw materials to match with the availability of capacity.

Electronic Business Models

It is important to focus on the *value proposition* of Electronic Business Models for which the participants in the b-web are working together to create competitive advantage. A (food) business-web can be based on three value propositions:

Network differentiation and market segmentation. As a b-web model, the purpose is to differentiate to meet the specific demands of customers in different segments.

Integrated quality. The objective is to meet with the increasing demand of consumers and governments for safe and environmentally friendly products.

Network optimization. The objective here is to achieve cost reduction through a streamlined chain with rational information management.

For each e-business initiative the value proposition should be determined, which then leads to the filling-in of the other elements of the business model.

Value Proposition

Roles of participants (Tapscott *et al.*, 2000) that are interacting with each other, exchanging information via the e-business hub can be summarized as:

- **context providers**, who deal with the rule-making activities of the system (they facilitate the interface between customers and b-web);
- **content providers**, who design, and deliver the value (goods, services or information) that satisfy the customer needs;
- **commercial service providers**, who enable the flow of business, including transactions and financial management, security and privacy, information and knowledge management, logistics and delivery, and regulatory services (examples are trusted third parties, technical support providers, financial service providers and logistics service providers).
- **customers**, who not only receive but also sometimes contribute value to the b-web (e.g. buyers at an e-market-place).
- ***Processes*** that are supported by the e-business initiative (the main processes are marketing and sales, quality control, procurement and supply chain planning).
- ***Functionalities*** that support these processes.
- ***Applications*** that enable these functionalities, that is, the ICT infrastructure.

Typology of Business-webs

All 16 e-business initiatives were analyzed to provide insight into the opportunities of e-business in food industry and agribusiness.

The main findings can be summarized as follows:

The ***value propositions*** of most cases relate to the specific characteristics of the food industry and agribusiness. Customers are concerned with food safety as they prefer certified products. Furthermore, the variability in quality, quantity and timing of agricultural products makes buyers search for ways to reduce supply risks. Both these characteristics are incentives for partners to set up e-business-driven supply chains.

Most initiatives are carried out exercising quality control over ***processes for*** food safety or by controlling risks at source through quality purchasing to reduce supply risks. The ability to track and trace goods is a definite order winner in food supply chains.

Several levels of the e-business hubs can be identified:

Hub 1: information transparency of the supply of goods
Hub 2: sending orders electronically
Hub 3: settling the financial flows
Hub 4: logistical services

The cases showed that inter-organizational tracking and tracing systems are found only when economic control is high. That is, when one partner takes the lead and sets the standards. In all cases the initiator in the supply chain was the partner closest to the consumers. Some initiatives have gone further towards the marketing, or branding, of certified products.

E-market-places bring together sellers and buyers. Hierarchical b-webs have a leader who controls the content of the value proposition, the pricing and the flow of transactions and positions itself as a value-adding intermediary between suppliers and buyers.

Conclusions

There is a shift from competition between organizations towards competition between supply chains (Christopher, 1998) through to competition between business webs. Information sharing is critical for competitive advantage. Supply chain collaboration and visibility are growing in importance, requiring central (value chain or b-web) databases. Another critical factor is consolidation of goods flows since smaller flows have to reach more dispersed networks. This will give more room for logistic service providers, who together with application service providers give companies facilities to focus on their core competencies.

References

Amit, R. & Zott, C. (2001), Value Creation in e-business, *Strategic Management Journal*, 22, (6± 7), pp. 493-520.

Chopra, S. & Meindl, P. (2001), *Supply Chain Management Strategy, Planning and Operations* (Englewood Cliffs, NJ, Prentice-Hall).

Christopher, M.G. (1998), *Logistics and Supply Chain Management; Strategies for Reducing Costs and Improving Services* (London, Pitman).

Holland, C., Bouwman, H. & Smidts, M. (2000), *Back to the Bottom Line*; onderzoek naar succesvolle e-business modellen, ECP.NL (http://www.ECP.NL) (in Dutch).

Janssen, M. & Sol, H.G. (2000), Evaluating the role of intermediaries in the electronic value chain, *Internet Research: Electronic Networking Applications and Policy*, 10, (5), pp. 406-417.

Kaplan, S. & Sawhney, M. (1999), B2B e-commerce hubs: towards a taxonomy of business models (netmarketmakers.com/documents).

Lancioni, R.A., Smith, M.F. & Oliva, T.A. (2000), The Role of the Internet in Supply Chain Management, *Industrial Marketing Management*, 29, pp. 45-56.

Lee, H.L. & Whang, S. (2001), *Supply Chain Integration Over the Internet* (Graduate School of Business, Stanford University).

Means, G. & Schneider, D. (2000), *Metacapitalism: The E-business Revolution and Design of the 21st Century Companies and Markets* (New York, John Wiley & Sons).

Mostafi, K. (2000), *Nederlands Bedrijfsleven: E-business is Van Strategisch Belang* (emerce.nl/archives/nieuws/Industrie) (in Dutch).

Porter, M.E. (2001), Strategy and the Internet, *Harvard Business Review*, March, pp. 63-78.

Ptak, C.A. (2001), E-business, *APICS Conference 2001*, Amsterdam, 4-6 April.

Rutten, W.G.M.M. (1995) The use of recipe flexibility in production planning and inventory control, Dissertation, Eindhoven University of Technology, The Netherlands.

Tapscott, D., Ticoll, D. & Lowy, A. (2000), *Digital Capital* (Boston, MA, Harvard Business School Press).

Thompson, S.J., Hayenga, M. & Hayes, D. (2000), E-agribusiness, *Proceedings of the IAMA Conference*, Chicago, 23-28 June.

Timmers, P. (1998), Business Models of Electronic Markets, *Electronic Markets*, 8, (2), pp. 318-335.

Vorst, J.G.A.J. Van Der (2000), Effective Food Supply Chains; Generating, Modelling and Evaluating Supply Chain Scenarios, PhD Thesis, Wageningen University, The Netherlands.

Weele, A.J. Van (1988), *Inkoop in Strategisch Perspectief* (Alphen aan den Rijn, Samson) (in Dutch).

Weele, A.J. Van (2001), Myths and Truths about e-procurement and Virtual Markets, *APICS Conference 2001*, Amsterdam, 4-6 April.

APPENDIX 1

E-Business Adoption and its Role in Supply Chain and Logistics Management

E-business, a term originally coined by Lou Gerstner, CEO of IBM, refers to the use of internet and related networks and information technologies to support e-commerce, enterprise communications and collaboration, web enabled business processes, both within the networked enterprise, and with its customers and business partners. E-business includes E-commerce, which involves buying and selling, and marketing and servicing of products, and information over the Internet and other networks. (O'brien, J. *et. al.*, 2010).

E-Business application Architecture(O,Brien, J., 2000)

In reality, E-commerce is more than buying and selling pf products because it encompasses the entire online process of developing, marketing, selling, delivering, servicing, and paying for products and services transacted on inter-networked global market places of customers with the active support of business partners. E-commerce also includes extranet access of inventory databases by customers and suppliers, intranet access of customer relationship management systems by sales and customer service departments/managers, and it includes customer collaboration in product development through e-mail exchange of ideas and suggestions. (O'brien, J. *et. al.*, 2010).

Impact on Global Economy

E-commerce, which uses various information and communication technologies (ICT), has the potential to improve trade efficiency across the globe and to integrate developing countries into the global economy. Most IT technologies, including e-commerce were developed in Western countries where the social and economic development is at higher peak than those of developing countries. The success of technology adoption depends on how it is used by the adopters and how it is found to be suitable and usable to the needs of the adopters. As a result of different levels of development, technology adoption rate has shown great variations in terms of success rates in the developing countries. In the global world today, understanding and adoption of IT technologies are important to drive the e-commerce between developed and developing and emerging economies. This, in turn, enables developed countries to trade with developing countries more efficiently (Kurnia, S., 2006).

Factors Influencing E-commerce Adoption in Developing Countries

Government Initiatives

Government initiatives are important in the adoption of e-commerce and other ICT technologies in the developing countries. This can be in terms of resource allocation in the national budgets, promotion of ICT usage, establishment of IT institutions and departments that oversee the development of IT education hubs across the country; incentives to the hardware companies in terms of concessions in excise duty and other taxes, setting up of software parks for establishing IT related businesses, promotion of software exports, Intellectual Property protections and spreading the use and adoption of IT technologies across various sectors such as banks, Government departments, and other businesses in all sectors of economy.

Political Environment

Government initiatives have higher chances of success due to favorable political and economic climate in the country.

Economic Environment

Economic environment is recognized as a major driver for e-commerce adoption by the consumers and industries. The GDP and per capita income are common indicators for the economic condition of a country. Since e-commerce relies on some technology infrastructures which are relatively expensive for many developing countries, countries with unfavourable economic condition are not likely to be involved in e-commerce (Dedrick et.al.1995; Kurnia, S., 2006).

Technology Infrastructure

E-commerce success relies heavily on a number of technology infrastructures. For example, for telecommunications, infrastructure need to be developed in various parts of the country by government or the private companies. The cost of accessing the infrastructures also influences the growth of e-commerce. E-commerce also relies on efficient logistic infrastructures within a country. Its growth further requires the establishment of reliable and secure payment systems to avoid frauds and other illegal actions (Kurnia, S, 2006).

Geographical Situation

Geographical condition of a region can be a motivation or barrier to technology infrastructure development. For example, setting up infrastructure in regions surrounded by mountains, or a country with small islands can be costly and difficult to develop. (Kurnia, S., 2006).

Socio-cultural Environment

The adoption of e-commerce also depends on the cultural and social environment as it affects the IT usage. Likewise, the level of education, the availability of IT skills, the level of penetration of personal computers and telephone within the society affect the growth of e-commerce (Kurnia, S., 2006).

External Influence

The growth of e-commerce in a country is also influenced by the technologically advanced countries with whom the host country has education, trading and intellectual links.

Role of E-commerce in Supply Chains, with Particular Reference to Logistics

E-commerce and the Internet have changed the nature of supply chains, and redefined businesses. E-commerce helps consumers choose, purchase, and use consumer and industrial products and services. As a result, there has been an emergence of new business-to business (B2B) supply chains that are customer-focused rather than product-focused. The ICT technologies also provide customized products and services.

E-commerce impacts supply chain management in a variety of ways. These include:

Cost efficiency, and streamlining business processes: E-commerce facilitates Logistic/transportation companies to exchange material/cargo documents electronically over the Internet. E-commerce enables shippers, freight forwarders and trucking firms to streamline document handling and save considerable time and costs vis-à-vis the traditional document handling cum delivery systems.

By using e-commerce, firms improve and streamline business processes, accelerate business cycles, and enhance customer service. Ocean carriers and their trading partners are able to exchange bill of lading instructions, freight invoices, container status, shipment instructions, and other documents with increased accuracy and efficiency. The only tools needed to take advantage of this solution are a personal computer and an Internet browser.

Changes in the distribution system: E-commerce gives businesses more flexibility in managing the complex movement of products and information between businesses, and their suppliers and customers.

Customer-orientation: E-commerce is a vital link in the logistics and transportation services for both internal and external customers. E-commerce helps companies to improve services to their customers, accelerate the growth of the e-commerce initiatives that are critical to their business, and lower their operating costs. Using the Internet for e-commerce will allow customers to access price or rate information, place delivery orders, track shipments and pay freight bills.

Ease in handling business processes: E-commerce makes it easier for customers to do business with commercial firms. Processes which simplify the transportation arrangements or services help in enhancing companies' image and revenues from increased sale of products. Also, through the website, the marketing firm/supplier of goods provides detailed information about the products and services offered. E-commerce functions are taking companies a substantial step forward by providing customers with a faster and easier way to do business with them.

Shipment tracking and shipping enquiry: E-commerce helps users in establishing an account and obtain accurate and timely information about cargo shipments. Parcel shipments can be tracked and proof of delivery can be confirmed. A customer can negotiate freight rates with the supplier rates, and improve delivery service.

Advance shipment information: E-commerce helps in transmitting a packing list ahead of the shipment. It also allows firms to record the relevant details of each pallet, parcel, and item being shipped. It reduces the need for manual intervention as document pertaining to standard bills of lading, shipping labels, and carrier are available through the internet and other elated IT networks. As a result, paperwork is reduced considerably.

REFERENCES

Bowersox, D., Closs, D., and Cooper, M.B. (2008), Supply Chain Logistics Management, 2nd ed., Special India edition, Tata-McGraw-Hill, New Delhi.

Dedrick, J., Goodman, S. & Kraemer, K. (1995), "Little Engines that could: Computing in Small Energetic Countries", *Association of Computing Machinery*, (35), 1995, pp. 21-26.

Kurnia, S. (2006), E-Commerce Adoption in Developing Countries: an Indonesian Study. Department of Information systems, University of Melbourne, Australia. *http://disweb.dis.unimelb.edu.au/staff*, accessed March 28, 2010.

O'Brien, J. (2000), Essentials for the internet worked E-business Enterprise—a PPT presentation In: Introduction to Information systems. 11th edition, Tata McGraw-Hill Education, New Delhi.

O'Brien, J., Marakas, and R. Behl (2010), Electronic Commerce systems, In: Management Information Systems, 9th ed., Tata McGraw-Hill Education, New Delhi.

O'Brien, J., Marakas, and R. Behl (2010), E-business systems, In: Management Information Systems, 9th ed., Tata McGraw Hill Education, New Delhi.

Sreenivas, M. (2007). Impact of e-commerce on Supply Chain Management. *http://www.ehtzilon.com/articles*, accessed March 27, 2010.

INFORMATION INTEGRATION IN MULTI-DIMENSIONAL FOOD SUPPLY CHAIN*

Background

The business environment of agri-food production has changed owing to consumer demand for quality and safe products which are free from disease and other contaminations. One of the strategies to face these twin challenges is to innovate and move towards a knowledge-based production systems where both tangible and intangible information is used. Tangible information relates mainly with physical inputs such as seeds, planting materials, fertilizers, and pesticides whereas intangible information is concerned with information on weather, varieties, government regulations, harvest timing, prices etc. Additionally, inputs in the form of advisory services and knowledge from Research Institutes are also utilized for developing processes to meet the production and market challenges.

This paper seeks to clarify that agri-food supply chains are not simple linear chains, but are characterized by multiple dimensions. The major dimensions include:

- Vertical dimension: consists of channel partners who develop, produce and distribute products to fulfill customer needs;

*Source: *Adapted from* Sjaak Wolfert[1,2], Cor Verdouw[1] Adrie Beulens[2] "Information integration in multi-dimensional agri-food supply chain networks: a service-oriented approach in the KodA program", In: Proceedings of the summer university on IT in agriculture and rural development.—Debrecen, Hungary : Hungarian Association of Agricultural Informatics.

[1] LEI, Wageningen UR, P.O. Box 29703, Den Haag, 2502 LS, The Netherlands,
[2] Information Technology Group, Wageningen University, P.O. Box 8130, Wageningen, 6700 EW, The Netherlands.

- Horizontal dimension: consists of producers who complement each other, and jointly develop resources and business processes;

In Agri-food supply chain networks (AFSCN), three basic forms of network governance are identified (Lazzarini et al., 2001). These relate to (1) Planning, (2) Standardization, and 3) Mutual Adjustment. Multi-dimensional networks put the emphasis on standardization and mutual adjustment, which require a high flexibility of processes and enterprises.

Objectives and Scope of the Study

The study objective was to find out what appropriate information integration meant for AFSCNs. This paper presents the results of this study that was carried out as part of the KodA program. In KodA, the farm is considered as the focal company in the AFSCN, which is a networked enterprise where several network dimensions come together.

KodA (Dutch abbreviation of 'Kennis op de Akker') means: 'From knowledge to practice in farming'. In KodA, about 60 arable farmers, along with their suppliers and processors (about 12 large companies), work together in a private-public partnership in association with the Ministry of Agriculture.

Theoretical Concepts and Methodology Used

(a) Framework for Information-Integration

Integration of information for a networked enterprise in multi-dimensional AFSCNs is complex. Therefore, distinction is made between different integration levels and types These are:

- Intra-enterprise: *within* enterprises to integrate and to tie the loose ends between organizational units;
- Inter-enterprise: *between* enterprises to develop a **virtual enterprise** that is integrated in multi-dimensional networks;
- Process Integration: alignment of tasks by coordination;
- Application Integration: alignment of software systems;
- Data Integration: alignment of data systems in order to share information;
- Physical Integration: Enabling communication and connectivity between hardware and operating systems.

(b) Integration Possibilities at Different Levels are as follows:

(i) Physical Integration Standardization

It relates to the standardization of the physical communication infrastructure, which includes hardware, and operating systems.

(ii) Data Integration Standardization

It deals with the standardization of data exchanges such as format of messages and databases at both intra- and inter-enterprise level.

(iii) Application Integration Standardization

This includes integration of software applications within the organization and/or from different organizations into one aligned system.

(iv) Process Integration Standardization

The integration of processes is done by coordination. Therefore, interactions between processes have to be defined in process and data models. Some well-known integrated intra-enterprise models include ERP reference models of SAP vis-a-vis inter-enterprise models such as SCOR (Supply Chain Operations Reference-model) and the CPFR-model (Collaborative Planning, Forecasting and Replenishment) model of VICS.

Survey of Agri-food Supply Chain Networks

Using the conceptual framework, a survey of Dutch arable AFSCNs was conducted, where a farm was considered as the focal company in a multi-dimensional network. Management of farms was divided into two categories: on-farm management and at field level management. Inter-enterprise information-exchange mainly took place at the farm level, while at the field level, intra-enterprise information-exchange took place. The connectivity between these two levels is important for the smooth operation of AFSCN. For example, a food processor, may want to know what plant protection chemicals or seed varieties were used for a particular crop/horticultural product.

Information from several channel/supply chain partners is combined, and put to use by multiple partners. Thus the use of common standards and properties of the inputs are important in information exchange processes. For example, the proper spraying advice for a particular plant protection can be provided by the advisory services of the Research Institute. The survey indicated that such conceptual or the desired information exchange is rare. Electronic formats or systems are not in use commonly, but in many cases information is still communicated by paper or verbally. For example, only 50% of the sugar beet farmers deliver their product information electronically. Besides, farmers use various applications (e.g. for production control, financial management and decision support), which are not integrated properly with each other.

Summary of Major Findings

Physical Integration at intra- and inter-enterprise level was found to be satisfactory, where Network technology e.g. internet was often used. Farm machinery and equipment e.g. tractors, harvesting machines also had standardized communication interfaces that included on-board computers as well.

Data Exchange between machines at field level and management systems was supported by widely adopted networks. However, data exchange between different systems at farm level was not adequate. In practice, farmers found it difficult to deliver the right standardized information, which resulted in a

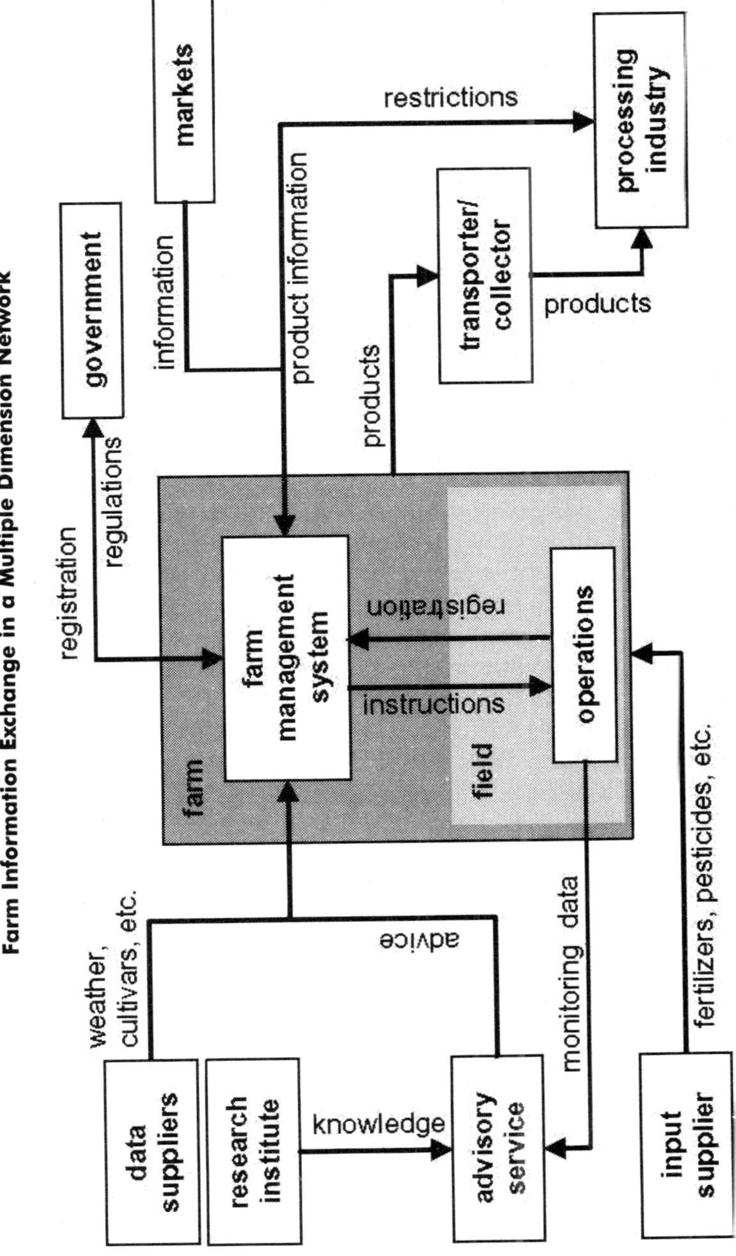

Farm Information Exchange in a Multiple Dimension Network

low adoption rate of automated systems. Farmers complained that the information they received from industry, was in a non-standardized data format e.g. on paper and it was difficult to integrate in their management system.

Application Integration at the intra-enterprise level adopted specific farm management systems, which are comparable with ERP-systems. At the inter-enterprise level, there was lack of common integration standard.

Process Integration was not supported systematically at the time of survey in the sample farms and industry players.

Conclusions

Since the effort for collecting, organizing, managing and exchanging necessary data was large, the level of standardization for data, application and process integration was not satisfactory. Also the decision support and decision-making were both below par. Further, accountability requirements led to administrative problems. In brief, knowledge-based production and flexibility was not possible due to the sub-standard information-integration.

Recommendations

As Agri-food companies increasingly participated as networked enterprises in multi-dimensional networks, they had to make new connections and employ the latest information smoothly in business operations. For setting-up and changing integrations quickly, re-configuration approach was proposed in which information integrations are set-up from standard components. This requires component-based information systems, independent components, and standardized interfaces between components.

A Service-Oriented Architecture (SOA) approach is very suitable to realize rapid (re-)configuration. It is a process-oriented and component-based approach in which service providers publish web services in a service directory. Service requestors search in this directory to find suitable services and use them based on information from the directory and standardized procedures (Leymann, 2003; Erl, 2005).

References

Erl, T. (2005), Service-Oriented Architecture (SOA): Concepts, Technology, and Design. Prentice Hall.

ESPRIT (1996), Computer-Integrated Agriculture. http://cordis.europa.eu/esprit/src/results/res_area/iim/iim5.htm

Giachetti, R.E. (2004), A Framework to Review the Information Integration of the Enterprise. International Journal of Production Research 42(6), 1147-166.

Lazzarini, S.G., Chaddad, F.R., Cook, M.L. (2001), Integrating supply chain and network analyses: the study of netchains. Journal on Chain and Network Sciences 1(1), 7-22.

Lee, J., Siau, K., Hong, S. (2003), Enterprise Integration with ERP and EAI. Communications of the ACM 46(2), 54-60.

Leymann, F. (2003), Web Services: Distributed Applications without Limits: An Outline, BTW, Leipzig.

Tan, P.S., Lee, E.W. (2004), Services Technology for the Industry. JSSL.

Wolfert, J., Schoorlemmer, H.B., Paree, P.G.A., Zunneberg, W., Van Hoven, J.P.C. (2005), KodA: from knowledge to practice for Dutch arable farming. In: Boaventura, J., Morais, R. (Eds.), Proceedings of the joint EFITA/WCCA 2005 conference, 25-28 July, Vila Real, Portugal, pp. 883-888.

Wolfert, J., Verdouw, C.N., Beulens, A.J.M. (2007), Integration and standardization in arable farming practice: a service-oriented approach. In: Parker, C., Skerratt, S., Park, C., Shields, J. (Eds.), EFITA Glasgow 2007: Proceedings of the 6th Biennial Conference of the European Federation of IT in Agriculture, Food and the Environment, 2-5 July 2007. Glasgow Caledonian University, Glasgow.

SUPPLY CHAIN MODELS—PROBLEMS AND PROSPECTS

A **business model** is a conceptual framework which expresses the underlying economic logic and system that proves how a business can deliver value to customers at an appropriate cost, and make money. A business model answers questions such as: Who are our customers? What do the customers value? How much will it cost to deliver that value to our customers? How do we make money in this business? (O"brien, J. *et. al.*, 2010).

Thus a business model specifies what value to offer to the chosen customer segments, what products and services will be supplied to customers, and what will be the price structure for the products/product-mix to be supplied. It also specifies as to how the business will be organized in order to operate successfully with all the capability, and sustain advantage while providing value to customers. A business model is a valuable planning tool because it focuses attention on how all the required components of business fit into a complete system. If it is implemented properly, it makes entrepreneurs and managers to think deeply about the viability of the business initiatives that they have planned. In this context, strategic planning can help in developing a unique business strategies of a firm's business model to help it gain competitive advantage over competitors in the industry as well as the market it wishes to target. (O'brien, J. *et. al.*, 2010).

Supply Chain Networks in Food Industry*

To assure consumers that the products they consume, conform to all the

**Source*: *Adapted from* Steinbauer C, and Hanf J.H. (2009) "New business model for quality supplies", In: Proceedings of the 19. World Food & Agribusiness Symposium. Budapest, Ungarn, June 20-23, 2009.
Johann Heinrich von Thünen-Institut (vTI) Federal Research Institute for Rural Areas, Forestry and FisheriesBundesallee 50, 38116 Braunschweig, Germany.
Jon H. Hanf, Leibniz Institute of Agricultural Development in Central and Eastern Europe (IAMO)Theodor-Lieser-Str. 206120 Halle (Saale), Germany.

desired specifications and standards, including those connected with hygiene and environment, the vertical linkages between supply chain partners are important. A food chain has multiple stages, including diversified global sourcing that leads to a complex network structure. The key driver for the designing, or re-designing of a food chain is the reliability factor of product quality and safety that passes through the vertical linkages to the consumer. As a result, many food products are produced in vertically cooperating organizations or networks. In this study, the focus is on a specific type of chain organization named **supply chain networks (SCN)** (Lambert and Cooper 2000; Hanf and Dautzenberg 2006).

Supply chain networks comprise collaboration of more than two firms (Omta *et. al.*, 2001). Strategic chain organizations possess a **focal firm** being the core element that is expected to manage the system (Jarillo 1988). The focal company determines the decisions of all network members. In general the focal firm is identified by the consumers as being 'responsible' for the specific food item, or a particular producer or retail brand.

Coordination and Cooperation among Firms

The challenge to a supply chain organization is to identify and choose the appropriate management mechanisms (Xu and Beamon, 2006). In this context, the role of collective strategies are important. A collective strategy is a systematic response by a group of organizations that collaborate in order to absorb the variation caused by the inter-organizational environment (Astley and Fombrun, 1983). Collective strategies can be re-active, which can absorb variation within an environment, or they can be pro-active which can prevent unpredictable behaviour by other organisations (Astley and Fombrun 1983). The adoption of collective strategies in SCN implies that the network pursues certain goals.

The focal company in a SCN is the strategy setting unit that sets network goals. To achieve the goals, the management of chain organizations has to orient towards organizing activities through inter-firm **coordination and cooperation** (Ménard 2004). Generally, cooperation refers to the alignment of interests. Conflicts of interests arise if self-interested individuals optimize their personal/individual benefits before they aim for collective benefits. Therefore, cooperation between actors (cooperating partners) requires the coordination of their activities with regard to resource and information flows aimed at timing, quantity, quality and specifications concerning product supplies in order to deliver value to the customers. On this account, coordination is attributed to the alignment of actions, which are interdependent with those of the others (Gulati *et al.* 2005).

Network Goals vs. Firm Level Goals

At times, it could be difficult to distinguish between the network level goals and the firm level goals. Under **network-level** goals, goals set within a network can only be realized if all networked firms are jointly working to achieve them-for example, total chain quality with regard to a product. **Firm-**

level goals are those goals that single firms want to achieve for their own firms. Examples could be higher sales, and higher profits. Therefore a collective strategy has to be regarded as a systematic approach that addresses the alignment of actions (coordination) and interests (cooperation) of independent but collaborating companies in order to achieve certain common network level goals.

Thus a successful chain management requires a change from managing individual functions of a firm to integrating activities into key processes of the network organization consisting of collaborating companies (Lambert and Cooper, 2000). This integration of key processes (named cooperation, coordination and the consideration of different levels) can be efficiently aligned by a sophisticated **management concept** (Bogaschewsky 1995).

Materials and Methods

Development of Strategic Management Model—Use of Balanced Scorecard (BSC) Concept

There are multiple strategic management systems for single companies to manage the firms´ processes in order to reach a well defined strategic goal. Kaplan and Norton in 1996 introduced a management framework called **Balanced Scorecard (BSC)** that has now been widely adopted as a strategic management system. The Balanced Scorecard is a multidimensional concept that combines financial and also non-financial parameters to link today's actions with tomorrow's goals (Kaplan and Norton, 1996). The BSC translates the firm's strategy into objectives which are classified in critical and important business perspectives. The limitation of the Balanced Scorecard in traditional management systems is its inability to link a company's long-term strategy with its short-term actions. Hence, building a BSC enables the company to align its management processes and focuses the entire organization on implementing long term strategy (Kaplan and Norton, 1996).

It has to be noted that the complexity and diversity of interests within a firm come in the way of implementation of the overall strategy in this single firm. Therefore, it is a very challenging task to create a strategy for networks that are composed of a multitude of firms (Kaplan and Norton, 2001). A prerequisite for the use of business management systems in chain networks is the comparability of firms and networks with conglomerates (Hanf and Andrea, 2005). Therefore similar concepts can be used to coordinate a SCN.

Supply Chain Network Management Model

In this study, the authors have combined the identified main strategic management objectives for SCN, named alignment of interests (cooperation), alignment of action (coordination) and alignment of goals (different levels) with the concept of Balanced Scorecard. In this context, the three perspectives must be linked to collective strategy. The This balanced approach of translating collective strategy into three strategic important perspectives helps the involved firms, especially the focal company, to acquire foresight about which

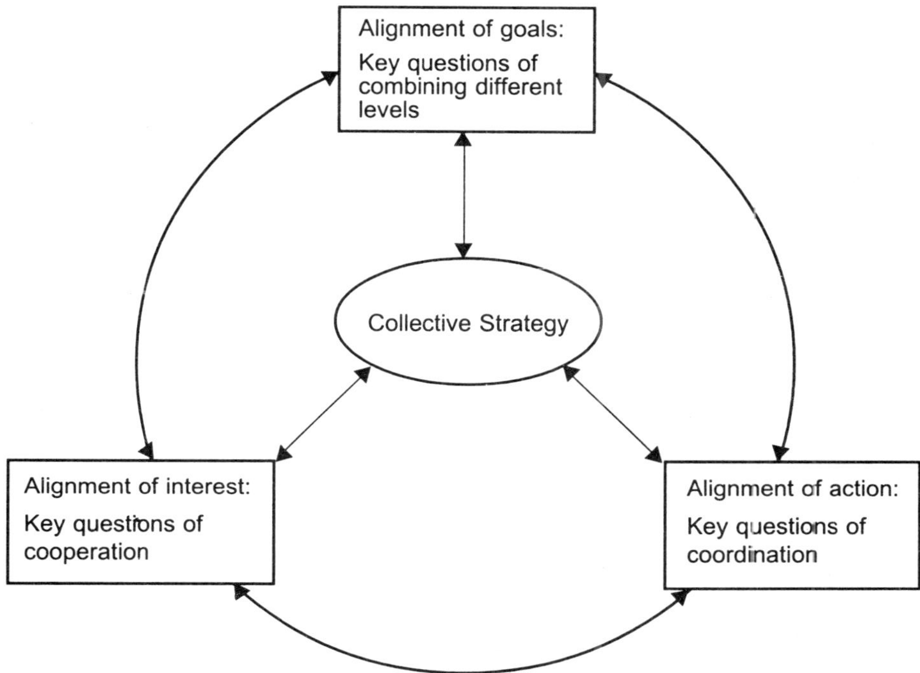

problems are most relevant in achieving the network goals and thus reduce conflicts.

Conclusion

The creation of a management system for a whole supply chain network is a tremendous organizational task that the focal firm has to accomplish. Therefore, a food chain can be called "supply chain network" if it highlights a collective strategy, that focuses on the alignment of interests, the alignment of action as well as on the alignment of different network goals. The implementation of a collective strategy has to be carried out in the interest of the whole chain, and translate strategy into network goals.

References

Astley, W.G. (1984), Towards an Appreciation of Collective Strategy. In: *Academy of Management Review*, 9: 526-535.

Astley, W.G.; Fombrun, C.J. (1983), Collective Strategy: Social Ecology of Organizational Environments. In: *Academy of Management Review*, 8 (3): 576-587.

Bogaschewsky, R. (1995), Vertikale Kooperationen—Erklärungsansätze der Transaktionskostentheorie und des Beziehungsmarketing. In: Schmalenbachs Zeitschrift für betriebswirtschaftliche Forschung, Sonderheft 35: 159-177.

Brewer, P.C., Speh, T.W. (2000), Using the Balanced Scorecard to Measure Supply Chain Performance. In: *Journal of Business Logistics*, 1 (21): 75-93.

Brewer, P.C., Speh, T.W. (2001), Adapting the Balanced Scorecard to Supply Chain Performance. In: *Supply Chain Management Review*, 2 (5): 48-56.

Burr, W. (1999), Koordination durch Regeln in selbstorganisierenden Unternehmensnetzwerken. In: Zeitschrift für Betriebswirtschaft, 69 (10): 1159-1179.

Carney, M.G. (1987), The Strategy and Structure of Collective Action. In: *Organization Studies*, 8: 341-362.

Duysters, G., Heimeriks, K.H., Jurriëns, J.A. (2004), An integrated Perspective on Alliance Management, In: *Journal on Chain and Network Science*, 4 (2): 83-94.

Edström, À., Högberg, B., Norbäck, L.E. (1984), Alternative Explanations of Interorganizational Cooperation: The Case of Joint Programmes and Joint Ventures in Sweden. In: *Organization Studies*, 5: 147-168.

Gagalyuk, T.; Hanf, J. (2008), The Importance of Network Goals for Strategic Chain Management. 12th Congress of the European Association of Agricultural Economists—EAAE 2008, Ghent.

Gulati, R., N. Nohria und A. Zaheer (2000), Strategic Networks. In: *Strategic Management Journal*, 21 (3): 203-216.

Gulati, R., Lawrence, P.R., Puranam, P. (2005), Adaptation in Vertical Relationships: Beyond Incentive Conflicts. In: *Strategic Management Journal*, 26: 415-440.

Hanf, J., Andreä, K. (2005), As a Consequence of Change—Supply Chain Networks in the Agri-Food Business. In: Schriften der Gesellschaft für Wirtschafts-und Sozialwissenschaften des Landbaus e. V. (GeWiSoLa), Band 40, 387-394.

Hanf, J., Dautzenberg, K. (2006), A Theoretical Framework of Chain Management. In: *Journal in Chain and Network Science*, 6 (1): 79-94.

Hanf, J., Hanf, C.H. (2007), Does Food Quality Management create a Competitive Advantage? In: Theuvsen, L., Spiller, A., Peupert, M., Jahn, G. (ed.), Quality Management in Food Chains. Wageningen Academic Publishers, 489-502.

Hanf, J.H., Kühl, R. (2003), Marketing Orientation and its Consequence for the Food Chain. In: Baourakis, Ed.G. (ed.): Marketing Trends for Organic Food in the Advent of the 21st Century". World Scientific Publishing, London, 116-135.

Hendrikse, G.W.J. (2003), Governance of Chains and Networks: A Research Agenda. In: *Journal on Chain and Network Science*, 3 (1): 1-6.

Jarillo, J.C. (1988). On Strategic Networks. In: *Strategic Management Journal*, 9: 31-41.

Kaplan, R.S., Norton, D.P. (1996), Using the BSC as a Strategic Management System. In: *Harvard Business Review*, 74 (1): 75-85.

Kaplan, R.S., D.P. Norton (2001), The Strategy Focused Organization. Harvard Business School Press, Boston, Mass.

Lambert, D.M., Cooper, M.C. (2000). Issues in Supply Chain Management. In: *Industrial Marketing Management*, 29: 65-83.

Lazzarini, S., F. Chaddad und M. Cook (2001), Integrating Supply Chain and Network Analysis: The Study of Netchains. In: *Journal on Chain and Network Science* 1 (1): 7-22.

Lindgreen, A., Hingley, M. (2003), The Impact of Food Safety and Animal Welfare Policies on Supply Chain Management. In: *British Food Journal*, 105 (6): 328-349.

Martinez, M.G., Poole, N., Skinner, C. (2006), Food Safety Performance in European Union Accession Countries: Benchmarking the Fresh Produce Import Sector in Hungary. In: *Agribusiness: An International Journal*, 22 (1): 69-89.

Matchette, J., Seikel, M.A. (2005), Inquiries and Insights on Supply Chain Collaboration. In: *Ascet*, 7: 148-151.

Ménard, C. (2004), The Economics of Hybrid Organizations. In: *Journal of Institutional and Theoretical Economics* (JITE), 160: 345–376.

Müller, M., Seuring, S., Goldbach M. (2003). Supply Chain Management—Neues Konzept oder Modetrend. In: *Die Betriebswirtschaft* 63 (4): 419-439.

Obrien, J.A, Marakas, and R.Behl (2010). Developing Business/IT strategies, In:

Management Information Systems, 9th edition, Tata McGraw Hill Education, New Delhi

Omta, A.W.F., Trienekens, J.H., Beers, G. (2001). Chain and Network Science: A Research Framework. In: *Journal on Chain and Network Science* 1 (1): 1-6.

Várdi, L. (2001), Review of Trends in the Development of European Inland Aquaculture Linkages with Fisheries. In: *Fisheries Management and Ecology*, 8: 453-462.

Werner, H. (2000), Die Balanced Scorecard im Supply Chain Management. In. *Distribution*, 31 (4): 8-15 (part I and II).

Wildemann, H. (1997), Koordination von Unternehmensnetzwerken. In: Zeitschrift für *Betriebswirtschaft*, 67 (4): 417-439.

Xu, L., Beamon, B.M. (2006). Supply Chain Coordination and Cooperation Mechanisms: An Attribute-Based Approach. In: *Journal of Supply Chain Management*, winter/ February 2006, 4-12.

Zylbersztajn, D., Farina, E.M.M.Q. (1999), Strictly Coordinated Food-Systems: Exploring the Limits of the Coasian Firm. In: *International Food and Agribusiness Management Review*, 2 (2): 249-265.

APPENDIX 1

Balanced Scorecard Method*

Origins

The Balanced Scorecard was developed by Robert Kaplan and David Norton (1992). In 1990, Kaplan and Norton led a research study of companies with the objective of exploring the new methods of performance measurement. The importance of the study was a growing belief that financial measures of performance were ineffective for the modern business enterprise. Representatives of the study companies, along with Kaplan and Norton, were convinced that reliance on financial measures of performance had an affect on their ability to create value. The group discussed a number of possible alternatives but settled on the idea of a scorecard, featuring performance measures capturing activities from throughout the organization—customer issues, internal business processes, employee activities, and of course shareholder concerns. Thus Kaplan and Norton introduced the new tool the **Balanced Scorecard (BSC),** which has been translated and effectively implemented in both the nonprofit and public sectors. Success stories are beginning to accumulate and studies suggest the Balanced Scorecard is of great benefit to both these organization types.

Factors Responsible for BSC Development

Most traditional management systems focus on the financial performance of an organization. According to those who support the balanced scorecard, the financial approach is unbalanced and has major limitations as highlighted below:

1. Financial data typically reflect an organization's past performance. Therefore, they may not accurately represent the current state of the organization or what is likely to happen to the organization in the future.
2. It is not uncommon for the current market value of an organization to exceed the market value of its assets. There are financial ratios that reflect the value of a company's assets relative to its market value. The difference between the market value of an organization and the current market value of the organization's assets is often referred to as intangible assets. Traditional financial measures do not cover these intangible assets.

What is a Balanced Scorecard?

The Balanced Scorecard can be understood as a management system, which is structured according to the logic of the management circle ("plan-

Source: Based on the Research work of Kaplan and Norton. *Information also adapted from* "The Balanced Scorecard Method: from theory to practice" by Margarita ISORAITĖ, Mykolas Romeris Universitety, Ateities str. 20, LT–08303 Vilnius, Lithuania.

do-check-act"). The Balanced Scorecard has become popular and brought about many changes in a variety of organizations.

The starting point of the Balanced Scorecard is the vision and the strategy of a company. The BSC takes the vision and the strategy as a given. The BSC should translate a business unit's mission and strategy into tangible objectives and measures. The measurement focus of the BSC is used to accomplish the following management processes: (1) clarifying and translating vision and strategy, (2) communicating and linking strategic objectives and measures, (3) planning, setting targets and aligning strategic initiatives, and (4) enhancing strategic feedback and learning. The measures function as a link between the strategy and operative action. The core question is the selection of goals and measures to monitor the implementation of the vision and the strategy. Kaplan and Norton recommend a nine-step process for creating and implementing the balanced scorecard in an organization.

1. Perform an overall organizational assessment.
2. Identify strategic themes.
3. Define perspectives and strategic objectives.
4. Develop a strategy map.
5. Drive performance metrics.
6. Refine and prioritize strategic initiatives.
7. Automate and communicate.
8. Implement the balanced scorecard throughout the organization.
9. Collect data, evaluate, and revise.

The BSC method is a strategic approach and performance management system that enables organizations to translate a company's vision and strategy into implementation, while working from four perspectives:

1. Financial perspective,
2. Customer perspective,
3. Business process perspective, and
4. Learning and growth perspective.

(1) The BSC/Financial Perspective: Kaplan and Norton do not disregard the traditional need for financial data. Timely and accurate funding data will always be a priority, and managers will do whatever necessary to provide it. In fact, often there is more than enough handling and processing of financial data. With the implementation of a corporate database, it is hoped that more processing can be centralized and automated. But the point is that the current emphasis on financials leads to the "unbalanced" situation with regard to other perspectives. There is perhaps a need to include additional financial-related data, such as risk assessment and cost-benefit data, in this category.

(2) The BSC/Customer Perspective: The recent management philosophy has shown an increasing realization of the importance of customer focus and customer satisfaction in any business. These are leading indicators: if customers are not satisfied, they will eventually find other suppliers that will meet their needs. Poor performance from this perspective is thus a leading indicator of future decline, even though the current financial picture may look good. In developing metrics for satisfaction, customers should be analyzed in terms of kinds of customers and the kinds of processes for which we are providing a product or service to those customer groups.

Balanced Score Card-Kaplan and Norton

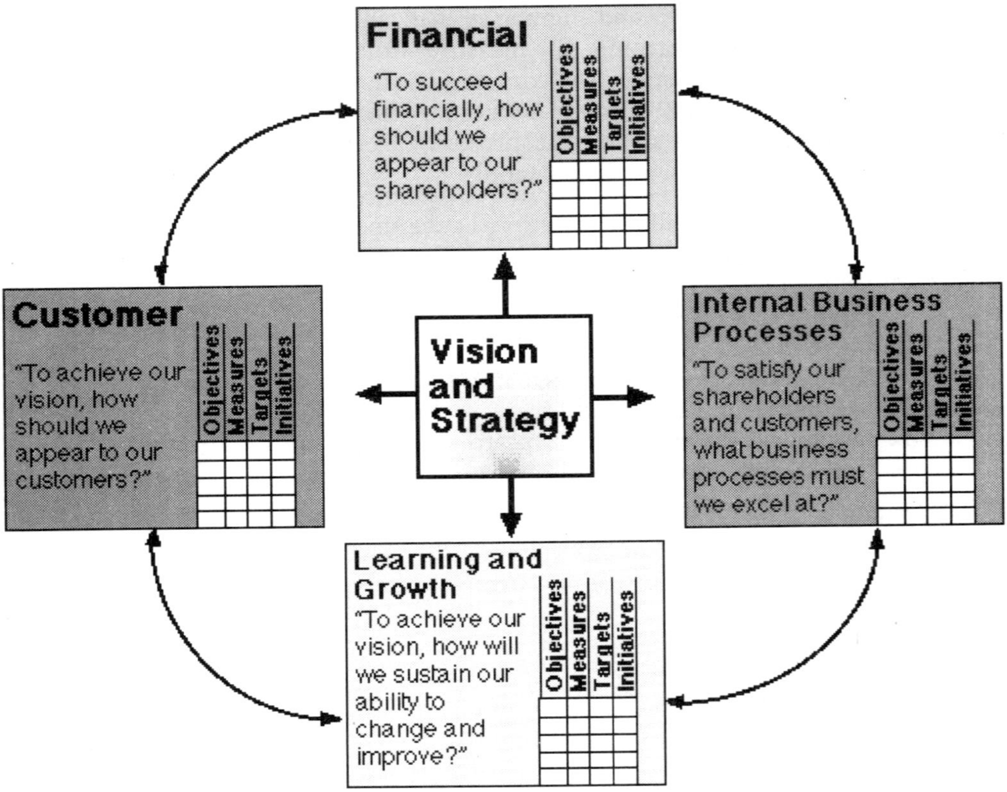

Financial
"To succeed financially, how should we appear to our shareholders?"
Objectives | Measures | Targets | Initiatives

Customer
"To achieve our vision, how should we appear to our customers?"
Objectives | Measures | Targets | Initiatives

Vision and Strategy

Internal Business Processes
"To satisfy our shareholders and customers, what business processes must we excel at?"
Objectives | Measures | Targets | Initiatives

Learning and Growth
"To achieve our vision, how will we sustain our ability to change and improve?"
Objectives | Measures | Targets | Initiatives

(3) The BSC/Business Process Perspective: It refers to internal business processes. Metrics based on this perspective allow the managers to know how well their business is running, and whether its products and services conform to customer requirements. These metrics have to be carefully designed by those who know these processes most intimately. In addition to the strategic management process, two kinds of business processes may be identified. These are : a) mission-oriented processes, and b) support processes. Mission-oriented processes are the special functions of government offices, and many unique problems are encountered in these processes. The support processes are more repetitive in nature, and hence easier to measure and benchmark using generic metrics.

(4) The BSC/Learning and Growth Perspective: It includes employee training and corporate cultural attitudes related to both individual and corporate self-improvement. In a knowledge-worker organization, people are the main resource. In the current climate of rapid technological change, it is becoming necessary for knowledge workers to be in a continuous learning mode. Government agencies often find themselves unable to hire new technical workers and at the same time they are showing a decline in training of existing employees. Kaplan and Norton emphasize that 'learning' is more than 'training'; it also includes things like mentors and tutors within the organization, as well as ease of communication among workers that allows them to readily get help on a problem when it is needed. It also includes technological tools such as an Intranet.

The integration of these four perspectives into a graphical appealing picture have made the Balanced Scorecard method a very successful methodology within the Value Based Management philosophy.

REFERENCES

IŠORAITE, Margarita, "The Balanced Scorecard method: From Theory to Practice" *Intellectual Economics*, No. 1(3), 2008, pp. 18–28.

Kaplan, R. and David Norton, "Clarifying and communicating vision and strategy into action: The BSC Framework" Value based management.net, updated Dec 2009, *http://www.valuebasedmanagement.net/methods*, accessed March 28, 2010.

Kaplan, R.S., Norton, D.P., "The Balanced Scorecard—Measures that Drive Performance," *Harvard Business Review*, January–February 1992, pp. 71–79.

Kaplan, R.S., Norton, D.P., *The Balanced Scorecard*, Boston: Harvard Business School Press, 1996.

Kaplan, R.S., Norton, D.P., *Balanced Scorecard: Strategien erfolgreich umsetzen, aus dem Amerikanischen von Horváth*, P., Stuttgart, 1997.

Kaplan, R.S., Norton, D.P., Strategy maps—Converting Intangible Assets Into Tangible Outcomes. *Harvard Business Review*, 2002.

Cross-Border Supply Chains and their Significance to Developing Countries*

Impact of Globalization on Supply Chains

Globalization offers opportunities to producers and exporters in developing countries, as fresh produce can be shipped at competitive costs to the markets where demand exists. As a result, multinational corporations, importers and retailers have expanded their international operations to meet new consumer demands with food safety as the one of the most important concerns.

Cross-border supply chains involve suppliers, or group of suppliers, or companies from a one particular country who export produce to the markets/ buyer organizations in importing countries. Through these cross-border chains, new forms of on-farm production technologies, labor processes and organizational networks are introduced in the supplier countries. Supply chains not only benefit the companies directly involved, they also stimulate social, and economic development within a region or country from where food in fresh or processed form is sourced. Besides, cross-border supply chain

Developed from Roekel, J. van, S. Willems, D.M. Boselie (2002). "Agri-Supply Chain Management: To Stimulate Cross-Border Trade in Developing Countries and Emerging Economies", Paper prepared for the Rural Development Department of the World Bank, Washington, DC.

Roekel, J. van Director, Agri Chain Competence center, The Netherlands, Sabine Willems, Agri Chain Competence center, The Netherlands, and Dave M. Boselie, Wageningen UR—Agricultural Economics Research Institute (LEI), The Netherlands.

stimulates the development of local agro-industry, imparts value addition to products, decreases product losses, and increases export earnings of the exporting (mostly developing) countries.

Integration of Small Farmers in Cross-border Supply Chains

In developing countries, small-scale producers are usually not able to adjust to new market conditions as they are often the least organized group in the supply chain. They are characterized by small-scale operations, use traditional techniques, depend on family labor, and do not have much capital to invest on their own. Producers with access to capital, technology and logistics may be best positioned to reap the benefits. As a result of increased competition, poor small-scale producers may turnout to be losers unless they become part of the supply chain.

To take advantage of new opportunities, chain partners in developing countries comprising producers, processors and exporters have to strategically plan their activities, and upgrade production systems to export improved products. In short, chain partners in developing countries/emerging economies must shift from an internal product or business orientation to an external market orientation.

Reasons for Collaboration

Supply chain partners collaborate in order to respond to :

(i) Various market segments based on product and service differentiation.
(ii) Value-added demand, coupled with consumers' demand for quality and safety.
(iii) Pursue low cost strategy by optimizing the chain costs.
(iv) Take advantage of global markets and to limit transaction costs.

The changing preference of western consumers' for organic, exotic, pre-cut, and ready-to-eat products at competitive prices is leading to supply chain collaboration among chain partners to offer value-added products and services to meet the requirements of a particular market segment. Interestingly this is leading to chain differentiation as well.

Consumer choices are increasingly influenced by food quality, safety, health and animal welfare issues. Owing to worldwide competition, the supply chain partners are forced to minimize costs to stay in business. The collaboration of the successive supply chain links to fine-tune processes and their activities to minimize costs by decreasing transaction costs optimizes the chain result.

Building Supply Chains

Supply chains are not developed easily as they require a lot of efforts and competencies of those involved. Certain steps have to be taken in order to formulate the right chain organization. Special care is required for the formation of cross-border supply chains as cultural and social differences in

Cross-border Supply Chain

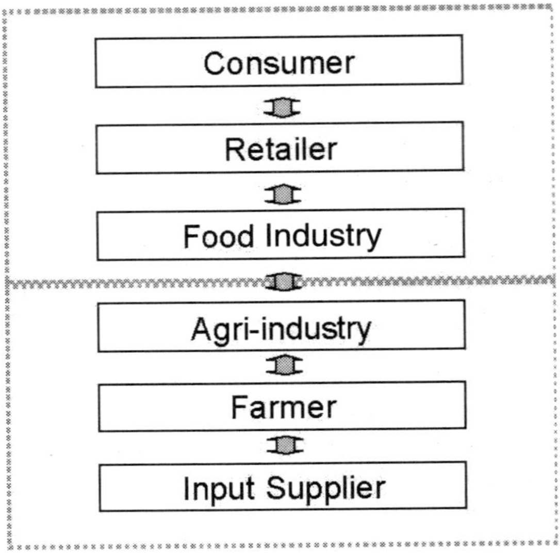

Consumer
⇕
Retailer
⇕
Food Industry
⇕
Agri-industry
⇕
Farmer
⇕
Input Supplier

Note: The upper half of the diagram represents chain in the importing country, and the lower half represents the chain in the supplier (usually developing) country.

business can have significant influence on the chain collaboration, and its performance.

The first step in agri supply chain development is the analysis of the existing trade system and the trade environment (product flow, exchange levels, factors affecting the operation of the supply chain such as government regulations and policies). From this analysis, potential supply chain players can be identified along with their functional and organizational roles in the trade system.

The success of a supply chain depends on a strong chain leader, who integrates or binds the chain organization together, and ensures mutual collaboration among supply chain partners.

Also, the performance indicators of the supply chain should be measured according to various parameters such as efficiency, flexibility, innovation, responsiveness, reduction in system-wide costs, etc. For international benchmarking, the present chain organization is compared with the best in the category, or best in its class. Through this benchmarking, the different aspects of the supply chains can be analyzed and the critical success factors can be determined. A SWOT-analysis is conducted to assess the strengths and weaknesses of the supply chain and the opportunities and threats of the supply chain environment.

Chain Competence

The development and smooth functioning of supply chains requires knowledge and expertise *about chains* and chains *within chains*. To determine the chain strategy, it is crucial to understand the consumer and the competitive environment. Chain partners still focus mainly on internal strategies such as cost-cutting strategies in order to respond to competition and low margins. Forecasting consumer demand is becoming very important (Rabobank International, 2002). At the developing stage of a supply chain, representatives of the chain partners formulate the strategy of their chain.

Cooperation and working out a common strategy prevents these chain partners from pitfalls in the process of chain formation and execution of chain functions. Chain organization knowledge helps in finding the appropriate partners who complement each other. Knowledge *about chains* is essential to develop a workable architecture but knowledge *within chains* is essential for assuring survival and sustainability to execute functions like chain marketing, logistics, information flow, etc. Key factors of success for supply chain development are partnerships and integration.

Cross-Border Chains

Cross-border chains, and especially chains that include partners from developing and developed countries, are rather complex since differences in social and commercial aspects exist between these partners. Trust and commitment are crucial elements to achieve partnerships and chain integration. Because of the different trade environments in which cross-border supply chains operate, chain partners have to deal with several trade regulations and laws (national and international), a large logistic network, and different levels of technologies. Awareness of each other's situation is a very important.

Supply Chain Management and its Benefits

Managing supply chains requires an integral approach in which chain partners jointly plan and control the flow of goods, information, technology and capital from the suppliers of raw materials to the final consumers and *vice versa*.

In order to react effectively and quickly to consumer's demand, supply chain management is consumer-oriented. It aims at coordination of production processes (Lambert and Cooper, 2000; Handfield and Nichols 1999). Supply chain management results in lower transaction costs and increased margins. Because of the many activities and aspects involved, it demands a multidisciplinary approach. The advantages of the supply chain management approach are numerous. Some important advantages are listed below:

- Reduction in product losses in transportation and storage.
- Increased sales.
- Dissemination of technology, advanced techniques, capital and knowledge among the chain partners.
- Better information about the flow of products, markets and technologies.

- Transparency of the supply chain.
- Tracking & tracing to the source.
- Better control of product safety and quality.
- Large investments and risks are shared among partners in the chain.

Supply Chain Management Tools

A range of new supply chain management tools have been developed over the past decade. 'Efficient consumer response' (ECR) has been developed to increase the consumer orientation and cost-effectiveness of supply chains (Kurt Salmon Associates, 1993). New-generation cooperatives are emerging, strengthening the position of farmers' groups (Cook *et. al.*, 2001) and strategic partnering and vertical alliances are cementing sustainable partnerships throughout the supply chain (Zylbersztajn & Farina, 1999).

Food safety concerns have led to the development of 'integral chain-care' tools such as social accountability, good agricultural practice (GAP), total quality management, and HACCP (hazard analysis at critical control points). Implementation of such tools throughout a cross-border supply chain enables chain partners to ensure the quality and safety of their products.

Retailers (e.g., Walmart, Carrefour, Royal Ahold, Tesco and Sainsbury) have increasingly established their own quality standards (e.g., EUREP-GAP and BRC) which suppliers must meet. Tracking and tracing systems are used to certify the quality of products and ensure transparency in the flow of goods throughout the supply chain. Implementing such standards and systems impacts not only the organization of supply chains, but also financial aspects of chain cooperation (Cook *et. al.*, 2001).

Role of Government in Agri-Chain Development

Governments can improve the environment for agri-chain development by:

- Organizing platforms for public and private cooperation to exchange information on bottlenecks in cross-border agricultural trade. The ultimate goal here is to formulate and implement policies (e.g., product and production standards, codes of conduct) to stimulate cross-border agri-chain development.
- Investing in transportation, communication and power infrastructure.
- Offering incentives for sustainable use of production resources.
- Offering subsidies or co-financing supply for high-risk investments.
- Establishing and enforcing a commercial code that includes property rights and expediting judicial processes for resolving contract conflicts/disputes.
- Ensure the availability of production, price, and industry information and statistics to facilitate market activity and to monitor market progress.

Public-Private Partnerships

Government support might take the form of a public private partnership in a supply chain. Public-private partnerships thus are beneficial for the society at large and for private sector entities (van der Meer, 2000). The public research institute might contribute by developing and testing new technologies, tools, models, and instruments to improve the performance of the supply chain. The private firms can access this knowledge. Government's role in public-private partnerships can be as co-financier of a supply chain project (Australia, Canada, the Netherlands, Thailand and South Africa), as creator of an enabling environment (e.g., through provision of research and physical infrastructure), and as mediator in trade negotiations (Newton, 2000).

International Organizations

International organizations such as the World Bank, World Trade Organization, Food & Agricultural Organization, international research institutes, etc. can assist national governments of developing countries and emerging economies with special and sustainable public interventions to upgrade cross-border trade. These interventions can include institutional capacity building, analysis of particular agro-systems, supply chain analysis of particular products, training courses in supply chain development.

The international organizations can also stimulate public-private partnerships by linking national and international research institutes.

REFERENCES

Andersen, O. and A. Buvik (2001), Inter-firm co-ordination: international versus domestic buyer-seller relationship. *Omega, The International Journal of Management Science* 29: 207-219.

Boehlje, M., L. Schrader and J. Akridgel (1998), Observations on formation of food supply chains. In: *Proceedings of the third international conference on chain management in the agribusiness and the food industry* edited by G.W. Ziggers, J.H. Trienekens and P.J.P. Zuurbier. Wageningen.

Buurma, J.S. *et al.* (2001), Developing countries and products affected by setting new maximum residue limits (MRLs) of pesticides in the EU. The Hague: Agricultural Economics Research Institute (LEI).

Cook, M.L., T. Reardon, C. Barrett and Joyce Cacho (2001), Agroindustrialization in emerging markets: overview and strategic context. *International Food and Agribusiness Management Review* 2(3/4): 277-288.

Farina, E.M.M.Q., and T. Reardon (2000), Agrifood Grades and Standards in the Extended Mercosur: Their Role in Changing Agrifood System, *American Journal of Agricultural Economics*, 82(5): 1170-1176.

Grievelink, J.W., L. Josten, and C. Valk (2001), State of the art in food: the changing face of the worldwide food industry. Amsterdam: Elsevier.

Gaisford, J.D. and W.A. Kerr (2001), Economic analysis for international trade negotiations: the WTO and agricultural trade. Northamptom: Edward Elgar.

Handfield, R.B. and E.L. Nichols (1999) Introduction to supply chain management. N.J.: Prentice Hall.

Itharattana, K. (1996), Market Prospects for Upland Crops in Thailand, Working Paper 21, CGPRT Center, Bogor.

Jaffee, S.M. (1994), Contract farming in the shadow of competitive markets: the experience of Kenyan horticulture. In: *Living under contract, contract farming and agrarian transformation in sub-Sahara Africa* edited by P.D. Little and M.J. Watts. Wisconsin: University of Wisconsin Press.

Kurt Salmon Associates (1993), Efficient Consumer Response: enhancing consumer value in the grocery industry, Washington, D.C.: Food Marketing Institute.

Lambert, D.M. and M.C. Cooper (2000), Issues in supply chain management. *Industrial Marketing Management* 29: 65-83.

Lazzarini, S.G., F.R. Chaddad and M.L. Cook (2001), Integrating supply chain and network analyses: the study of netchains. *Chain and Network Science*, 1(1): 7-22.

Little, P.D. and M.J. Watts (eds) (1994) Living under contract: contract farming and agrarian transformation in sub-Sahara Africa. Wisconsin: University of Wisconsin Press.

van der Meer, C. (2000), Public-private cooperation: examples from agricultural research in the Netherlands. Washington, D.C.: World Bank.

Newton, D. (2000), Supply chain learning for Australian agribusiness, chain reversal and shared learning for global competitiveness. Canberra: Department of Agriculture, Fisheries & Forestry.

Oyejide, A., I. Elbadawi, P. Collier (eds) (1997), Regional integration and trade liberalization in sub-Saharan Africa. Vol. 1: framework, issues and methodological perspectives. Houndmills: Macmillan.

van Roekel, J., R. Kopicki, J.E. Broekmans and D.M. Boselie (2002), Building agri-supply chains: issues and guidelines. In: *A guide to developing agricultural markets and agro-enterprises* edited by Daniele Giovannucci. Washington, D.C.: World Bank.

Silver, E.A. and D.F. Pyke, R. Peterson (1998), Inventory management and production planning and scheduling. Chichester: John Wiley & Sons.

Unnevehr, L.J., and H.H. Jensen (1999), The Economic Implications of Using HACCP as Food Safety Regulatory Standard, Food Policy 24 (6): 625-635.

Vieira, L.F. and F. Hartwich (forthcoming) Approaching public-private partnerships for agroindustrial research: a methodological framework. The Hague/San José: International Service for National Agricultural Research.

Watts, M.J. (1994) Life under contract: contract farming, agrarian restructuring and flexible accumulation. In: *Living under contract, contract farming and agrarian transformation in sub-Sahara Africa* edited by P.D. Little and M.J. Watts. Wisconsin: University of Wisconsin Press.

Zylbersztajn, D., and E.M.M.Q. Farina (1999), Strictly co-ordinated food-systems: exploring the limits of the Coasian firm, *International Food and Agribusiness Management Review*, Vol. 2 (2): 249-265.

Managing and Controlling International Food Supply Chains*

Since the 1990s, Western retailers have increased their demands on suppliers of fresh produce from developing countries. In late nineties, British Retail Consortium (BRC) formulated common food safety and quality standards for suppliers of food. The BRC standard and other standards, like Eurep-Gap (a primary producers' standard supported by major retailers), are used by supermarkets and are applicable world over to coordinate supply chain activities and control food safety. The introduction of these standards implies that producers and processors have to implement requirements in the supply chain that forbid the use of some crop protection chemicals/agents and fertilizers, and recommand adherence to production and processing methods, including labour conditions (Marsden, 2000) prevailing at farms.

Study Objectives

To analyze international food chain development and its contribution to innovation and new governance structures in supply chains in developing countries.

*Source: *Adapted from* Jacques Trienekens[1] and Sabine Willems[2]

"Innovation and Governance in International Food Supply Chains : The Cases of Ghanaian Pineapples and South African Grapes", International Food and Agribusiness Management Review, Volume 10, Issue 4, 2007

[1]Professor, Management Studies Group, Wageningen University, Hollandseweg 1, Wageningen, 6706 KN, The Netherlands.

[2]Professor, Management Studies Group, Wageningen University, Hollandseweg 1, Wageningen, 6706 KN, The Netherlands

Methodology

The methodology used was based on the analysis of two case studies from developing countries.

The first one was **pineapple export chain from Ghana** and the second one was **table grape export chain from South Africa.** Both supply chains are characterized by the involvement of a large number of producers who had to comply with international market demands in order to participate at the global market level.

Data Collection

For data and information collection, key stakeholders in and around the pineapple export chain in Ghana and the table grape export chain in South Africa were interviewed in 2003. Both supply chains were export oriented. Producers are targeting different international markets (mainly in Europe) as these markets offer greater opportunities than the local markets. The two cases were chosen because they present different stages of chain development. The more advanced South African chain, with its advanced production and distribution technologies and well-developed market relationships, was compared with the emerging but still weakly developed Ghanaian chain, with its low level of technology use and lowly developed market relationships.

Case Facts and Analysis

Organization and Structure of Ghanaian Pineapple Chain

It consisted of four categories of farms.

Specialized Plantations with Out-growers

These were large (>500 ha) farms specializing in pineapple production. Farms are often run by farmer-exporters who have integrated production and export trade. In general, specialized plantations have a vertically integrated business from the farm to the port. They have direct contact with their customers in Europe, their own trucks and their own shaded pack houses, thus controlling all the activities necessary for exporting.

Medium-scale (diversified) Export Farms

Farms with less than 500 hectares, and producing less than 90% pineapples are categorized as medium-scale (diversified) export farms. These farms often grow a diversified portfolio of crops (mangoes, papayas, pineapples and vegetables). They export these products themselves to the European market or sell them to the local processing industry which exports the processed products.

Organized Small Holders

With the support of the World Bank in 1998, 178 farmers and two pineapple exporters (namely Gabrho Limited and Kokobin Farms) formed a cooperative called Farmapine. The World Bank granted a loan facility to Farmapine, which was partly used to purchase and supply inputs to farmers.

Farmapine has built a central packing facility for all pineapple exports. Currently, Farmapine has over 200 members, all of whom own between 0.5 and 10-15 hectares.

Non-organized Small Holders

These farmers produce normally for the local market, and occasionally for larger farmers when there is sufficient demand. Ghana has hundreds of small pineapple farmers who cultivate up to 4 hectares of land. These out-growers(when they supply regularly to large farmers) are often supplied with seeds and in return promise to sell their crops to the exporter. Sometimes they also receive other inputs or cash in advance but in general there is no written contract. The estimated number of non-organized pineapple producing smallholders is 1000.

Role of Middlemen

A number of middlemen collect pineapples from small-scale farmers for the export to Europe. These middlemen pay the farmers a farm-gate price and handle the products from the farm-gate onwards.

Logistics and Transportation Arrangements

There are **two types of transport** available to carry pineapple produce from farm to port.

The first one is privately owned trucks and the second one are contracted trucks. Privately owned trucks are mainly used by export firms and by organized smallholders. Most of these trucks are in good condition and some have a cooling facility (Pegge, 2003). The contracted trucks were mainly operated by one-man businesses and transported all types of loads. These trucks were found to be in poor condition and lacked cooling facilities.

Means of Export Arrangements

Around 95% of the total pineapple export is transported by boat.

Due to relatively small scale of the Ghanaian exporters, they were often forced to accept the residual space available on ships and cargo airplanes. The piecemeal export consignments this way resulted in delays and increase in transportation costs. Lack of cooperation among exporters and inadequate long-range planning further compounded the problem of managing sea/air freight available space (Pegge, 2003).

Trading and Export

Most traders acquired pineapple farms to ensure regular and sufficient supply. The number of exporters fluctuated between 50 and 70 during the last decade, although just 10 companies accounted for 80% of all exports. These 10 larger exporters were the specialized plantations with out-growers and the cooperative Farmapine.

South African Table Grape Chain

The South African fruit industry has seen some dramatic changes over

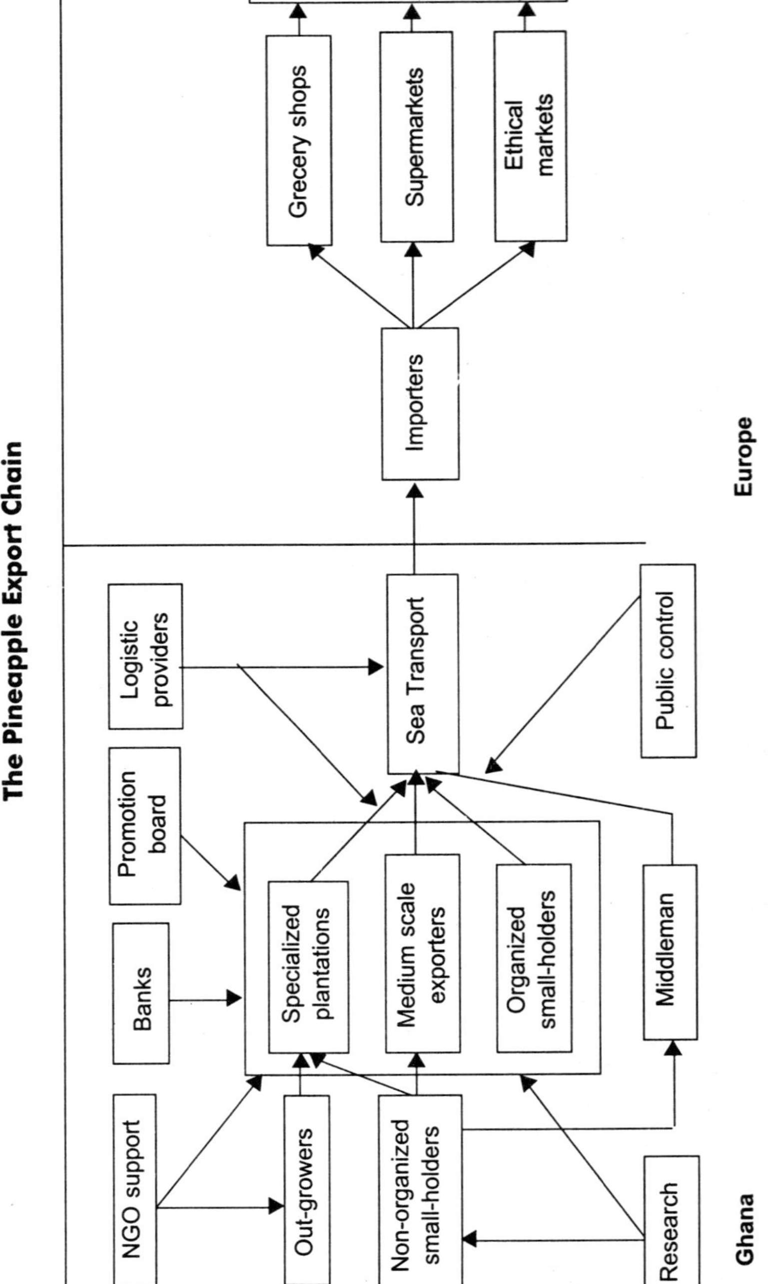

The Pineapple Export Chain

the past ten years, moving from a fully regulated market environment towards a free market system (McDonald and Punt, 2001). Prior to deregulation in South Africa in 1997, there was one single marketing channel for most of the commodities. This meant that the supply chain was relatively simple and it was relatively easy to manage and optimize the chain. (Vos, 2003). The fresh fruit and wine industries have gained the most from the opening up of export opportunities.

Currently the South African table grape sector is under high competitive forces due to oversupply of fruit world wide, and new competitors such as Argentina, Brazil, and Peru.

The South African table grape chain can be described as follows.

Producers

In 2003 there were 974 table grape producers in South Africa. Farms are in most cases modern-enterprises that use high-quality input materials and production methods. During the period of Apartheid most workers lived on the farm estates throughout the year. In recent years, the number of producers has slightly decreased and more efficient production in larger units has developed in response to movement of labour force in search for better opportunities and higher wages in a more democratic South Africa.

Cold Stores

After the harvest, grapes are first stored in cold stores that belong to an individual farmer or are cooperatively owned . Every grape-producing region has a number of cold stores. In the near future a further increase in the number of cooling/storage facilities is expected.

Logistics and Transporter Facilities

South Africa's transport infrastructure (air, road, rail and sea) is well developed. The road, rail and air transport services are good in most parts of the country. The quality of infrastructure in the rural areas varies. Most grapes are destined for export. Grapes for export are transported to the harbor by modern transportation companies with cooled trucks.

Exporters

Since the industry in South Africa was deregulated and the overseas market for fresh fruit opened up for South African producers, the number of exporters has increased enormously to about 400.

Export Markets

Because of the good long-term connections with UK retailers, market share of south African grapes has declined for Europe, owing to increased international competition. South-east Asian markets, especially Indonesia might become a new market for South African grapes, as quality and safety demands in Asia are still much lower than in the EU. Other potential markets in Asia are India, China and Japan. The South African table grape export chain is depicted in the diagram on next page.

The Table Grape Export Chain

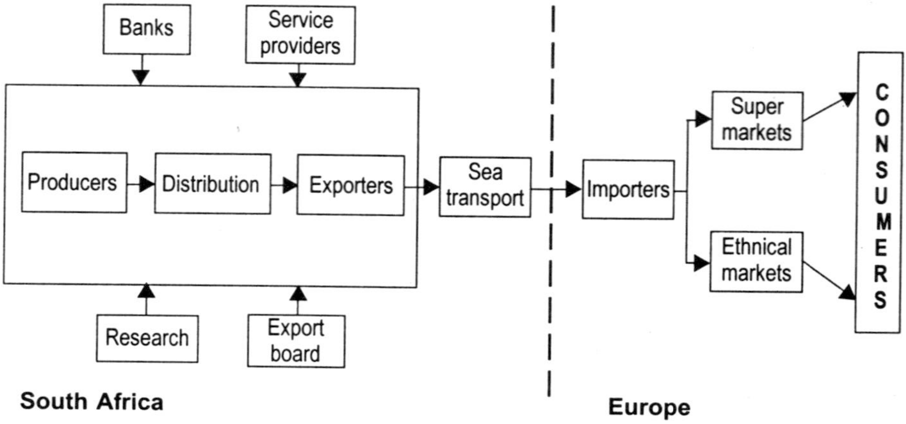

Banks
Service providers
Producers → Distribution → Exporters → Sea transport → Importers → Super markets / Ethnical markets → CONSUMERS
Research
Export board
South Africa
Europe

From the two diagrams, we can observe the differences between the two chains. The South-African table grape chain has a less complex (more "straightforward") structure than the Ghanaian pineapple chain, if we include the small-holders in this chain. There are no "middleman" in the South-African chain.

Results and Discussion

Stimulus of Market Demand on Chain and Facility Development

Technology and System Innovations

Respondents in both countries reported a very strong increase of market demands on quality and safety of produce, consistency in terms of quantity, on-time deliveries, traceability, selection of input materials and labour conditions. Compared to Ghana, South-Africa is at higher level of development as their produce (grapes in the present case) satisfy many demands. Consequently, the grape sector faces fewer requirements to develop the sector due to better infrastructure that is already in place.

As per market requirements, farmers in both South African and Ghana are changing their production technology by restricting the use of pesticides and fertilizers (Eurep-Gap requirements). Further, in both sectors more attention is now being paid to Eurep-Gap compliant quality systems, cooling facilities (although in Ghana this is restricted to a limited number of cooled trucks), bar-coding, farm equipment (tractors) and harvesting and packaging facilities (sheds). In line with these findings, increases in investment in Ghana were found in land equipment (tractors to prepare the land, plastics to protect produce from bugs and investments in new pineapple varieties), packaging sheds, bar-coding (by a few large producers) and to a lesser extent in cooling. South African producers have focused their investments on packaging facilities, cooling facilities (smaller units) and bar-coding, thereby complying with international standards. Respondents in South Africa underlined the importance of manual labour in dealing with the delicate table grapes. In Ghana we see these changes especially amongst the large producers, whilst in South Africa all types of producers are involved.

At the chain level in South Africa we see innovations in packaging and packaging standards (pallets, food safety related issues, carton sizes), IT standards (e.g. traceability), quality standards in general and cooling technology development. A constraint with regard to the development of new packaging materials is that the costs of these innovations cannot be easily included in the product price, because of strong price competition in consumer markets. There is no innovation 'owner' in the South African table grape chain (contrary to the situation before deregulation where Capespan "the" exporter was involved in packaging innovation). In Ghana, except for Eurep-Gap induced innovations, no innovations at the chain level have been introduced so far.

A direct effect of international retail demands on local production systems can be identified in the South African table grape chain. Quality and safety are currently receiving high priority in South Africa, with the export sector taking a leading role in these developments. Compared to the Ghanaian pineapple chain, the investments and innovations in the South African table grape sector are far more advanced, including modern cooling systems, coding technology, etc. An important innovative role in South Africa is played by the exporters, who invest in chain-wide information systems and also perform educational activities for parties throughout the chain.

Effects on Governance Structure

Chain integration has been emerging in South Africa for some time now. Increasing demands of Western retailers and (slowly) growing long-term relationships between parties (retailers, exporters—and to a lesser extent producers) are structuring the chain towards hybrid, contract based, governance structures. This form of governance is strongly supported by the exporter-link, where initiatives for information and quality system integration are taken to better attune processes in the chain. Moreover, direct relationships with Western retailers stimulate the emergence of efficient (fast, responsive) and flexible chains. At the same time chains are being consolidated through reductions in the number of parties in different links, which also may lead to more balanced relationships and strengthening of the chains as a whole. Respondents also expect that more producers will become exporter-producers as a way to try to lower costs and exert control over the supply chain. These developments are enforced by transaction-related investments of exporters (such as investments in cold stores and credits to producers) to ensure deliveries (whereas in Ghana banks are reluctant to finance perishable produce). Transportation is another activity that is developing in line with these integrating developments. Respondents expect that transport providers increasingly will become chain service providers, covering the chain from pack house to cold store and from cold store to ship or plane. However, a major barrier to the further development of these integrated chains is the opportunistic sales behaviour of producers, which is also a barrier to increased efficiency in the chain (information asymmetry leads to bad planning by exporters and transporters, according to most respondents).

One large challenge for the South African table grape sector is the still large distinction and lack of trust between black and white employees on the farms. 'Transformation' of a black-white economy into an integrated economy is progressing (too) slowly. Greater effort and educational initiatives have to be undertaken.

In the emerging Ghanaian pineapple chain, market demands have led to a fragmented production system, with a few large integrated producer-exporters and many small producers (out-growers). Although many exporters seek long-term relationships with retailers to ensure demand, this is still constrained by weak market opportunities, a very weak infrastructure and the opportunistic behaviour of chain participants. Contrary to the South African table-grape chain there is no (horizontal) collaboration between exporters. In Ghana many small-scale producers depend on large-scale producers for input supplies, market access and credits. Furthermore, transportation is increasingly organized by exporters. These dependency relationships between large producer/exporters and smallholders lead to chains in which smallholders are forced to find market access through large producers in an imbalanced buyer-supplier relationship. Therefore, the existence of a large cooperative like Farmapine, with many smallholder members and out-growers, is promising.

With regard to the credit structure, in general, respondents reported that banks are not eager to finance perishable products because of the high risks involved. Small-scale producers need a guarantee from a large-scale producer or an importer to be able to receive credits from banks. Farmers receive credits more easily if they are members of Farmapine.

Conclusion and Outlook

The South African table grape chain is a mature chain in which concentration and consolidation of parties is taking place. The Ghanaian pineapple chain is a newly emerging supply chain, with many constraints to overcome. Both export chains are constrained by external factors.

References

Bowersox, D.J. and Closs D.J. (1996), Logistical Management: The integrated supply chain process. New York: Macmillan.

Coleman J.S. (1990), Foundations of Social Theory. Cambridge, MA: Harvard University Press.

Cooper, M.C., Lambert, D.M. and Pagh, J.D. (1997), Supply Chain Management: More than a new name for logistics. *International Journal of Logistics Management*, 8 (1), 1-14.

David, R.J. and Han, S.-H. (2004), A systematic assessment of the empirical support for transaction cost economics. *Strategic Management Journal*, 25(1), 39-58.

Deciduous Fruit Producers Trust (DFPT) (2002), Key Deciduous Fruit Statistics, DFPT, Paarl South Africa.

Fafchamps, M. (2004), Market institutions in Sub-Saharan Africa. Theory and Evidence, Boston: The MIT Press.

Folkerts, Henk and Hans Koehorst (1997), Challenges in international food supply chains: Vertical coordination in the European Agribusiness and Food Industries, *Supply Chain Management*, 2 (1), 11-14.

Fresh Producers Exporters Forum (FPEF) (2003), Market Forces Affecting Industry Returns, Lecture S. Symington, Cape Town South Africa.

Friedland, W.H. (1994), The Global Fresh Fruit and Vegetable System: An Industrial Organization Analysis, In: McMichael, P. (ed.) (1994), The Global Restructuring of Agro-Food Systems, Ithaca, New York: Cornell University Press.

Gereffi, G., Korzeniewicz, K. Korzeniewicz, R. (1994), Introduction: Global Commodity Chains. In: G. Gereffi and M. Korzeniewicz (eds.), Commodity chains and global capitalism, Westport: Greenwood Press.

Ghana Export Promotion Council (GEPC), (2002), Exporter performance, non-traditional exports by exporter for 2001, Accra.

Ghana Export Promotion Council (GEPC), (2003), Export of fresh pineapples in 2002, 2001, Accra.

Giovanucci, D. and Reardon, T. (2001), Understanding grades and standards and how to apply them, In: A guide to developing agricultural markets and ago-enterprises, Edited by Daniele Giovannuci, Washington: The World Bank.

Grover, V. and Malhotra, M.K. (2003), Transaction cost framework in operations and supply chain management research: theory and measurement. *Journal of Operations Management*, 21(4), 457-473.

Handfield, R.B. and E.L. Nichols (1999), Introduction to Supply Chain Management, New Jersey: Prentice Hall.

Hueth, B., E. Ligon, S. Wolf & S. Wu (1999), Incentive instruments in fruit and vegetable contracts: input control, monitoring, measuring and price risk, *Review of Agricultural Economics*, 21 (2), 374-389.

Humphreys, P.K., Li, W.L. and Chan, L.Y. (2004), The impact of supplier development on buyer-supplier performance, *Omega*, 32(2), 131-143.

Lambert, D.M. and Cooper, M.C. (2000), Issues in Supply Chain Management, *Industrial Marketing Management*, 29, 65–83.

Lancioni R., Smith M., and Oliva, T. (2000), The Role of the Internet in Supply Chain Management, *Industrial Marketing Management*, 29, 45-56.

Lazzarini, S.G., Chaddad, F.R. and Cook, M.L. (2001), Integrating supply chain and network analyses: the study of netchains, *Journal on Chain and Network Science*, 1 (1), 7-22.

Marsden, T. (2000), Food Matters and the Matter of Food: Towards a New Food Governance?, *Sociologia Ruralis*, 40 (1), 21-29.

McDonald, S. and Punt, C. (2001), The Western Cape of South Africa: Export Opportunities, Productivity Growth and Agriculture, 4th Global Economic Analysis Conference, Purdue University, June.

Omta, S.W.F., Trienekens, J.H. and Beers, G. (2001), Chain and Network Science: a Research Framework, *Journal on Chain and Network Science*, 1 (1), 1-6.

Pegge, S. (2003), Pineapple and Partners, MSc Thesis, Management Studies Group, Wageningen University, The Netherlands.

Perishable Products Export Control Board (PPECB), (1999), Deciduous fruit exports from South Africa, 1996-1999, South Africa.

Porter, M.E. (2001), Strategy and the internet, *Harvard Business Review*, 79, March, 62-78.

Reardon, T. and Timmer, C.P. (2005), Transformation of Markets for Agricultural Output in Developing Countries since 1950: How has Thinking Changed? Chapter in R. Evenson and P. Pingali (eds), Handbook of Agricultural Economics, Volume 3A, Amsterdam: Elsevier Press.

Ruben R., M. van Boekel, A. van Tilburg, J. Trienekens (2007), Governance for Quality in Tropical Food Chains, Wageningen: Wageningen Acadamic Publishers, p. 309.

Sarpong, D.B. (2002), Farm-size, resource use efficiency and rural development: technoserve and small-scale pineapple farmer groups in Ghana, Issues in African Rural Development, Monograph Series, Winrock International, Arlington, VA, USA. (Data March 1999).

Spiegel van der, M. (2004), Measuring effectiveness of food quality management, Ponsen & Looijen, Wageningen, The Netherlands.

Stern, L.W., El-Ansary, A.I. and Coughlan, A.T. (1996), Marketing channels, London: Prentice Hall-International, (5th ed.).

Thorpe, Andy and Elizabeth Bennett (2004), Market-driven international fish supply chains: the case of Nile-perch from Africa's Lake Victoria, *International Food and Agribusiness Management Review*, 7 (4), 40-57.

Trienekens, J.H. and A.J.M. Beulens (2001), Views on inter-enterprise relationships, *Production Planning & Control*, 12 (5), 466-477.

Uzzi, B. (1997), Social Structure and Competition in Interfirm Networks: the Paradox of Embeddedness, *Administrative Science Quarterly*, 42, 35-67.

Vellema, S. and D. Boselie (2003), Cooperation and competence in global food chains. Perspectives on food quality and safety, Shaker Publishing, Maastricht.

Vos, T. de (2003), Information exchange and collaboration in the South African fresh produce export supply chain, PPECB, Cape Town South Africa.

Williamson, O.E. (1985), The Economic Institutions of Capitalism: Firms, Markets, Relational Contracting, Free Press, New York.

Williamson, O.E. (1999), Strategy research: governance and competence perspectives, *Strategic Management Journal*, 20, 1087-1108.

Yin, R.K. (1994), Case study research: Design and methods (second edition), Thousand Oaks, CA, USA: Sage Publications.

Factors Affecting the Food Quality and Safety in Agri-food Supply Chains

This chapter briefly presents the factors at various stages of agri-food supply chain, which affect the food quality and safety, especially in horticultural products in the developing and fast emerging economies.

These factors can be production related, harvest and post-harvest-related, besides market and packaging-related.

Production Factors

Production factors affecting quality and health safety include:

Variety. Some varieties are more prone to pest attacks during production phase, or damage during transportation. Additionally, genetically modified varieties such as **Bt cotton** and **Bt Brinjal** are facing public debates in India owing to safety issues. Therefore such varieties need to be carefully selected after considering pros and cons of their benefits.

Soils. Soils with high salt content, presence of harmful organisms and minerals in soils can affect the product quality and cause health problems upon their consumption.

Irrigation. Excessive irrigation and quality of water e.g. water with industrial effluents or sewerage water damages the product quality, and the products obtained from those areas cause health problems. Too little irrigation or deficient water application to crops from lack of precipitation also causes damage to the products.

Location. Both airborne and water borne contamination can occur when agricultural farms located near to production units especially those dealing with chemicals are exposed to their gases, wastes and effluents.

Pesticide use. Since consumers purchase products on the basis of appearance, they are not aware of pesticides use by farmers owing to pressure on the latter from the downstream members of the supply chain. In some countries, there is clear evidence of overuse of pesticides.

Harvest and Post-harvest Handling

Harvest-related problems include:

Early harvest. Sometimes produce is harvested early to provide consumers with the supply of products from early on in the season. Early harvesting may not result in perfectly ripe or mature products and consumers may avoid buying it. However, some products may be stored for ripening such as bananas, pineapples and papayas, and distributed through the chain to the final consumer, as they become mature.

Harvesting techniques Poor harvesting techniques can lead to skin breakages, crushing and bruising, thus promoting physiological damage and disease infection to the horticultural products.

Time of harvesting. The best time to harvest is in the mornings when the temperature is low. Harvesting must be synchronized or matched with the transportation facilities otherwise produce is spoiled when it lies in open under the sun throughout the day. Farmers and their agents tend to spray water and put it under sheds to provide coolness and shade until the transport arrives to pick them up for transfer to cooling stations or warehouses. For example, Mother dairy' procurement operations of fruits and vegetables from producing areas around Delhi or from channel partners in other states. The produce is transported in specialized trucks to the centralized warehouse in New Delhi where cool temperatures are maintained.

Handling the produce for the market. Excessive washing and humidity during storage, rainy season, or transit to the market can lead to fungus and bacterial infestation. Handling by infected people, workers with dirty hands, or who have handled harmful wastes can spoil the quality of produce. Also, workers have to be trained to handle the sensitive horticultural produce with care.

Packaging, Transport and Storage

Produce that leaves the farmer in perfect condition can still reach the consumer in extremely bad condition. Factors contributing to this include:

Packaging quality. The quality of packaging materials is on improvement side in India due to availability of plastic crates, and other paper/card board based materials coming in all shapes for packaging the delicate horticultural products. However, packaging shows variations at the farmer levels unless they are instructed by channel members as to how to pack them, and what materials to use.

Non-availability of clean vehicles. Farmers and transporters may use the same vehicles which are used for transporting other products like organic manure, fertilizers and even livestock. Lack of cleanliness results in contamination, particularly of produce that is transported in bulk and without proper packaging.

Transport practices. Produce is often damaged when transporter or farmer tries to load the truck or vehicle to its fullest capacity to minimize the number of trips in order to reduce transportation costs.

Storage practices. With the exception of onions, garlic and a few other vegetables which can survive in normal storage conditions, products like potatoes and chillies (some special varieties like "Bydagi" famous for their food grade color value) are stored under cool refrigerated conditions. Most of the horticultural produce is perishable in nature, and they cannot be stored for long term. Ripe, and ethylene-emitting fruit should be separated from other fruit. Pesticide usage particularly of harmful and banned pesticides like DDT should be avoided.

Produce Handling by the Supply Chain

Traders usually indulge in grading, cleaning, waxing, and using water to make produce look fresh. Some cases of colouring the produce as natural green particularly leafy vegetables have been reported. Such practices compromise with the customer concern for food safety.

Food Standards in the Global Supply Chains

Private standards have become common in governing and controlling global agriculture sector/food sector products' supply chains in the last 10 to 15 years. Private firms and NGOs, have created and adopted standards for food safety, and quality besides environmental and social aspects of agri-food production. These are usually monitored and enforced through third party certification.

It is also possible for governments to set standards with which compliance should be made mandatory. Many organizations create and adopt standards, and there is an active interchange between the public and private sectors. Global standards setting bodies such as Codex are a central part of the complex multi-layered structure of public and private standards that currently governs global production and trade in the agri-food sector. There are five different functions that are involved in standard schemes. These are: *standard-setting; adoption; implementation; conformity assessment; and enforcement*. These can be carried out by a range of public and/or private organizations/agencies/ associations as per nature of the standard. (Henson and Humphrey, 2009).

There are four key factors for increasing control in agri-food value chains. These must be related to the restructuring of global agricultural and food markets.

(1) Reforms of food safety regulatory systems should respond to real and/or perceived risks in food production, transport and processing systems.
(2) Increased interest among consumers and businesses towards food production processes is due to changes in their perception of food

safety and quality on account of competitive strategies of firms that focus on environmental and social impacts.

(3) Globalization of food supply and coordination in defining competitiveness create new risks and new challenges for value chain coordination and control.

(4) Responsibility for ensuring food safety has gone from the state to the private sector.

The integration of these four factors create an environment in which businesses are under more pressure to deliver food safety and work hard to maintain the integrity of their brands.(Henson and Humphrey, 2009).

Revision of Food Regulations in India

In tune with the international requirements, the Government of India is working on improving the food quality and safety standards in the country. The Ministry of Food Processing Industries, Government of India declared 2008-09 as "Food Safety & Quality year". Since the concept of food safety and quality is important in the supply chain starting from farmers-processors-wholesalers-retailers to the consumers, the Ministry has taken policy initiative to meet certain requirements of the food sector. This initiative is meant to bring together the proposed initiatives of Food processing Ministries with the schemes of Ministry of Agriculture, Department of Commerce, Ministry of Health, and Department of Consumer Affairs, all of which are directly involved in the implementation of the Food Safety and Standards Act, 2006.

In order to implement safety standards effectively, the active cooperation and involvement of Indian Council of Agricultural Research (ICAR), Bureau of Indian Standards (BIS), Federation of Indian Chambers of Commerce (FICCI), Confederation of Indian Chambers of Commerce and Industry(CII), Agricultural and Food Products Export Development Authority (APEDA), and other industry associations, and state governments and the recognized agencies will be undertaken.

Implementation of Food Safety and Quality Year under 11th Five Year Plan Schemes

(i) Under the new scheme of up-gradation of hygiene and quality of street food of the Ministry, 10,000 street vendors across the nation would be identified, profiled and methodology would be designed to upgrade the safety and quality of food they sell. They would also be granted quality certification on the basis of standards which have already been worked out by the Ministry.

Further, 10 "food streets" with ethnic cuisine would also be identified in order to upgrade them in terms of quality and hygiene; support would be given for creation of infrastructure such as drainage, water supply, lighting, etc., so that these efforts result in more hygienic and safe conditions of food preparations.

(ii) National and regional industry associations would identify units and launch a program for capacity building through the implementation of HACCP or ISO 22000 for the food processing units who are members of their Organizations. Upto 10,000 units would be taken up, profiled and detailed programs drawn up for their up-gradation. Certification would be achieved within a period of 18 months.

(iii) A protocol based on best international and trade standards would be prepared and benchmarked against the protocols of HACCP certified units. The field protocol will be evaluated and companies graded into Platinum, Gold and Silver categories.

(iv) 50 food safety laboratories will be identified who would be benchmarked against industry best practices and a plan of action drawn up for their up-gradation. Steps would be initiated to bring them up to best practice levels within 2 years.

(v) Good Agricultural Practices (GAP) have already been identified as a thrust area for improving traceability, hygiene and safety of food items. Over the country as a whole, 10,000 farmers would be identified (approximately 500 in each State) who would be taken in a step by step process to achieve certification of GAP or for organic food. Commercially viable projects would be created for agricultural cum horticultural produce to be produced in these farms.

(vi) Under the Central Food Authority, "Fruit Products Order" and "Meat & Meat Food Products Order" would be reviewed to link them with international standards.

(vii) The existing Food Safety Standards under the Prevention of Food Adulteration Act would be reviewed and sent for approval to Central Food Authority.

(viii) A study will be commissioned to identify the standards prescribed under ***Codex Alimentarius*** which are relevant to Indian markets.

REFERENCES

Government of India (2008), *"Action plan-Food safety and quality"*, Ministry of Food processing industries, New Delhi, www: mofpi.nic.in/FSQY_0809/ Action Plan, accessed March 23, 2010.

Henson, Spencer and John Humphrey (2009), *The Impacts of Private Food Safety Standards on the Food Chain and on Public Standard-Setting Processes*, Joint FAO/WHO Food standards program, paper prepared for Codex Alimentarius Commission, 32nd session, FAO, Rome, June 29-July 4, 2009.

Shepherd, A.W. (2006), *Quality and safety in the traditional horticultural marketing chains of Asia*, Agricultural Management, Marketing and Finance, Occasional paper, FAO, Rome.

APPENDIX 1

Hazard Analysis and Critical Control Point (HACCP) System

Hazard Analysis and Critical Control Point (HACCP) is the major tool for international legislation concerning Good Manufacturing Practices (GMP) for all sectors of the food industry. HACCP is also a key component of many certified standards, and is recognized as a main element of international trade in food products.

HACCP is a risk management tool recognized internationally for use in the management of food safety issues. A HACCP system helps in identifying hazards that affect food safety by hazard identification and to establish critical control limits at critical points during the production process.

Hazard Analysis and Critical Control Point (HACCP) is a systematic and preventive approach applied to food products safety, including pharma industry products, that aims at preventing physical, chemical, and biological hazards as opposed to finished product inspection. After HACCP has identified potential food safety hazards, the key actions, known as critical control points (CCPs) can be taken to reduce or eliminate the risk of the hazards from the production and handling processes. The system is used at all stages of food production and preparation processes including packaging, distribution, etc.

HACCP and its Seven Principles

Principle 1: Conduct a hazard analysis. Determine the food safety hazards and identify the preventive measures which can be applied to control these hazards.

Principle 2: Identify critical control points. A Critical control point (CCP) is a point or procedure in a food manufacturing process at which control can be applied to prevent food safety hazard.

Principle 3: Establish critical limits for each critical control point. A critical limit is the maxima or minima value which can be decided to control, prevent and eliminate physical, biological, or chemical hazard.

Principle 4: Establish critical control point monitoring requirements. Monitoring activities are necessary to ensure that the process is under control at each critical control point.

Principle 5: Establish corrective actions. These are corrective actions that should be taken in the even a critical limit is not met. Corrective actions are intended to ensure that no product is injurious to health or otherwise adulterated.

Principle 6: Establish record keeping procedures. The HACCP regulation requires that all plants maintain certain documents pertaining to hazard analysis and the HACCP plan. Records must be maintained that provide evidence to the monitoring of critical control points, critical limits, verification activities, and the handling of processing deviations.

Principle 7: Establish procedures for ensuring the HACCP system is

working properly. Validation ensures that the plants operate as per specifications and the intended objectives Plants will be required to validate their own HACCP plans. International agencies like the U.S. food safety and inspection service (FSIS) will review HACCP plans for conformance to the rules and regulations.

Verification ensures the HACCP plan is adequate, and working as intended.

Standards

The seven HACCP principles are included in the international ISO 22000. This standard is a complete food safety management system along with HACCP and quality management systems which together form an organization's Total Quality Management (TQM) system.

HACCP Application

HACCP is relevant to all sectors of the food industry, including primary producers, manufacturers, processors and food service operators who want to demonstrate their compliance with national or international food safety legislation requirements.

HACCP Implementation

It involves monitoring, verifying and validating the daily work that is compliant with regulatory requirements in all the stages and all the time.

Website References

http://en.wikipedia.org/wiki/Hazard_Analysis_and_Critical_Control_Points

http://www.bsigroup.co.in/en-in/Assessment-and-certification-services/Management-systems/Standards-and-schemes/HACCP/

http://www.fda.gov/Food/FoodSafety/HazardAnalysisCriticalControlPointsHACCP/

Using Innovation as a Tool for Improving Supply Chain Coordination with the Help of CPFR Model

INTRODUCTION

Innovation is about knowledge for creating new possibilities through combining different knowledge sets. These can be in the form of knowledge about what is technically possible or what particular configuration of this would meet a latent need. Successful innovation management requires that we get hold of and use knowledge about components but also know about how to put those together, which is termed as an architecture of an innovation. (Tidd, Bessant and Pavitt, 2005). Most of the time innovation takes place within a set of rules which are clearly understood by all players who are involved in innovating the product, or its processes to make it a better or improved one by doing generally the incremental or marginal innovations. These can be in the form of variations around the central innovation. But sometimes rules of the game change, and a completely new innovation comes through which dislocates the established rules of the game. This happens with the experimentations by either the new players or existing players who are trying to face up to the new market conditions for survival and growth. Such experimentations are usually accompanied by failures till a dominant design, or organizational format is accepted and begins to set up the new rules of game. Such a process is referred to as a Discontinuous innovation when the existing rules of game are replaced by new rules of game to establish new technology, product or process design.

In this chapter, an attempt has been made to understand as to how the concept of supply chain management has undergone a change through a series of innovations, which has its roots in the 1960s concept of logistics management—a planning tool that seeks to develop a system-wide, integrated view of the firm. Subsequently, supply chain management extends the concept of logistics management to external integration of the firm. The supply chain is conceived as "a series of linked suppliers and customers" (Handfield and Nichols Jr., 1999). It encompasses all activities associated with the flow and transportation of goods from the raw materials stage through the end user plus the required information and financial flows. Supply chain management refers to the coordination and alignment of materials, financial, and information flows for all activities and processes involved in a supply chain (Simchi-Levi *et. al.*, 2003).

Companies are facing difficult business environment and as a result they are not able to make forecasts in medium to long-term. Consumer constraints are becoming more obvious as they require and purchase smaller quantities, exhibit higher variation in their buying practices, go for increased customization, prefer higher quality, and shorter delivery products. It is therefore important for companies to be able to adapt quickly to achieve an overall efficiency. Overall efficiency is the purpose of integration and co-ordination among supply chain partners. A change in coordination has been observed among companies from an earlier version of supply chain where each partner-company operated independently in its self-interest by using only locally available information, to a supply chain with a fully coordinated decision-making approach, in which all information and decisions are aligned to accomplish the system-wide objectives. However, even in such networks, the supply chain partners remain autonomous entities and are governed by their individual objectives and constraints. On the other hand, a well coordinated supply chain management can be a tremendous asset for companies as it can reduce inventories and costs, improve the profit margin, and offer a better return on investments. However, companies may still require to overcome problems related to data, technology, and or vendors. Obtaining and using quality data requires a few considerations. In order to do proper forecasting, the predictions must be based on data from a large sample. If few orders are used as the basis for the predictions, the results are likely to be quite unreliable. Additionally, managers generally do not realize that data can change or show variations in short period of time. For these reasons, SCM data must be continuously re-evaluated in order to make it realistic. Also, a proper training can go a long way to improve the data collection and processing to improve the overall effectiveness of SCM. While vendors, suppliers, and other processors are the necessary elements of the supply chain, companies need to meet with the decision-makers in those companies and outline clearly what benefits supply chain coordination will bring for them(Affonso, *et. al.*, 2006).

Supply Chain Management: A Complex Coordination Problem

Supply chains consist of networks of organizations which are involved, through upstream and downstream linkages, in the different processes and activities that produce value for the ultimate customer in the form of products and services. SCM is also a coordination and integration of entire range of activities associated with moving of raw materials, components or goods from the basic stage through to the end-user. This includes activities like procurement, in-bound and out-bound transportation, production scheduling, order processing and fulfillment, inventory management, warehousing, and customer service. When it comes to decision making, the understanding of the co-ordination mechanisms helps in selecting the best available alternative. The supply chain partners when forming a collaborative supply chain bring with them new resources and constraints. Collaboration can also contribute to the reduction in local shortcomings if tasks and responsibilities are well managed by supply chain partners (Affonso *et. al.*, 2006).

Demand Management

Demand management is generally related to estimation and management of customer's demand with a view to use this information to streamline and enhance operational effectiveness. The traditional supply chains usually start at the point of manufacture or assembly point and end-up with the sale of product to individual consumers or business buyers. In spite of understanding of the supply chain performance enhancement metrics such as use of technology, information sharing, inventory turnover, delivery efficiency, the manufacturers continue to play a major role in determining what product-mix will be available for sale, at what point, in how much quantity and for what duration of time. However, in reality there might be a mismatch between manufacturing and demand at the point of consumption-regardless whether it is at retailers, retail customers or business consumers' level. If the members of the supply chain pay any attention to the demand management, the efforts are likely to bring-in results for the entire supply chain.

The key point here is that there should be collaboration between supply chain members—right from the manufacturing through the customer. They must collaborate on activities related to product flows, services, information and capital. The desired result should be to create additional value for the end-user or consumer for whom all supply chain operations have been constituted.

In order to develop an effective demand management, a manager must identify the problems and needs of the consumers; this information must be shared with other supply chain members. They should be in position to develop products and services which have the capacity to solve customers' problems. The supply chain members should also make use of reliable and efficient transportation facilities, logistics and employ distribution methods and strategies to deliver products to the consumers in the desired format.

Key Supply Chain Management Issues

These mainly relate to :

Network Configuration: This refers to the re-organization of distribution network consisting of production facilities, distribution centers, warehouses, cross-docks and customers. This may happen on account of changing demand patterns, location of production plants or warehouses, addition of new suppliers and/or demand centers.

Distribution strategy which includes:

decision-making with respect to operational control—whether it should be centralized, decentralized or shared;

delivery systems—whether direct shipment, cross-docking, or direct store delivery system would be appropriate;

mode of transportation—how the supplies/consignments should be dispatched—whether by land—rail or road route, or by sea or air carriers. Besides, managers have to work on trade-offs between freight, delivery time and customer satisfaction.

Replenishment strategy is used to decide whether pull, push or combination of both systems to replenish inventory.

Logistics control—This refers to the transportation ownership whether a firm should have owner-operated, contract carrier or use 3 PL logistics.

In order to achieve the lowest net logistics cost, the above activities must be coordinated well. Trade-offs exist that increase the total cost if only one of the activities is optimized. For example, full truckload (FTL) freight rates are more economical on a per unit cost basis rather than paying more for less than truckload (LTL) shipments, which turn out to be expensive in terms of freight costs and effective or net price of the consignment. On the other hand, FTL consignment may result in increase in inventory holding costs. It is therefore important to take a systems approach when planning logistical activities. These trade-offs are key to developing the efficient and effective Logistics and SCM strategy.

Other important supply chain management issues are :

- **Information:** It refers to the Integration of processes through the supply chain to share information, including customer demand, forecasts, inventory, transportation, and possibility of collaboration as well.
- **Inventory management:** This mainly relates to Quantity and location of inventory-be it raw materials, work-in-process (WIP) or finished goods inventory.
- **Cash-Flow:** It aims at finalizing the payment terms and the methodologies for exchanging funds between trading partners across the supply chain.

Since supply chain execution is managing and coordinating the movement of materials, information and funds across the supply chain, the flow of information, and planning activity takes place in both upstream and downstream directions.

Role of Forecasting

A major component of demand management is **forecasting**—the quantity of product that will be purchased by consumers or end-users. The main focus of the forecasting is to determine the primary demand. One of the key objectives is to anticipate and respond to the primary demand across the supply chain. There are short term forecasts and they extend to medium term to long-term forecasts. One of the objectives of integrated supply chain management is to anticipate and respond to primary demand as it unfolds itself in the market.

Collaboration

Collaboration between different members of supply chain is now recognized as a joint activity to plan, forecast and replenish the stocks/ inventories ranging from raw materials/goods, components, sub-assemblies, and assemblies to finished products across the supply chain.

Firms may pursue collaboration because it creates strategic advantages resulting in revenue and profit growth through increased market share, access to strategic knowledge or operational effectiveness through risk-sharing and by achieving economies of scale. One of the initiatives which is aimed at achieving realistic supply chain integration is **Collaborative Planning, Forecasting and Replenishment (CPFR®).** It is a business model that takes a collective approach to supply chain management and information exchange among trading partners. It uses common metrics, standard language, and firm agreements to improve supply chain efficiencies for all participants. The driving force of CPFR is a synchronized forecast of supply chain members. Every member or the trading partner in a CPFR process—supplier, manufacturer, distributor, retailer—can view and amend forecast data to optimize the process from end to end. Essentially, CPFR puts a break to guesstimates in forecasting. It means that manufacturers and retailers share their plans, with detailed knowledge of each others' assumptions and constraints.

An Overview of the Model

Collaborative Planning, Forecasting and Replenishment (CPFR) is a business practice that aims at planning and fulfillment of customer demand by combining the inputs of multiple trading partners. This practice started in 1995 as a pilot program between Wal-Mart and Warner Lambert called CFAR, for "Collaborative Forecasting and Replenishment." In 1997, the **Voluntary inter-industry Commerce Solutions Association (VICS)** developed the CPFR model and in 1998 published the first CPFR guidelines. A joint committee of **Voluntary Inter-industry Commerce Solutions Association** (VICS) and the **Efficient Consumer Response (ECR)** organization revised the guidelines in 2001 to incorporate global requirements, sanctioned by the Global Commerce Initiative (GCI).

Since then, according to the VICS, more than 300 companies have implemented the CPFR process in the USA. As these companies worked with CPFR, shortcomings were identified and innovations were developed, which were included in a 2004 major model revision by the VICS CPFR committee.

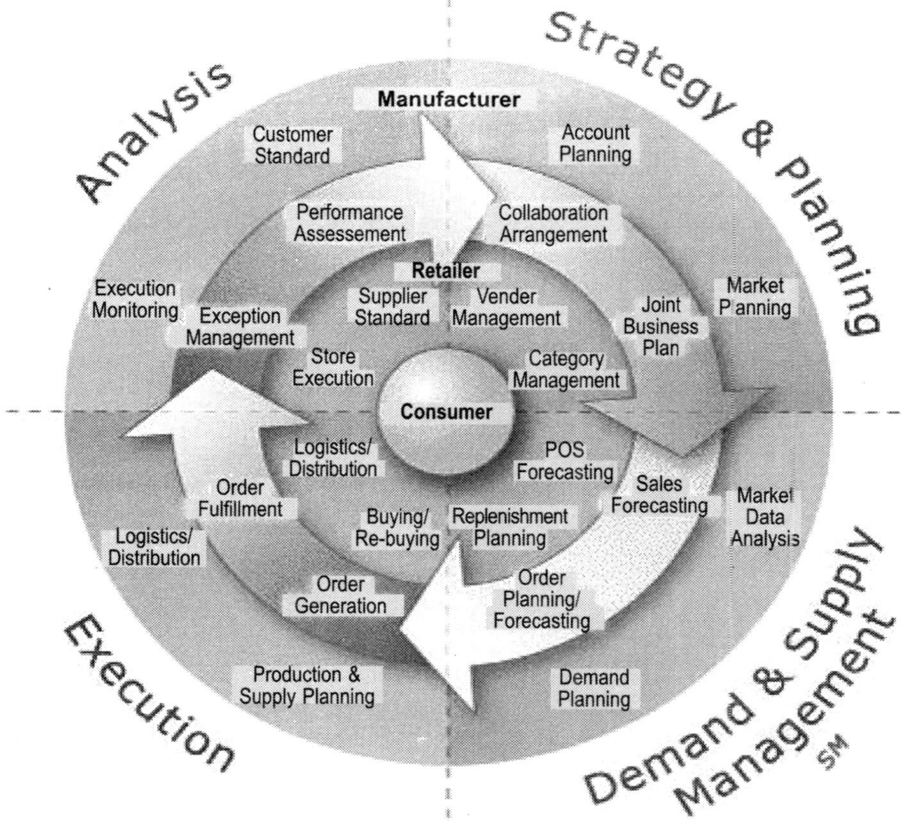

By linking sales and marketing to supply chain planning and execution processes, CPFR increases products' availability while reducing inventory, transportation and logistics costs. The experience gained from pilot projects and production planning as per CPFR guidelines has provided many insights.

Over time, the VICS initiative reported benefits of CPFR in terms of inventory reductions of 10 to 40 per cent across supply chains. However, several barriers to adoption of CPFR have been noticed, which include difficulties in information exchange, investments in human resources as CPFR is process-intensive.

Salient Features of Collaborative Planning, Forecasting and Replenishment (CPFR) Model

CPFR is a business practice that combines the intelligence of multiple trading partners in planning and fulfillment of customer demand.

- Links sales and marketing practices to supply chain planning and execution processes

- Objective is to increase product availability to the customer while reducing inventory, transportation and logistics costs
- The consumer is the ultimate focus of all efforts
- "Buyers" (retailers) and "sellers" (manufacturers) collaborate at every level
- Joint forecasting and order planning reduces fluctuations in the supply chain
- The timing and quantity of physical flows is synchronized across all parties
- Exception management is made systematic.

CPFR is an initiative that facilitates the reengineering of the relationships between trading partners and their transactions. This initiative is based on an industry-recognized set of standards. CPFR model provides platform for supply chain partner collaboration.

CPFR creates a win-win scenario, by bringing the buyer and seller together so that their goals are compatible. By competing in the market as one, the buyer and seller form a value chain that comes out ahead of other buyers and sellers who are still negotiating prices.

CPFR has evolved from a previously tried Supply Chain Solutions. CPFR is considered to be the next stage in the evolution of supply chain initiatives. Older supply chain operations had gaps in their practices, including financial plans taking precedence over forecasts and non-integrated supply chain planning. This resulted in higher inventory levels, and lower order execution rates. Companies were not realizing the benefits that they had expected. For successful CPFR adoption and implementation, the following points are summarized:

(1) ***Collaboration is the foundation.*** The real key to a successful implementation of CPFR is the forging of cultural alliances rather than traditional supplier-customer relationship . Such alliances involve peer-to-peer relationships, common goals and measures, and governance through formal communication points. Collaborative efforts should begin by first developing internal cross-functional teams and measures and then linking them to the participant's comparable teams and measures. Linked performance measures should focus on common goals.

(2) ***Both participants must be ready.*** Both participants must be focused on deeper supply chain visibility such as data on sales to the end consumer. Participant readiness must be assessed to determine the appropriate business model. A standardized model might not work with every customer. No single business process fits all customers; thus, collaborative processes must be customized. Assessments of customer readiness should gauge management stability, high-level ownership of distribution and the current or potential share of the manufacturer's sales going to each customer.

(3) ***Customer service focus is critical to success***. Customer intimacy is

a real strength to sales team. The company must learnt to adapt to the customer wants to conduct business—regionally or locally.

(4) ***Time-based decision-making is key.*** Both participants must adopt a common calendar for planning. In addition, a firm must standardize the decision-making dates, and ensure that both participants have appropriate information and plans ready for concurrent decision-making.

(5) ***Collaboration is focused on building relationships.*** The strength of these relationships determines how long collaboration will continue and how successful it will be. One of the most significant determinants will be the development of one-to-one relationships.

(6) ***Organizational roles must change.*** The organization must change to become customer-focused rather than product-focused. Customer- and supplier-focused teams help develop the strong relationships that form the basis of all interactions.

Limitations of CPFR Model

The weakness of CPFR efforts has been due to its over-emphasis on replenishment. While streamlined replenishment is main objective, effort directed towards planning and forecasting is an important input. Many CPFR projects fail due to lack of executive support, lack of collaboration effort or because of unclear objectives at the outset, or they cannot work consistently with many of the company's key trading participants. It is especially true when they involve many items and locations, high degrees of required automated processing and lots of exception management. **Exception management** is the practice of investigating, resolving and handling such occurrences either by using skilled staff or through the application of software tools. Good exception management can contribute to efficiency of business processes.

Reasons for Slower Rate of CPFR Adoption and its Implementation

CPFR pilot projects undertaken between companies, such as Nabisco and Wegman's, Kimberly-Clark and Kmart, and Wal-Mart and Sara Lee, have resulted in significant improvements in product availability, increased sales and reduced inventory (VICS, 1999). However, the adoption rate has been slower than expected. Most implementations involve only two or a few parties, and only a limited number of products. Large-scale implementations were not observed, especially in Europe. Several reasons have been presented to explain the difficulties in implementing CPFR. There have been problems related to trust and information sharing by adversaries, change management and the difficulty in reaching critical mass. The single most important obstacle in Europe, might be due to the retailer's lack of forecasting processes and resources.

The CPFR model was developed based on work done by Wal-Mart, a retailer with exceptional logistics processes, in the area of demand planning and forecasting (Smaros, 2002).

REFERENCES

Affonso, R., Marcotte, and Grabot, B. (2006), "Coordination model in supply chain" in Intelligent Production Machine Systems, Conference. *http://conference.iproms.org* accessed Dec. 27, 2009.

Aqua Management Consulting Group, Five Essential Elements of integrated Supply Chain Management-How best in class manage their supply chains", a White paper, *www.aquamcg.com*, accessed, Nov. 18, 2009.

Bowersox, D., Closs, D., and Cooper, M.B. (2008), "Customer accommodation", In *Supply Chain Logistics Management*, 2nd ed., TMH, New Delhi.

Businessweek (2009). "Supply Chain Collaboration-CPFR means process and practice", http:*//www.businessweek/adsections/chain/2*, accessed June 16, and September 21, 2009.

Cederlund J., Kohli, R., Sherer, S., and Yao, Yuliang (2007), "How Motorola put CPFR into action", *Supply Chain Management Review*, October 2007.

Coyle et al. (2009). "Demand management and customer service", In *A Logistics approach to Supply Chain Management*, Cengage Learning, New Delhi.

Handfield, R. and Nicholas, E., Jr. (1999), "Introduction to Supply Chain Management" Prentice-Hall, New York.

J.D. Edward and Company (2003), "CPFR-Collaborative, Planning, Forecasting and Replenishment, Delivering results for manufacturers-serving the retail, A white paper", Denver, CO, USA. *http://wwwjdedwards.com*, accessed June 16, 2009.

Power, D. (2008), "Capability and practice in procurement collaboration: a vendor's perspective of benefits", *Operations and Supply Chain Management*, Vol. 1, No. 2, pp. 72-84.

Simchi-Levi, D., Kaminsky, P., Simchi-Levi, E. (2003), "Designing and managing the Supply Chain-concepts, strategies and case studies", Tata-McGraw-Hill, New Delhi.

Smaros, J. (2002), "Collaborative Forecasting in practice", a paper presented at the *Logistics Research Network Conference*, Birmingham, U.K.

Tidd, J., Bessant, J., and Pavitt (2005), "Managing Innovation-Integrating technological, market and organizational Change", 3rd ed. Wiley India, New Delhi.

VICS CPFR Committee. (2007). *http://www.vics.org/committees/cpfr/*, accessed Aug. 21, 2009.

Trends and Challenges in Supplies of Primary Agri-Food Products in India

India's agriculture sector has an impressive track record in managing the food supplies despite population increases, and several droughts the country has gone through. This has been possible due to the development of infrastructure, establishment of Research and Development (R&D) institutions, technology application at field level aimed at increasing yields, multiple cropping systems, extension activities for educating the farmers on crop/dairy/livestock management practices, and policy support of the successive Governments. These initiatives have resulted in tripling of food grains yields, and food grains production increased from 51 million metric tons in 1950–51 to 217 million metric tons in 2006–07. Production of oilseeds, sugarcane, and cotton have also increased more than four-fold over the period, reaching 24 million tons and 355 million tons and 23 million bales, respectively, in 2006–07 (Planning Commission, GOI, 2008).

Agriculture provides significant support to the overall economic growth of the country. As one of the world's largest agricultural economies, the agriculture sector (including allied sectors comprising forestry and fishing) accounted for 15.7 per cent of the GDP (at constant 2004-05 prices), in 2008-09, compared to 16.4 per cent a year ago, and 18.9 per cent in 2004-05, and contributed approximately 10.2 per cent of total exports during 2008-09 *vis-à-vis* 12.05 per cent in 2007-08. Notwithstanding the fact that the share of this sector in the GDP has been declining over the years, its role remains critical as it provides employment to around 52 per cent of the workforce. The share of agriculture alone in GDP during 2008-09 was 13.2 per cent, a slight decline from 13.9 per cent in 2007-08. The growth of GDP for agriculture sector during 2008-09 declined to 1.1 per cent (1.6 per cent inclusive of agriculture and allied sectors) compared with 5 per cent during 2007-08 (4.7 per cent inclusive of agriculture and allied sectors)(Economic Survey, 2009-10).

Crop Production: 2008-09

For three consecutive years, from 2005-06 to 2008-09, food grains, production recorded an average annual increase of over 8 million tons. Total food grains production in 2008-09 was estimated at 233.88 million tons as against 230.78 million tons in 2007-08. The share of rice and wheat are estimated at 99.2 and 80.6 million tons in 2008-09 compared with 96.7 and 78.6 million tons in 2007-08. However, the production of major commercial crops-oilseeds, sugarcane, cotton declined to 28.2 million tons (MT), 273.9 million tons, and 23.2 million bales in 2008-09 compared to 29.75 MT, 348.2 MT and 25.9 million bales respectively in 2007-08 levels (Economic Survey, 2009-10).

Crop Production: 2009-10—*Kharif* (summer) Season Prospects

Deficit rainfall during the south-west monsoon season in 2009, particularly in July and August, severely affected prospects of *kharif* crops, especially paddy. The recovery of monsoon in September, which was followed by post-monsoon (October-December) cumulative rainfall of 8 per cent above normal proved to be slightly beneficial for the *kharif* crops, and improved the prospects of *Rabi* (winter) season crops in 2009-10. As per the first advance estimates (*kharif* season only) for 2009-10, production of food grains is estimated at 98.83 million tones which is lower than the target of 125.15 million tones set for the year as also lower than the fourth advance estimates (*kharif* only) of 117.70 million tons for 2008-09 (Economic Survey, 2009-10).

Note: Total food grains production in India is a sum of *Kharif* (summer season) and *Rabi* (winter season) crops. While *Kharif* crops are planted in July and harvested in Oct-November, Rabi crops are planted in November and harvested in the March-April following year, thus completing the planting to harvest cycle in the same agricultural year. Both planting and harvesting dates can show variations of plus/minus of 2-3 weeks. In case of paddy (rice is obtained after milling), the nursery can even start before July due to the availability of irrigation facility. Also, due to variations in agro-climatic conditions in India, a crop like rice can be planted in some regions during months when it is winter season in North India. The fiscal year in India is on April-March basis, while the calendar year is from January to December.

Rainfall

More than 75 per cent of annual rainfall is received during the southwest monsoon season (June-September). In January-February 2009, the cumulative rainfall all over the country was 46 per cent less rainfall than the LPA (Long period Average). In the pre-monsoon period between March-May 2009, rainfall was 32 per cent below the LPA. During the 2009 south-west monsoon, the country as a whole received 23 per cent less rainfall than the LPA. Central

India, north-east India, north-west India and the southern peninsula received 20 per cent, 27 per cent, 36 per cent and 4 per cent deficient rainfall respectively. At district level, 9 per cent of districts received excess rainfall, 32 per cent normal rainfall, 51 per cent deficient rainfall and 8 per cent scanty rainfall.

Out of 36 subdivisions, 23 recorded deficient rainfall during the south-west monsoon in 2009. Out of the remaining 13 subdivisions, only three recorded excess rainfall and the remaining 10 normal rainfall. Out of 526 meteorological districts for which data are available, 215 (41 per cent) received excess/ normal rainfall and the remaining 311 (59 per cent) received deficient/ scanty rainfall during the season. During the post-monsoon season (October-December) of 2009, the country as a whole has received 8 per cent above normal rainfall (Economic Survey, 2009-10).

Price Policy for Agricultural Produce

The Government of India's (GOI's) price policy for agricultural commodities aims to ensure remunerative prices to the farmers for their produce with a view to encouraging higher investment in agriculture and consequently production. On the other hand, GOI also tries to safeguard the interests of consumers by making supplies available at reasonable prices. The price policy also seeks to develop a balanced and integrated price structure for the economy. In this context, the Government announces minimum support prices (MSPs) each season for major agricultural commodities and organizes purchase operations through public and cooperative agencies. The designated Central nodal agencies intervene in the market to undertake procurement operations with the objective of ensuring that market prices do not fall below the MSPs fixed by the Government.

The Government fixes the support prices for various agricultural commodities which are based on the recommendations of the Commission for Agricultural Costs and Prices (CACP), the views of State Governments and Central Ministries, besides other relevant factors that are considered important for fixation of support prices (Economic Survey, 2009-10).

Food Management

The main objectives of food management include procurement of food grains from farmers at remunerative prices, distribution of food grains to consumers, particularly the vulnerable sections of society, at affordable prices and maintenance of food buffers for food security and price stability. The instruments used are the MSP and central issue price (CIP). The central agency which undertakes procurement, distribution and storage of food grains is the Food Corporation of India (FCI). Procurement at MSP is open-ended, while distribution is governed by the scale of allocation and its off-take by the beneficiaries. The off-take of food grains is primarily under the targeted public distribution system (TPDS) and for other welfare schemes of the Government of India. Off-take of food grains under the TPDS has been increasing in the last five years and has gone up from 29.7 million tons in 2004-05 to 34.8 million tons in 2008-09(Economic Survey, 2009-10).

Procurement of Food Grains

Overall procurement of rice and wheat which was 35.8 million tons in 2006-07, increased marginally to 37.6 million tons in 2007-08. However, increased MSP along with various other steps taken by the Government resulted in record wheat procurement of 22.69 million tons in 2008-09 and 25.38 million tons in 2009-10 (April to December). In case of rice, the procurement in 2008-09 was 32.8 million tons and 22.9 million tons in 2009-10 (April-December). The record procurement of rice and wheat during 2007-08, 2008-09 and 2009-10 (April-December) has resulted in comfortable food stock availability to meet the TPDS needs and buffer stocks norms.

As in earlier years, procurement of food grains by the FCI continues to be higher in Punjab, Haryana, Uttar Pradesh and Andhra Pradesh states. These four States accounted for nearly 69.7 per cent of the rice procured for the Central Pool in 2006-07, 69.46 per cent in 2007-08 and 67.47 per cent in 2008-09. Punjab and Haryana which accounted for 91.1 per cent of procurement of wheat for the Central Pool in 2007-08, contributed 66.88 per cent in 2008-09 and 69.53 per cent in 2009-10, which indicated an increased share in procurement by other contributing states (Economic Survey, 2009-10).

Buffer Stock

The stock position of food grains as on January 2010 was 47.4 million tons comprising 24.3 million tons of rice and 23.1 million tons of wheat against buffer norms of 11.8 million tones and 8.2 million tons respectively. This is adequate to meet the requirements under the TPDS and welfare schemes during the current financial year. Earlier, the stock of food grains in the Central Pool at 15.7 million tons as on April 1, 2006 was marginally lower than the minimum buffer norm of 16.2 million tons. This increased to 17.9 million tons on April 1, 2007, and 19.6 million tons on April 1, 2008, and 35.0 million tons of food grains as on April 1, 2009, which consisted of 21.6 million tons of rice and 13.4 million tons of wheat against the buffer norm of 12.2 million tons and 4.0 million tons respectively (Economic Survey, 2009-10).

Open Market Sale Scheme

In order to check inflationary trends in the food economy, the Government took a decision in August 2008 to release wheat into the open market under the Open Market Sales Scheme (OMSS -Domestic). These releases have been made through (a) allocation to State/UT Governments for distribution to retail consumers; and (b) sale to bulk consumers by the FCI through open tenders. The release of wheat under the OMSS has helped stabilize wholesale prices of wheat (Economic Survey, 2009-10).

Recent Trends in Economic Growth

The fiscal year 2009-10 started on a difficult note for India. There was a significant slowdown in the growth rate in the second half of 2008-09, after the financial crisis of industrialized nations in 2007, which later spread to the world economy. The growth rate of the gross domestic product (GDP) in 2008-

09 was 6.7 per cent, compared with growth rate of around 6 per cent in the last two quarters of this fiscal. There was an expectation that this trend would continue for some time as the impact of the economic slowdown in the developed world was felt in the system. A delayed and severely subnormal monsoon added to the overall uncertainty. The continued recession in the developed world, for the better part of 2009-10, meant a sluggish export recovery and a slowdown in financial flows into the economy. Despite all these negatives, the economy posted a remarkable recovery both in terms of overall growth but also in terms of certain fundamentals (Economic Survey, 2009-10).

As per the advance estimates of GDP for 2009-10, released by the Central Statistical Organisation (CSO), the economy is expected to grow at 7.2 per cent in 2009-10, with the industrial and the service sectors growing at 8.2 and 8.7 per cent respectively. The fast-paced recovery of the economy underscores the effectiveness of the policy response of the Government in the wake of the financial crisis. A major concern during the year 2009-10, especially in the second half, was the emergence of high double-digit food inflation. On a year-on-year basis, wholesale price index (WPI) inflation in December 2009 was 7.3 per cent. The upsurge in prices in the second half of 2009-10 had been confined to food items only. For the week ending January 30, 2010, the inflation in primary food articles was at 17.9 per cent, and that in fuel, power light and lubricants at 10.4 per cent. A significant part of this inflation could be explained by supply-side bottlenecks in a few essential commodities, precipitated by the delayed and sub-normal southwest monsoons (Economic Survey, 2009-10).

Challenges Facing the Indian Agriculture

The Mid-Term Appraisal (MTA) for the Tenth Five Year Plan(2002-2007) drew the attention to the fact that agriculture, inclusive of allied sectors, had lost its dynamism after the mid-1990s. During the last decade, Indian agriculture has faced a number of serious challenges, and recent trends have raised concern regarding food security, farmers' income, and poverty, etc.

The main issues which were highlighted by the MTA of agriculture sector pertained to the following:

- Slowdown in growth.
- Widening of performance differences between irrigated and rain-fed areas.
- Increased vulnerability of agricultural sector to volatility of world commodity prices after the trade liberalization of 1990's. This adversely affected the regions cultivating commercial crops such as cotton and oilseeds.
- Uneven and slow development of technology.
- Inefficient use of available technology and inputs.
- Lack of adequate incentives and appropriate institutions.
- Degradation of natural resource base.
- Rapid and widespread decline in groundwater table, with negative impact on small and marginal farmers.

- Increased non-agricultural demand for land and water as a result of the higher level of urbanization, and GDP growth.

The supply side performance of agriculture is affected by a large number of factors, which interact with each other. These factors relate to the natural resource base, including rainfall, technology, infrastructure, irrigation, besides the economic environment and prices. Analysis by the Steering Group for the Eleventh Plan has identified technological change(using yield potential of varieties of major crops released by the National Agricultural Research System), public investment (including investment on irrigation), and diversification (represented by area under fruits and vegetables) as the most important determinants of growth. The following table summarizes the changes in growth rates of major indicators in eighties, nineties, and from mid-nineties to 2005-06. (Planning Commission, 2008)

Trends in Growth Rates of Selected Indicators of Indian Agriculture: 1980–81 to 2005–06

(% per Year)

Period	*1980–81 to 1990–91*	*1990–91 to 1996–97*	*1996–97 to 2005–06*
Technology#	3.3	2.81	0.00
Gross irrigated area	2.28	2.62	0.51*
Public sector net fixed capital stock	3.86	1.92	1.42*
Terms of trade	0.190	0.95	-1.69*
Area under fruits and vegetables	5.60	5.60	2.71@
NPK use	8.17	2.45	2.30
Credit supply	3.72	7.51	14.37*
Electricity consumed in agriculture	14.07	9.44	-0.53@
Total cropped area	0.43	0.43	–0.10
Net sown area	–0.08	0.04	–0.22
Cropping intensity	0.51	0.39	0.12

Note: # Yield potential of new varieties released of paddy, rapeseed/mustard, groundnut, wheat, maize, and cotton; * Upto 2003–04;

Additionally, the Eleventh Plan advocated an increase in public investment from 3% of agricultural GDP to about 4%, and to ensure that future growth was more efficient, sustainable, and inclusive. This could be achieved by focusing on the following:

- With availability of land and water as fixed variables, growth in agriculture can be achieved only by increasing productivity per unit of these natural resources through an effective use of improved technology. The research system has so far focused mainly on breeding varieties that increase the yield potential of individual crops by enabling more intensive use of inputs. Although such research did increase potential yields substantially in the past, it put less emphasis on efficient and sustainable use of soil nutrients and water. The research also has to identify location-specific farming systems with proper mix of crops and livestock, especially for rain-fed areas. Besides, the potential yields of new varieties being released appear to have reached limits, suggesting that the 'technology fatigue' has to be countered by changing research priorities suitably.

- At the same time, yield gaps between what is achievable under R&D trials and what can be achieved at the farmer's field with adoption of available technology needs to be reduced. Since yield gaps vary considerably from crop-to-crop and from region-to-region, the strategy must enable specific plans for each agro-climatic region. This will also require much stronger links between research, extension, and farmers.
- The pressing need to accelerate agriculture growth should not be at the cost of sustainability of limited natural resource base. Deforestation has affected both soils and water along with soil degradation and overexploitation of groundwater. In addition to erosion, salinity, and alkalinity, soils are losing soil carbon and micronutrients due to irrational and unbalanced fertilizer use. Rapid expansion of groundwater use for irrigation was a key factor in the relatively rapid growth of agriculture between the mid-1960s and late 1980s. But further expansion should be strictly monitored, especially in regions where water levels have dropped causing concern about future sustainability (Planning Commission, 2008).

Challenges facing agricultural research can be summarized as follows:

- Orientation of public sector research with adequate funding has to be re-introduced for crops like pigeon pea, soybean, and mustard.
- Indigenous plant types that inherently possess genes responsible for higher nutritive value (more protein, micronutrients, etc.) need to be identified for enriching nutrients in rain fed crops.
- A major research thrust is warranted in areas of balanced and site-specific nutrient supply and efficient water management strategies.
- Integrated Pest Management (IPM) needs greater emphasis. The existing package of practices is not fully integrated between various plant protection sciences. There is a need for interdisciplinary research in plant protection sciences.
- In Horticulture, the research agenda needs to emphasize survey of indigenous biodiversity for resistance to various biotic and abiotic stresses for improvement in production, productivity, and quality of produce.
- With regard to animal feeds, research should explore technologies to augment feed resources, including genetic modification of microorganism to utilize high lignin in forage grasses.
- The health of the human population is connected to the health of the animal with several diseases being common to both man and

animal. Serious attention to animal health care, disease diagnosis, and prophylactics will go a long way in ensuring human health also.

- Overall, there is a need to identify integrated farming systems in different agro-ecological regions, internalizing synergies of different components to enhance resource utilization, income, and livelihood generation and minimize environmental loading (Planning Commission, 2008).

Horticulture

The horticulture sector contributes around 28 per cent of the GDP in agriculture from about 13 per cent of the area. It also provides 37 per cent of the total exports of agricultural commodities. The sector covers a wide range of fruit crops, vegetables crops, potato and tuber crops, ornamental crops, medicinal and aromatic crops, spices, and plantation crops. Introduction of new crops such as mushroom, bamboo, and bee keeping (for improving the crop productivity) has further expanded the scope of horticulture.

India accounts for an area of 4.96 million hectares (MH) under fruit crops with a production of 49.3 million metric tons (MMT). During the period 1991–92 to 2001-02, growth in area, production, and productivity of fruits was recorded at the rate of 3.4 per cent, 4.2 per cent, and 0.7 per cent respectively. Area growth accelerated between 2001–02 and 2004–05 to 7.4 per cent but with negligible acceleration in production growth. Among various States, Maharashtra ranks first and contributes 27 per cent in area and 21.5 per cent in production. Andhra Pradesh ranks second in area and production contributing 13 per cent and 16 per cent of fruits in the country.

Total vegetable production in India before independence was 15 million metric tons (MMT) and since independence for decades the growth rate was stabilized around 0.5%. The impetus on vegetable research and policy intervention to promote vegetable crops witnessed a sudden spurt in growth rate of 2.5 per cent, a hike of five times during the last decade. The production in this period increased from 58.53 million metric tons in 1991-92 to 101.43 million metric tons in 2004-05. During the period, productivity of vegetables increased from 10.5 mt/hectare to 15.0 mt/hectare. While West Bengal continues to be the leading State in area and production, the productivity is higher in Tamil Nadu followed by Uttar Pradesh and Bihar (Planning Commission, 2008).

Post-harvest Management (PHM)

At present, the post-harvest losses are about 20–30 per cent in different horticultural crops. This is due to inadequate infrastructure development for PHM including pre-cooling facilities. Packing materials like corrugated fibre-board boxes, cling films, sachets, wraps, etc., have been standardized for fresh horticultural produce. Tetra packs of different products are now available freely.

Agro-processing

Demand for horticultural products will be supported by developments in agro-processing. In fact, there is a rising demand for new products such as dried powder based milk mix, juice punches, banana chips and fingers, essential oils from citrus, fruit wines, dehydrated products from grape, pomegranate, mango, apricot and coconut, grape wines, value-added coconut products like tender coconut, milk powder, and pouched tender coconut water. Improved blending and packaging of tea and coffee have opened new markets. Consumer-friendly products such as frozen green peas, ready-to-use salad mixes, vegetable sprouts, and ready-to-cook fresh cut vegetables are major retail items. The private corporate sector has a major role to play in developing this aspect of the agriculture–consumer linkage.

REFERENCES

Government of India (2009-10), "Economic Survey", *http://economic survey*, accessed March 24 and 26, 2010.

Government of India (2008-09), "Economic Survey", *http://economic survey*, accessed January 12, 2010.

Planning Commission (2008), "Eleventh Five Year Plan, 2007-12, Vol. III, Agriculture, Rural Development, Industry, Services, and Physical Infrastructure, GOI, New Delhi.

Reserve Bank of India (2010), "RBI Bulletin", March 2010, Vol. LXIV (3).

STATISTICAL TABLES

APPENDIX TABLE 1

Area under Cultivation—Foodgrains

(Million hectares)

Year	*Cereals*				*Pulses*	*Total Foodgrains (5+6)*
	Rice	*Wheat*	*Coarse Cereals*	*Total (2+3+4)*		
1	*2*	*3*	*4*	*5*	*6*	*7*
1950-51	30.81	9.75	37.67	**78.23**	19.09	**97.32**
1951-52	29.83	9.47	38.88	**78.18**	18.78	**96.96**
1952-53	29.97	9.83	42.45	**82.25**	19.84	**102.09**
1953-54	31.29	10.68	45.37	**87.34**	21.73	**109.07**
1954-55	30.77	11.26	43.92	**85.95**	21.91	**107.86**
1955-56	31.52	12.37	43.45	**87.34**	23.22	**110.56**
1956-57	32.28	13.52	42.02	**87.82**	23.32	**111.14**
1957-58	32.30	11.73	42.91	**86.94**	22.54	**109.48**
1958-59	33.17	12.62	44.66	**90.45**	24.31	**114.76**
1959-60	33.82	13.38	43.79	**90.99**	24.83	**115.82**
1960-61	34.13	12.93	44.96	**92.02**	23.56	**115.58**
1961-62	34.69	13.57	44.73	**92.99**	24.24	**117.23**
1962-63	35.69	13.59	44.29	**93.57**	24.27	**117.84**
1963-64	35.81	13.50	43.93	**93.24**	24.18	**117.42**
1964-65	36.46	13.42	44.35	**94.23**	23.88	**118.11**
1965-66	35.47	12.57	44.34	**92.38**	22.72	**115.10**
1966-67	35.25	12.84	45.09	**93.18**	22.12	**115.30**
1967-68	36.44	14.99	47.34	**98.77**	22.65	**121.42**
1968-69	36.97	15.96	46.24	**99.17**	21.26	**120.43**
1969-70	37.68	16.63	47.24	**101.55**	22.02	**123.57**
1970-71	37.59	18.24	45.95	**101.78**	22.54	**124.32**
1971-72	37.76	19.14	43.57	**100.47**	22.15	**122.62**
1972-73	36.69	19.46	42.21	**98.36**	20.92	**119.28**
1973-74	38.29	18.58	46.24	**103.11**	23.43	**126.54**
1974-75	37.89	18.01	43.15	**99.05**	22.03	**121.08**
1975-76	39.48	20.45	43.80	**103.73**	24.45	**128.18**
1976-77	38.51	20.92	41.94	**101.37**	22.98	**124.35**
1977-78	40.28	21.46	42.28	**104.02**	23.50	**127.52**
1978-79	40.48	22.64	42.23	**105.35**	23.66	**129.01**
1979-80	39.42	22.17	41.36	**102.95**	22.26	**125.21**
1980-81	40.15	22.28	41.78	**104.21**	22.46	**126.67**
1981-82	40.71	22.14	42.45	**105.30**	23.84	**129.14**
1982-83	38.26	23.57	40.43	**102.26**	22.83	**125.09**

(Contd.)

1	2	3	4	5	6	7
1983-84	41.24	24.67	41.71	**107.62**	23.54	**131.16**
1984-85	41.16	23.56	39.21	**103.93**	22.74	**126.67**
1985-86	41.14	23.00	39.47	**103.61**	24.42	**128.03**
1986-87	41.17	23.13	39.74	**104.04**	23.16	**127.20**
1987-88	38.81	23.06	36.55	**98.42**	21.27	**119.69**
1988-89	41.73	24.11	38.68	**104.52**	23.15	**127.67**
1989-90	42.17	23.50	37.69	**103.36**	23.41	**126.77**
1990-91	42.69	24.17	36.32	**103.18**	24.66	**127.84**
1991-92	42.65	23.26	33.42	**99.33**	22.54	**121.87**
1992-93	41.78	24.59	34.42	**100.79**	22.36	**123.15**
1993-94	42.54	25.15	32.82	**100.51**	22.25	**122.76**
1994-95	42.81	25.70	32.17	**100.68**	23.03	**123.71**
1995-96	42.84	25.01	30.88	**98.73**	22.28	**121.01**
1996-97	43.43	25.89	31.81	**101.13**	22.45	**123.58**
1997-98	43.45	26.70	30.83	**100.98**	22.87	**123.85**
1998-99	44.80	27.52	29.34	**101.66**	23.50	**125.16**
1999-00	45.16	27.49	29.34	**101.99**	21.12	**123.11**
2000-01	44.71	25.73	30.26	**100.70**	20.35	**121.05**
2001-02	44.90	26.34	29.52	**100.76**	22.01	**122.77**
2002-03	41.18	25.20	26.99	**93.37**	20.50	**113.87**
2003-04	42.59	26.60	30.80	**99.99**	23.46	**123.45**
2004-05	41.91	26.38	29.03	**97.32**	22.76	**120.08**
2005-06	43.66	26.48	29.04	**99.18**	22.39	**121.57**
2006-07 AE	43.62	28.04	28.71	**100.37**	23.11	**123.48**

AE : Advance Estimates.

Source : Ministry of Agriculture, Government of India.

APPENDIX TABLE 2

Area under Cultivation—Major Commercial Crops

(Million hectares)

Year	Oilseeds				Sugarcane	Tea	Coffee	Cotton (Lint)	Jute and Mesta	Tobacco
	Ground-nut	Rapeseed and Mustard	Soyabean	Total #						
1	2	3	4	5	6	7	8	9	10	11
1950-51	4.49	2.07	—	**10.73**	1.71	—	—	5.88	0.57	0.36
1951-52	4.92	2.40	—	**11.69**	1.94	—	—	6.56	0.79	0.29
1952-53	4.80	2.11	—	**11.18**	1.73	—	—	6.36	0.93	0.36
1953-54	4.25	2.24	—	**10.99**	1.41	—	—	6.99	0.68	0.37
1954-55	5.54	2.44	—	**12.52**	1.62	—	—	7.55	0.68	0.35
1955-56	5.13	2.56	—	**12.09**	1.85	—	—	8.09	0.94	0.41
1956-57	5.53	2.54	—	**12.49**	2.05	—	—	8.02	1.07	0.42
1957-58	6.42	2.41	—	**12.66**	2.07	—	—	8.01	1.02	0.36
1958-59	6.25	2.45	—	**13.00**	1.95	—	—	7.96	1.10	0.38
1959-60	6.44	2.91	—	**13.95**	2.14	—	—	7.30	0.98	0.41
1960-61	6.46	2.88	—	**13.77**	2.42	—	—	7.61	0.90	0.40
1961-62	6.89	3.17	—	**14.77**	2.46	—	—	7.98	1.34	0.42
1962-63	7.28	3.13	—	**15.34**	2.24	—	—	7.73	1.24	0.41
1963-64	6.89	3.05	—	**14.82**	2.25	—	—	8.22	1.27	0.44
1964-65	7.38	2.91	—	**15.26**	2.60	—	—	8.37	1.21	0.41
1965-66	7.70	2.91	—	**15.25**	2.84	—	—	7.96	1.11	0.38
1966-67	7.30	3.01	—	**15.00**	2.30	—	—	7.84	1.12	0.42
1967-68	7.55	3.24	—	**15.67**	2.05	—	—	8.00	1.20	0.42
1968-69	7.09	2.87	—	**14.47**	2.53	—	—	7.60	0.81	0.44
1969-70	7.13	3.17	—	**14.81**	2.75	—	—	7.73	1.09	0.44
1970-71	7.33	3.32	0.03	**16.64**	2.62	0.35	0.14	7.61	1.08	0.45
1971-72	7.51	3.61	0.03	**17.27**	2.39	0.36	0.14	7.80	1.11	0.46
1972-73	6.99	3.32	0.03	**15.79**	2.45	0.36	0.15	7.68	0.99	0.45
1973-74	7.02	3.46	0.05	**16.90**	2.75	0.36	0.16	7.57	1.16	0.46
1974-75	7.06	3.68	0.07	**17.31**	2.89	0.36	0.16	7.56	0.98	0.38
1975-76	7.22	3.34	0.09	**16.92**	2.76	0.36	0.17	7.35	0.91	0.37
1976-77	7.04	3.13	0.13	**16.47**	2.87	0.36	0.14	6.89	1.09	0.43
1977-78	7.03	3.58	0.20	**17.17**	3.15	0.37	0.15	7.87	1.16	0.50

1978-79	7.43	3.54	0.31	**17.71**	3.09	0.37	0.16	8.12	1.27	0.41
1979-80	7.17	3.47	0.50	**16.94**	2.61	0.37	0.17	8.13	1.22	0.43
1980-81	6.80	4.11	0.61	**17.60**	2.67	0.38	0.19	7.82	1.30	0.45
1981-82	7.43	4.40	0.48	**18.91**	3.19	0.38	0.19	8.06	1.15	0.44
1982-83	7.22	3.83	0.77	**17.76**	3.36	0.39	0.21	7.87	1.02	0.50
1983-84	7.54	3.87	0.84	**18.69**	3.11	0.40	0.21	7.72	1.05	0.44
1984-85	7.17	3.99	1.24	**18.92**	2.95	0.40	0.21	7.38	1.13	0.44
1985-86	7.12	3.98	1.34	**19.02**	2.85	0.40	0.21	7.53	1.50	0.40
1986-87	6.98	3.72	1.53	**18.63**	3.08	0.41	0.22	6.95	1.07	0.39
1987-88	6.84	4.62	1.54	**20.13**	3.28	0.41	0.22	6.46	0.96	0.32
1988-89	8.53	4.83	1.73	**21.90**	3.33	0.41	0.22	7.34	0.92	0.38
1989-90	8.71	4.97	2.25	**22.80**	3.44	0.41	0.22	7.69	0.91	0.41
1990-91	8.31	5.78	2.56	**24.15**	3.69	0.42	0.22	7.44	1.02	0.41
1991-92	8.67	6.55	3.18	**25.89**	3.84	0.42	0.22	7.66	1.11	0.43
1992-93	8.17	6.19	3.79	**25.24**	3.57	0.42	0.22	7.54	0.93	0.42
1993-94	8.32	6.29	4.37	**26.90**	3.42	0.42	0.23	7.32	0.89	0.38
1994-95	7.85	6.01	4.32	**25.30**	3.87	0.43	0.23	7.87	0.93	0.38
1995-96	7.52	6.55	5.04	**25.96**	4.15	0.43	0.24	9.04	0.93	0.39
1996-97	7.60	6.55	5.45	**26.34**	4.17	0.43	0.25	9.12	1.10	0.43
1997-98	7.09	7.04	5.99	**26.12**	3.93	0.43	0.29	8.87	1.11	0.46
1998-99	7.40	6.51	6.49	**26.23**	4.05	0.47	0.30	9.34	1.03	0.51
1999-00	6.87	6.03	6.22	**24.28**	4.22	0.49	0.31	8.71	1.04	0.43
2000-01	6.56	4.48	6.42	**22.77**	4.32	0.50	0.31	8.53	1.02	0.26
2001-02	6.24	5.07	6.34	**22.64**	4.41	0.51	0.32	9.13	1.05	0.35
2002-03	5.94	4.54	6.11	**21.49**	4.52	0.52	0.33	7.67	1.04	0.33
2003-04	5.99	5.43	6.56	**23.66**	3.93	0.52	0.33	7.60	1.00	0.37
2004-05	6.64	7.32	7.57	**27.52**	3.66	0.52	0.33	8.79	0.92	0.37
2005-06	6.74	7.28	7.71	**27.86**	4.20	0.56	0.34	8.68	0.90	0.37
2006-07 AE	5.64	6.60	8.33	**26.05**	4.86	0.57	0.34	9.14	0.94	0.37
2007-08	—	—	—	—	—	0.57	0.34	—	—	

AE : Advance Estimates.

: For nine oilseeds out of eleven in all.

Notes: 1. Data from 1950-51 to 1969-70 relate to total of five major oilseeds, *viz.* , groundnut, castorseed, sesamum, rapeseed and mustard, and linseed.

2. Data from 1950-51 and 1951-52 relate to Jute crop only.

Source : Ministry of Agriculture, Government of India.

APPENDIX TABLE 3

Agricultural Production—Foodgrains

(Million tonnes)

Year	*Cereals*				*Pulses*	*Total Foodgrains (5+6)*
	Rice	*Wheat*	*Coarse Cereals*	*Total (2 to 4)*		
1	*2*	*3*	*4*	*5*	*6*	*7*
1950-51	20.58	6.46	15.38	**42.42**	8.41	**50.83**
1951-52	21.30	6.18	16.09	**43.57**	8.42	**51.99**
1952-53	22.90	7.50	19.61	**50.01**	9.19	**59.20**
1953-54	28.21	8.02	22.97	**59.20**	10.62	**69.82**
1954-55	25.22	9.04	22.82	**57.08**	10.95	**68.03**
1955-56	27.56	8.76	19.49	**55.81**	11.04	**66.85**
1956-57	29.04	9.40	19.87	**58.31**	11.55	**69.86**
1957-58	25.53	7.99	21.23	**54.75**	9.56	**64.31**
1958-59	30.85	9.96	23.18	**63.99**	13.15	**77.14**
1959-60	31.68	10.32	22.87	**64.87**	11.80	**76.67**
1960-61	34.58	11.00	23.74	**69.32**	12.70	**82.02**
1961-62	35.66	12.07	23.22	**70.95**	11.76	**82.71**
1962-63	33.21	10.78	24.63	**68.62**	11.53	**80.15**
1963-64	37.00	9.85	23.72	**70.57**	10.07	**80.64**
1964-65	39.31	12.26	25.37	**76.94**	12.42	**89.36**
1965-66	30.59	10.40	21.42	**62.41**	9.94	**72.35**
1966-67	30.44	11.39	24.05	**65.88**	8.35	**74.23**
1967-68	37.61	16.54	28.80	**82.95**	12.10	**95.05**
1968-69	39.76	18.65	25.18	**83.59**	10.42	**94.01**
1969-70	40.43	20.09	27.29	**87.81**	11.69	**99.50**
1970-71	42.22	23.83	30.55	**96.60**	11.82	**108.42**
1971-72	43.07	26.41	24.60	**94.08**	11.09	**105.17**
1972-73	39.24	24.74	23.14	**87.12**	9.91	**97.03**
1973-74	44.05	21.78	28.83	**94.66**	10.01	**104.67**
1974-75	39.58	24.10	26.13	**89.81**	10.02	**99.83**
1975-76	48.74	28.84	30.41	**107.99**	13.04	**121.03**
1976-77	41.92	29.01	28.88	**99.81**	11.36	**111.17**
1977-78	52.67	31.75	30.02	**114.44**	11.97	**126.41**
1978-79	53.77	35.51	30.44	**119.72**	12.18	**131.90**
1979-80	42.33	31.83	26.97	**101.13**	8.57	**109.70**
1980-81	53.63	36.31	29.02	**118.96**	10.63	**129.59**
1981-82	53.25	37.45	31.09	**121.79**	11.51	**133.30**
1982-83	47.12	42.79	27.75	**117.66**	11.86	**129.52**
1983-84	60.10	45.48	33.90	**139.48**	12.89	**152.37**
1984-85	58.34	44.07	31.17	**133.58**	11.96	**145.54**
1985-86	63.83	47.05	26.20	**137.08**	13.36	**150.44**
1986-87	60.56	44.32	26.83	**131.71**	11.71	**143.42**
1987-88	56.86	46.17	26.36	**129.39**	10.96	**140.35**
1988-89	70.49	54.11	31.47	**156.07**	13.85	**169.92**
1989-90	73.57	49.85	34.76	**158.18**	12.86	**171.04**

(Contd.)

1	2	3	4	5	6	7
1990-91	74.29	55.14	32.70	**162.13**	14.26	**176.39**
1991-92	74.68	55.69	25.99	**156.36**	12.02	**168.38**
1992-93	72.86	57.21	36.59	**166.66**	12.82	**179.48**
1993-94	80.30	59.84	30.82	**170.96**	13.30	**184.26**
1994-95	81.81	65.77	29.88	**177.46**	14.04	**191.50**
1995-96	76.98	62.10	29.03	**168.11**	12.31	**180.42**
1996-97	81.73	69.35	34.11	**185.19**	14.24	**199.43**
1997-98	82.54	66.35	30.40	**179.29**	12.98	**192.27**
1998-99	86.08	71.29	31.33	**188.70**	14.91	**203.61**
1999-00	89.68	76.37	30.34	**196.39**	13.41	**209.80**
2000-01	84.98	69.68	31.08	**185.74**	11.07	**196.81**
2001-02	93.34	72.77	33.37	**199.48**	13.37	**212.85**
2002-03	71.82	65.76	26.07	**163.65**	11.13	**174.78**
2003-04	88.53	72.15	37.60	**198.28**	14.91	**213.19**
2004-05	83.13	68.64	33.46	**185.23**	13.13	**198.36**
2005-06	91.79	69.35	34.06	**195.20**	13.39	**208.59**
2006-07	93.35	75.81	33.92	**203.08**	14.20	**217.28**
2007-08 AE	96.43	78.40	40.73	**215.56**	15.11	**230.67**

AE : Advance Estimates.

Source : Ministry of Agriculture, Government of India.

APPENDIX TABLE 4

Agricultural Production—Major Commercial Crops

(Million tonnes)

Year	*Oilseeds*				*Sugarcane*	*Tea $ (Jan.-Dec.)*	*Coffee $*	*Cotton (Lint)@*	*Jute and Mesta**	*Tobacco*
	Ground-nut	*Rapeseed and Mustard*	*Soyabean*	*Total #*						
1	2	3	4	5	6	7	8	9	10	11
1950-51	3.48	0.76	—	**5.16**	57.05	—	—	3.04	3.31	0.26
1951-52	3.19	0.94	—	**5.03**	61.63	—	—	3.28	4.72	0.21
1952-53	2.93	0.86	—	**4.73**	51.00	—	—	3.34	5.32	0.25
1953-54	3.45	0.87	—	**5.37**	44.41	—	—	4.13	3.77	0.27
1954-55	4.25	1.04	—	**6.40**	58.74	—	—	4.45	3.86	0.26
1955-56	3.86	0.86	—	**5.73**	60.54	—	—	4.18	5.39	0.30
1956-57	4.37	1.04	—	**6.36**	69.05	—	—	4.92	5.81	0.31
1957-58	4.71	0.93	—	**6.35**	71.16	—	—	4.96	5.33	0.24
1958-59	5.18	1.04	—	**7.30**	73.36	—	—	4.88	6.91	0.32
1959-60	4.56	1.06	—	**6.56**	77.82	—	—	3.68	5.69	0.29
1960-61	4.81	1.35	—	**6.98**	110.00	—	—	5.60	5.26	0.31
1961-62	4.99	1.35	—	**7.28**	103.97	—	—	4.85	8.24	0.34
1962-63	5.06	1.30	—	**7.39**	91.91	—	—	5.54	7.19	0.34
1963-64	5.30	0.92	—	**7.13**	104.23	—	—	5.75	7.98	0.36
1964-65	6.00	1.47	—	**8.56**	121.91	—	—	6.01	7.66	0.36
1965-66	4.26	1.30	—	**6.40**	123.99	—	—	4.85	5.78	0.29
1966-67	4.41	1.23	—	**6.43**	92.83	—	—	5.27	6.58	0.35
1967-68	5.73	1.57	—	**8.30**	95.50	—	—	5.78	7.59	0.37
1968-69	4.63	1.35	—	**6.85**	124.68	—	—	5.45	3.84	0.36
1969-70	5.13	1.56	—	**7.73**	135.02	—	—	5.56	6.79	0.34
1970-71	6.11	1.98	0.01	**9.63**	126.37	419.00	110.20	4.76	6.19	0.36

1971-72	6.18	1.43	0.01	**9.08**	113.57	435.00	69.00	6.95	6.84	0.42
1972-73	4.09	1.81	0.03	**7.14**	124.87	456.00	91.10	5.74	6.09	0.37
1973-74	5.93	1.70	0.04	**9.39**	140.81	472.00	86.40	6.31	7.68	0.46
1974-75	5.11	2.25	0.05	**9.15**	144.29	489.00	92.50	7.16	5.83	0.36
1975-76	6.76	1.94	0.09	**10.61**	140.60	487.00	84.00	5.95	5.91	0.35
1976-77	5.26	1.55	0.12	**8.43**	153.01	512.00	102.30	5.84	7.10	0.42
1977-78	6.09	1.65	0.18	**9.66**	176.97	556.00	125.10	7.24	7.15	0.49
1978-79	6.21	1.86	0.30	**10.10**	151.66	564.00	110.50	7.96	8.33	0.45
1979-80	5.77	1.43	0.28	**8.74**	128.83	544.00	149.80	7.65	7.96	0.44
1980-81	5.01	2.30	0.44	**9.37**	154.25	569.60	118.70	7.01	8.16	0.48
1981-82	7.22	2.38	0.35	**12.08**	186.36	560.40	152.10	7.88	8.37	0.52
1982-83	5.28	2.21	0.49	**10.00**	189.51	560.70	130.00	7.53	7.17	0.58
1983-84	7.09	2.61	0.61	**12.69**	174.08	581.50	105.00	6.39	7.72	0.49
1984-85	6.44	3.07	0.95	**12.95**	170.32	639.90	195.10	8.51	7.79	0.49
1985-86	5.12	2.68	1.02	**10.83**	170.65	656.20	122.50	8.73	12.65	0.44
1986-87	5.88	2.60	0.89	**11.27**	186.09	624.60	192.10	6.91	8.62	0.46
1987-88	5.85	3.45	0.90	**12.65**	196.74	674.30	122.70	6.38	6.78	0.37
1988-89	9.66	4.38	1.55	**18.03**	203.04	701.10	214.70	8.74	7.86	0.49
1989-90	8.10	4.13	1.81	**16.92**	225.57	684.10	118.10	11.42	8.29	0.55
1990-91	7.51	5.23	2.60	**18.61**	241.05	720.30	169.70	9.84	9.23	0.56
1991-92	7.09	5.86	2.49	**18.60**	254.00	754.20	180.00	9.71	10.29	0.58
1992-93	8.56	4.80	3.39	**20.11**	228.03	703.90	169.40	11.40	8.59	0.60
1993-94	7.83	5.33	4.75	**21.50**	229.66	760.80	212.10	10.74	8.43	0.56
1994-95	8.06	5.76	3.93	**21.34**	275.54	752.90	180.10	11.89	9.08	0.57
1995-96	7.58	6.00	5.10	**22.11**	281.10	756.00	223.00	12.86	8.81	0.54
1996-97	8.64	6.66	5.38	**24.38**	277.56	780.10	205.00	14.23	11.13	0.62
1997-98	7.37	4.70	6.46	**21.32**	279.54	810.00	228.30	10.85	11.02	0.64
1998-99	8.98	5.66	7.14	**24.75**	288.72	874.10	265.00	12.29	9.81	0.74
1999-00	5.25	5.79	7.08	**20.71**	299.32	825.90	292.00	11.53	10.55	0.52
2000-01	6.41	4.19	5.28	**18.44**	295.96	846.90	301.20	9.52	10.56	0.34

(Contd.)

APPENDIX TABLE 4 (*Contd.*)

1	*2*	*3*	*4*	*5*	*6*	*7*	*8*	*9*	*10*	*11*
2001-02	7.03	5.08	5.96	**20.66**	297.21	853.90	300.60	10.00	11.68	0.55
2002-03	4.12	3.88	4.66	**14.84**	287.38	838.50	275.30	8.62	11.28	0.49
2003-04	8.13	6.29	7.82	**25.19**	233.86	878.10	270.50	13.73	11.17	0.55
2004-05	6.77	7.59	6.88	**24.35**	237.09	893.00	275.50	16.43	10.27	0.55
2005-06	7.99	8.13	8.27	**27.98**	281.17	945.97	274.00	18.50	10.84	0.55
2006-07	4.86	7.44	8.85	**24.29**	355.52	955.90	280.00	22.63	11.27	0.52
2007-08 AE	9.36	5.80	9.99	**28.82**	340.56	944.68	262.00	25.81	11.17	—

AE : Advance Estimates.
: For nine oilseeds out of eleven in all.
$: Million kg.
@ : Production in million bales of 170 kg. each.
* : Production in million bales of 180 kg. each.

Notes :

1. Data from 1950-51 to 1969-70 relate to total of five major oilseeds, *viz.*, groundnut, castorseed, sesamum, rapeseed and mustard, and linseed.
2. Data from 1950-51 and 1951-52 relate to Jute crop only.

Source : Ministry of Agriculture, Government of India.

APPENDIX TABLE 5

Minimum Support Price for Foodgrains According to Crop Year (Fair Average Quality)

(Rupees per quintal)

Year	*Paddy Common #*	*Coarse Cereals*	*Wheat*	*Gram*	*Arhar (Tur)*	*Moong*	*Urad*
1	*2*	*3*	*4*	*5*	*6*	*7*	*8*
1975-76	74	74	105	90	—	—	—
1976-77	74	74	110	95	—	—	—
1977-78	77	74	112	125	—	—	—
1978-79	85	85	115	140	155	165	—
1979-80	95	95	117	145	165	175	175
1980-81	105	105	130	—	190	200	200
1981-82	115	116	142	—	—	—	—
1982-83	122	118	151	235	215	240	230
1983-84	132	124	152	240	245	250	245
1984-85	137	130	157	—	275	275	275
1985-86	142	130	162	260	300	300	300
1986-87	146	132	166	280	320	320	320
1987-88	150	135	173	290	325	325	325
1988-89	160	145	183	325	360	360	360
1989-90	185	165	215	421	425	425	425
1990-91	205	180	225	450	480	480	480
1991-92	230	205	280	500	545	545	545
1992-93	270	240	330 $	600	640	640	640
1993-94	310	260	350 $	640	700	700	700
1994-95	340	280	360	670	760	760	760
1995-96	360	300	380	700	800	800	800
1996-97	380	310	475 *	740	840	840	840
1997-98	415	360	510 @	815	900	900	900
1998-99	440	390	550	895	960	960	960
1999-00	490	415	580	1015	1105	1105	1105
2000-01	510	445	610	1100	1200	1200	1200
2001-02	530	485	620	1200	1320	1320	1320
2002-03	530	485	620	1220	1320	1330	1330
2003-04	550	505	630	1400	1360	1370	1370
2004-05	560	515	640	1425	1390	1410	1410
2005-06	570	525	650 @	1435	1400	1520	1520
2006-07	580 †	540	750 $$	1445	1410	1520	1520
2007-08	645 $$	600	1000	1600	1550 ‡	1700 ‡	1700 ‡

: From 1997-98, Minimum Support Price (MSP) is announced for two varieties of paddy—common and Grade 'A', as against the earlier three categories of common, fine and super fine.

$: Including a Central bonus of Rs. 25 per quintal. Quintal = 100 kgs.

$$: An additional incentive bonus of Rs. 100 per quintal is payable over the MSP.

* : Including a Central bonus of Rs. 60 per quintal payable up to June 30, 1997.

@ : Including a Central bonus of Rs. 50 per quintal payable over the MSP.

† : An additional incentive bonus of Rs. 40 per quintal on procurement between Oct. 1, 2006 to March 31, 2007.

‡ : A bonus of Rs. 40 per quintal is payable over and above the MSP.

Source : Ministry of Agriculture, Government of India.

APPENDIX TABLE 6

Minimum Support Price For Non-foodgrains According To Crop Year (Fair Average Quality)

(Rupees per quintal)

Year	*Sugarcane@*	*Cotton #*	*Jute*	*Groundnut (in shell)*	*Soyabean Black*	*Soyabean Yellow*	*Sunflower Seed*	*Rape Seed/ Mustard*	*Safflower*
1	*2*	*3*	*4*	*5*	*6*	*7*	*8*	*9*	*10*
1975-76	—	—	135	—	—	—	—	—	—
1976-77	8.5	—	136	140	—	—	150	—	—
1977-78	8.5	—	141	160	145	—	165	225	—
1978-79	10	—	150	175	175	—	175	245	—
1979-80	12.5	—	155	190	175	—	175	—	—
1980-81	13	—	160	206	183	198	183	—	—
1981-82	13	—	175	270	210	230	250	—	—
1982-83	13	—	175	295	220	245	250	355	—
1983-84	13.5	527	185	315	230	255	275	360	—
1984-85	14	535	195	340	240	265	325	385	—
1985-86	16.5	535	215	350	250	275	335	400	400
1986-87	17	540	225	370	255	290	350	415	415
1987-88	18.5	550	240	390	260	300	390	430	415
1988-89	19.5	600	250	430	275	320	450	460	440
1989-90	23	690	295	500	325	370	530	575	550
1990-91	22	750	320	580	350	400	600	600	575
1991-92	26	840	375	645	395	445	670	670	640
1992-93	31	950	400	750	475	525	800	760	720
1993-94	34.5	1050	450	800	525	580	850	810	760
1994-95	39.1	1200	470	860	570	650	900	830	780
1995-96	42.5	1350	490	900	600	680	950	860	800
1996-97	45.9	1380	510	920	620	700	960	890	830
1997-98	48.45	1530	570	980	670	750	1000	940	910
1998-99	52.7	1650	650	1040	705	795	1060	1000	990
1999-00	56.1	1775	750	1155	755	845	1155	1100	1100
2000-01	59.5	1825	785	1220	775	865	1170	1200	1200
2001-02	62.05	1875	810	1340	795	885	1185	1300	1300
2002-03	69.5	1875	850	1355	795	885	1195	1330	1300
2003-04	73	1925	860	1400	840	930	1250	1600	1500
2004-05	74.5	1960	890	1500	900	1000	1340	1700	1550
2005-06	79.5	1980	910	1520	900	1010	1500	1715	1565
2006-07	80.25	1990 $	1000	1520	900	1020	1500	1715	1565
2007-08	81.18	2030 $	1055	1550	910	1050	1510	1800	1650

@ : Up to 2004-05 Statutory Minimum Price (SMP) linked to a basic recovery of 8.5 per cent of sugar with proportionate premium for every 0.1 per cent increase in recovery above that level. The SMP for 2002-03 includes the one-time drought relief.

: Minimum Support Price (MSP) of cotton for H-4.

$: Long Staple. Quintal = 100 kgs

Sources: 1. Ministry of Agriculture, Government of India.

2. Economic Survey 2004-05, Government of India.

APPENDIX TABLE 7

Pattern of Land Use and Select Inputs for Agricultural Production

(Area in million hectares)

Year	*Net Sown Area*	*Gross Sown Area*	*Net Irrigated Area*	*Gross Irrigated Area*	*Area under High Yielding Varieties*	*Consumption of Fertilisers $ (N+P+K)* (lakh tonnes)*	*Consumption of Pesticides (Technical grade material) ('000 tonnes)*
1	*2*	*3*	*4*	*5*	*6*	*7*	*8*
1950-51	118.75	131.89	20.85	22.56	—	0.69	2.35
1951-52	119.40	133.23	21.05	23.18	—	0.66	—
1952-53	123.44	137.68	21.12	23.31	—	0.66	—
1953-54	126.81	142.48	21.87	24.36	—	1.05	—
1954-55	127.85	144.09	22.09	24.95	—	1.21	—
1955-56	129.16	147.31	22.76	25.64	—	1.31	—
1956-57	130.85	149.49	22.53	25.71	—	1.54	—
1957-58	129.08	145.83	23.16	26.63	—	1.84	—
1958-59	131.83	151.63	23.40	26.95	—	2.24	—
1959-60	132.94	152.82	24.04	27.45	—	3.05	—
1960-61	133.20	152.77	24.66	27.98	—	2.92	8.62
1961-62	135.40	156.21	24.88	28.46	—	3.38	—
1962-63	136.34	156.76	25.67	29.45	—	4.52	—
1963-64	136.48	156.96	25.89	29.71	—	5.43	—
1964-65	138.12	159.23	26.60	30.71	—	7.73	—
1965-66	136.20	155.28	26.34	30.90	—	7.85	—
1966-67	137.23	157.36	26.91	32.68	—	11.01	—
1967-68	139.88	163.74	27.19	33.21	—	15.39	—
1968-69	137.31	159.53	29.01	35.48	—	17.61	—
1969-70	138.77	162.27	30.20	36.97	—	19.82	—
1970-71	140.27	165.79	31.10	38.20	15.38	21.77	24.32
1971-72	139.72	165.19	31.55	38.43	18.17	26.57	29.54
1972-73	137.14	162.15	31.83	39.06	22.32	27.68	35.16
1973-74	142.42	169.87	32.55	40.28	26.04	28.39	50.43
1974-75	137.79	164.19	33.71	41.74	27.33	25.73	—
1975-76	141.65	171.30	34.59	43.36	31.89	28.94	—
1976-77	139.48	167.33	35.15	43.55	33.56	34.11	—
1977-78	141.95	172.23	36.55	46.08	38.93	42.86	—
1978-79	142.98	174.80	38.06	48.31	40.13	51.17	—
1979-80	138.90	169.59	38.52	49.21	38.38	52.55	—
1980-81	140.00	172.63	38.72	49.78	43.08	55.16	45.00
1981-82	141.93	176.75	40.50	51.41	46.49	60.64	47.00
1982-83	140.22	172.75	40.69	51.83	47.49	63.88	50.00
1983-84	142.84	179.56	41.95	53.82	53.74	77.10	55.00
1984-85	140.89	176.33	42.15	54.53	54.14	82.11	56.00
1985-86	140.90	178.46	41.87	54.28	55.42	84.74	52.00
1986-87	139.58	176.41	42.57	55.76	56.17	86.45	50.00
1987-88	134.09	170.74	42.89	56.04	54.10	87.84	66.90
1988-89	141.89	182.28	46.15	61.13	60.11	110.40	75.89

(Contd.)

1	2	3	4	5	6	7	8
1989-90	142.34	182.27	46.70	61.85	61.17	115.68	72.00
1990-91	143.00	185.74	48.02	63.20	64.98	125.46	75.00
1991-92	141.63	182.24	49.87	65.68	64.71	127.28	72.13
1992-93	142.72	185.70	50.29	66.76	65.40	121.55	70.79
1993-94	142.34	186.58	51.34	68.26	66.99	123.66	63.65
1994-95	142.96	188.05	53.00	70.65	70.93	135.64	61.36
1995-96	142.20	187.47	53.40	71.35	72.11	138.76	61.26
1996-97	142.81	189.59	55.05	73.25	76.40	143.08	56.11
1997-98	142.08	190.57	54.99	73.00	76.00	161.88	52.24
1998-99	142.58	193.03	57.08	75.95	78.35	167.98	49.16
1999-00	140.96	189.44	57.11	78.81	—	180.70	46.20
2000-01	141.16	185.70	54.84	75.82	—	167.02	43.58
2001-02	141.42 P	189.75 P	56.30 P	78.07 P	—	173.60	47.02
2002-03	132.66 P	175.66 P	53.88 P	72.89 P	—	160.94	48.30
2003-04	140.95 P	190.37 P	56.00 P	77.11 P	—	167.99	41.00
2004-05	141.32 P	190.91 P	58.54 P	79.51 P	—	183.98	40.67
2005-06	—	—	—	—	—	203.40	—
2006-07	—	—	—	—	—	220.45	—

P : Provisional.
$: Data relate to February-January up to 1982-83 and April-March from 1983-84 onwards.
* : N : Nitrogen, P : Phosphorus, K : Potassium.
Source : Ministry of Agriculture, Government of India.

APPENDIX TABLE 8

India's Foreign Trade—US Dollars

(US $ million)

Year	Exports			Imports			Trade Balance		
	Oil	Non-oil	Total	Oil	Non-oil	Total	Oil	Non-oil	Total
1	2	3	4	5	6	7	8	9	10
1970-71	11	2020	**2031**	180	1983	**2162**	-169	38	**-131**
1971-72	14	2138	**2152**	260	2182	**2442**	-246	-44	**-290**
1972-73	38	2531	**2569**	266	2167	**2433**	-228	364	**136**
1973-74	16	3223	**3238**	719	3074	**3793**	-703	149	**-554**
1974-75	17	4175	**4192**	1457	4234	**5691**	-1440	-59	**-1499**
1975-76	22	4627	**4649**	1412	4652	**6064**	-1390	-25	**-1415**
1976-77	21	5708	**5728**	1574	4077	**5652**	-1554	1630	**77**
1977-78	18	6280	**6299**	1806	5205	**7012**	-1788	1075	**-713**
1978-79	17	6943	**6960**	2038	6241	**8279**	-2021	703	**-1318**
1979-80	23	7903	**7926**	4035	7256	**11291**	-4011	647	**-3364**
1980-81	32	8453	**8485**	6655	9212	**15867**	-6623	-758	**-7382**
1981-82	246	8458	**8704**	5786	9387	**15173**	-5540	-929	**-6469**
1982-83	1278	7830	**9108**	5816	8970	**14787**	-4538	-1141	**-5679**
1983-84	1536	7914	**9449**	4673	10638	**15311**	-3137	-2724	**-5862**
1984-85	1529	8349	**9878**	4550	9863	**14412**	-3020	-1514	**-4534**
1985-86	527	8378	**8905**	4078	11989	**16067**	-3551	-3611	**-7162**
1986-87	322	9423	**9745**	2200	13527	**15727**	-1878	-4104	**-5982**
1987-88	500	11588	**12089**	3118	14038	**17156**	-2618	-2450	**-5067**
1988-89	349	13622	**13970**	3009	16488	**19497**	-2660	-2867	**-5527**
1989-90	418	16194	**16613**	3768	17452	**21219**	-3349	-1258	**-4607**
1990-91	523	17623	**18145**	6028	18044	**24073**	-5505	-422	**-5927**
1991-92	415	17451	**17865**	5325	14086	**19411**	-4910	3365	**-1545**
1992-93	476	18061	**18537**	6100	15782	**21882**	-5624	2279	**-3344**
1993-94	398	21841	**22238**	5754	17553	**23306**	-5356	4288	**-1068**
1994-95	417	25914	**26331**	5928	22727	**28654**	-5511	3187	**-2324**
1995-96	454	31341	**31795**	7526	29150	**36675**	-7072	2192	**-4880**
1996-97	482	32988	**33470**	10036	29096	**39132**	-9554	3892	**-5663**
1997-98	353	34654	**35006**	8164	33321	**41485**	-7811	1333	**-6478**
1998-99	89	33129	**33219**	6399	35990	**42389**	-6309	-2861	**-9170**
1999-00	39	36784	**36822**	12611	37059	**49671**	-12573	-276	**-12848**
2000-01	1870	42691	**44560**	15650	34886	**50537**	-13780	7804	**-5976**
2001-02	2119	41708	**43827**	14000	37413	**51413**	-11881	4295	**-7587**
2002-03	2577	50143	**52719**	17640	43773	**61412**	-15063	6370	**-8693**

(Contd.)

APPENDIX TABLE 8 (*Contd.*)

1	*2*	*3*	*4*	*5*	*6*	*7*	*8*	*9*	*10*
2003-04	3568	60274	**63843**	20570	57580	**78149**	-17001	2695	**-14307**
2004-05	6989	76547	**83536**	29844	81673	**111517**	-22855	-5127	**-27982**
2005-06	11640	91451	**103091**	43963	105203	**149166**	-32324	-13752	**-46075**
2006-07 R	18679	107683	**126362**	57144	128606	**185749**	-38465	-20923	**-59388**
2007-08 P	24869	134138	**159007**	79641	160009	**239651**	-54772	-25872	**-80644**

P : Provisional R : Revised.
Source : Directorate General of Commercial Intelligence and Statistics.

APPENDIX TABLE 9

Exports of Principal Commodities—US Dollars

(US $ million)

Commodity/Year	*1970-71*	*1971-72*	*1972-73*	*1973-74*	*1974-75*	*1975-76*	*1976-77*	*1977-78*	*1978-79*
1	*2*	*3*	*4*	*5*	*6*	*7*	*8*	*9*	*10*
Food and live animals	**546.0**	**583.3**	**690.9**	**871.1**	**1283.5**	**1443.1**	**1448.7**	**1810.9**	**1759.7**
1 Fish and fish preparations	40.4	55.4	70.1	113.1	81.9	144.4	198.8	199.1	269.1
2 Cereals and cereal preparations	14.5	40.1	111.5	14.8	31.6	22.1	17.2	75.1	154.9
3 Fruits and vegetables	82.1	94.1	105.7	116.3	171.3	151.1	181.6	229.3	175.9
(a) Cashew kernels	68.9	82.1	89.7	95.5	148.8	110.7	118.1	174.2	97.5
(b) Others	13.2	12.1	16.1	20.8	22.5	40.4	63.6	55.1	78.4
4 Coffee	33.2	29.5	42.9	59.0	64.7	76.8	140.4	226.4	177.4
5 Tea	196.2	209.2	191.9	187.4	287.2	272.7	326.5	663.5	413.8
6 Spices	51.4	48.4	38.0	70.7	77.3	81.7	83.5	159.7	179.8
(a) Pepper black	21.6	22.4	19.1	38.4	43.8	42.7	45.6	63.1	58.9
(b) Others	29.7	26.0	18.9	32.2	33.5	39.0	37.9	96.5	120.9
7 Feeding stuff for animals	78.0	58.8	103.0	240.5	130.4	110.9	298.7	182.8	169.6
8 Sugar and honey	38.8	41.5	17.9	55.6	427.9	546.8	167.1	24.4	164.3
9 Others	11.5	6.2	9.9	13.7	11.3	36.7	34.7	50.7	57.2
Beverages and tobacco	**43.1**	**60.4**	**83.5**	**91.1**	**103.6**	**113.4**	**114.7**	**137.1**	**142.3**
1 Tobacco, unmanufactured	41.5	56.5	79.6	87.8	101.2	107.2	107.9	131.9	134.6
2 Others	1.5	3.8	3.9	3.3	2.4	6.2	6.8	5.3	7.7
Crude materials, inedible, except fuels	**333.0**	**322.0**	**331.4**	**465.1**	**544.4**	**626.8**	**670.7**	**569.0**	**623.6**
1 Hides, skins and fur skins, raw	5.0	0.9	1.1	2.0	0.5	0.2	0.9	0.7	0.7
2 Wool and other animal hair	6.7	5.7	9.1	10.9	11.0	5.8	9.0	1.9	1.5
3 Cotton textile fibre and waste	21.7	24.5	32.1	47.1	21.5	51.3	43.2	4.4	24.4

(Contd.)

APPENDIX TABLE 9 (*Contd.*)

1	*2*	*3*	*4*	*5*	*6*	*7*	*8*	*9*	*10*
4 Jute textile fibre and waste	5.7	17.5	6.4	5.7	22.6	12.0	1.8	2.8	1.8
5 Mica	20.6	20.6	21.6	16.3	22.9	16.8	19.3	21.0	23.9
6 Iron ore and concentrates	155.2	140.1	143.0	170.5	202.0	246.2	265.7	280.5	283.1
7 Manganese ore	18.5	14.2	11.3	11.5	21.7	20.2	21.3	12.6	18.7
8 Lac	6.6	8.8	8.1	18.5	30.6	14.4	10.9	7.4	10.9
9 Others	93.0	89.7	98.6	182.6	211.6	259.7	298.7	237.7	258.5
Mineral fuels, lubricants and related materials	**16.6**	**15.5**	**41.9**	**19.7**	**25.7**	**42.1**	**36.7**	**32.4**	**24.1**
1 Petroleum crude and partly refined	0.0	2.2	20.4	0.0	0.0	0.0	0.0	0.0	0.0
2 Petroleum products	11.3	11.8	17.4	15.7	17.2	21.7	20.8	18.3	17.2
3 Others	5.3	1.4	4.1	4.0	8.6	20.4	16.0	14.1	6.8
Animal and vegetable oils and fats	**9.4**	**10.6**	**34.3**	**41.2**	**43.4**	**42.5**	**58.5**	**29.0**	**21.7**
1 Fixed vegetable oils and fats	0.1	10.1	33.2	40.6	42.4	38.3	56.2	24.1	16.5
2 Others	9.3	0.5	1.1	0.6	1.0	4.1	2.3	5.0	5.2
Chemicals	**48.1**	**47.4**	**52.8**	**74.7**	**131.2**	**104.4**	**132.7**	**145.6**	**189.1**
1 Chemical elements and compounds	10.4	9.6	10.1	19.2	34.2	27.7	35.0	31.0	43.3
2 Dyeing, tanning and colouring materials	9.6	7.3	12.1	14.8	29.2	21.6	37.3	41.4	40.5
3 Medicinal and pharmaceutical products	11.2	12.9	13.5	19.4	28.9	25.5	26.9	36.3	68.6
4 Essential oils and perfume materials	9.4	11.7	13.1	15.2	20.2	16.4	21.3	26.8	24.6
5 Plastic materials, regenerated cellulose and artificial resins	4.2	1.5	1.3	2.0	2.4	1.4	4.6	3.3	2.6
6 Others	3.3	4.5	2.7	4.0	16.3	11.8	7.6	6.8	9.4

Manufactured goods classified chiefly by material	**815.0**	**890.0**	**1063.6**	**1284.0**	**1471.9**	**1599.8**	**2362.7**	**2555.7**	**2848.9**
1 Leather and manufactures *n.e.s.* and dressed fur skins	95.5	121.5	227.4	221.0	182.6	231.8	294.3	288.8	398.3
2 Cotton manufactures excluding yarn and thread and clothing	129.0	133.9	165.1	307.8	270.9	245.5	308.9	272.1	272.6
3 Textile yarn and thread	45.6	37.6	48.7	39.2	47.4	26.1	61.6	56.2	48.3
4 Jute manufactures excluding twist and yarn	250.3	352.3	322.1	289.7	370.3	282.5	224.0	285.7	203.3
5 Woollen carpets and rugs	13.5	17.3	28.6	31.7	44.8	9.7	74.9	103.7	123.1
6 Pearls, precious and semi-precious stones	55.5	71.0	103.1	138.2	123.9	141.6	319.7	635.7	867.5
7 Manufacture of metals *n.e.s.*	37.0	32.7	39.4	51.0	86.3	95.5	148.4	189.6	241.3
8 Iron and steel	119.9	54.8	54.4	77.9	111.3	134.9	443.3	326.3	271.9
9 Non-ferrous metals	16.0	10.7	10.9	21.5	114.1	232.7	220.1	115.7	139.7
10 Others	52.7	58.3	64.0	106.1	120.3	159.3	267.5	281.9	282.8
Machinery and transport equipment	**110.2**	**101.1**	**113.8**	**151.9**	**271.4**	**298.9**	**336.6**	**392.9**	**485.5**
1 Machinery, other than electric	37.6	33.1	40.3	60.9	115.1	127.3	133.3	156.4	216.3
2 Electrical machinery, apparatus and appliances	21.4	25.1	30.9	37.3	72.1	74.1	93.3	100.7	113.0
3 Transport equipment	51.2	43.0	42.6	53.7	82.7	97.1	104.4	135.8	154.1
Miscellaneous manufactured articles	**100.9**	**113.8**	**147.7**	**229.8**	**307.3**	**365.0**	**551.5**	**600.7**	**839.6**
1 Footwear	15.1	15.7	16.8	17.4	26.1	25.4	33.7	28.0	31.9
2 Clothing	40.0	50.5	73.1	127.8	173.9	233.5	371.1	383.7	553.9
3 Others	45.8	47.6	57.9	84.6	107.3	106.2	146.7	189.0	253.8
Commodities and transactions ***n.e.s.***	**9.0**	**7.8**	**8.9**	**9.8**	**9.8**	**12.7**	**15.6**	**25.3**	**25.9**
Total Exports	**2031.3**	**2151.9**	**2568.7**	**3238.3**	**4192.1**	**4648.7**	**5728.4**	**6298.6**	**6960.3**

APPENDIX TABLE 9 (*Contd.*)

(*US $ million*)

Commodity/Year	*1979-80*	*1980-81*	*1981-82*	*1982-83*	*1983-84*	*1984-85*	*1985-86*	*1986-87*
1	*11*	*12*	*13*	*14*	*15*	*16*	*17*	*18*
Food and live animals	**2103.5**	**2155.9**	**2139.9**	**1962.5**	**2001.7**	**2054.5**	**2051.0**	**2177.3**
1 Fish and fish preparations	308.0	269.2	312.6	376.7	347.5	320.8	334.3	414.3
2 Cereals and cereal preparations	254.9	307.1	429.6	237.6	121.3	168.4	209.5	192.6
3 Fruits and vegetables	224.3	277.8	320.6	299.2	281.2	305.2	326.4	411.2
(a) Cashew kernels	145.9	177.2	202.4	140.0	145.8	151.1	184.0	256.3
(b) Others	78.4	100.6	118.2	159.1	135.4	154.0	142.4	154.9
4 Coffee	201.7	270.9	163.1	193.6	175.8	176.8	223.5	232.2
5 Tea	454.3	538.0	440.7	382.5	498.2	644.9	511.9	451.4
6 Spices	184.5	140.8	110.1	97.8	112.8	173.8	227.1	218.3
(a) Pepper black	51.1	56.0	35.6	46.9	51.7	60.7	149.8	161.2
(b) Others	133.3	84.8	74.6	50.9	61.2	113.2	77.3	57.1
7 Feeding stuff for animals	207.9	200.2	172.9	194.1	197.3	144.4	125.7	176.5
8 Sugar and honey	201.1	50.4	71.1	69.8	169.1	29.9	13.7	1.3
9 Others	66.9	101.6	119.2	111.3	98.4	90.2	79.1	79.5
Beverages and tobacco	**142.9**	**178.7**	**263.6**	**257.5**	**172.9**	**150.8**	**139.4**	**146.1**
1 Tobacco, unmanufactured	126.3	157.3	228.5	221.8	150.5	126.6	111.9	113.8
2 Others	16.6	21.4	35.1	35.7	22.3	24.2	27.5	32.3
Crude materials, inedible, except fuels	**823.2**	**1029.8**	**863.4**	**845.1**	**861.8**	**842.5**	**914.6**	**928.1**
1 Hides, skins and fur skins, raw	0.7	0.9	0.5	0.2	0.2	0.0	0.0	0.7
2 Wool and other animal hair	1.7	1.2	2.2	1.3	1.6	1.3	1.3	1.3
3 Cotton textile fibre and waste	106.2	223.9	49.0	112.8	161.2	53.0	56.9	163.7
4 Jute textile fibre and waste	2.7	6.7	14.0	9.6	0.8	0.9	3.6	4.8
5 Mica	26.6	24.0	34.3	22.4	19.0	19.8	20.9	18.8
6 Iron ore and concentrates	352.3	383.5	392.2	393.6	388.4	386.5	473.1	427.8
7 Manganese ore	16.2	16.0	16.5	15.0	13.0	19.9	16.6	7.2

8 Lac	14.1	17.1	20.2	14.1	13.2	26.3	33.4	22.0
9 Others	302.7	356.3	334.5	276.0	264.4	334.9	308.8	281.9
Mineral fuels, lubricants and related materials	**26.2**	**35.2**	**250.8**	**1283.3**	**1537.8**	**1533.4**	**535.3**	**326.8**
1 Petroleum crude and partly refined	0.0	0.0	218.8	1100. 1	1190.6	1314.8	110.5	0.0
2 Petroleum products	23.3	31.5	27.5	177.9	345.2	214.5	416.5	321.8
3 Others	2.9	3.7	4.4	5.3	1.9	4.0	8.4	4.9
Animal and vegetable oils and fats	**64.7**	**24.4**	**22.3**	**26.9**	**46.0**	**49.6**	**39.7**	**24.9**
1 Fixed vegetable oils and fats	51.6	18.6	19.4	26.1	29.0	46.4	38.2	23.5
2 Others	13.1	5.8	2.9	0.8	17.0	3.2	1.5	1.4
Chemicals	**257.5**	**297.7**	**418.7**	**360.4**	**316.9**	**406.1**	**322.1**	**380.6**
1 Chemical elements and compounds	39.2	40.5	44.3	49.2	46.6	57.4	43.6	62.9
2 Dyeing, tanning and colouring materials	54.3	64.1	61.3	62.0	65.0	67.5	60.9	94.9
3 Medicinal and pharmaceutical products	108.0	85.2	136.0	116.1	150.1	197.0	129.0	126.2
4 Essential oils and perfume materials	41.5	93.9	162.1	120.0	42.6	61.1	55.1	61.3
5 Plastic materials, regenerated cellulose and artificial resins	3.6	3.2	3.9	2.2	1.8	3.7	5.2	8.7
6 Others	10.9	10.7	11.1	10.9	10.6	19.4	28.3	26.6
Manufactured goods classified chiefly by material	**2963.8**	**2933.7**	**2879.7**	**2731.6**	**2857.9**	**3035.6**	**3033.0**	**3546.0**
1 Leather and manufactures *n.e.s.* and dressed fur skins	599.6	426.3	411.8	372.5	414.8	527.5	528.5	572.2
2 Cotton manufactures excluding yarn and thread and clothing	354.9	349.6	328.4	280.9	294.7	378.9	323.9	345.1
3 Textile yarn and thread	59.3	63.7	54.8	58.7	59.4	65.6	68.8	109.3
4 Jute manufactures excluding twist and yarn	416.7	417.4	289.1	212.4	165.5	287.1	214.4	191.2
5 Woollen carpets and rugs	164.8	207.7	169.7	—	—	—	—	—
6 Pearls, precious and semi-precious stones	640.9	761.0	348.6	982.8	1167.7	970.1	1 153.8	1561.1
7 Manufacture of metals *n.e.s.*	252.4	234.9	246.1	203.0	189.8	167.7	124.3	129.1

(Contd.)

APPENDIX TABLE 9 (*Contd.*)

1	*11*	*12*	*13*	*14*	*15*	*16*	*17*	*18*
8 Iron and steel	131.1	88.1	89.0	52.6	46.9	63.7	45.9	43.9
9 Non-ferrous metals	19.2	19.6	13.5	26.8	20.9	14.9	34.6	19.0
10. Others	325.0	365.4	428.5	542.0	498.2	560.2	538.9	575.2
Machinery and transport equipment	**554.2**	**664.9**	**689.0**	**605.2**	**523.0**	**557.8**	**575.0**	**654.3**
1 Machinery, other than electric	221.2	272.4	303.8	258.3	266.4	281.7	292.4	333.6
2 Electrical machinery, apparatus and appliances	119.9	144.6	148.8	157.2	108.3	116.0	129.7	163.0
3 Transport equipment	213.1	247.9	236.3	189.6	148.3	160.1	152.9	157.7
Miscellaneous manufactured articles	**956.8**	**1100.7**	**1158.9**	**1012.2**	**1108.3**	**1224.0**	**1279.7**	**1530.3**
1 Footwear	41.9	50.7	40.3	33.8	33.2	40.7	40.7	63.5
2 Clothing	616.3	715.3	733.3	625.8	716.7	828.3	905.6	1100.2
3 Others	298.6	334.8	385.3	352.6	358.4	355.0	333.4	366.6
Commodities and transactions *n.e.s.*	**33.6**	**63.7**	**17.7**	**22.9**	**23.4**	**23.7**	**14.6**	**30.4**
Total Exports	**7926.4**	**8484.7**	**8703.9**	**9107.6**	**9449.4**	**9878.1**	**8904.5**	**9744.7**

APPENDIX TABLE 9 (*Contd.*)

(*US $ million*)

Commodity/Year	*1987-88*	*1988-89*	*1989-90*	*1990-91*	*1991-92*	*1992-93*	*1993-94*	*1994-95*	*1995-96*
1	*19*	*20*	*21*	*22*	*23*	*24*	*25*	*26*	*27*
I. Primary products	**3160.5**	**3242.5**	**3883.2**	**4324.0**	**4132.2**	**3873.5**	**4915.7**	**5214.4**	**7256.9**
A. Agriculture and allied products	**2560.7**	**2417.3**	**2852.7**	**3354.4**	**3202.5**	**3135.8**	**4027.5**	**4226.1**	**6081.9**
1 Tea	463.7	420.8	550.7	596.4	491.5	337.2	337.7	310.7	350.1
2 Coffee	201.7	202.7	208.5	140.6	134.7	129.9	173.9	335.3	449.3
3 Rice	261.2	228.9	256.2	257.2	306.5	336.8	410.2	384.0	1365.7
4 Wheat	27.3	2.1	1.3	17.3	51.5	3.5	0.1	13.5	109.6
5 Cotton raw including waste	84.5	14.8	77.1	471.4	123.7	62.8	208.4	44.5	60.8
6 Tobacco	104.2	87.0	105.1	146.8	152.9	163.7	147.0	81.1	133.6
7 Cashew including cashew nut shell liquid	243.1	190.5	220.8	249.1	274.0	258.5	334.2	397.2	369.9
8 Spices	259.6	190.0	166.4	130.4	151.0	135.8	181.4	195.0	237.2
9 Oil meals	164.6	282.2	366.5	339.1	373.8	533.5	740.9	572.6	702.1
10 Fruits and vegetables	98.9	117.7	121.3	118.9	141.6	107.9	132.1	139.1	157.7
11 Processed fruits, juices, miscellaneous processed items	134.3	122.3	126.4	118.5	77.3	78.8	90.6	115.0	265.4
12 Marine products	411.3	435.0	412.7	535.0	585.2	601.9	813.6	1126.4	1010.8
13 Sugar and mollases	9.1	6.7	19.5	20.9	63.8	122.1	56.8	19.8	151.4
14 Meat and meat preparations	67.7	64.9	68.3	77.9	93.6	88.8	109.8	128.3	187.4
15 Others	29.9	51.9	152.0	134.7	181.4	174.6	290.8	363.6	530.8
B. Ores and minerals	**599.8**	**825.3**	**1030.5**	**969.6**	**929.7**	**737.8**	**888.2**	**988.3**	**1174.9**
1 Iron ore	427.7	464.8	557.1	584.7	582.3	381.2	438.0	413.1	514.5
2 Mica	18.0	20.3	18.0	19.4	14.3	8.3	8.8	7.1	8.2
3 Others	154.1	340.2	455.3	365.5	333.2	348.3	441.4	568.1	652.2

(*Contd.*)

APPENDIX TABLE 9 (*Contd.*)

1		19	20	21	22	23	24	25	26	27
II.	**Manufactured goods**	**8195.1**	**10110.3**	**11971.5**	**12996.4**	**13148.4**	**14038.8**	**16656.7**	**20404.4**	**23747.0**
A.	**Leather and manufactures**	**964.4**	**1051.0**	**1171.5**	**1449.2**	**1268.8**	**1277.5**	**1299.5**	**1610.6**	**1752.2**
B.	**Chemicals and Related products**	**791.6**	**1090.5**	**1553.8**	**1728.0**	**1868.8**	**1786.1**	**2377.2**	**3066.8**	**3597.0**
1	Basic chemicals, Pharmaceuticals & cosmetics	529.0	773.0	1128.5	1235.1	1400.7	1148.0	1373.1	1762.9	2169.2
2	Plastic and linoleum products	50.3	74.7	97.5	111.2	112.1	149.4	335.9	478.3	585.4
3	Rubber, glass, paints, enamels and products	174.0	201.3	266.4	310.0	277.4	408.1	563.8	633.1	652.6
4	Residual chemicals and allied products	38.3	41.4	61.3	71.7	78.6	80.7	104.4	192.6	189.8
C.	**Engineering goods**	**1152.3**	**1601.3**	**1997.7**	**2250.4**	**2253.1**	**2480.8**	**3038.1**	**3508.0**	**4391.0**
1	Iron & steel	21.6	52.1	98.9	161.1	153.5	306.1	568.4	528.4	696.7
2	Manufacture of metals	222.3	305.1	445.7	456.3	484.2	560.2	663.2	706.2	826.4
3	Machinery and instruments	397.0	509.5	603.9	696.2	581.4	541.6	638.9	726.7	829.8
4	Transport equipnment	195.2	250.7	316.0	400.6	496.4	533.7	591.9	771.3	924.9
5	Electronic goods	154.1	200.5	302.7	232.4	265.2	212.3	303.6	412.2	670.1
6	Others	162.1	283.3	230.4	303.8	272.3	326.9	272.2	363.3	443.1
D.	**Textile and textile products**	**3013.8**	**3037.7**	**3746.5**	**4342.6**	**4693.1**	**5007.4**	**5472.3**	**7117.7**	**8031.6**
1	Cotton yarn, fabrics, madeups, *etc.*	882.8	797.6	905.1	1170.3	1299.3	1350.5	1537.1	2233.8	2576.6
2	Natural silk yarn, fabrics, madeups, *etc.*, incl. silk waste	106.6	128.0	123.1	131.0	142.0	138.6	127.2	136.2	133.2
3	Manmade yarn, fabrics, madeups, *etc.*	88.2	115.4	187.1	226.7	333.2	372.6	425.7	613.9	750.8
4	Manmade staple fibre	—	—	—	—	—	21.5	12.2	25.6	21.1
5	Woolen yarn, fabrics, madeups, *etc.*	6.1	14.2	17.0	11.8	30.0	39.2	50.2	60.7	62.5
6	Readymade garments	1403.4	1451.4	1937.9	2236.1	2199.2	2393.0	2586.2	3281.9	3675.6
7	Jute & jute manufactures	185.6	160.7	178.0	166.3	158.5	122.6	124.0	150.6	185.7
8	Coir & coir manufactures	22.9	21.8	24.9	26.8	28.5	31.2	41.4	55.0	62.9

9	Carpets	318.3	348.7	373.2	373.7	502.4	538.2	568.2	560.0	563.4
	(a) Carpet handmade	253.3	285.2	301.4	289.3	407.4	434.8	453.7	441.5	420.4
	(b) Carpet millmade	65.0	63.5	71.8	84.4	95.0	85.5	100.3	105.6	126.0
	(c) Silk carpets	—	—	—	—	—	17.9	14.2	12.8	16.9
E.	**Gems and jewellery**	**2015.1**	**3032.8**	**3180.7**	**2924.1**	**2738.2**	**3071.7**	**3995.8**	**4500.4**	**5274.8**
F.	**Handicrafts (excluding handmade carpets)**	**174.3**	**205.9**	**222.9**	**223.9**	**241.5**	**275.9**	**318.5**	**386.3**	**433.9**
G.	**Other manufactured goods**	**83.5**	**91.2**	**98.5**	**78.2**	**84.9**	**139.3**	**155.3**	**214.5**	**266.5**
III.	**Petroleum products**	**500.4**	**348.7**	**418.4**	**522.7**	**414.7**	**476.2**	**397.8**	**416.9**	**453.7**
IV.	**Others**	**232.6**	**268.9**	**339.3**	**302.2**	**170.1**	**148.6**	**268.0**	**294.7**	**337.3**
Total Exports		**12088.5**	**13970.4**	**16612.5**	**18145.2**	**17865.4**	**18537.2**	**22238.3**	**26330.5**	**31794.9**

APPENDIX TABLE 9 (*Contd.*)

(*US $ million*)

	Commodity/Year	*1996-97*	*1997-98*	*1998-99*	*1999-00*	*2000-01*	*2001-02*	*2002-03*	*2003-04*	*2004-05*	*2005-06*	*2006-07R*	*2007-08P*
1		*28*	*29*	*30*	*31*	*32*	*33*	*34*	*35*	*36*	*37*	*38*	*39*
I.	Primary products	8035.1	7687.3	6927.9	6524.2	7126.2	7163.6	8706.1	9901.8	13553.3	16377.4	19686.0	27064.6
A.	**Agriculture and allied products**	**6862.7**	**6626.2**	**6034.5**	**5608**	**5973.2**	**5901.2**	**6710.0**	**7533.1**	**8474.7**	**10213.8**	**12683.5**	**18059.9**
1	Tea	292.1	504.9	538.4	411.9	391.5	360.5	341.4	356.3	409.6	390.9	435.3	502.3
2	Coffee	401.9	456.4	410.7	331.1	259.4	229.6	205.4	236.3	237.9	358.8	435.1	464.0
3	Rice	893.6	907.0	1492.9	721.4	641.8	665.6	1204.9	907.0	1506.5	1405.2	1554.9	2913.8
4	Wheat	196.7	0.1	0.3	0.0	90.9	278.9	363.6	520.4	324.9	125.9	7.8	0.1
5	Cotton raw including waste	443.5	221.1	49.2	17.8	48.4	9.0	10.4	205.1	94.0	656.0	1349.8	1987.0
6	Tobacco	213.2	288.0	181.1	232.8	189.8	169.4	211.4	238.6	279.2	300.6	372.4	479.0
7	Cashew including cashew nut shell liquid	362.9	378.6	387.8	567.9	449.5	376.2	426.0	371.0	554.0	585.8	553.9	555.1
8	Spices	338.6	379.3	388.0	407.9	354.1	313.9	342.1	336.0	419.1	477.9	697.9	1037.3
9	Oil meals	984.6	924.3	461.5	378.0	447.6	474.5	307.3	728.7	707.2	1101.1	1216.4	1975.6
10	Fruits and vegetables	163.0	158.7	128.4	148.4	184.6	221.1	245.5	389.9	398.7	481.9	681.1	760.8
11	Processed fruits, juices, miscellaneous processed items	307.1	173.5	169.5	196.9	288.4	259.3	306.7	305.2	284.3	359.0	405.8	523.2
12	Marine products	1128.9	1207.3	1038.4	1182.6	1393.8	1236.8	1431.6	1328.7	1439.8	1589.2	1768.2	1702.6
13	Sugar and mollases	303.6	68.6	5.8	9.3	110.6	373.6	374.9	269.0	34.5	135.0	720.6	1404.4
14	Meat and meat preparations	199.7	217.5	187.3	189.1	321.7	250.2	284.6	373.1	424.0	621.2	732.4	927.6
15	Others	633.1	740.9	595.0	813.1	801.2	682.8	654.3	967.8	1360.9	1625.3	1751.6	2827.4
B.	**Ores and minerals**	**1172.4**	**1061.1**	**893.4**	**916.1**	**1153.0**	**1262.4**	**1996.0**	**2368.7**	**5078.6**	**6163.6**	**7002.5**	**9004.7**
1	Iron ore	480.7	476.2	384.0	271.2	357.6	426.4	867.9	1125.8	3277.3	3801.1	3902.0	5745.1
2	Mica	7.0	10.8	10.3	9.8	9.1	11.7	8.4	23.0	14.1	17.4	16.8	21.6
3	Others	684.6	574.1	499.1	635.1	786.3	824.3	1119.7	1219.9	1787.1	2345.1	3083.7	3238.0

II.	Manufactured goods	24613.4	26546.6	25791.5	29714.4	34335.2	33369.7	40244.5	48492.1	60730.7	72562.8	84920.6	101099.3
A.	**Leather and manufactures**	**1605.8**	**1656.7**	**1660.7**	**1590.2**	**1944.4**	**1910.1**	**1848.3**	**2163.0**	**2421.6**	**2697.7**	**3016.7**	**3431.6**
B.	**Chemicals and related products**	**3912.8**	**4396.3**	**4009.2**	**4706.5**	**5885.9**	**6051.8**	**7455.3**	**9445.9**	**12443.7**	**14769.5**	**17335.5**	**20453.5**
1	Basic chemicals, pharmaceuticals & cosmetics	2497.4	2821.8	2654.6	3088.2	3664.0	3697.0	4658.4	5845.6	7139.1	9127.1	10958.9	13346.6
2	Plastic and linoleum products	539.4	514.3	471.7	603.8	915.2	987.4	1221.7	1752.7	3032.8	2819.3	3252.6	3352.7
3	Rubber, glass, paints, enamels and products	683.1	712.0	631.3	693.7	936.5	984.5	1198.3	1488.0	1759.5	2105.2	2372.8	2820.4
4	Residual chemicals and allied products	192.9	348.1	251.6	320.9	370.1	382.9	377.0	359.6	512.3	717.9	751.2	933.8
C.	**Engineering goods**	**4962.7**	**5336.2**	**4463.9**	**5152.1**	**6818.6**	**6957.8**	**9033.0**	**12405.4**	**17348.3**	**21718.8**	**29567.2**	**36722.0**
1	Iron & steel	769.8	874.7	579.1	833.0	1028.3	898.1	1856.0	2477.8	3921.0	3548.3	5238.6	5447.7
2	Manufacture of metals	913.5	1023.2	1040.0	1225.6	1577.7	1604.0	1847.6	2426.5	3401.5	4233.2	5081.2	7023.9
3	Machinery and instruments	1057.1	1195.7	1154.8	1183.2	1580.1	1734.1	2008.4	2776.3	3719.4	5077.5	6722.8	8720.3
4	Transport equipnment	968.7	929.1	761.8	810.2	991.9	1020.9	1333.9	1956.0	2829.7	4323.0	4949.9	7025.5
5	Electronic goods	783.7	759.6	502.8	681.0	1051.5	1171.3	1252.7	1728.3	1831.8	2173.1	2854.0	3299.1
6	Others	469.9	554.0	425.5	419.1	589.1	529.4	734.3	1040.5	1644.9	2363.7	4673.8	5275.5
D.	**Textile and textile products**	**8635.8**	**9050.4**	**8866.3**	**9822.1**	**11285.0**	**10206.5**	**11617.0**	**12791.5**	**13555.3**	**16402.1**	**17373.2**	**19015.1**
1	Cotton yarn, fabrics, madeups, *etc.*	3121.7	3264.3	2771.9	3089.6	3460.7	3072.9	3351.0	3394.8	3450.1	3944.8	4218.7	4511.2
2	Natural silk yarn, fabrics, madeups, *etc.*, incl. silk waste	128.8	176.4	178.2	245.4	316.6	285.9	314.1	379.8	405.0	432.6	441.9	381.9
3	Man made yarn,fabrics, madeups, *etc.*	702.7	804.9	700.0	811.4	1058.5	1065.0	1371.9	1761.2	1962.7	1957.8	2204.4	2858.8

(Contd.)

APPENDIX TABLE 9 (*Contd.*)

1		*28*	*29*	*30*	*31*	*32*	*33*	*34*	*35*	*36*	*37*	*38*	*39*
4	Manmade staple fibre	18.8	17.9	19.6	43.7	36.6	23.5	45.6	60.1	88.0	81.8	196.4	276.9
5	Woolen yarn, fabrics, madeups, *etc.*	103.7	109.7	74.6	50.0	62.4	52.2	50.9	58.3	69.8	85.3	85.2	93.1
6	Readymade garments	3753.3	3876.2	4364.9	4765.1	5568.9	5006.6	5689.9	6231.4	6561.4	8617.7	8892.3	9491.8
7	Jute & jute manufactures	155.4	186.8	138.2	125.7	151.2	128.3	187.6	242.4	276.3	296.3	260.4	322.9
8	Coir & coir manufactures	61.0	68.6	75.2	46.1	48.3	61.8	73.4	77.8	105.6	133.3	145.9	158.9
9	Carpets	590.5	545.6	543.5	645.1	581.7	510.2	532.6	585.7	636.4	852.6	928.0	919.7
	(a) Carpet handmade	436.3	410.6	409.3	498.6	446.9	374.8	401.0	559.5	608.1	829.2	898.7	905.7
	(b) Carpet millmade	134.8	105.5	102.4	112.9	110.5	99.3	111.7	0.0	0.0	0.0	0.0	0.0
	(c) Silk carpets	19.4	29.5	31.9	33.6	24.3	36.1	19.9	26.2	28.4	23.3	29.3	14.0
E.	**Gems and jewellery**	**4752.7**	**5345.5**	**5929.3**	**7502.3**	**7384.0**	**7306.3**	**9029.9**	**10573.3**	**13761.8**	**15529.1**	**15977.0**	**19657.4**
F.	**Handicrafts (excluding handmade carpets)**	**475.7**	**525.9**	**633.1**	**668.6**	**661.5**	**549.0**	**785.3**	**499.7**	**377.4**	**462.0**	**438.0**	**460.7**
G.	**Other manufactured goods**	**267.9**	**235.6**	**228.9**	**272.6**	**355.8**	**388.3**	**475.6**	**613.3**	**822.6**	**983.7**	**1213.0**	**1359.1**
III.	**Petroleum products**	**481.8**	**352.8**	**89.4**	**38.9**	**1869.7**	**2119.1**	**2576.5**	**3568.4**	**6989.3**	**11639.6**	**18678.7**	**24869.2**
IV.	**Others**	**339.4**	**419.8**	**410.0**	**544.9**	**1229.2**	**1174.3**	**1192.3**	**1880.3**	**2262.6**	**2510.7**	**3076.2**	**5973.5**
	Total Exports	33469.7	35006.4	33218.7		44560.3	43826.7	52719.4	63842.6	83535.9	103090.5	126361.5	159006.7

P : Provisional R : Revised *n.e.s.* : not elsewhere specified or included.

Note : Due to change in commodity classification by DGCI&S, data on 'Chemical elements and compounds', 'Machinery other than electric', and 'Electrical machinery, apparatus and appliances' from 1970-71 to 1975-1976 and 1976-77 to 1986-87 may not be strictly comparable.

Source : Directorate General of Commercial Intelligence and Statistics.

APPENDIX TABLE 10

Imports of Principal Commodities—US Dollars

(US$ million)

Commodity/Year	*1970-71*	*1971-72*	*1972-73*	*1973-74*	*1974-75*	*1975-76*	*1976-77*	*1977-78*	*1978-79*
1	*2*	*3*	*4*	*5*	*6*	*7*	*8*	*9*	*10*
Food and live animals	**359.6**	**263.5**	**208.1**	**702.0**	**1077.0**	**1645.8**	**1064.6**	**270.8**	**298.2**
1 Cereals and cereal preparations	281.8	175.6	105.3	607.2	961.9	1546.5	966.4	142.7	105.7
(a) Wheat	229.4	137.3	62.7	444.1	879.2	1394.2	890.3	109.0	80.3
(b) Rice	39.5	24.2	14.0	8.3	15.3	53.6	51.2	7.2	1.2
(c) Others	13.0	14.1	28.6	154.8	67.3	98.7	24.9	26.5	24.1
2 Cashew nuts raw	38.9	37.3	41.4	37.0	46.1	38.7	20.4	20.9	11.1
3 Spices	0.6	1.2	1.1	1.1	1.1	1.3	1.6	8.6	11.1
4 Others	38.2	49.4	60.4	56.8	67.9	59.2	76.2	98.6	170.3
Beverages and tobacco	**0.4**	**0.4**	**0.4**	**0.6**	**1.3**	**1.1**	**0.8**	**1.7**	**0.8**
1 Tobacco, unmanufactured	0.0	0.0	0.1	0.0	0.3	0.0	0.1	0.4	0.0
2 Others	0.4	0.3	0.3	0.5	1.1	1.1	0.6	1.3	0.8
Crude materials, inedible, except fuels	**265.0**	**284.9**	**247.4**	**236.3**	**277.1**	**244.9**	**383.2**	**748.4**	**702.6**
1 Crude rubber including synthetic and reclaimed	5.1	4.8	4.8	5.2	8.8	8.1	9.3	12.6	36.1
2 Cotton	130.8	151.7	118.4	66.8	34.5	32.5	144.2	231.6	32.1
3 Jute	0.2	0.0	1.5	15.7	4.7	3.8	7.5	0.0	1.9
4 Wool and other animal hair excluding wool tops	21.3	19.0	15.5	26.9	34.6	29.9	31.1	35.0	38.7
5 Manmade fibres and waste thereof	—	—	—	—	—	—	17.9	95.1	92.8
6 Synthetic fibres suitable for spinning #	9.5	6.2	6.4	3.3	3.4	7.3	15.7	128.2	147.4
7 Metalliferrous ores and metal scrap	14.4	13.3	8.6	17.1	7.5	23.3	34.6	52.6	82.3
8 Crude fertilisers and crude minerals	46.7	48.7	49.2	65.6	143.3	96.3	96.6	131.1	138.6
9 Others	37.1	41.1	43.0	35.7	40.2	43.8	26.1	62.1	132.7

(Contd.)

APPENDIX TABLE 10 (*Contd.*)

1	*2*	*3*	*4*	*5*	*6*	*7*	*8*	*9*	*10*
Mineral fuels, lubricants and related materials	**180.0**	**260.4**	**266.1**	**719.5**	**1457.1**	**1412.1**	**1574.3**	**1807.4**	**2050.5**
1 Petroleum crude and partly refined	140.1	197.3	188.7	535.2	1202.5	1211.4	1282.8	1451.5	1511.0
2 Petroleum products	39.7	62.5	77.1	183.8	254.4	200.3	291.5	355.0	527.2
3 Others	0.2	0.6	0.3	0.5	0.1	0.4	0.0	1.0	12.3
Animal and vegetable oils and fats	**50.9**	**62.2**	**32.5**	**83.3**	**43.9**	**19.6**	**131.4**	**859.5**	**671.4**
1 Vegetable oils, fixed	30.5	37.7	20.2	73.1	15.5	16.3	112.1	828.8	652.8
2 Others	20.4	24.5	12.3	10.2	28.4	3.2	19.3	30.6	18.5
Chemicals	**254.4**	**292.4**	**337.3**	**458.7**	**920.7**	**875.2**	**493.0**	**754.7**	**1016.8**
1 Chemical elements and compounds	89.9	96.1	119.1	140.7	234.5	207.5	153.5	228.9	280.6
2 Dyeing, tanning and colouring materials	12.2	11.2	11.9	13.3	14.4	13.6	16.8	20.3	28.4
3 Medicinal and pharmaceutical products	32.1	35.5	30.3	33.9	43.1	41.8	47.0	74.1	96.2
4 Fertilisers, manufactured	81.0	108.7	125.4	209.0	549.3	540.6	213.4	300.6	450.7
5 Others	39.2	40.8	50.6	61.8	79.5	71.6	62.2	130.8	160.8
Manufactured goods classified chiefly by material	**456.1**	**589.4**	**585.7**	**692.1**	**971.5**	**714.1**	**754.1**	**1132.8**	**1795.7**
1 Pearls, precious and semi-precious stones	32.5	35.2	54.2	95.0	66.7	97.0	201.2	385.1	567.4
2 Paper, paper board and manufactures thereof	33.2	46.7	40.9	37.5	75.0	66.4	69.3	95.3	127.3
(a) Newsprint paper	24.8	36.9	26.7	23.7	56.7	44.1	52.6	70.9	97.7
(b) Others	8.4	9.8	14.1	13.8	18.3	22.3	16.7	24.4	29.6
3 Textile yarn, fabrics, made-up articles and related products	10.4	13.4	8.1	7.6	16.3	14.4	8.5	23.7	57.6
4 Iron and steel	194.6	317.9	294.2	320.1	533.6	359.2	244.4	306.1	562.1
5 Non-ferrous metals	158.0	137.0	142.1	180.1	225.0	115.7	175.0	223.8	298.4
6 Manufactures of metal, *n.e.s.*	12.3	16.2	24.5	28.1	34.8	38.2	35.5	44.3	56.0
7 Others	15.1	22.8	21.6	23.7	20.1	23.2	20.2	54.6	126.9

Machinery and transport equipment	**522.2**	**629.7**	**693.3**	**836.2**	**876.1**	**1076.4**	**1166.9**	**1293.3**	**1531.5**
1 Machinery, other than electric	341.1	362.4	388.2	547.5	508.2	664.2	857.1	809.1	935.4
2 Electrical machinery, apparatus and appliances	93.1	140.7	174.6	166.8	202.7	231.2	119.5	221.8	235.3
3 Transport equipment	88.0	126.6	130.4	121.9	165.2	181.0	190.2	262.4	360.7
(a) Railway vehicles	18.5	26.7	33.0	32.5	32.1	39.5	19.3	21.2	15.2
(b) Others	69.5	99.9	97.5	89.4	133.2	141.4	170.9	241.2	345.5
Miscellaneous manufactured articles	**73.6**	**58.7**	**62.4**	**64.0**	**65.9**	**74.5**	**83.5**	**143.3**	**211.2**
Total Imports	**2162.3**	**2441.5**	**2433.1**	**3792.6**	**5690.6**	**6063.7**	**5651.7**	**7011.8**	**8278.7**

APPENDIX TABLE 10 (*Contd.*)

(*US $ million*)

Commodity/Year	*1979-80*	*1980-81*	*1981-82*	*1982-83*	*1983-84*	*1984-85*	*1985-86*	*1986-87*
1	*11*	*12*	*13*	*14*	*15*	*16*	*17*	*18*
Food and live animals	**345.7**	**480.6**	**769.5**	**661.7**	**1005.9**	**617.1**	**717.6**	**587.1**
1 Cereals and cereal preparations	130.7	127.0	387.1	386.1	781.9	203.6	90.1	68.0
(a) Wheat	104.1	96.8	334.2	363.9	622.2	109.0	49.9	34.5
(b) Rice	0.9	4.7	16.4	4.0	97.1	76.0	11.2	1.3
(c) Others	25.6	25.5	36.5	18.2	62.7	18.6	29.0	32.2
2 Cashew nuts raw	14.3	11.0	20.5	1.5	21.4	32.7	19.9	55.7
3 Spices	14.2	23.1	21.9	28.8	39.7	25.2	19.8	26.0
4 Others	186.5	319.6	340.0	245.4	162.9	355.7	587.8	437.4
Beverages and tobacco	**0.7**	**1.0**	**1.3**	**1.2**	**3.0**	**1.3**	**3.0**	**2.4**
1 Tobacco, unmanufactured	0.1	0.0	0.1	0.0	0.6	0.0	0.0	0.1
2 Others	0.7	0.9	1.2	1.2	2.4	1.3	3.0	2.3
Crude materials, inedible, except fuels	**658.6**	**714.9**	**940.4**	**793.6**	**922.0**	**944.9**	**1227.9**	**1271.4**
1 Crude rubber including synthetic and reclaimed	66.2	39.9	84.8	66.1	79.8	73.4	82.2	84.1
2 Cotton	0.1	0.0	13.2	0.1	0.0	0.0	10.3	0.1
3 Jute	0.6	2.6	2.7	8.8	6.3	30.0	5.0	2.0
4 Wool and other animal hair excluding wool tops	39.4	64.2	48.9	57.6	74.8	69.1	84.0	68.9
5 Manmade fibres and waste thereof	70.3	84.9	137.7	93.5	48.3	27.6	17.2	4.8
6 Synthetic fibres suitable for spinning#	64.3	37.2	55.4	57.2	53.0	23.1	38.9	41.4
7 Metalliferrous ores and metal scrap	114.1	146.1	226.1	200.3	186.7	156.0	296.5	369.4
8 Crude fertilisers and crude minerals	227.3	263.4	267.1	211.0	291.7	347.8	381.2	329.1
9 Others	76.3	76.7	104.5	98.9	181.4	218.0	312.7	371.6

Mineral fuels, lubricants and related materials	**4114.7**	**6692.2**	**5831.9**	**5957.4**	**4703.4**	**4595.9**	**4260.8**	**2370.8**
1 Petroleum crude and partly refined	2701.5	4234.3	4165.9	4183.5	3424.6	2885.4	3013.3	1659.2
2 Petroleum products	1333.2	2420.6	1620.3	1632.7	1248.5	1664.4	1064.7	540.3
3 Others	80.0	37.3	45.6	141.2	30.3	46.1	182.8	171.3
Animal and vegetable oils and fats	**562.3**	**889.9**	**767.1**	**463.2**	**772.0**	**847.7**	**629.4**	**513.6**
1 Vegetable oils, fixed	551.1	863.4	697.2	410.4	709.9	799.5	612.3	496.4
2 Others	11.2	26.5	69.9	52.7	62.0	48.2	17.1	17.2
Chemicals	**1196.4**	**1674.7**	**1476.2**	**1023.0**	**1360.2**	**2044.9**	**2348.1**	**2063.4**
1 Chemical elements and compounds	399.6	452.9	541.0	437.1	638.2	720.6	890.4	896.3
2 Dyeing, tanning and colouring materials	31.4	26.3	27.7	29.1	30.3	34.9	46.1	52.0
3 Medicinal and pharmaceutical products	91.3	106.9	94.2	91.9	142.1	115.4	144.8	167.3
4 Fertilisers, manufactured	458.5	824.7	568.3	211.6	197.8	846.7	860.5	450.7
5 Others	215.6	263.9	245.0	253.3	351.9	327.4	406.3	497.2
Manufacture goods classified chiefly by material	**2434.6**	**2834.7**	**2896.6**	**2919.3**	**3091.6**	**2498.2**	**3090.4**	**3409.6**
1 Pearls, precious and semi-precious stones	429.0	526.9	443.1	754.4	1061.8	868.2	898.8	1165.5
2 Paper, paper board and manufactures thereof	196.1	235.8	273.6	165.0	151.4	164.4	184.7	169.9
(a) Newsprint paper	136.6	145.4	202.1	122.2	109.0	118.3	106.6	95.0
(b) Others	59.6	90.4	71.5	42.8	42.4	46.1	78.1	74.9
3 Textile yarn, fabrics, made-up articles and related products	65.0	75.1	107.9	131.6	131.6	94.7	124.7	118.1
4 Iron and steel	1072.7	1077.8	1342.0	1212.7	1014.2	791.6	1139.9	1218.0
5 Non-ferrous metals	436.4	603.6	442.8	356.5	377.8	346.3	442.8	404.4
6 Manufactures of metal, *n.e.s.*	93.5	113.1	128.8	148.7	143.8	118.5	164.7	163.6
7 Others	141.8	202.4	158.4	150.5	211.0	114.5	134.9	170.2

(Contd.)

APPENDIX TABLE 10 (*Contd.*)

1	*11*	*12*	*13*	*14*	*15*	*16*	*17*	*18*
Machinery and transport equipment	**1707.6**	**2302.1**	**2208.5**	**2661.5**	**3069.2**	**2546.2**	**3238.0**	**4913.5**
1 Machinery, other than electric	873.9	1377.0	1503.9	1488.6	1983.9	1622.0	2119.3	3335.8
2 Electrical machinery, apparatus and appliances	415.6	328.3	364.5	511.1	653.1	613.9	753.8	948.9
3 Transport equipment	418.1	596.7	340.1	661.7	432.2	310.3	464.8	628.9
(a) Railway vehicles	31.5	58.8	61.6	71.3	42.9	27.3	27.8	32.6
(b) Others	386.6	538.0	278.5	590.5	389.3	283.0	437.0	596.2
Miscellaneous manufactured articles	**270.0**	**276.4**	**281.4**	**305.7**	**383.5**	**316.1**	**451.6**	**594.8**
Total Imports	**11290.6**	**15866.5**	**15172.9**	**14786.6**	**15310.9**	**14412.3**	**16066.9**	**15726.6**

APPENDIX TABLE 10 (*Contd.*)

(*US $ million*)

	Commodity/Year	*1987-88*	*1988-89*	*1989-90*	*1990-91*	*1991-92*	*1992-93*	*1993-94*	*1994-95*	*1995-96*	*1996-97*
1		*19*	*20*	*21*	*22*	*23*	*24*	*25*	*26*	*27*	*28*
I.	**Bulk imports**	**7019.1**	**7886.1**	**8539.4**	**10848.0**	**8562.8**	**9829.8**	**9112.2**	**11320.6**	**14314.3**	**16365.1**
A.	**Petroleum, crude and products**	**3118.1**	**3009.0**	**3767.5**	**6028.1**	**5324.8**	**6100.0**	**5753.5**	**5927.8**	**7525.8**	**10036.2**
B.	**Bulk consumption goods**	**1140.6**	**1304.0**	**556.1**	**556.5**	**274.7**	**506.7**	**326.7**	**1144.1**	**969.7**	**1214.0**
1	Cereals and cereal preparations	50.9	534.2	234.0	101.6	70.3	333.5	92.6	29.4	24.0	137.2
2	Edible oils	747.2	503.9	125.4	181.6	100.5	57.6	53.1	198.8	676.2	825.1
3	Pulses	193.6	265.8	138.4	268.2	103.5	115.5	180.7	188.8	205.0	250.8
4	Sugar	148.9	0.1	58.3	5.2	0.3	0.0	0.2	727.1	64.5	0.9
C.	**Other bulk items**	**2760.4**	**3573.1**	**4215.9**	**4263.3**	**2963.2**	**3223.1**	**3032.0**	**4248.6**	**5818.9**	**5114.8**
1	Fertilisers	391.8	644.7	1082.9	984.3	954.2	977.7	825.9	1052.4	1682.7	911.2
	(a) Crude	107.9	131.4	161.4	193.2	184.5	158.4	122.0	152.6	156.8	134.5
	(b) Sulphur and unroasted iron pyrites	139.1	173.4	180.3	155.1	124.4	120.9	72.2	135.8	144.4	91.0
	(c) Manufactured	144.9	340.0	741.2	636.0	645.3	698.4	631.7	763.9	1381.5	685.7
2	Non-ferrous metals	492.8	535.8	712.9	614.1	340.6	394.8	479.2	717.9	903.9	1105.6
3	Paper, paper boards, manufactures including news prints	208.3	209.6	209.3	254.2	197.9	177.2	221.9	246.2	473.3	498.7
4	Crude rubber, including synthetic and reclaimed	92.9	119.4	104.4	126.1	73.8	90.0	109.0	118.1	215.0	177.3
5	Pulp and waste paper	184.0	179.3	184.5	255.2	121.2	141.2	158.6	202.3	275.3	231.7
6	Metalliferrous ores, metal scrap, etc.	372.9	549.4	569.5	851.7	476.5	663.6	442.4	748.1	822.4	819.6
7	Iron and steel	1017.8	1335.0	1352.4	1177.6	798.9	778.6	795.0	1163.6	1446.2	1370.6
II.	**Non-bulk imports**	**10136.6**	**11611.1**	**12679.8**	**13224.6**	**10847.8**	**12051.8**	**14194.0**	**17333.8**	**22361.0**	**22767.4**
A.	**Capital goods**	**5063.8**	**4803.0**	**5288.1**	**5835.6**	**4232.6**	**4531.6**	**6242.8**	**7638.1**	**10330.2**	**9922.0**
1	Manufactures of metals	123.8	133.5	144.8	168.5	130.4	145.8	178.3	206.2	278.2	316.4
2	Machine tools	163.2	173.8	191.8	263.2	172.8	166.1	154.6	213.6	371.9	525.0
3	Machinery except electrical and electronic	2016.5	1809.5	1929.9	2100.0	1457.5	1652.6	1881.9	2727.8	3924.4	3644.3

(*Contd.*)

APPENDIX TABLE 10 (*Contd.*)

1		19	20	21	22	23	24	25	26	27	28
4	Electrical machinery except electronic	843.2	1079.0	1088.4	948.7	629.8	826.9	204.1	251.4	386.4	325.3
5	Electronic goods	—	—	—	—	—	—	912.4	1228.1	1752.3	1423.8
6	Computer goods	—	—	—	—	—	—	18.0	43.6	120.8	84.4
7	Transport equipment	586.1	519.8	889.3	930.5	371.2	461.8	1270.4	1113.6	1105.1	1484.3
8	Project goods	1330.9	1087.5	1043.9	1424.7	1471.0	1278.5	1623.1	1853.6	2391.0	2118.3
B.	**Mainly export related items**	**2584.8**	**3729.0**	**3960.9**	**3680.0**	**3581.0**	**4148.2**	**4387.5**	**4316.6**	**5257.5**	**6138.0**
1	Pearls, precious and semi-precious stones	1556.7	2192.8	2554.6	2083.1	1957.1	2442.1	2634.5	1629.7	2106.0	2925.0
2	Organic and inorganic chemicals	834.4	1307.9	1153.8	1275.6	1378.7	1427.5	1370.7	2137.1	2565.5	2660.9
3	Textile yarn, fabrics, made-ups, etc.	144.0	185.9	202.7	246.7	137.1	148.7	228.4	329.6	358.7	358.5
4	Cashew nuts	49.7	42.4	49.8	74.7	108.2	129.9	153.9	220.2	227.2	193.7
C.	**Others**	**2488.0**	**3079.1**	**3430.8**	**3709.0**	**3034.2**	**3372.0**	**3563.7**	**5379.1**	**6773.3**	**6707.4**
1	Gold and silver	—	—	—	—	—	—	—	712.6	867.1	991.5
	(a) Gold	—	—	—	—	—	—	—	—	—	—
	(b) Silver	—	—	—	—	—	—	—	—	—	—
2	Artificial resins and plastic materials, etc.	437.4	558.3	599.4	610.0	568.7	420.5	434.5	606.2	803.4	796.0
3	Professional, scientific controlling instruments, photographic optical goods	385.4	469.1	404.0	590.6	407.2	501.4	422.3	491.9	669.1	552.6
4	Coal, coke and briquittes, etc.	168.9	290.0	337.5	440.0	420.4	477.6	466.5	708.4	925.5	994.9
5	Medicinal and pharmaceutical products	129.4	163.3	240.0	261.1	226.6	280.8	257.9	298.5	406.0	306.8
6	Chemical materials and products	147.5	129.1	131.3	159.4	137.2	169.5	167.0	201.9	245.5	263.6
7	Non-metallic mineral manufactures	80.8	113.4	102.3	113.1	88.8	89.1	86.8	131.5	151.5	120.9
8	Others	1138.6	1356.0	1616.3	1534.9	1185.2	1433.0	1728.8	2228.1	2705.2	2681.1
	Total Imports	**17155.7**	**19497.2**	**21219.2**	**24072.5**	**19410.5**	**21881.6**	**23306.2**	**28654.4**	**36675.3**	**39132.4**

APPENDIX TABLE 10 (*Contd.*)

(*US $ million*)

	Commodity/Year	*1997-98*	*1998-99*	*1999-00*	*2000-01*	*2001-02*	*2002-03*	*2003-04*	*2004-05*	*2005-06*	*2006-07 R*	*2007-08 P*
1		*29*	*30*	*31*	*32*	*33*	*34*	*35*	*36*	*37*	*38*	*39*
I.	**Bulk imports**	**14790.1**	**13230.1**	**19646.1**	**20815.7**	**20263.1**	**24299.5**	**29461.5**	**42400.7**	**61086.1**	**84434.2**	**112686.5**
A.	**Petroleum, crude and products**	**8164.0**	**6398.6**	**12611.4**	**15650.1**	**14000.3**	**17639.5**	**20569.5**	**29844.1**	**43963.1**	**57143.6**	**79641.3**
B.	**Bulk consumption goods**	**1483.4**	**2524.2**	**2416.9**	**1443.2**	**2043.2**	**2411.0**	**3072.8**	**3104.6**	**2766.6**	**4294.2**	**4574.6**
1	Cereals and cereal preparations	291.5	287.7	221.9	19.1	18.2	24.5	19.4	26.4	36.1	32.1	45.0
2	Edible oils	743.9	1803.9	1856.8	1308.2	1355.6	1814.2	2542.5	2465.3	2024.0	2108.3	2558.0
3	Pulses	321.4	168.5	81.9	109.1	662.6	565.6	497.2	395.6	559.3	860.1	1311.0
4	Sugar	126.5	264.1	256.3	6.8	6.8	6.8	13.6	217.3	147.2	0.8	0.6
C.	**Other bulk items**	**5142.8**	**4307.3**	**4617.8**	**3722.4**	**4219.6**	**4249.0**	**5819.2**	**9452.0**	**14356.5**	**22996.5**	**28470.6**
1	Fertilisers	1116.6	1076.4	1399.1	751.8	679.0	625.8	720.8	1377.1	2127.0	3144.1	5405.7
	(a) Crude	178.2	198.3	204.2	222.3	166.8	184.8	133.8	289.5	317.8	361.1	467.3
	(b) Sulphur and unroasted iron pyrite	94.3	66.6	116.0	89.0	57.4	83.3	86.2	128.1	136.0	109.3	362.0
	(c) Manufactured	844.1	811.4	1079.0	440.5	454.8	357.6	500.8	959.5	1673.3	2673.6	4576.4
2	Non-ferrous metals	920.3	597.4	546.9	533.8	647.3	666.5	948.8	1310.3	1844.4	2604.9	3490.5
3	Paper, paper boards, manufactures including news prints	502.1	465.1	447.2	451.1	446.9	449.4	657.7	727.7	944.1	1206.8	1429.7
4	Crude rubber, including synthetic and reclaimed	160.4	145.4	143.3	151.9	174.3	182.5	280.8	409.2	414.1	630.8	785.7
5	Pulp and waste paper	283.9	235.5	255.2	281.7	294.7	343.4	409.1	489.5	572.9	639.3	769.6
6	Metalliferrous ores, metal scrap, *etc.*	738.4	723.9	874.5	774.2	1143.7	1037.8	1295.9	2468.5	3881.8	8345.8	7905.5
7	Iron and steel	1421.1	1063.5	951.7	777.8	833.7	943.7	1506.1	2669.7	4572.2	6424.7	8684.0

(*Contd.*)

APPENDIX TABLE 10 (*Contd.*)

1		*29*	*30*	*31*	*32*	*33*	*34*	*35*	*36*	*37*	*38*	*39*
II.	**Non-bulk imports**	**26694.4**	**29158.6**	**30024.6**	**29720.8**	**31150.2**	**37112.6**	**48687.6**	**69116.7**	**88079.6**	**101315.1**	**126964.0**
A.	**Capital goods**	**9796.1**	**10064.4**	**8965.5**	**8941.1**	**9882.2**	**13498.2**	**18278.9**	**25135.0**	**37666.2**	**47069.2**	**58393.2**
1	Manufactures of metals	325.3	380.1	405.0	390.3	407.0	488.3	689.7	918.7	1211.1	1603.6	2657.6
2	Machine tools	422.2	346.9	261.5	219.1	193.0	246.9	460.1	620.4	1076.2	1481.3	2210.7
3	Machinery except electrical and electronic	3621.9	3044.5	2745.0	2708.8	2970.8	3565.6	4743.6	6817.8	10009.8	13850.4	19660.8
4	Electrical machinery except electronic	378.2	421.0	437.8	481.0	594.4	664.1	872.2	1195.0	1504.3	1959.8	2982.8
5	Electronic goods	2087.8	2223.0	2796.6	3508.5	3782.0	5599.4	7506.1	9993.2	13241.7	15972.6	20324.3
6	Computer goods	170.1	162.5	197.0	186.0	216.5	493.8	383.2	666.3	901.9	967.0	1019.6
7	Transport equipment	1051.3	798.2	1136.6	700.3	1149.4	1897.4	3227.9	4327.4	8838.5	9438.6	8248.2
8	Project goods	1739.4	2688.1	986.0	747.2	569.0	542.7	396.0	596.2	882.7	1795.9	1289.2
B.	**Mainly export related items**	**6913.3**	**7131.1**	**9117.3**	**8058.6**	**8260.0**	**10313.7**	**12716.8**	**17095.5**	**18641.0**	**17871.7**	**20758.1**
1	Pearls, precious and semi-precious stones	3342.1	3760.3	5436.0	4807.7	4622.6	6062.8	7128.7	9422.7	9134.4	7487.5	7975.1
2	Organic and inorganic chemicals	2956.1	2683.7	2866.3	2443.9	2799.6	3025.2	4031.9	5699.9	6984.1	7830.7	9878.7
3	Textile yarn, fabrics, made-ups, *etc.*	408.6	456.8	538.4	596.8	747.5	970.4	1257.8	1571.2	2050.5	2151.2	2478.5
4	Cashew nuts	206.4	230.3	276.5	210.3	90.4	255.4	298.5	401.7	471.9	402.4	425.8
C.	**Others**	**9984.9**	**11963.2**	**11941.8**	**12721.1**	**13008.0**	**13300.7**	**17691.9**	**26886.2**	**31772.4**	**36374.2**	**47812.7**
1	Gold and silver	3169.3	5072.1	4706.1	4638.0	4582.3	4288.3	6856.4	11150.0	11317.7	14646.0	17845.8
	(a) Gold	—	—	4151.8	4121.6	4170.4	3844.9	6516.9	10537.7	10830.5	14461.9	16716.4
	(b) Silver	—	—	554.3	516.5	411.9	443.3	339.5	612.3	487.2	184.1	1129.4
2	Artificial resins and plastic materials, *etc.*	692.6	675.7	719.5	554.9	674.1	781.8	1082.0	1456.9	2267.7	2584.8	3684.7

3	Professional, scientific controlling instruments, photographic optical goods	745.7	820.2	844.5	878.8	1041.1	1133.2	1230.3	1530.4	1972.7	2341.0	3060.9
4	Coal, coke and briquittes, *etc.*	1192.5	979.7	1008.1	1103.1	1143.3	1239.6	1410.8	3198.4	3868.7	4576.8	6411.9
5	Medicinal and pharmaceutical products	389.4	383.9	373.0	374.7	424.9	592.0	643.7	705.4	1027.9	1296.5	1663.9
6	Chemical materials and products	298.8	389.8	360.8	334.5	444.4	452.0	631.6	819.4	1052.5	1321.6	1624.1
7	Non-metallic mineral manufactures	138.5	160.3	163.9	173.7	219.9	234.7	327.4	471.9	621.9	780.0	1046.6
8	Others	3358.1	3481.5	3765.9	4663.4	4478.0	4579.1	5509.8	7553.9	9643.2	8827.5	12474.8
	Total Imports	**41484.5**	**42388.7**	**49670.7**	**50536.5**	**51413.3**	**61412.1**	**78149.1**	**111517.4**	**149166.0**	**185749.0**	**239651.0**

P : Provisional R : Revised *n.e.s.* : not elsewhere specified or included.

: Data prior to 1976-77 relate to synthetic and regenerated fibres (man-made fibres).

Notes: Due to change in commodity classification by the DGCI&S, data on 'Chemical elements and compounds', 'Machinery, other than electric and electrical machinery apparatus and appliances' from 1970-71 to 1975-76 and 1976-77 to 1986-87 may not be strictly comparable.

Source: Directorate General of Commercial Intelligence and Statistics.

BIBLIOGRAPHY

Accenture, 2010, High Performance in a Volatile World-Seven Imperatives for Achieving Dynamic Supply Chains. http://microsite.accenture.com accessed July 18, 2010.

ACMA, 2010, Indian Auto Component Industry—An Overview, www.acmainfo.com, accessed June 28, 2010.

Air India, 2006, Cargo—Products and Services. www.ia-cargo.com accessed Dec 14, 2008, and July 5, 2010.

Balasubramanian, P., 2005, Supply Chain Management—Supply Chain Metrics, Collaboration Models and Innovation Imperatives, PPT presentation at Tata Tea Executive Conference, August 26. www.citeseerx.ist.psu.edu accessed June 26, 2009.

Balcet, G. and Enrietti, A., 2002, Partnership and Global Production: Fiat's Strategies in Turkey. www.gerpisa.univ-evry.fr accessed August 21, 2009, and July 18, 2010.

Banga, M.S., 2004, HLL is Re-inventing Distribution. www.hul.co.in accessed March 16, 2008.

Blackburn J, and Scudder, G., 2008, Supply Chain Strategies for Perishable Products: The Case of Fresh Produce, Vanderbilt University, Nashville, Tennessee, USA. http://mba.vanderbilt.edu accessed July 15, 2010.

Bloomberg, D.J., Lemay, S. and Hanna, J.E., 2005, Logistics, Prentice Hall of India, New Delhi.

Bowersox, D., Closs, D., and Cooper, M.B., 2008, Supply Chain Logistics Management, 2nd ed., Special India edition, Tata-McGraw-Hill, New Delhi.

Brown *et. al.* 2005, The Automotive Industry—Supply Chain Management for Honda and Foreign Automakers, a PPT Presentation, www.fisher.osu.edu, accessed Oct 17, 2008 and July 11, 2010.

Carlsson, D., D'Amours, S., Martel, A. and Ronnquist, M., 2006, Supply Chain Management in the Pulp and Paper Industry, Working paper DT-2006-AM-3. *Interuniversity Research Center on Enterprise Networks, Logistics and Transportation,* (CIRRELT), University Laval, Quebec, Canada.

Chase, R.B., Jacobs, R.F., Aquilano, N. and Agarwal, N.K., 2006, Inventory Control in *Operations Management for Competitive Advantage*, Tata-McGrraw-Hill, New Delhi.

Chaudhary. R., 2008, Supply Chain Strategies, *Logistics Management*. pp. 30-36, April issue.

Chopra and Meindl, 2001, Supply Chain Management: Strategy, Planning, and Operation, 3rd edition, Prentice Hall, India.

Coyle, J.J., Langley, J.C., Gibson, B.J., Novack, R.A., and Bardi, E.J. 2009. "Demand Management and Customer Service", in *A Logistics Approach to Supply Chain Management*, Cengage Learning, New Delhi.

Cygnus, 2006, Background Note on Supply Chain Management in Automotive Industry, paper presented at auto SCM Conference held at Chennai, Cygnus Business Consultative and Research, www.cygnusindia.com accessed May 26, 2008.

Cygnus, 2006, Background note-Logistics paper presented at CII, Kolkata Conference, Cygnus Business Consultative and Research, www.cygnusindia.com accessed October 12, 2008.

Finch, B.J., 2008, Supply Chain Management: Managing Business-to-Business Interactions In: *Operations Now: Supply Chain profitability and performance*, Tata-McGraw-Hill, New Delhi.

Flower Council, Holland. 2005. Logistics. http://www.flowercouncil.org, accessed October 12, 2005.

Gati, 2009, Green Logistics, In: *Gati Express*, Vol. 3, www.Gati.com, accessed July 13, 2010.

Gati, 2009, Through the ages-Logistics as it Evolved, In: *Gati Express*, www.Gati.com, Vol. 3, accessed July 13, 2010.

Gaucher, S., Le Gal, P.Y., and Soler, G., 2003, Modelling supply chain management in Sugar industry In: *Proceedings of South African Technology Association*, CIRAD and Centre for Rural Development Systems, University of Natal, Scottsville, South Africa.

Government of India (GOI), 2008, Annual Report, 2007-08, Department of Shipping, GOI, New Delhi.

Gordon, L.C., Kung, D. and Dyck, H., 2006, IT deployment assessment: A Two Dimensional Supply Chain Life-cycle Management Framework for Strategic Analysis, *E-leader*, Slovakia. www.g-case.com accessed October 21, 2008.

Greater Western Sydney, 2009, Industry Capability Profile; Automotive and Transport Equipment. www.gws.org.au accessed Nov10, 2009.

Gujarat Cooperative Milk Marketing Federation Limited (GCMMF), 2006, Report of the Board of Directors, *In: Chairman's Speech*, 32nd Annual Report 2005-06, Anand, June, 2006.

Gupta, I., and Rajshekhar, M., 2004, HLL-Remaking Lever-cover Story, www.businessworld.com accessed November 17, 2008, and July 18, 2010.

Handfield, R. and Nicholas, E., Jr., 1999, Introduction to Supply Chain Management, Prentice-Hall, New York.

Jadhav, S. 2010. Supply Chain Management at Hindustan Unilever. http://www.mindtree.com, accessed July 18, 2010.

Krajewski, L.J., Ritzman, L.P. and Malhotra, M.K., 2007, Lean Systems In: *Operations Management, Processes and Value Chains*, 8th edition, Prentice Hall of India, New Delhi.

Krajewski, L.J., Ritzman, L.P. and Malhotra, M.K., 2007, Supply Chain Strategy In: *Operations Management, Processes and Value Chains*, 8th edition, Prentice Hall of India, New Delhi.

Kurien, V., 2005, *Chairman's Speech: 31st Annual General Body Meeting*, Gujarat Cooperative Milk Marketing Federation Limited (GCMMF) on 23rd June 2005, In Report of the Board of Directors, 31st GCMMF Annual Report 2004-05, Anand.

Kurnia, S. and Johnston, R., 2006, Identifying Critical Success Factors for Efficient Consumer Response Based on Australian Experience, *School of Business Systems*, Monash University, Clayton, Victoria, Australia.

Light Lift Industries, 2009, Material Handling Equipment. *Manufacturer and Exporter*. Faridabad, Haryana, India. www.lightlift.com accessed Dec. 24, 2009, and July 19, 2010.

Maruti-Suzuki, 2008, *Industry Overview—Management discussion and analyses*. www.marutisuzuki.com, accessed 11th September 2009.

Moily, H., 2008, A Supply Chain Model for Dairy Farming and Health Care in *Mint*, www.livemint.com, October 20.

Molla, A. and Peszynski, K., 2009, E-business Diffusion among Australian Horticulture Firms. *Australasian Agribusiness Review*, Vol. 17, 2009, Paper 4. School of Business Information Technology, RMIT University, Australia.

NDTV Profit, 2008, Gujarat Potato is McDonald's Indian French Fry, Indo-Asian News Service, www.ndtv.com, March 20.

O'Brien, J.A., Marakas, G.M., and Behl, R., 2010, Management Information Systems, Ninth edition, Tata McGraw-Hill, New Delhi.

Ram Kumar, V.G., 2008, Using e-Commerce Portals to Link Rural Communities in *Mint*, www.livemint.com, October 20.

Russell, Roberta S., and Bernard Taylor, 2004, Supply Chain Management In: *Operations Management*, 4th edition, New Delhi: Prentice Hall of India.

Simchi-Levi, D., Kaminsky, P., Simchi-Levi, E., 2003, "Designing and Managing the Supply Chain—Concepts, Strategies and Case Studies", Tata McGraw-Hill, New Delhi.

Singh, Abhinav, 2007, FMCG/Consumer Durables—Under Pressure to Structure Supply Chain and Storage, Expresscomputer, May 28. www.expresscomputeronline.com accessed April 12, 2008.

Singru, N., 2007, Profile of the Indian Transport Sector. *A Report by Asian Development Bank*, pp. 18, August.

Stevenson, W.J., 2006, Inventory Management in *Operations Management*, Tata McGraw-Hill, New Delhi.

Stevenson, W.J., 2006, Supply Chain Management in *Operations Management*, Tata McGraw-Hill, New Delhi.

Veloso, F. and Rajiv Kumar, 2002, The Automotive Supply Chain: Global Trends and Asian Perspectives, Economics and Research Department, working paper No. 3, *Asian Development Bank*, January, www.adb.org, accessed 15th December 2009.

Vieira, V., Ferreira, Jr. S.C. and Yoshizaki, H.T.Y., 2003, Collaborative Planning, Forecasting and Replenishment: State of Art in Brazil, University of Sao Paulo, Brazil.

Zailani, S., Premkumar, R., and Fernando, Y., 2008, Factors Influencing the Effectiveness of Operational Information Sharing within Supply Chain Channels in Malaysia, *Operations and Supply Chain Management*, Vol. 1 (2), September, pp. 85-100.

INDEX